William Camden

The Visitation of the County of Leicester in the Year 1619

Salzwasser

William Camden

The Visitation of the County of Leicester in the Year 1619

1. Auflage | ISBN: 978-3-84604-944-0

Erscheinungsort: Frankfurt, Deutschland

Erscheinungsjahr: 2020

Salzwasser Verlag GmbH

Reprint of the original, first published in 1870.

THE

PUBLICATIONS

OF

The Harleian Society.

ESTABLISHED A.D. MDCCCLXIX.

Volume II.

FOR THE YEAR MDCCCLXX.

The Visitation of the County of

Leicester

In the Year

1619.

TAKEN BY

WILLIAM CAMDEN

Clarenceux King of Arms.

EDITED BY

JOHN FETHERSTON, F.S.A.

LONDON:

1870.

At a Meeting of the Council of the HARLEIAN SOCIETY, *held at 8, Danes Inn, London, W.C., on the 22nd day of November, 1869,* JOHN MACLEAN, ESQ., *F.S.A., in the Chair, it was resolved that—*

"The Second Publication of the Society be THE HERALDIC VISITATION OF LEICESTERSHIRE *in 1619, by William Camden, Clarenceux King of Arms; to be edited by* JOHN FETHERSTON, ESQ., *F.S.A."*

Preface.

The Visitation comprised in the ensuing pages was taken by William Camden, Clarenceux King of Arms, in 1619, Sampson Lennard and Augustine Vincent being his deputies, by the former of whom it was in great part written, and whose arms are stamped upon the cover. The pedigrees registered in it are nearly all marked with crosses of red chalk or blacklead pencil, signifying that they were copied from hence for the use of the heralds. Since the book was written, several entrances and insertions have been made by other persons. At fo. 4 is an erroneous pedigree of Cater, put down by Henry Parker. At fo. 42 are the arms of Sir Arthur Haselrigg as they were marshalled A.D. 1644, tricked also by the same Henry Parker. At fo. 56 will be found the following "Account of the Fees and Rewards given to the Officers of Arms, 24th March, A.D. 1619, by Prince Charles and several Lords at their first Entrance into the Tilt Yard":—

"Prince Charles for his first entring into the Tilt gaue to the Kings of Armes Heralds and Pursuivants of Armes twelue scarffes of his colers being those colers, nine yards a peece, of rich taffata, fringed wth deepe golde fringe, and to euerie one a white beuer hat wth siluer bands and feathers of his coulers. and twentie pounds in monie the 24 of March 1619. and all brought him into the tilt yeard from Somerset house the 24. of March afforesaid 1619.

"The Marquesse Buckingham gaue the same time 1619 for his entrance into the tilte twentye markes in monie to the officers of Armes but no coulors bycause all the companie did attend the Prince.

"The Marquesse Hamilton for his first entrance into the tilt gaue to the officers of Armes twentye marks at the same time but no coulors, bycause none did attend him into the tilt.

"The Earle of Oxford gaue for his first entrance into the tilt the same tyme ten pounds in monie but no coulors.

"The Earle of Salisberie gaue for his first entrance into the tilt the same time 1619 the sume of ten pounds in monie to the officers of Armes and six yards of taffata sarcenet for two officers of Armes although he had none to attend him.

"The yeare following 1620 the Earle of Lincolne gaue for his first entrance into the tilt to 4. officers of Armes 6 yards of taffata sarcenet a peece and ten pounds in monie who brought him from the muse into the tilt & gaue them also fethers of his colour.

"The Lord Compton sonne to the Earle of Northampton gaue to 4 officers of Armes 3^{li} a peece in monie to buy them scarffs of his colours & 20^{s} to buy them feathers of his coulers and vj^{li} xiij^{s} iiij^{d} as a fee to the whole companie wch foure did attend him from the muse into the tilt the 24 of March 1620.

"The yeare following 1621 the Viscount Mansfeild gaue to 3 officers of Armes 3 pounds a peece to buy them scarffes of his colours and viij^{li} in monie as a fee to the whole companie But through the fowle wether the daye being twice putt of. In the end the King would haue no tilting that yeare.

"The lord Stanhop the same time 1621 gaue to 3. officers of Armes 3. pounds a peece to buy them scarffes of his colours & vi^{li} xiij^{s} iiij^{d} in monie to ye whole companie, But ther was no tilting that yeare by reason of the fowle weather as is aforesayd.

"The Lord Montioye of Ireland gaue for his first entrance into the tilt the same time 1621 scarffes of taffata sercenet for 3. officers to bring him into the tilt and vi^{li} xiij^{s} iiij^{d} in monie to the whole companie but nothing was done that yeare by reason of the fowle weather as afforesaid, yet they all had the monie before hand, and the scarffes."

At (fo. 77, pencil,) will be found inserted an escocheon of Sir Beaumont Dixie, second Baronet of Market Bosworth, impaling the arms and quarterings of his wife Mary, the sister and sole heiress of Sir William Willoughby, Baronet, of Selston, co. Notts. Only one original subscription is to be found, that of "Wylliam Noell," at fo. 5 b; but in Harl. MSS. 1195 (from fo. 72) is a number of the original loose sheets, signed by those who gave the information for the Visitations of Leicestershire and Warwickshire, and facsimiles of forty-four signatures of the county of Leicester are appended to this work. Several pedigrees have been continued, chiefly by the hands of Henry Parker and Robert Fisher, arms painter, whose autograph is to be seen on the first page. One Richard Mundy, who perhaps accompanied the heralds at this Visitation, seems to have tricked the arms and seals used by the Corporation of Leicester, and to have entered the descent of Wellesborough; that of Beaumont at fo. 34 is in the hand of Augustine Vincent. All these additions, and words written in pencil, are distinguished from the original entries by being in Brevier type. The headings of pedigrees *within* brackets are so written in the original manuscript; those *without* have been supplied.

The first Visitation of the County of Le'cester was that of Harvey in 1563, by Robert Cooke, Chester Herald. A copy of this, written narratively, is in the national collection (Add. MS. 17,065, fo. 125) and contains the following pedigrees :—

"The dessent of Robert Brokesby of Sholesby in the . . . of Leycester. And in the hondreth of Goscott."

Of " Henry Kebyll of Homerston."

"John Danvers of Swythland."

"George Sherard of Stapullford."

"John Ashbye of Lowesbye."

"Will'm Peche of Kingthorpe."

"Edmond Wynter of Wordington."

"Thomas Graye of Langlaye."

"Thomas Rosse of Ingmanthorpe."

"Thomas Ffarnham of   "

"Will'm Lacye of Melton Mowbraye."

"Ffrauncys Cave of Baggrave."

"Bryan Cave of Ingusbye."

"Morrys Barklaye lord of Womandham."

"George Pochen of Barkbye."

"Nicholas Sevyll of Blabye."

"Richard Turvyll of Normanton Turvoyle."

"John Nowell of Wellesborow."

"Sʳ Thomas Nevyll Knight lord of Hoult & Roliston."

"Will'm Skevington of Skevington."

"George Vincent of Pekleton."

"Robert Belgrave."   .

"George Pureffey of Dreyton."

Two others are in the College of Arms, also narratively written, the one marked G. 11, the other by Turpin H. 12. There is likewise a book of pedigrees from Cooke's Visitations of Somerset, Warwick, and Leicester, marked F. 7.

A small volume in the possession of the Honorary Treasurer of the Harleian Society is worthy of note, since it gives some information relative to the quarterings of Leicestershire families at this period, and calls attention to a collection of genealogical manuscripts, collected by Henry Ferrers, not one of which unfortunately now remains in the possession of his lineal male heir at Baddesley Clinton.

" The Armes and the names
of Knigtes Esquyres and

Gentilmen within the Coun-
tie of leicester liuing in y^e
yeere of our lord God
1564
Sett oute as it was performed by Robarte
Cooke then Chester herauld of armes,
the originall (that this was
Copied forth of) was
doun on vellam in
Coullers being in the hands
of Henrie fferrers
of baddisley Clin
ton in Warwik
shire 1593.

In the British Museum, in addition to the manuscript printed here, are others of the second Visitation (1619) :—

Harl. MSS. 6125.

     6183.

     1431.

     1187, bound up with the Visitation of Northamptonshire in 1618, beginning at fo. 97, (pencil,) and extending with alphabetical index to the end of the book,

  and 1189, which commences with a list of names and trickings of arms of justices of the county of Leicester in 1601.

The Library of the College of Arms has two copies :—C. 8, containing about one hundred and twenty-eight pedigrees; and Vincent's Leicester, No. 127. Leicester Visitations are also preserved in both Universities :— Caius College, Cambridge, MSS. 519; New College, Oxford, MSS. CCCXXX.; Queen's College, Oxford, MSS. LXXXIX.

The third and last Visitation of Leicestershire was taken "by Sir Henry St. George, Knt., Clarenceux King at Arms; begun by Thomas May Chester and Gregory King, Rougedragon, in Trinity Vacation, 168½, and finished by Henry Dethick Richmond and the said Rouge Dragon in Trinity Vacation following, 1683." It forms one of the series of later Visitations, marked K, in the College of Arms, and consists of about one hundred and forty genealogies. In addition to families already recorded, it introduces many others who had become possessed of property in the county since the year 1619, or whose descents had not been registered in the *earlier* Visitations. The following list, in the order in which they occur, may prove useful :—

Manners (Earls of Rutland).	Pate of Sisonby.	Curl of Melton.
Crewe.	Fullwood of Hemington.	Palmes of Melton.
Hudson of Melton Mowbray.	Powell of Belvoir.	Bowdon of Melton.

Herick of Beaumanor.
Gery of Stony Stanton.
Toone of Belton.
Shenton of Barwell.
Harpur of Bilston.
Paget of Barwell and Croft.
Oneby of Barwell.
Rooe of Normanton Turvile.
Capper of Burbage.
Sacheverell of Rearsby.
Welles of Thrussington.
Verney of Allexton.
Andrewes of Great Bowdon.
Allington of Burbage.
Hewet of Dunton Basset.
Palmer of Onlip.
Dixwell of Coton.
Edwards of Kibworth.
Packe of Prestwold.
Wileman of Burton.
Lister of Thorpe Arnold.
Calcott, *alias* Caldecott, of Catthorp.
Greene of Rylston (Rolleston).
Cole of Lutterworth.

Street of Halloughton.
Billers of Leicester.
Palmer of Osgathorp.
Alefounder.
Burrough of Burrough.
Wilson of Knighthorp.
Maior of Leicester.
Barwell of Garradon.
Roby of Castle Donnington.
Rayson of Barrow upon Soar.
Wright of Barwell.
Bradgate of Ullesthorp.
Byerley of Belgrave.
Henslie of Lutterworth.
Briggs of Hinckley.
Hill of Netherseale.
Bate of Ashby-de-la-Zouch.
Woodcock of Cayham.
Smart of Ashby-de-la-Zouch.
Staunton.
Stephens of Leicester.
Estwick.
Mordaunt of Medborn.
Boothby of Marston.

Levinge of Shepey.
Firebrace.
Stanley.
Street of Orton-sup'-Monte' (Orton-on-the-Hill).
Thickbrome.
Bodle of Markfield.
Hayes of Burton-Lazers.
Pratt of Cotesback.
Holland of Waltham-on-y^e- Wolds.
Saunders of Foxton.
Bradgate of Peatlin.
Harley of Osgathorp.
Wodland of Medborn.
Sergeant of Melton-Mowbray.
Hacket of Abkettleby.
Bennet of Welby.
Goodall.
Hilton of Billinghurst.
Leek of Wymeswold.
Cox.
Clerk of Hoby.
Whatton.

The Editor begs to acknowledge his great obligation to John Davidson, Esq., for the very elaborate and useful Index attached to this Volume.

ERRATA.

———◆———

BERKLEY OF WYMONDHAM (page 2).

Quartering 1.—To *Gules, a chevron between ten cinquefoils argent*, add *six in chief and four in base.*

NOELL OF DALBY (page 3).

Quartering 4.—For *trumpets*, read *organ-pipes.*

SKEUINGTON (page 7).

Quartering 11.—For *at the top*, read *in dexter chief.*

SHERARD OF STAPLEFORD (page 10).

Quartering 2.—In the MSS. the drawing resembles *trefoils*, but the Arms of Hawberk are *on a bend nine annulets, three, three, and three, interlaced in triangle.*

EUERARD OF SHENTON (page 12).

"*Sup Cathedra' in Domo Rici' Euerard de Shenton*," read *impaling argent, on a fess between three bears' heads erased sable, muzzles (untinctured), as many bezants.*

HASELRIG OF NOSELEY (pages 15 and 16).

Quartering 5.—For *Bendy of six gules and argent*, read *Gules, three bendlets argent.*
Omit mark of descent to "Dorothy, sister to the Lord Brooke."

DIGBY (page 40).

Quartering 6.—Read *Argent, on a fess between three martlets sable as many mullets of the field.*

BROKESBY (page 49).

Quartering 4.—Read *Or, a bend gobonée argent and azure between three torteaux.*

HUMPHREY (page 62).

Omit mark of descent from *Sir Tho. Humphrie of Shipson in Com' Leyc.* and *Mary Da. of Wm Meringe of Meringes in com' Northam.*

POULTNEY (page 70).

Quartering 4.—For *Barry of six*, read *eight.*
Quartering 5.—For *fess*, read *chevron.*

SHERRARD (page 88).

Quartering 2.—For *three trefoils*, read *nine annulets, three, three, and three interlaced in triangle* (as at page 10).

NOBLE (page 114).

Quartering 2.—After *barry*, read *nebulée.*

CAVE (page 120).

Omit mark of descent to "Phillippa fil. unica hæres Rob'ti Braham de Barrow sup' Sore.

CAVE (page 125).

Mark of descent should be to Maria fil. et hæres Alexandri Caue militis, instead of to her husband, Sir Alexander Lounde, Kt., etc.

CARRINGTON, *alias* SMITH (page 145).

Quartering 4.—For *a . . . ?*, read *a lymphad.*

CHIPPINGDALE (page 157).

Arms.—After *erased*, omit *paleways.*

GILBERT (page 189).

After *broken spears*, read *erect.*

BABINGTON (page 205).

Crest.—After *rere-mouse*, omit *in pale affrontée displayed.*

NAMES OF QUARTERINGS AND IMPALEMENTS TRICKED IN THE VISITATION OF LEICESTER, 1619.

———◆———

BERKLEY OF WYMONDHAM (p. 2).

1. Berkley.
2. Hamelyn.
3. De la Laund.
4. Welles.
5. Engaine.
6. Waterton.

NOELL OF DALBY (p. 3).

1. Noell.
2. Hopton.
3. Heavon.
4. Downton.
5. St. Ouen.
6. Tirrell.

STARESMORE OF FROLESWORTH (p. 5).

1. Staresmore.
2. Partridge.
3. Willoughby (Burton's Leic. N. window of chancel of Frollesworth church, ed. 1767, fo. 102).
4. Wolfe.
5. Comberford.
6. Staresmore.

SKEFFINGTON (p. 7).

1. Skeffington.
2. Oldbeef.
3. English.
4. Stanhope.
5. Maulovell.
6. Rochford.
7. Lisley.
8. Jenney.
9. Doiley.
10. Cambridge.
11. Downe.
12. Childe.
13. Colsell.

SHERRARD OF STAPLEFORD (p. 10).

1. Sherrard.
2. Hawberk.
3. Woodford.

SHERRARD—*continued*.

4. Brabazon.
5. Foluile.
6. Helwell.
7. Brow.
8. Woodvile.

EVERARD OF SHENTON (p. 12).

1. Everard.
2. Waterton.
3. Grimsby.
4. Moton.
5. Basset.
6. Colvile.
7. Malory.
8. Bugg.
9. Champaine.

ASHBY OF QUENBY (p. 13).

1. Ashby.
2. Mallet?

ASHBY OF LOSEBY (p. 14).

1. Ashby.
2. Zouch of Lubbesthorpe (Nicholls Leic. vol. iii. fo. 298).
3. Burdet.
4. Houghton.
5. Stapleford.

HASELRIGG OF NOSELEY (p. 15).

1. Haselrigg.
2. Stanton.
3. Southill.
4. Boiville.
5.

LEGARD (p. 19).

1. Legard.
2. Moyne.
3. Whitworth.
4. Wodham.

NEVILL OF HOLT (p. 21).

1. Smith.

NEVILL—*continued*.

2. Laneham.
3. Hinde.
4. Raby.
5. Nevill.
6. Bulmer.
7. Blanchminster.
8. Rolleston.
9. Palmer.
10. Inglebeard.
11. Bishopston.
12. Fencotes.
13. Croftes.

BURDET (p. 23).

1. Burdet.
2. Camvile.
3. Bruin?
4.

FAUNT (p. 28).

1. Faunt.
2. Moyne   } Harl. MSS.
3. Clairvaulx } 1113, fo. 7.

VILLIERS (p. 29).

1. Villiers (modern).
2. Villiers (ancient) (Harl. MSS. 1113, fo. 7).
3. Pakeman (Notitia Anglicana, p. 89).
4. Bellers.
5. Howby (Not. Angl.) (Harl. MS. 1113 calls it Sellingham).
6. Kirkby.

PURIFOY (p. 32).

1. ——
2. Waver.
3. Shireford.
4.
5. Whellesborow.
6. ——
7. Waver.
8. Shireford.
9.
10. Ayott.
11. Bingham.

PURIFOY—*continued*.

12. Charnells.
13. Charnells.
14. Strelley.
15. ——

PALMER AND HARECOURT (p. 39).

1. Pochin.
2. Palmer.
3. Willoughby.

DIGBY (p. 40).

1. Digby.
2. Waleys.
3. Danvers.
4.
5.
6. Digby.

WINTER (p. 42).

1. Winter.
2. Hardwick.

REPINGTON (p. 42).

1. Repington.
2. Goldsmith.
3.

WHETHILL (p. 44).

1. Whethill.
2. Flanders.
3. Shepey.

NEELE (p. 45).

1. Neele.
2. Sutton.

BROKESBY (p. 49).

1. Brokesby.
2. Sapcot.
3. Denham.
4. Courtenay.
5. Moels.
6. Newmarch.
7. Arches.
8. Francis.
9. Plesington.

VINCENT (p. 50).

1. Vincent.
2. Grimsby.
3. Vullis.
4. Moton.
5. Basset.
6. Colville.
7. Champaine.
8. Bugg.

CHAMBERS (p. 51).

1. Chambers.
2. Dannet.
3.
4.

DRAPER (p. 52).

1. Draper.
2. Draper.

DRAPER—*continued*.

3. Aucher.
4. Urswick.

TURVILE (p. 53).

1. Turvile.
2. Flamvile.
3. Bugg.
4. Foucher.
5. Champaine.
6. Stanton.

KEBELL (p. 56).

1. Kebell.
2. Etton of Warwicksh. (Harl. MSS. 1189, f. 3).

BURTON (p. 56).

1. Curteys.
2. ——
3. Cotton (Harl. MSS. 1113, fo. 2).
4. Ridware.
5. Hardwick.
6. Lindley (Harl. MSS. 6128, fo. 61 b).
7. Funden.
8. Flanders.
9. Limsey.
10. Ashbrooke.
11. Champaine.
12. Stevens.

HUMPHREY (p. 62).

1. Humphrey.
2. Humphrey.

DANNET (p. 64).

1. Dannet.
2. De la Hay.
3. Belknap.
4. Sudley.
5. Reade.
6. Montfort.
7. Butler.
8. Shareshull.

BROOKE (p. 65).

1. Brooke.
2. Parker of Coppenhall.

SMITH *alias* HARRIS (p. 66).

1. Smith.
2. Coe.

BELGRAVE (p. 67).

1. Belgrave.
2. Shipton.
3. Shelton.
4. Glene or Glenfield.
5. Swyke.
6. Chauntrell.

TURPIN (p. 69).

1. Turpin.
2. Kinsman.
3. Tilley.

TURPIN—*continued*.

4. Pawcoe.
5. Gobion.

POULTNEY (p. 70).

1. Poultney.
2. Whymall MSS. (Lucells?).
3. Daniel MSS. (Massy?).
4. Thorpe.
5. Derby.
6. Morley.
7.
8. Davall (Ferrers MSS. *penes* J. J. Howard).
9. Walshe.
10. Byron.

HASELRIGG (p. 70).

1. Haselrig.
2.
3. Heron.
4. Sadington.
5. Martivall.
6. Staunton.
7. Eccleshall.
8. Meynell.
9. Warde ⎱ Nicholls Leic.
10. Everden ⎰ vol. ii. pt. 2, p. 753.
11. Entwisell.
12. Gorges (ancient).
13. Gorges (modern).
14. Russell (Falkiners Chelsea, p. 235).
15. Oldhall.
16. Inglowese.

HASTINGS (p. 72).

1. Hastings.
2. Pole.
3. France and England (Clarence).
4. Nevill.
5. Montacute.
6. Monthermer.
7. Holland.
8. Edmund, Earl of Kent.
9. Beauchamp.
10. Newburgh.
11. Spencer.
12. Clare.
13. Wake.
14. Hungerford.
15.
16. Moels.

GREY (p. 74).

1. Grey.
2. Hastings.
3. Valence.
4. Astley.
5. Ferrers.
6. Wydvile.
7. Bonvile.
8. Harington.

DANVERS (p. 86).

1. Danvers.
2. Walcote.
3. Wallis.
4.

SHERRARD (p. 88).

1. Sherrard.
2. Hawberk.
3. Isley.
4. Burgh.
5. Woodford.
6. Preston.
7. Brabazon.
8. Folvile.

YARDE (p. 91).

1. Yarde.
2. Ferrers (Harl. MSS. 889, fo. 73.)

SAVILL (p. 93).

1. Savill.
2. Blaby.

TURNER (p. 95).

1. Turner ⎫ impaling
2. Masterson ⎭ Breton.

BELGRAVE (p. 95).

1. Belgrave.
2. Shipton.
3. Shelton.
4. Glene or Glenfield.

PEPER (p. 103).

1. Peper.
2. Bugg.
3. Sheffield.

RUDING (p. 104).

1. Ruding.
2. Clerke.
3. Watercroftes.

POCHIN (p. 106).

1. Pochin.
2. Willoughby.
3. Lincoln.
4. ——
5. Palmer.
6. Brett.

SKEFFINGTON (p. 111).

1. Skeffington.
2. Oldbeef.
3. Cambridge.
4. Donne.
5. Childe.
6. Colsell.
7. English.
8. Lisley (?).

NOBLE (p. 114).

1. Noble.
2. Kebell.
3. Palmer.
4. Eaton.

DIXIE (p. 115).

1. Dixie.
2. Beridge.
3. Crathorne.
4. Thoresby ⎫ Harl. MSS.
5. Esterby ⎬ 1550, fo's.
6. Moigne ⎭ 190, 53, 174.
7. Beaumont.
8. Comyn.
9. Quincy.
10. Bellamont.
11. De Grentesmainil.
12. Alan, Earl of Galloway.
13. Scotland (ancient).
14. Nevill.
15. Hugh Lupus.
16. Everingham.
17. Maureward.
18. Hastings.

IMPALING.

1. Willoughby.
2. Green or Rotherham?
3. Pusey,
4. Clay of Crich co. Derby.
5. Calton.
6.
7. Strelley.
8. Ashton.
9. Wardell.

DIXIE (p. 116).

1. Dixie.
2. Beridge.

STURTON (p. 119).

1. Sturton.
2. Cowley.
3. Smith.

BURTON (p. 121).

1. Burton.
2. Curteys.
3. Cotton.
4. Ridware.
5. Hardwick.
6. Rodvile.
7. Funden.
8. Flanders.
9. Limesey.
10. Ashbrook.
11. Champaine.
12. Stevens.

PLUMBE, IMPALING FORTESCUE (p. 121).

CAVE (p. 122).

1. Cave.
2. Gilliott.
3. Cliffe.

CHARNELLS (p. 122).

1. Charnells.
2. Bereford.

CHARNELLS—*continued.*

3. Shevesby.
4. Francis (?).

DUPORT (p. 123).

1. Duport.
2. Montague.

CARRINGTON *alias* SMITH (p. 130).

1. Smith.
2. Laneham.
3. Harewell.
4. Morton.
5. Woodford.
6. Preston.
7. Brabazon.
8. Rolleston.
9. Folvile.
10.
11.
12.

ASHBY (p. 132).

1. Ashby.
2. Mallet ?.

CROFT (p. 140).

1. Croft.
2. Harvey.
3. Burdet.
4. Willoughby.

BALE (p. 141).

1. Bale.
2.

EVERARD (p. 142).

1. Everard.
2. Everard of Shenton.
3. Langham.

BRUDNELL (p. 143).

1. Brudnell.
2. Atte Grove.
3. Raan (Harl. MSS. 1095, fo. 35).
4. Blaket of Castleton, co. Oxon.
5. Bulstrode.
6. Knife.
7. Thorne (Harl. MSS. 1095, fo. 35).
8. Entwisell.

CARRINGTON *alias* SMITH (p. 145).

1. Smith.
2. Laneham.
3. Raby.
4. Nevill.
5. Bulmer.
6. Blanchminster.
7. Rolleston.
8. Palmer.
9. Inglebeard.

List of Pedigrees.

The Visitation of the County of Leicester,

TAKEN A.D. 1619 BY SAMPSON LENNARD BLUE MANTLE AND AUGUSTINE VINCENT ROUGE ROSE POURSUIVANTS, BEING MARSHALLS AND DEPUTIES TO WILLIAM CAMDEN, CLARENCEUX. (HARL. MSS., 1180.)

(Cater.)*

ARMS. *Ermine, on a pile gules a lion passant guardant or.*

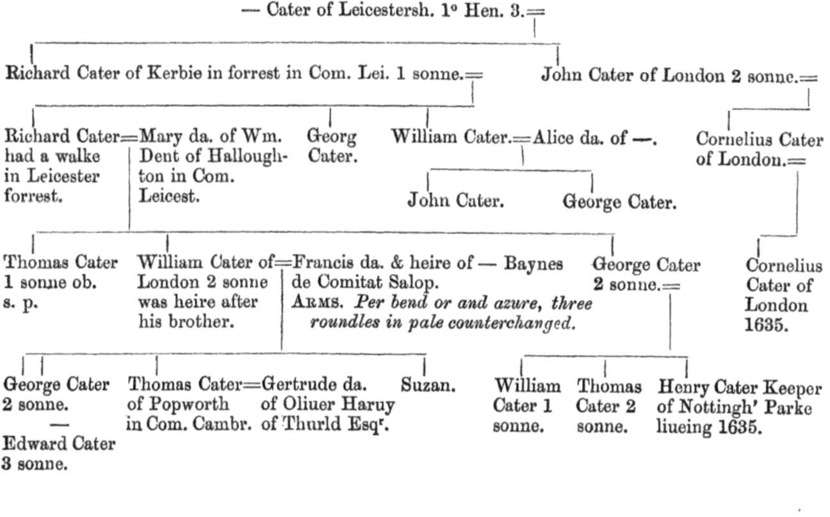

---

* This erroneous descent of Cater of Leicestershire was put down by Henry Parker.

Berkley of Wymondha' Leyc.

ARMS. *Quarterly :—1. Gules, a chevron between ten cinquefoils argent.* (BERKLEY.)
    2. Gules, a lion rampant ermine, crowned or. (HAMELYN.) *3. Argent, a fess
    dancettée between three billets gules.* (DE LA LAUND.) *4. Or, a lion rampant,
    double queuée sable.* (WELLES.) *5. Gules, a fess dancettée between six cross
    crosslets or.* (ENGAINE.) *6. Barry of six, ermine and gules, over all three
    crescents sable.* (WATERTON.)
ANOTHER COAT. *Quarterly, a chevron between ten cinquefoils (untinctured); and
    gules a lion rampant ermine, crowned or.*
CREST. *A bear's head couped argent, muzzled gules.*

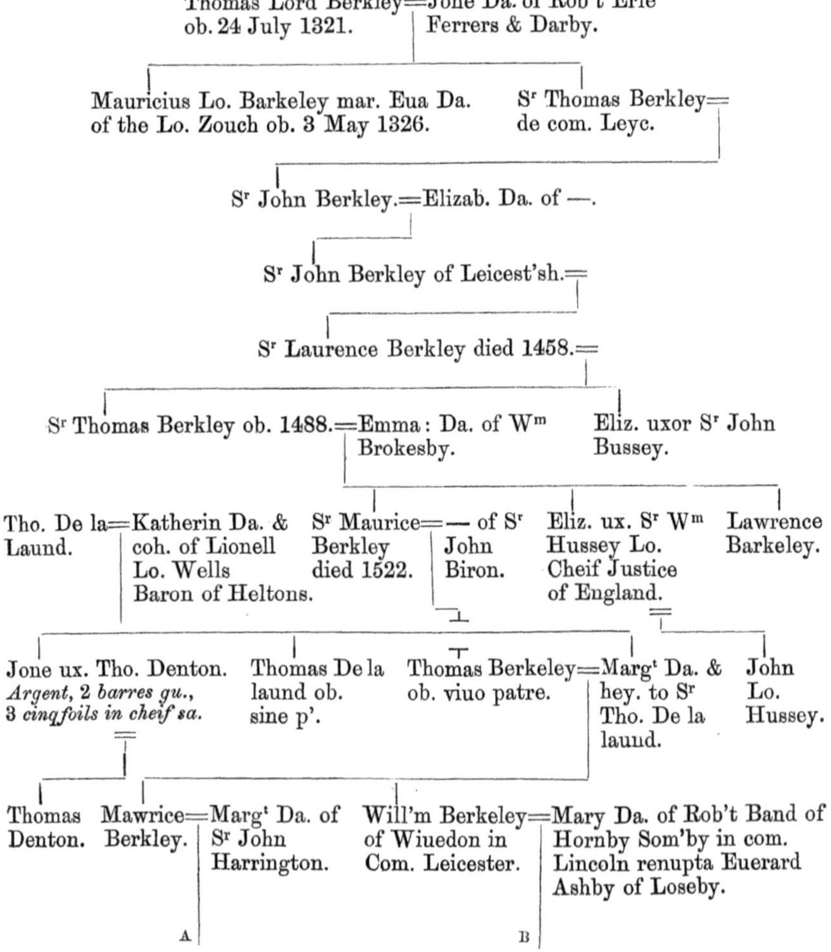

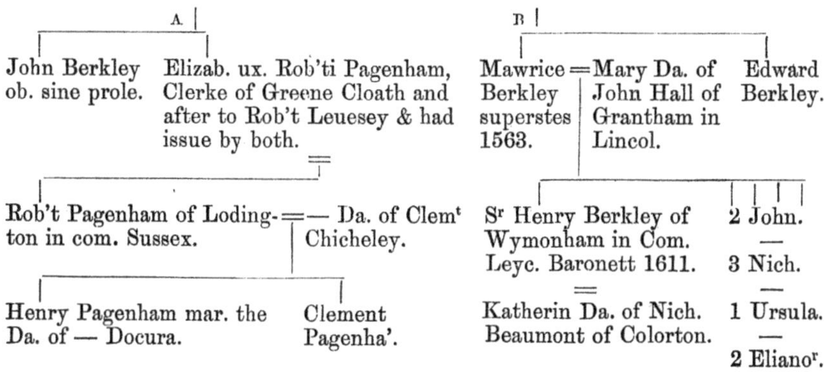

A. |

John Berkley ob. sine prole.	Elizab. ux. Rob'ti Pagenham, Clerke of Greene Cloath and after to Rob't Leuesey & had issue by both.
Rob't Pagenham of Loding- = ton in com. Sussex.	— Da. of Clem' Chicheley.
Henry Pagenham mar. the Da. of — Docura.	Clement Pagenha'.

B. |

Mawrice = Mary Da. of Berkley John Hall of superstes Grantham in 1563. Lincol.

Edward Berkley.

S' Henry Berkley of Wymonham in Com. Leyc. Baronett 1611.
=
Katherin Da. of Nich. Beaumont of Colorton.

2 John.
—
3 Nich.
—
1 Ursula.
—
2 Eliano'.

𝔑oell of 𝔇alby 𝔏eic.

ARMS. *Quarterly :—1. Or, fretty gules, a canton ermine. 2. Gules, semée of cross crosslets fitchée, a lion rampant or, charged on the shoulder with a crescent for difference. 3. Azure, three boars' heads argent, between nine cross crosslets or. 4. Azure, two trumpets in pile between nine cross crosslets or. 5. Barry of six, or and gules. 6. Azure, a lion rampant argent within a bordure engrailed or.*
CREST. *A buck statant argent, attired or.*

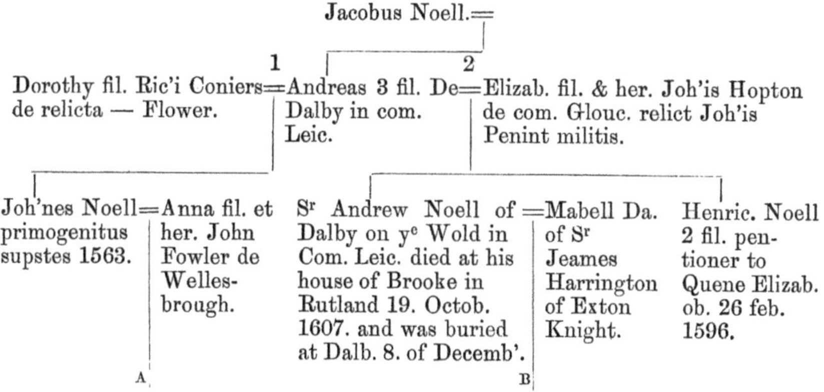

Jacobus Noell. =

1   2

| Dorothy fil. Ric'i Coniers = Andreas 3 fil. De = Elizab. fil. & her. Joh'is Hopton de relicta — Flower. | Dalby in com. Leic. | de com. Glouc. relict Joh'is Penint militis. |

| Joh'nes Noell = Anna fil. et primogenitus her. John supstes 1563. Fowler de Welles- brough. | S' Andrew Noell of = Mabell Da. Dalby on y' Wold in of S' Com. Leic. died at his Jeames house of Brooke in Harrington Rutland 19. Octob. of Exton 1607. and was buried Knight. at Dalb. 8. of Decemb'. | Henric. Noell 2 fil. pen- tioner to Quene Elizab. ob. 26 feb. 1596. |

A   B

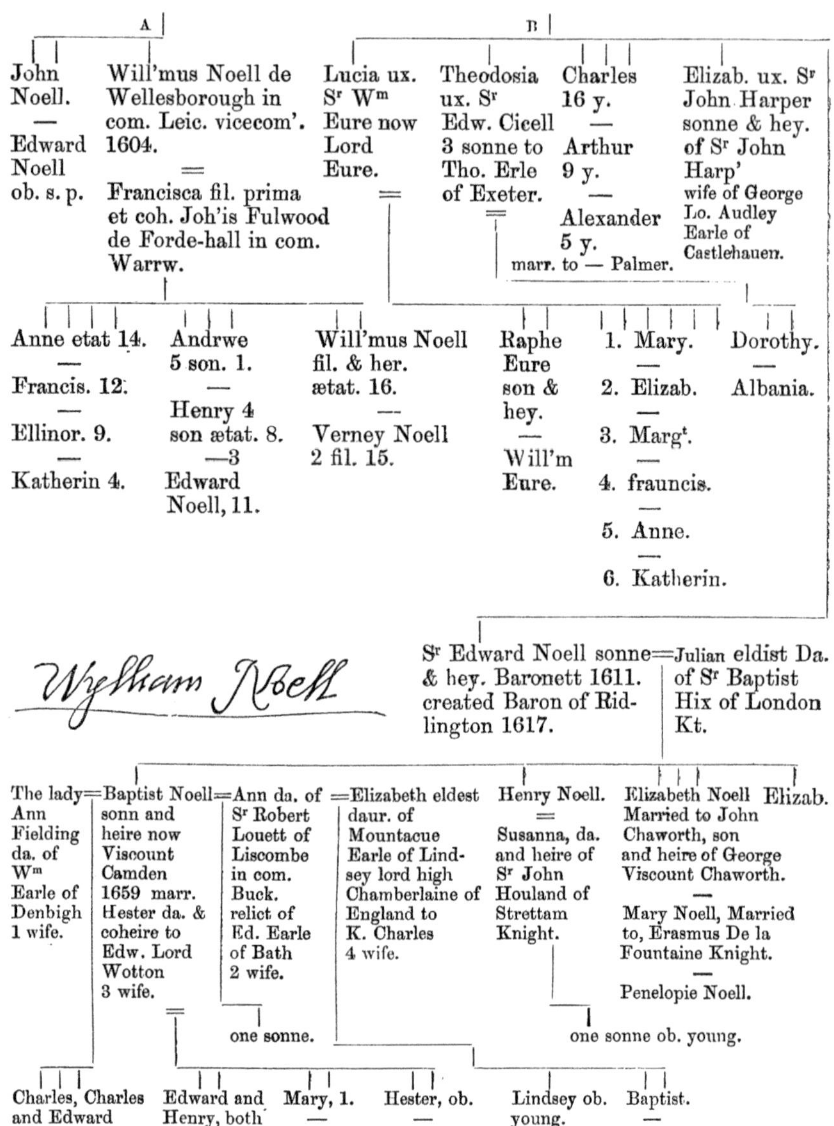

A |

John Noell. — Edward Noell ob. s. p.

Will'mus Noell de Wellesborough in com. Leic. vicecom'. 1604. = Francisca fil. prima et coh. Joh'is Fulwood de Forde-hall in com. Warrw.

Lucia ux. Sr Wm Eure now Lord Eure. =

B |

Theodosia ux. Sr Edw. Cicell 3 sonne to Tho. Erle of Exeter. =

Charles 16 y. — Arthur 9 y. — Alexander 5 y. marr. to — Palmer.

Elizab. ux. Sr John Harper sonne & hey. of Sr John Harp' wife of George Lo. Audley Earle of Castlehauen.

Anne etat 14. — Francis. 12. — Ellinor. 9. — Katherin 4.

Andrwe 5 son. 1. — Henry 4 son ætat. 8. —3 Edward Noell, 11.

Will'mus Noell fil. & her. ætat. 16. — Verney Noell 2 fil. 15.

Raphe Eure son & hey. — Will'm Eure.

1. Mary. — 2. Elizab. — 3. Marg^t. — 4. frauncis. — 5. Anne. — 6. Katherin.

Dorothy. — Albania.

Sr Edward Noell sonne & hey. Baronett 1611. created Baron of Rid-lington 1617. = Julian eldist Da. of Sr Baptist Hix of London Kt.

The lady Ann Fielding da. of Wm Earle of Denbigh 1 wife. = Baptist Noell sonn and heire now Viscount Camden 1659 marr. Hester da. & coheire to Edw. Lord Wotton 3 wife. = Ann da. of Sr Robert Louett of Liscombe in com. Buck. relict of Ed. Earle of Bath 2 wife. = Elizabeth eldest daur. of Mountacue Earle of Lindsey lord high Chamberlaine of England to K. Charles 4 wife.

Henry Noell. = Susanna, da. and heire of Sr John Houland of Strettam Knight.

Elizabeth Noell Married to John Chaworth, son and heire of George Viscount Chaworth. — Mary Noell, Married to, Erasmus De la Fountaine Knight. — Penelopie Noell.

Elizab.

one sonne.

one sonne ob. young.

Charles, Charles and Edward all ob. young.

Edward and Henry, both liuing 1659.

Mary, 1. — Julian, 2.

Hester, ob. — Elizabeth.

Lindsey ob. young.

Baptist. — Katherine.

Staresmore of Frolesworth in Com. Leic.

ARMS. *Quarterly* :—1. *Argent, a chevron vert between three torteaux.* (STARESMORE.) 2. *Argent, three partridges gules.* (PATRICH.) 3. *Gules, a cross moline argent.* 4. *Argent, a wolf saliant sable.* (WOLFE.) 5. *Gules, on a cross engrailed or five roses.* (COMBERFORD.) 6. *A fess between three roundles (untinctured).*

CREST. *A stare or starling proper.*

— Staresmore.== — Da. of — Malory.

— Staresmore.== — Da. of — Eiton.

Thomas Staresmore of Staresmore in com. Stafford == — Da. of — Partrich of Norfolk.

— Walshall.==

Ar., 6 tortuaux, 3 & 3 in pale.

Sr Will'm Walshall sine p'le.

Rob't Walshall of== — Da. of Geo. Peirpoint of Holm p' point.
Walshall & frolesworth.

Will'm Staresmore obijt== — Da. of Sr Robert Cresses de Comitat Salop.
1509.

Katherin ux. Edmon' Ringley de Tilton com. Staff. Captaine Calesij. ==

Maria fil. & coh. ux. Wilkes de Wikenhall.

Elizab. Da. &==John Staresmore ma. to his 2 wife== — Da. of — Perefoy
cohey. | Cassandra Da. of — Foulke of | 3. wife.
Brewood.

fil. ux. Lawley de Com. Staff.

Nicholas 2 sonne.

Francis Staresmore of Frolesworth==Mary Da. of Geo. Vincent of Pekelton supstes 1604.
in com. Leic. ob. 1582.

Mary ux. Berwell de com. Leyc.

Edmond.

—

Elizab. si. p.

A

B

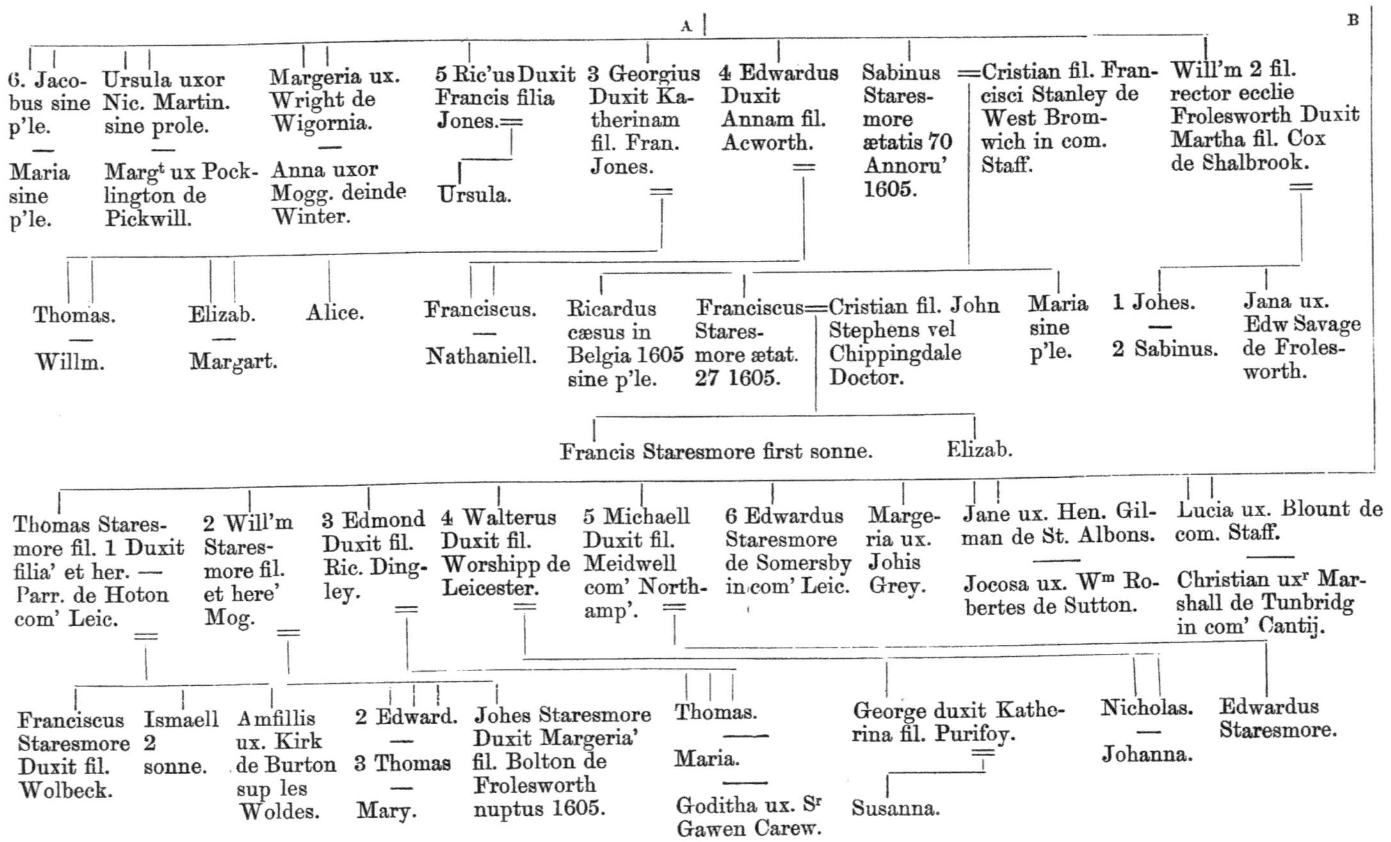
A
B

6. Jacobus sine p'le.
—
Maria sine p'le.

Ursula uxor Nic. Martin. sine prole.
—
Marg^t ux Pocklington de Pickwill.

Margeria ux. Wright de Wigornia.
—
Anna uxor Mogg. deinde Winter.

5 Ric'us Duxit Francis filia Jones.=
Ursula.

3 Georgius Duxit Katherinam fil. Fran. Jones.

4 Edwardus Duxit Annam fil. Acworth.

Sabinus Staresmore ætatis 70 Annoru' 1605.

=Cristian fil. Francisci Stanley de West Bromwich in com. Staff.

Will'm 2 fil. rector ecclie Frolesworth Duxit Martha fil. Cox de Shalbrook.

Thomas.
—
Willm.

Elizab.
—
Margart.

Alice.

Franciscus.
—
Nathaniell.

Ricardus cæsus in Belgia 1605 sine p'le.

Franciscus=Cristian fil. John Stephens vel Chippingdale Doctor.
Staresmore ætat. 27 1605.

Maria sine p'le.

1 Johes.
—
2 Sabinus.

Jana ux. Edw Savage de Frolesworth.

Francis Staresmore first sonne.

Elizab.

Thomas Staresmore fil. 1 Duxit filia' et her. Parr. de Hoton com' Leic.

2 Will'm Staresmore fil. et here' Mog.

3 Edmond Duxit fil. Ric. Dingley.

4 Walterus Duxit fil. Worshipp de Leicester.

5 Michaell Duxit fil. Meidwell com' Northamp'.

6 Edwardus Staresmore de Somersby in com' Leic.

Margeria ux. Johis Grey.

Jane ux. Hen. Gilman de St. Albons.
Jocosa ux. Wm Robertes de Sutton.

Lucia ux. Blount de com. Staff.
Christian ux^r Marshall de Tunbridg in com' Cantij.

Franciscus Staresmore Duxit fil. Wolbeck.

Ismaell 2 sonne.

Amfillis ux. Kirk de Burton sup les Woldes.

2 Edward.
—
3 Thomas
—
Mary.

Johes Staresmore Duxit Margeria' fil. Bolton de Frolesworth nuptus 1605.

Thomas.
Maria.
Goditha ux. Sr Gawen Carew.

George duxit Katherina fil. Purifoy.
Susanna.

Nicholas.
—
Johanna.

Edwardus Staresmore.

𝔖keuington.

ARMS. *Quarterly :—1. Argent, three bulls' heads erased sable. (SKEUINGTON). 2. Azure, a bend cotised between six mullets or. (OLDBEIFFE.) 3. Ermine, a bend azure. (ENGLISH.) 4. Quarterly, ermine and gules. (STANHOP.) 5. Vert, three greyhounds courant in pale or. (MALOUELL.) 6. Quarterly, or and gules within a bordure sable bezantée. (ROCHFORD.) 7. Gules, an eagle displayed or. (LISLEY.) 8. Argent, three Cornish choughs sable. (JENNEY.) 9. Argent, a fess dancettée between three crescents gules. (DOILEY.) 10. Sable, three garbs argent. (CAMBRIDG.) 11. Azure, a bend or, at the top an annulet gules. (DOWNE.) 12. Ermine, on a chief indented gules three escallops or. (CHILDE.) 13. Or, a pale azure, a chief vert. (COLSELL.)*

CREST. *A mermaid proper, crined or, holding in the dexter hand a looking-glass of the last, and in the sinister a comb (untinctured).*

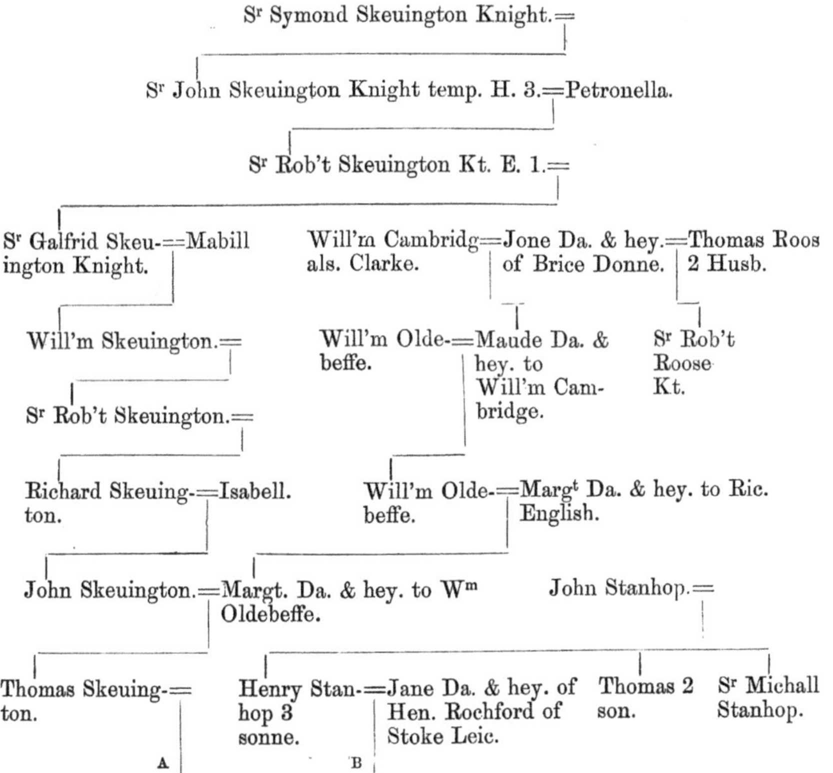

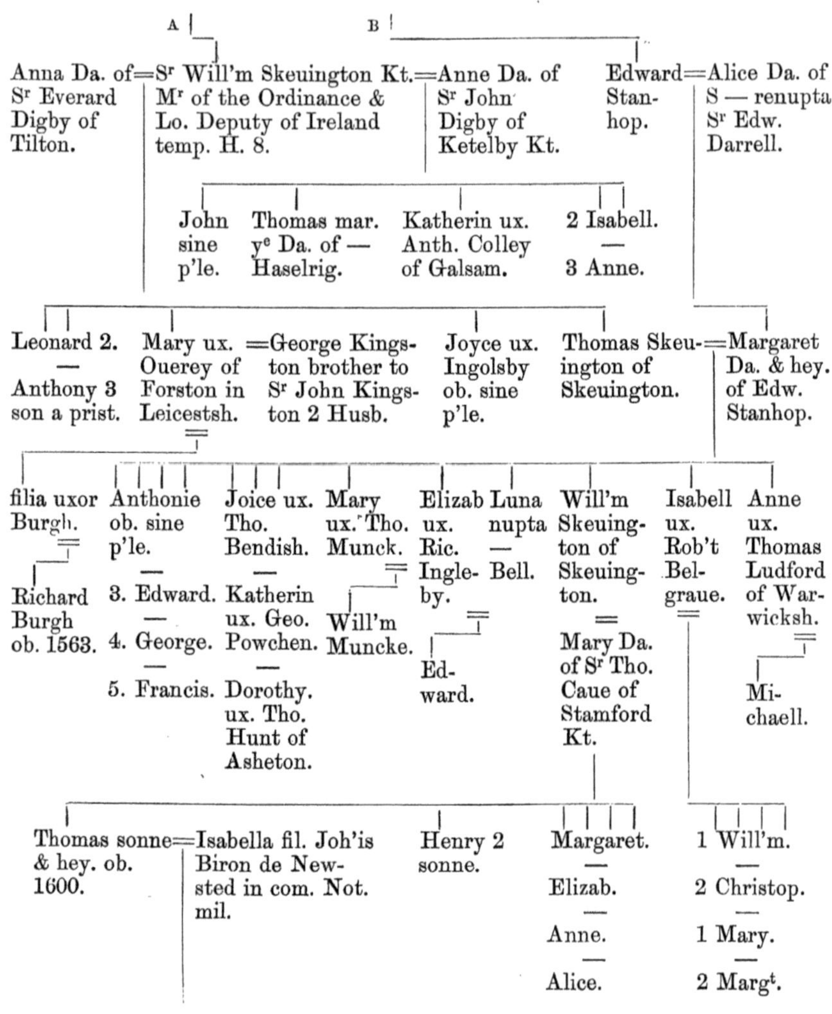

A
B
Anna Da. of=Sr Will'm Skeuington Kt.=Anne Da. of
Sr Everard | Mr of the Ordinance & | Sr John
Digby of | Lo. Deputy of Ireland | Digby of
Tilton. | temp. H. 8. | Ketelby Kt.
Edward=Alice Da. of
Stan- | S — renupta
hop. | Sr Edw.
| Darrell.

John | Thomas mar. | Katherin ux. | 2 Isabell.
sine | ye Da. of — | Anth. Colley | —
p'le. | Haselrig. | of Galsam. | 3 Anne.

Leonard 2. | Mary ux. =George Kings- | Joyce ux. | Thomas Skeu-=Margaret
— | Ouerey of ton brother to | Ingolsby | ington of | Da. & hey.
Anthony 3 | Forston in Sr John Kings- | ob. sine | Skeuington. | of Edw.
son a prist. | Leicestsh. ton 2 Husb. | p'le. | | Stanhop.

filia uxor | Anthonie | Joice ux. | Mary | Elizab Luna | Will'm | Isabell | Anne
Burgh. | ob. sine | Tho. | ux. Tho. | ux. nupta | Skeuing- | ux. | ux.
| p'le. | Bendish. | Munck. | Ric. — | ton of | Rob't | Thomas
Richard | 3. Edward. | Katherin | | Ingle- Bell. | Skeuing- | Bel- | Ludford
Burgh | — | ux. Geo. | Will'm | by. | ton. | graue. | of War-
ob. 1563. | 4. George. | Powchen. | Muncke. | | | | wicksh.
| — | — | | Ed- | Mary Da. | |
| 5. Francis. | Dorothy. | | ward. | of Sr Tho. | | Mi-
| | ux. Tho. | | | Caue of | | chaell.
| | Hunt of | | | Stamford | |
| | Asheton. | | | Kt. | |

Thomas sonne=Isabella fil. Joh'is | Henry 2 | Margaret. | 1 Will'm.
& hey. ob. | Biron de New- | sonne. | — | —
1600. | sted in com. Not. | | Elizab. | 2 Christop.
| mil. | | — | —
| | | Anne. | 1 Mary.
| | | — | —
| | | Alice. | 2 Margt.

Will'm Skefington de Skefing.=Katherina fil. Ric'i Chetwood
mil. ob. s. p. | de Woodhull in com.
| Bedf. mil.

Hartop of Burton Lazers in Com' Leyc.

Raphe Hartop temp. R. 2.=— Da. of Alexander Moyne.

Precilla ux. Oliuer Cooke.

Philippa ux. Geo. Holleys.

Alexander=Ellin Da. Hartope. of —.

Mariona Da.

Autheria 4 Da.

John Hartop.=Margaret Da. of Thomas Brideamaine.

Mary mar. to Hen. Leibourne Esq.

John Hartop 2 sonne mar. Cristian Da. of John Williams.

Henry =Barbara Da. of Hartop. Raphe fitz Randall.

Marg* eldist Da. mar. to Thomas Broxby.

Ursula mar. to John Ashley.

Rob't Hartop 2 son mar. Anne Da. of John Porter of Betton.

John Hartop.=Jane Da. of W** Inglebeard.

Isabell mar. to Thomas Blasbye.

Richard Hartop.=— Da. of Raph Chamberlayne.

John Hartop mar. Grace Da. of Will'm Blewet.

Thomas Hartop.=— Da. of John Allen.

Joane mar. to Octauian Fisher of Threkingham in Com. Lincoln.

Will'm =Ellianor Da. Hartop. & hey. of — Adcot postea ux. — Odingselles.

Valentine =Anne Da. & Hartop hey. of 2 son. Will'm Goodman Com. Leyc.

Richard student of the middle Temple ob. sine prole.

Judith. — Susan. — Elizab. — Anne.

4 Richard. — 5 Georg.

Valentine Hartop 2 sonne mar. the Da. of — Pratt of Lutterworth in Com. Leic.

Edward=Mary Da. Hartop of Eras- of Frith- mus Dry- by in den de Com. Ashby in Leic. Com. Northam'.

Thomas=— Da. of Hartop Tho. Caue first son. of Stan- ford in Com. Northam.

S* Will'm =Mary Da. of Hartop John Rolt of Burton of Milton Lazers in Herneis in Com. Leic. Com. Bedford. Kt.

Samuell Hartop 2 son : mar. Briget Da. of W** Mason of Egmondton in com. Nott.

Mary mar. to Nic. Stringer of Eaton in Com. Nott.

Elizab. mar. to Geo. Bale of Carlton Curlew in Com. Leic.

Jone mar. to W** Stret of De Com. Leic.

Thomas son & hey.

Sherard of Stapleford in Com. Leyc.

ARMS. *Quarterly* :—1. *Argent, a chevron between three torteaux.* (SHERARD.) 2. *On a bend three trefoils slipped (untinctured).* (HAUBERK.) 3. *Argent, three leopards' heads jessant-de-lis sable.* (WODFORD.) 4. *Ermine, a talbot passant sable.* (PRESTON.) 5. *On a bend three martlets (untinctured).* (BRABSON.) 6. *Per fess argent and or, a cross moline gules.* (FOLUILE.) 7. *Argent, on a chevron sable three bezants within a bordure engrailed gules.* (HELWELL.) 8. *Gules, on a chevron argent three roses of the field.* (BROW.) 9. *Argent, a fess and canton conjoined gules within a bordure bezantée.* (WOODUILE.)

CREST. *On a wreath azure a peacock's tail erect proper, banded checquy argent and gules. On the dexter side is written "pecocks tayle"; on the sinister, "pecocks plum."*

Tho. Sherard de Com' Lancash. miles.=

Rob't Sherard of Stapleford in=Anna Da. & hey. of — Hubarke
com. Leyc. 2 filij.   Dni de Stapleford.

filia — Foluile ux. 1.=Lawrence Sherard.= — Da. & hey. of — Woodford.

Galfred Sherard.=Joice Da. of Tho. Ashbye of Losebye.

Thomas =Margerit Da. & hey. of   3 Laurence.   Rob't Sherard 2 sonne mar.
Sherard. | John Helwell Knight.   —   Da. of — Digby of Welby.
      4 William.

2
Anna ux.   Marg^t ux.   Ricardus   Georg =Roisia Da. of   Rowland Sherard
Anth. Ellis   Black de   2 filius.   Sherard | Sr Tho.   mar. the Da. of
de Panton   Granth'.   sup'stes | Poultney of   Austin Porter of
in Com'   1563. | Misterton in   Beeton in Lin-
Leic.   Com. Leic.   colnsh.=

Susan   Thomas   1 Ellin.   4. Elizab.   Marg^t ux. W^m   Francis=Anne Da. of
6   2   —   —   Durant de   Sher- | Grigory
filia.   sonne.   3. Joyce.   5. Dorothie.   Coltesmor in   ard. | More de
                             Com. Leic.   Com. Lin-
                                             coln.

Willm's Sher- =Abigall filia Cicell   Sr Phillip Sherard=Isabell 4 Da.   2 George
rard miles | Caue gen relicta   of Stapleford | of Sr John   et heres.
pentioner | Hen. Tresham fil.   Knighted by King | Harpur of   —
to King | et hey. Tho. Tres-   James 1602 ætat. | Swarston in   3. Willm.
James supstes | ham de Nenton in   34. 1604. sup'stes | Darbish. ob.   —
1622. | Com. Northton.   1622. ob. s. p. | s.p.   Rose.

Benet Sherrard fil.   Francis Da. of John=Sr Willm. Sherard=Bridget Da. of
et heres æt. unius   Harrinton Witham | of Loyingthorpe | Kenolm Digby
anni et dimidij 1622.   on y^e Hill.   in Lincolnsh. | of Stok.

John Sherard.   Will'm Sherard.   Rowland.   Katherin.

𝕬pleby of 𝕬pleby.

ARMS. *Azure, six martlets or, three, two, one.*

Henricus Aplebye of Apleby in Com. Leicest.═

Sʳ Edmond Apleby 53 H. 3.═

Sʳ Will'm Apleby ═   Alice ux. John Hardwick of Lindley.

Sʳ John Apleby 4. & 27. Ed. 3.═

Sʳ Edmond Apleby.═

Sʳ John Apleby 1. R. 2. et 6. H. 4.═

Thomas Apleby 5. H. 5.═

Edmond Apleby 21. H. 6.═ — Da. & hey. of Wᵐ Peehet.   ARMS. *A fleur-de-lis* (*untinctured*).

John Aplebye.═

Rich. Apleby 21. H. 7. ob. 1528.═Elizab. Da. of Rob't Langham of Gopshill.

George Apleby Slayne at═Jocosa Da. of Tho. Curson de═Tho. Lewes de
Muskleborowe   Croxhall combusta propter   Manceter Com'
feild.   religione' 1557.   War.

Richard Apleby.═

Francis Apleby 1605.   Neuill.   Barbara.

Euerard of Shenton in Com' Leic.

ARMS. *Quarterly :*—1. *Gules, on a fess three mullets between as many étoiles argent.*
(EUERARD.) 2. *Barry of six ermine and gules, over all three crescents sable.*
(WATERTON). 3. *Barry nebulée of six sable and or, on a chief argent three birds
of the first.* (GRIMSBY.) 4. *Argent, a cinquefoil azure.* (MOTON.) *Or, three
piles meeting in base gules, a canton vair.* (BASSET.) 6. *Or, a fess gules.*
(COLUILE). 7. *Or, a lion rampant double queuée gules.* (MALORY.) 8. *Or,
on a fess three water bougets.* (BUGG.) 9. *Or, fretty (untinctured).* (CHAM-
PANIE.)

ARMS OF LANGHAM. *Argent, three bears' heads couped sable, muzzled or.*

Sup Cathedra' in Domo Rici' Euerard de Shenton.

*Gules, a fess nebulée between three étoiles argent, impaling argent, on a fess sable three
bezants between as many bears' heads erased, muzzled.*

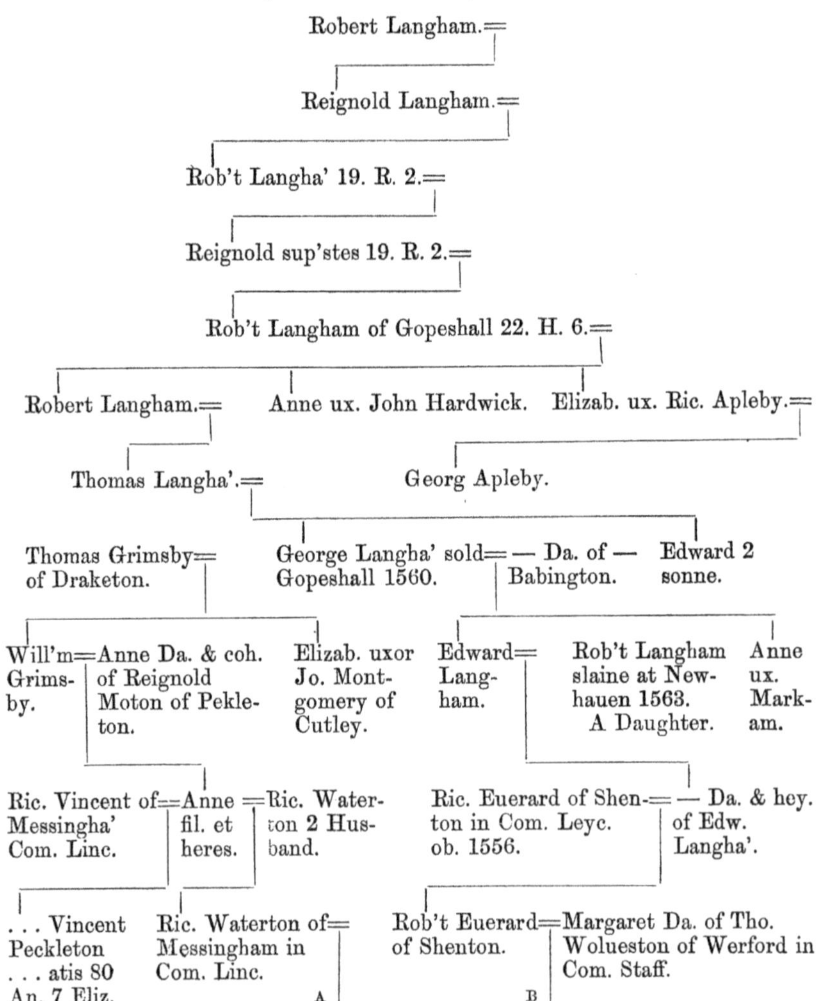

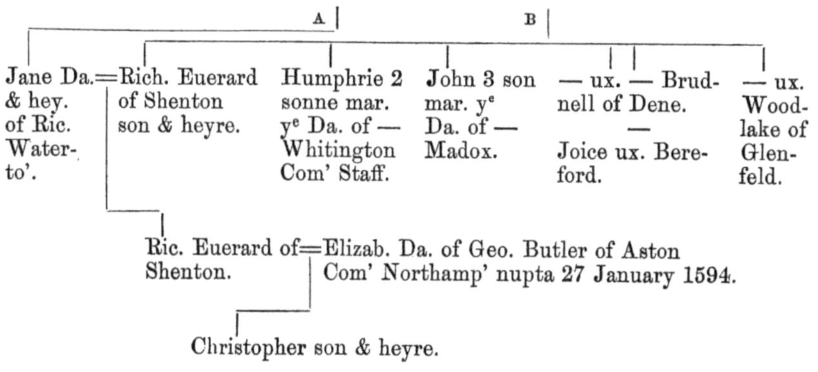

Ashby of Quenby in Com' Leyc.

ARMS. *Quarterly:—Azure, a chevron ermine between three leopards' faces or; and Gules, three mallets argent. "The first coat should be p'te p' pale b. g. the lybards' heads ar."*
CREST. *Out of a mural coronet argent, a leopard's face or.*

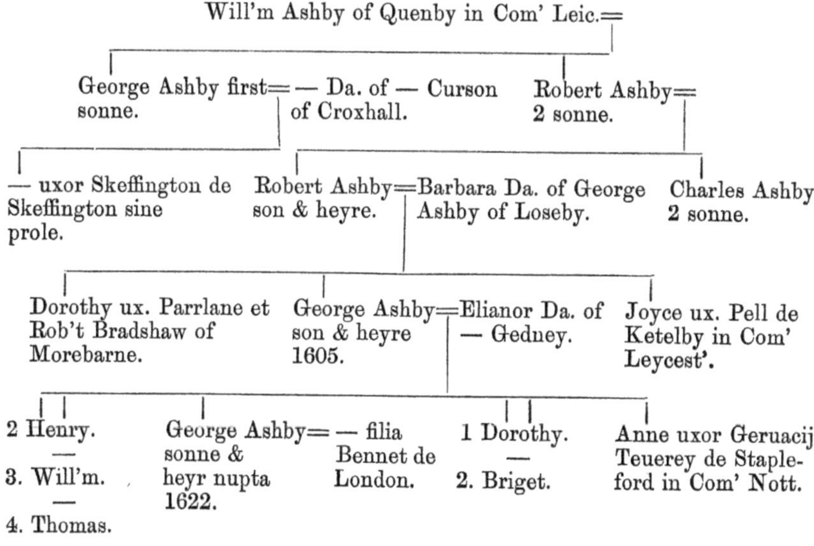

Ashby of Loseby in Leic.

ARMS. *Quarterly :—1. Argent, a lion rampant sable, a chief gules.   2. Azure, five bezants.   3. Azure, on two bars or six martlets gules.   4. Ermine, a cross engrailed sable.   5. Argent, a chevron gules between three door-staples sable.*
CREST. *A ram's head couped argent, attired or.*

"In the Parish Church of Loseby in Com' Leic.

1. *Argent, a lion rampant sable, a chief gules* (ASHBY), *impaling argent, a chevron gules between three door-staples sable.   2. A lion rampant (untinctured), a chief gules ; impaling ermine a cross engrailed gules.   3. The same ; impaling ermine on a bend azure three quatrefoils or.   4. Quarterly :—A lion rampant (untinctured), a chief gules ; and azure, two bars or ; impaling a chevron engrailed sable between three cross crosslets fitchée.*

Thomas Ashby of Loseby in Com' Leic. ob. 1422.==Elizab.

Thomas Ashby ob. 1433.==Katherin Da. of Rob't Brett of Addington.

1
Agnes Da. of Sʳ==Will'm Ashby==Agnes Da. of Sʳ Ric. Illingworth   Jocosa uxor
Tho. Poultney. ob. viuo patre Cheif Boron of the Exchequer   Galfredi
Kt. 1. ux.   1427.   ob. 1492.   Sherard.

2

2 Thomas.   Euerard==Mary Da. of   George==— Parnel Da.   — uxor Sercole.
—   Ashby   Robt. Baud   Ashby   of Sʳ John
3. Robert   of   of Somerby   2   Digby of   Elizab. ux Penbery
obiere s. p.   Loseby.   relicta   sonne.   Kettleby in   de Com' Northton.
   Will'm   Com' Leic.
   Berkley of   Ciceley uxor
   Wymondham.   Heirik de North.

Francis Ashby Duxit relict Browne de Walcott   Will'm sans   Eliza ux. Hen.
in Com. Northam' et obijt sine prole.   issue.   Naunton of Suff.

   2   **1**
John ==Eliz. Da. of Wᵐ Tan-   Thomas bis   Barbara ux. Rob't   Agnes ux.
Asby.   feild of Euerto' in   nupta filia   Ashby of Quenby.   Brokesby of
   Com. Hunt.   Witterantes.   Godeby.

Thomas Ashby==Anne Da. of John Beau-   John et Ursula   1 John.   Elizab.
sold Loseby   mont of Gracedieu Mʳ   both sans   —   —
et ob. 1604.   of yᵉ Rolles.   issue.   2 Thomas.   Anne.

Bridget ux.   George   Will'm==— Da. of —   Mary   Francis ux. Rob't
— Fox.   2 sonne.   Ashby   Minors of   uxor —   Throckmorton filij
—   sonne   Staffordsheir.   Eaton.   Junioris Nicholai
Elizab.   & hey.   militis.

Will'm Ashby sonne & hey. 1605.   Anne.

Haselrig of Noseley Com. Leyc.

ARMS. *Quarterly:*—1. *Argent a chevron sable between three hazel leaves vert.* (HESELRIG.) 2. *Vair sable and argent, a canton gules.* (STANTON.) 3. *Gules, an eagle displayed argent.* (SUTHELL.) 4. *Gules, a fess or between three saltires couped argent.* (BOIVILE.) 5. *Bendy of six gules and argent.*
CREST. *A maiden's head couped at the shoulders proper, with hair dishevelled or.*

Simon de Hasilirgg D'ns de Wotteslade et West Brunton in Com. Northumb' cui Ed. 1. dedit maneria de Yetham Corbet et Yetha' maner A° 1280.⚊

Symon Haselrig D'ns de Haselreg.⚊

Gulielmus⚊— fil. et her. Rob'ti Esselington militis. Haselrig.

Radus Hastings⚊ miles.

Robtus de Soding-⚊filia et her. — Mortinall. ton.

Radus Hastings⚊Isabella fil. et her. Robti miles 4 fil. de Sodington.

Tho. Haselreg⚊Isab. filia et coh. Rog. Heron militis. son & hey.

Johes Broket.⚊Margareta fil. et heres Robti Hastings.

Tho. Hasilrig sonne⚊Mabilia fil. & her. Johis Broket. & hey.

Tho. Stanton⚊

Willm. Hasel-⚊Elizab. Da. & hey.⚊Thomas⚊Edith sister Margeria Elizab. rigge of Nose- of Tho. Stanton Ent- to Ric. ux. — uxor ley in Com. de Stanton wisell. Bracebrige Villers. Willi Leic. Harold in Com' of Kinsburie. Turuill Leic. militis.

Katherina ux. John Robert Hasillridge — uxor to Thomas Hasel-⚊Lucia Thomæ Hasel- mar. Eliz. sist. Richard rigg Armiger Ent- Ashby de rigge. to Sr Raph Neale. p' corpore wisell. Quenby. Shirley. H. 8. 1535.

Elizab. Bartram⚊Anne da. & coh. 1 Herald 2 Anne ux. Edw. Milicent ux. Hesel- of Sr Hen. ux. David Catesby Com' uxor Walter Robert rigg Southill of Williams Rutland. Kebell de Coling- 1563. Stoberston in of Aber- ——— Humerston wood. Com. Leic. gauenie. 3 Editha ux. Com. Leic.
                                                    John Thorney.

A

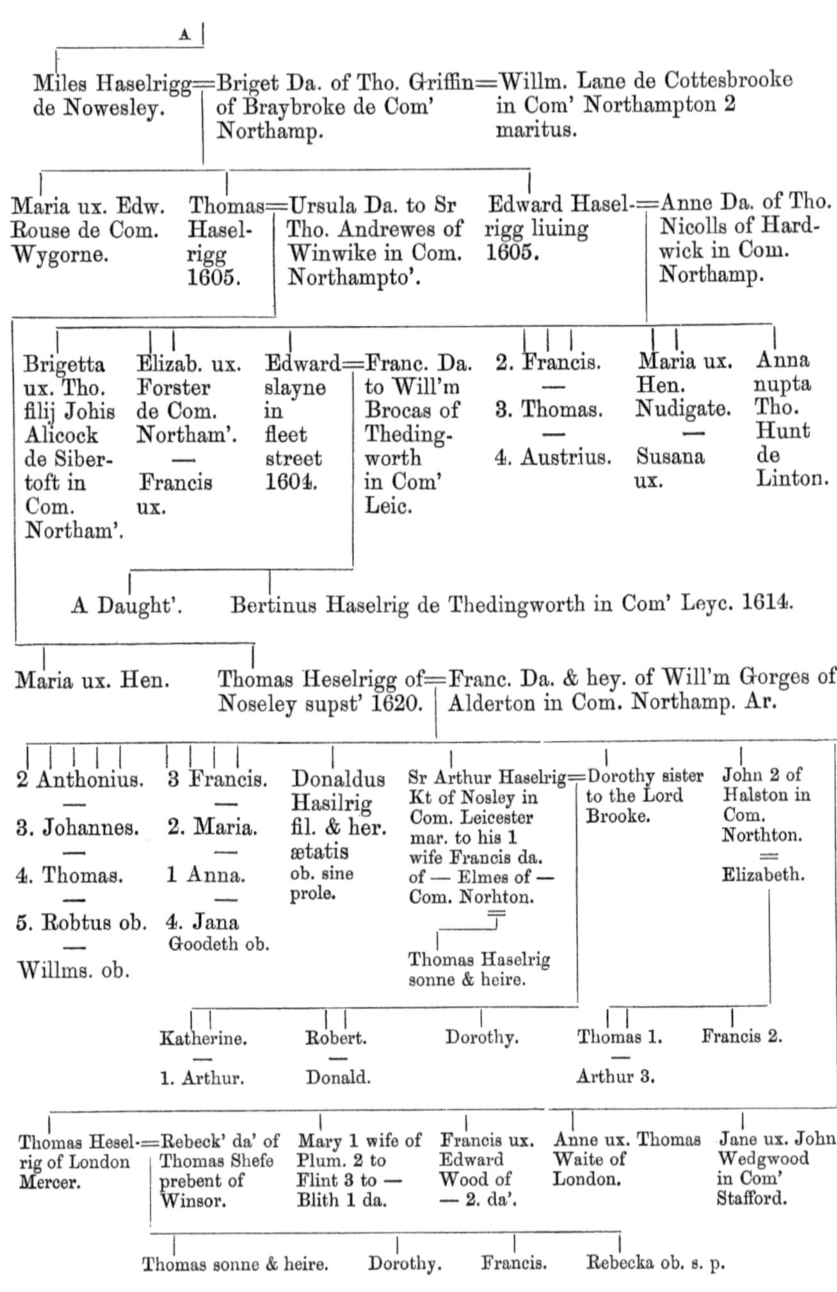

A

Miles Haselrigg=Briget Da. of Tho. Griffin=Willm. Lane de Cottesbrooke
de Nowesley.   of Braybroke de Com'   in Com' Northampton 2
                Northamp.   maritus.

Maria ux. Edw.   Thomas=Ursula Da. to Sr   Edward Hasel-=Anne Da. of Tho.
Rouse de Com.   Hasel- Tho. Andrewes of   rigg liuing   Nicolls of Hard-
Wygorne.   rigg   Winwike in Com.   1605.   wick in Com.
                 1605.   Northampto'.   Northamp.

Brigetta   Elizab. ux.   Edward=Franc. Da.   2. Francis.   Maria ux.   Anna
ux. Tho.   Forster   slayne to Will'm   —   Hen.   nupta
filij Johis   de Com.   in   Brocas of   3. Thomas.   Nudigate.   Tho.
Alicock   Northam'.   fleet   Theding-   —   —   Hunt
de Siber-   —   street worth   4. Austrius. Susana   de
toft in   Francis   1604.   in Com'   ux.   Linton.
Com.   ux.   Leic.
Northam'.

      A Daught'.   Bertinus Haselrig de Thedingworth in Com' Leyc. 1614.

Maria ux. Hen.   Thomas Heselrigg of=Franc. Da. & hey. of Will'm Gorges of
                     Noseley supst' 1620. Alderton in Com. Northamp. Ar.

2 Anthonius.   3 Francis.   Donaldus   Sr Arthur Haselrig=Dorothy sister   John 2 of
—   —   Hasilrig   Kt of Nosley in   to the Lord   Halston in
3. Johannes.   2. Maria.   fil. & her.   Com. Leicester   Brooke.   Com.
—   —   ætatis   mar. to his 1   Northton.
4. Thomas.   1 Anna.   ob. sine   wife Francis da.   =
—   —   prole.   of — Elmes of —   Elizabeth.
5. Robtus ob. 4. Jana   Com. Norhton.
—   Goodeth ob.   =
Willms. ob.   Thomas Haselrig
                                          sonne & heire.

       Katherine.   Robert.   Dorothy.   Thomas 1.   Francis 2.
       —   —   —
       1. Arthur.   Donald.   Arthur 3.

Thomas Hesel-=Rebeck' da' of   Mary 1 wife of   Francis ux.   Anne ux. Thomas   Jane ux. John
rig of London Thomas Shefe   Plum. 2 to   Edward   Waite of   Wedgwood
Mercer.   prebent of   Flint 3 to —   Wood of   London.   in Com'
               Winsor.   Blith 1 da.   — 2. da'.   Stafford.

       Thomas sonne & heire.   Dorothy.   Francis.   Rebecka ob. s. p.

Grey of Barwell in Com. Leyc.

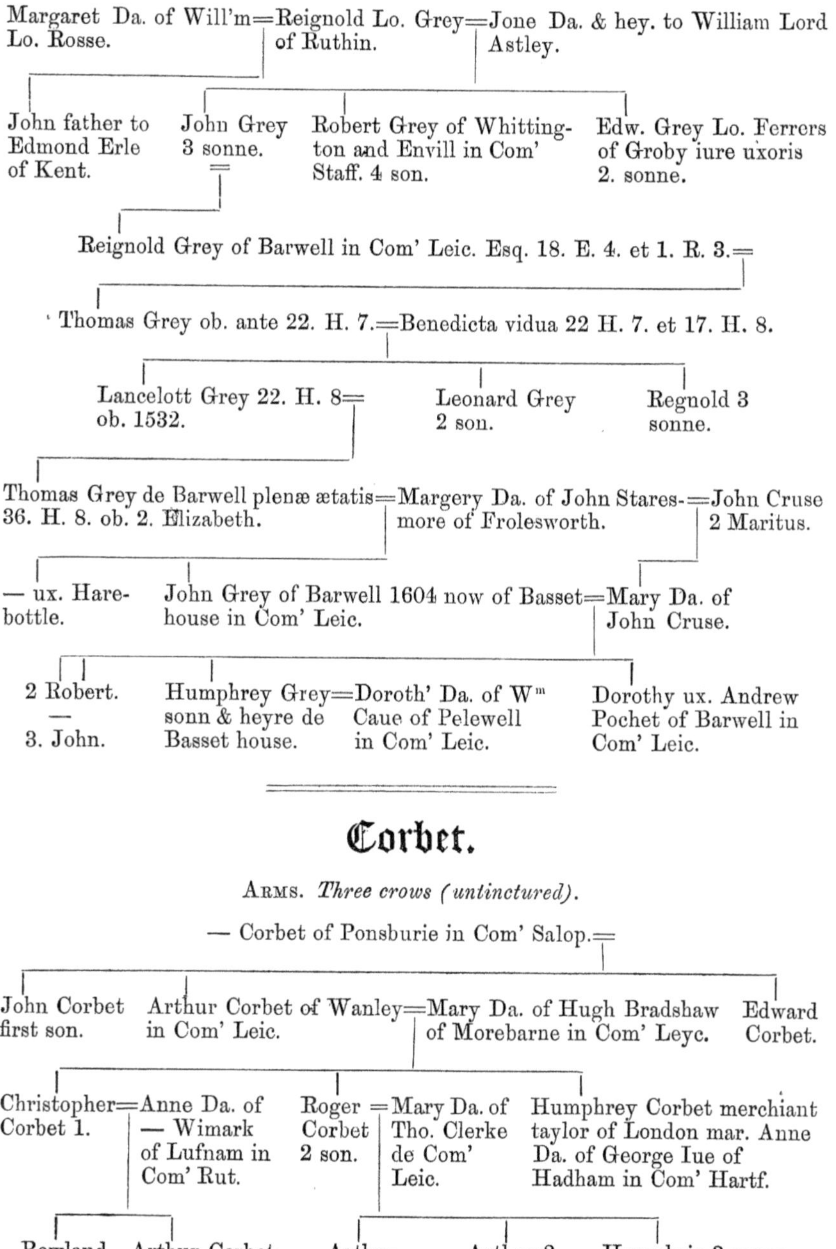

Margaret Da. of Will'm=Reignold Lo. Grey=Jone Da. & hey. to William Lord
Lo. Rosse.   of Ruthin.   Astley.

John father to   John Grey   Robert Grey of Whitting-   Edw. Grey Lo. Ferrers
Edmond Erle   3 sonne.   ton and Envill in Com'   of Groby iure uxoris
of Kent.   =   Staff. 4 son.   2. sonne.

Reignold Grey of Barwell in Com' Leic. Esq. 18. E. 4. et 1. R. 3.=

Thomas Grey ob. ante 22. H. 7.=Benedicta vidua 22 H. 7. et 17. H. 8.

Lancelott Grey 22. H. 8=   Leonard Grey   Regnold 3
ob. 1532.   2 son.   sonne.

Thomas Grey de Barwell plenæ ætatis=Margery Da. of John Stares-=John Cruse
36. H. 8. ob. 2. Elizabeth.   more of Frolesworth.   2 Maritus.

— ux. Hare-   John Grey of Barwell 1604 now of Basset=Mary Da. of
bottle.   house in Com' Leic.   John Cruse.

2 Robert.   Humphrey Grey=Doroth' Da. of W   Dorothy ux. Andrew
—   sonn & heyre de   Caue of Pelewell   Pochet of Barwell in
3. John.   Basset house.   in Com' Leic.   Com' Leic.

Corbet.

ARMS. *Three crows (untinctured).*

— Corbet of Ponsburie in Com' Salop.=

John Corbet   Arthur Corbet of Wanley=Mary Da. of Hugh Bradshaw   Edward
first son.   in Com' Leic.   of Morebarne in Com' Leyc.   Corbet.

Christopher=Anne Da. of   Roger =Mary Da. of   Humphrey Corbet merchiant
Corbet 1.   — Wimark   Corbet Tho. Clerke   taylor of London mar. Anne
        of Lufnam in   2 son.   de Com'   Da. of George Iue of
        Com' Rut.   Leic.   Hadham in Com' Hartf.

Rowland   Arthur Corbet   Arthur   Arthur 2   Humphrie 3 sonne.
Corbet.   2 sonne.   Corbet.   son.

Derby.

ARMS. *Argent, a fess between three sinister wings sable.*

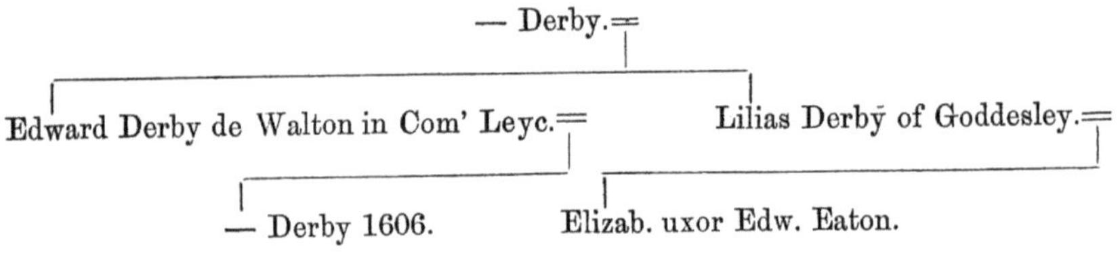

Segrave.

ARMS. *Argent, a lion rampant sable, crowned or.*

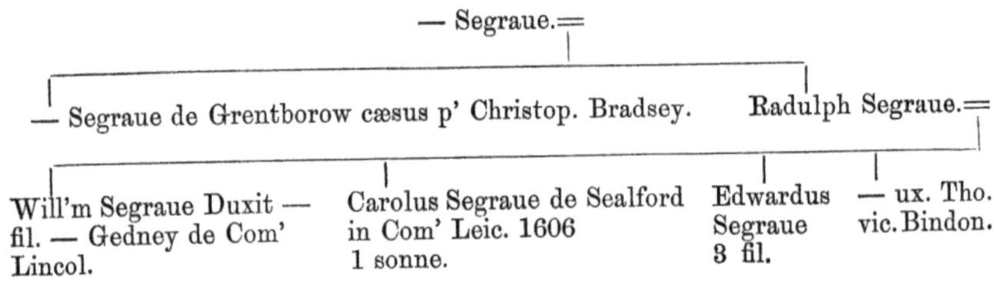

Burdet.

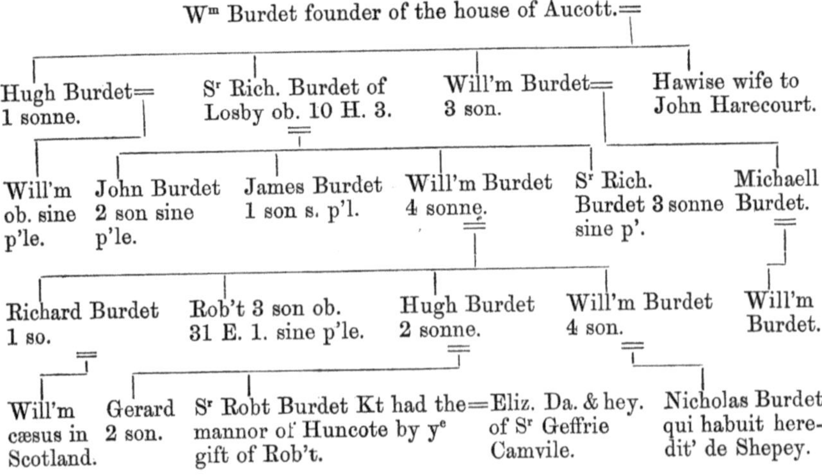

𝕷𝖊𝖌𝖆𝖗𝖉.

ARMS. *Quarterly :—1. Argent, on a bend between six mullets gules a cross pattée or.*
  2. Argent, on a bend gules three crescents of the field. 3. Gules, a bend or.
  4. Argent, three water bougets sable.
CREST, *A greyhound statant collared or, studded gules.*

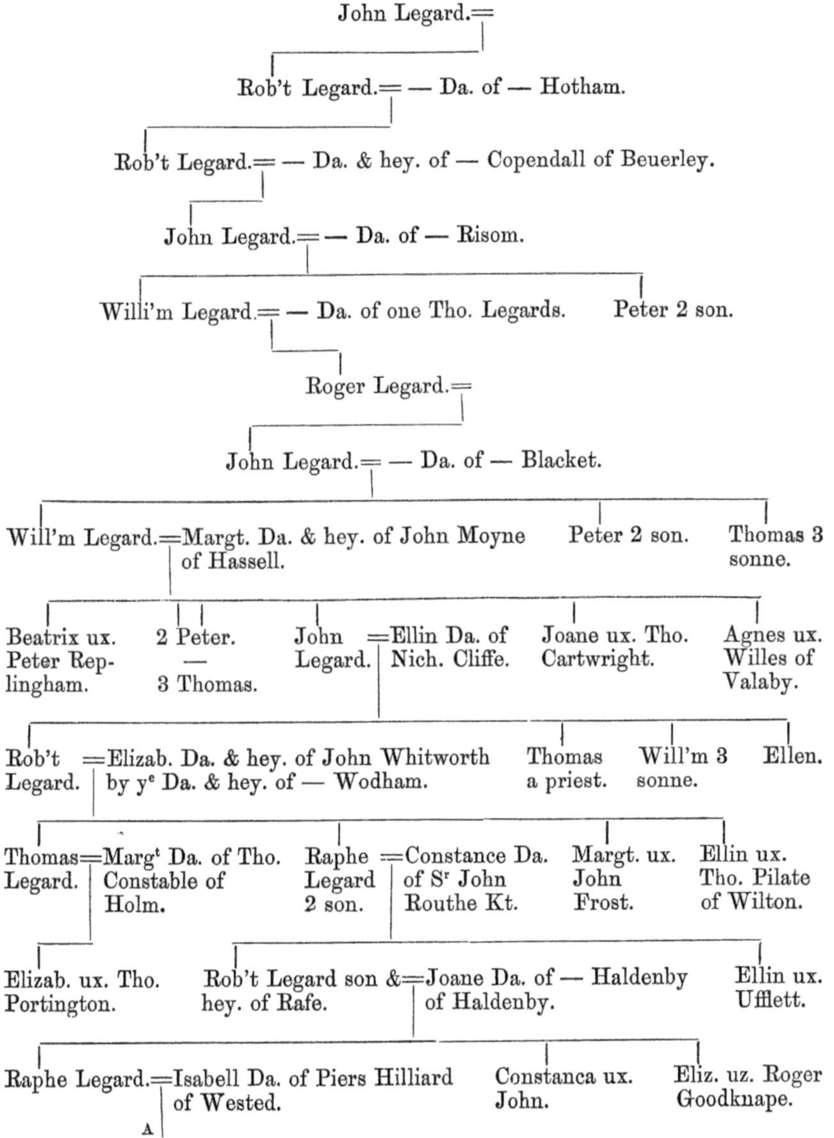

A

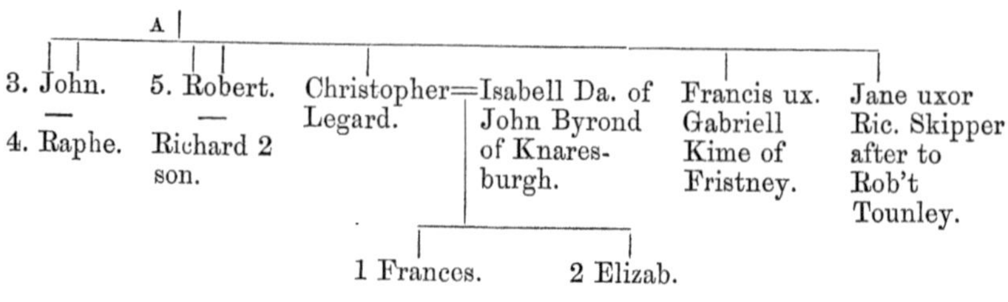

Cheselton.

ARMS. *A chevron between three crosses moline (untinctured).*
CREST. *A dog couchant, with collar and line reflexed, nowed at the end (untinctured).*

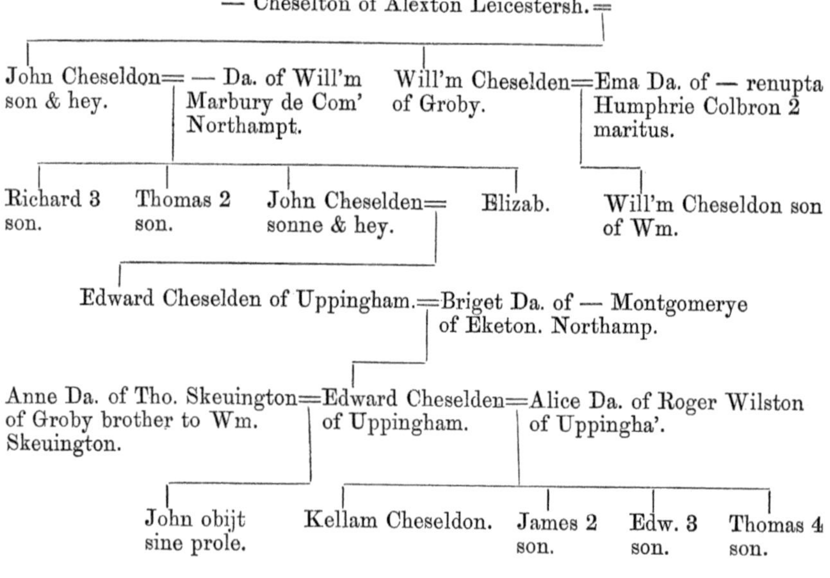

Neuill of Holte, Leic.

ARMS. *Quarterly*:—1. *Sable, a cross gules between four peacocks argent.* (SMITH.)
2. *Quarterly argent and sable, in the first quarter a fleur-de-lis of the last, and
in the fourth an ermine spot.* (LANEHAM.) 3. *Argent, on a chevron azure three
escallops of the field, on a chief of the second a lion passant of the first.* (HINDE.)
4. *Gules, a saltire ermine.* (RABY.) 5. *Or, fretty gules on a canton per pale
(untinctured) a lymphad.* (NEUILL.) 6. *Gules, a lion rampant or.* (BULMER.)
7. *Bendy of six gules and vert, over all a chevron ermine.* (BLANCHMINSTER.)
8. *Or, two bars nebulée sable, a canton ermine.* (ROLLESTON.) 9. *Azure, a
fleur-de-lis or.* (PALMER.) 10. *Bendy of six (untinctured), over all a chevron
ermine.* (INGLEBERD.) 11. *Bendy of six or and azure, a canton ermine.*
(BISHOPSTON.) 12. *Or, a chevron gules, a chief indented vert.* (FENCOTES.)
13. *Lozengy argent and sable.* (CROFTES.)

Robt. Lo. of Raby.=Isabell Da. & hey. of Galfred Neuill.

Galfred surnamed Neuill Lo[r] of Raby.=Margt. fil. Jo. Longuillers.

Robt. Lo.=Isabella fil. Rogeri Bartra'
Neuill. | D'ni de Mitford.

Jolanus Neuill Senior=Maud Da. & coh.
Lo. of Holt & Pichall. | to La. Eua Gray.

Robt. Lo.=Mary D'na de Midleham
Neuill. | fil. & her.

Jolanus Neuill=Amphelicia Lady of
iunior. | Rolleston.

Ranulphus=Eufemia fil. et
Lo. | her. Johis D'ni
Neuill. | de Clauering.

S[r] Andrew Neuill Lo.=Cicilia Da. & coh. to Raphe
of Holt, Pichall & | Blanchminster Lo. of Silly
Rolleston. | & S[t] Mary Wike.

Radulphus Neuill D'ns=Alicia fil. Hugo
de Raby et Mid. | D'ni de Audley.

S[r] Will'm Neuill=— Da. & coh. to
of Holt &c. | S[r] Tho. Fencotts.

Johes Neuill=Matilda fil.
D'ns de | Dni Hen.
Raby. | de Percy.

S[r] Raphe Neuill=
of Condall.

S[r] Rob't Neuill=— Da. of S[r]
of Holt in | Raphe Lang-
Com' Leic. | ford Kt.

Raphe Neuill
first Erle of
Westmerland.

S[r] Alexander=
Neuill of
Thornton-
brige.

S[r] Thos. Neuill=Elizab. Da. of
of Rolleston in | W[m] Babing-
Com' Nott. | ton Justice.

Tho. Palm'
ob. 3 Sept.
15. E. 4.

Will'm=Katherin
Neuill | Da. &
of Rol- | hey. to
ston & | Tho.
Holt. | Palmer of
| Holt in
| Com' Leic.

Katherin ux. Raffe
Marshall of
Carlton.
—
— ux. Stukeley.
—
Eliz. ux. W.
Mering.

Alice ux. S[r]
Geruice
Clifton &
after to —
Thurland.

— ux. Knight.
—
Mary ux. —
Disney.
—
John mar. Anne
Da. & hey of —
Mablethorp.

A   B

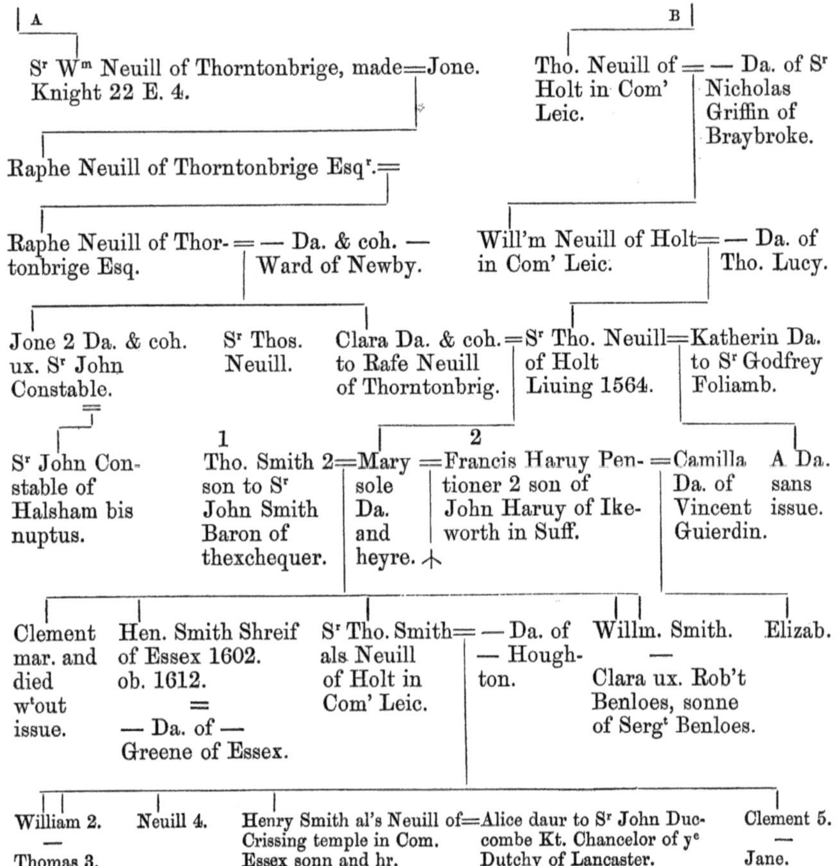
| A   B |
Sʳ Wᵐ Neuill of Thorntonbrige, made=Jone.
Knight 22 E. 4.
Tho. Neuill of = — Da. of Sʳ
Holt in Com'   Nicholas
Leic.   Griffin of
                  Braybroke.
Raphe Neuill of Thorntonbrige Esqʳ.=
Will'm Neuill of Holt= — Da. of
in Com' Leic.   Tho. Lucy.
Raphe Neuill of Thor-= — Da. & coh. —
tonbrige Esq.   Ward of Newby.
Jone 2 Da. & coh.   Sʳ Thos.   Clara Da. & coh.=Sʳ Tho. Neuill=Katherin Da.
ux. Sʳ John   Neuill.   to Rafe Neuill   of Holt   to Sʳ Godfrey
Constable.   of Thorntonbrig. Liuing 1564. Foliamb.
Sʳ John Con-   1   2
stable of   Tho. Smith 2=Mary =Francis Haruy Pen- =Camilla   A Da.
Halsham bis   son to Sʳ   sole tioner 2 son of   Da. of   sans
nuptus.   John Smith Da.   John Haruy of Ike-   Vincent   issue.
                Baron of   and   worth in Suff.   Guierdin.
                thexchequer. heyre.
Clement   Hen. Smith Shreif   Sʳ Tho. Smith= — Da. of   Willm. Smith.   Elizab.
mar. and   of Essex 1602.   als Neuill   — Hough-   —
died   ob. 1612.   of Holt in   ton.   Clara ux. Rob't
w'out   =   Com' Leic.   Benloes, sonne
issue.   — Da. of —   of Sergᵗ Benloes.
           Greene of Essex.
William 2.   Neuill 4.   Henry Smith al's Neuill of=Alice daur to Sʳ John Duc-   Clement 5.
—   Crissing temple in Com.   combe Kt. Chancelor of yᵉ   —
Thomas 3.   Essex sonn and hr.   Dutchy of Lancaster.   Jane.

ARMS. *Quarterly:*—1. *Azure, on two bars or six martlets gules.* 2. *Azure, three lions passant in pale argent.* 3. *Gules, a lion rampant ermine.* 4. *Gules, a fess or between six martlets argent.*
CREST. *A lion's head erased sable.*

Will'm Burdet fundato' Monast de Aucot in Com' Warw. temp. H. 2.=

vide Plus in fol. 12.

Willm's de Camvile sans date=

Will'm de Camvile 16 H. 3.=Albreda fil. et her. Galfredi Marmion 4 H. 3.

Ric. Burdet de Loseby in Com' Leic. ob. 10. H. 3.=

Will'mus de Camvile D'ns de Sekendon=Isend ux. eius. et Arow in Com' Warw.

Galfrid's Camvile de Clifton=Camvile in Com' Staff.

Willm. Burdet de Loseby.=

Thom. Camvile de Sekendon 6 E. 1.=

Will'mus Camville.=

Ric. Burdet de Loseby ob. 16 E. 1.=

Will'm Burdet de Shepey in Com' Leyc.=

Rob'tus D'ns manerij de Huncot com' Leic. ex dono patris dedit p'dc'm maneriu' Rob'to nepoti suo et obijt s. p'le. 31 E. 1.

Hugo Burdet 2 son.=

Galfredus Camvile 16 E. 1.=

Galfredus Camvile 6 E. 1.=Matilda fil. et her. Guy de Brian ætatis 33. 2 E. 1.

Willmus. cæsus apud Dundre in Scotia.

Nicholaus= 32 E. 1.

Robertus Burdet miles D'ns de Huncote=Elizab. fil. et hæres ex dono patrui sui ob. 7 E. 3 1333. Galfridi Camvil.

Will'ms Camvile de=Clifton.

Joh'es Burdet de Loseby 20 E. 3 a quo Ashby de losby.

Ric. Burdet 12 E. 3.=

Rob'tus Burdet de=Elizab. fil. et her. Huncote in Com' Robti Garshull Leyc. 20 E. 3. de Ibstoke in Com. Leic.

Gerardus Burdet D'ns maner. de Sakendon et Arow ex dono parentu' sup'stes 20 E. 3.=Elinora fil. Rob'ti soror et her. Joh'is Veal de Lodin in Com' Warw.

Matild. fil. et hær. nupta Ric. Stafford de Pipe militis.=

Joh'es Burdet de Shepey in Com' Leic.=
A

Rob'tus Burdet de Huncote= in Com' Ley.
B

Felicia.

Johannes Burdet Miles= 44 E. 3.
C

Matilda fil. et her. ux. Tho. Ardern militis 15 R. 2.

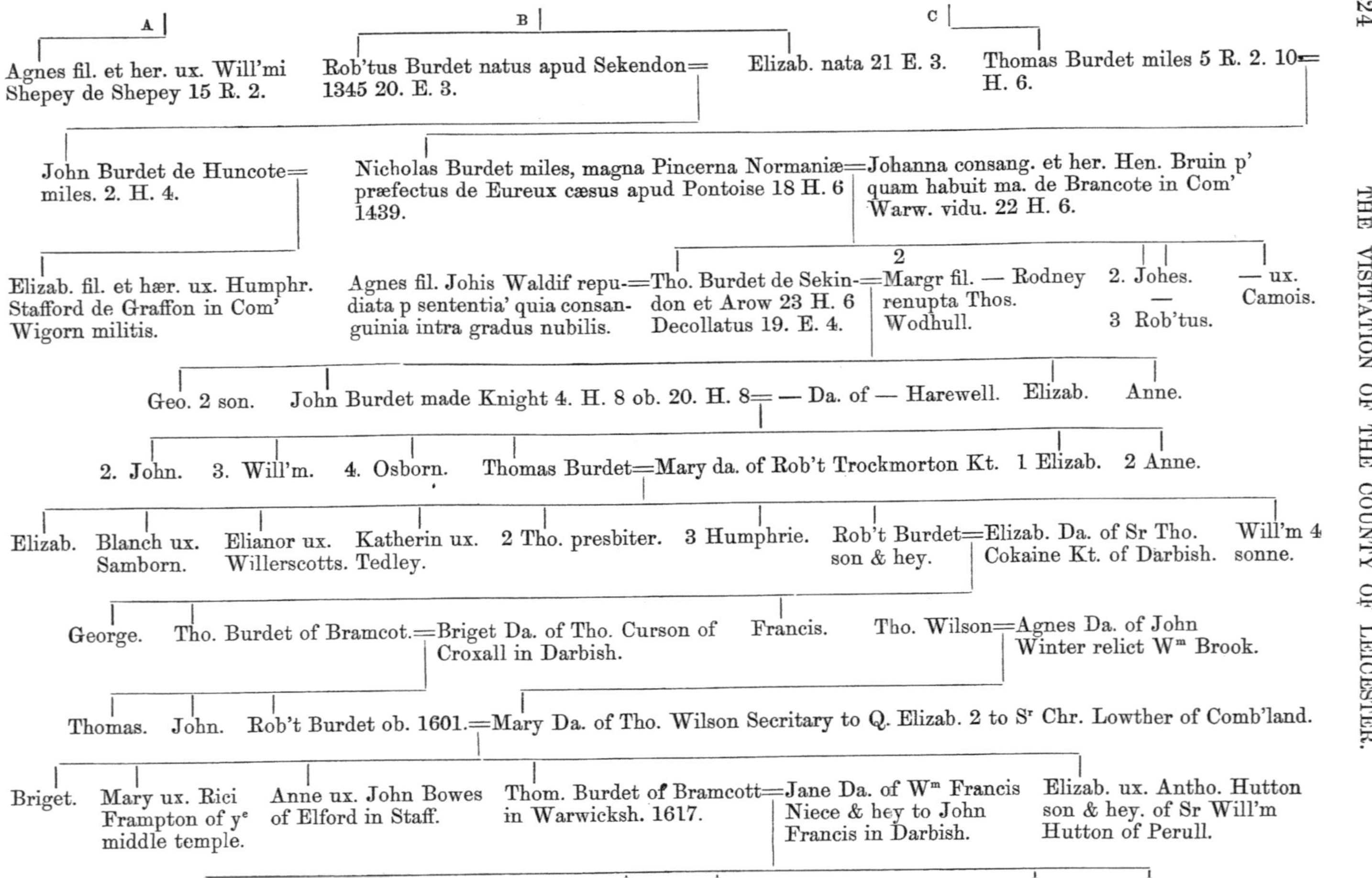
A
B
C
Agnes fil. et her. ux. Will'mi Shepey de Shepey 15 R. 2.
Rob'tus Burdet natus apud Sekendon=1345 20. E. 3.
Elizab. nata 21 E. 3.
Thomas Burdet miles 5 R. 2. 10 H. 6.
John Burdet de Huncote= miles. 2. H. 4.
Nicholas Burdet miles, magna Pincerna Normaniæ= præfectus de Eureux cæsus apud Pontoise 18 H. 6 1439.
Johanna consang. et her. Hen. Bruin p' quam habuit ma. de Brancote in Com' Warw. vidu. 22 H. 6.
Elizab. fil. et hær. ux. Humphr. Stafford de Graffon in Com' Wigorn militis.
Agnes fil. Johis Waldif repu-=diata p sententia' quia consan-guinia intra gradus nubilis.
Tho. Burdet de Sekin-=don et Arow 23 H. 6 Decollatus 19. E. 4.
2
Margr fil. — renupta Thos. Wodhull.
Rodney
2. Johes.
3 Rob'tus.
— ux. Camois.
Geo. 2 son.
John Burdet made Knight 4. H. 8 ob. 20. H. 8=— Da. of — Harewell.
Elizab.
Anne.
2. John.
3. Will'm.
4. Osborn.
Thomas Burdet=Mary da. of Rob't Trockmorton Kt.
1 Elizab.
2 Anne.
Elizab.
Blanch ux. Samborn.
Elianor ux. Willerscotts.
Katherin ux. Tedley.
2 Tho. presbiter.
3 Humphrie.
Rob't Burdet=Elizab. Da. of Sr Tho. son & hey. Cokaine Kt. of Darbish.
Will'm 4 sonne.
George.
Tho. Burdet of Bramcot.=Briget Da. of Tho. Curson of Croxall in Darbish.
Francis.
Tho. Wilson=Agnes Da. of John Winter relict Wm Brook.
Thomas.
John.
Rob't Burdet ob. 1601.=Mary Da. of Tho. Wilson Secritary to Q. Elizab. 2 to Sr Chr. Lowther of Comb'land.
Briget.
Mary ux. Rici Frampton of ye middle temple.
Anne ux. John Bowes of Elford in Staff.
Thom. Burdet of Bramcott=Jane Da. of Wm Francis in Warwicksh. 1617. Niece & hey to John Francis in Darbish.
Elizab. ux. Antho. Hutton son & hey. of Sr Will'm Hutton of Perull.

𝕾𝖍𝖎𝖗𝖑𝖊𝖞.

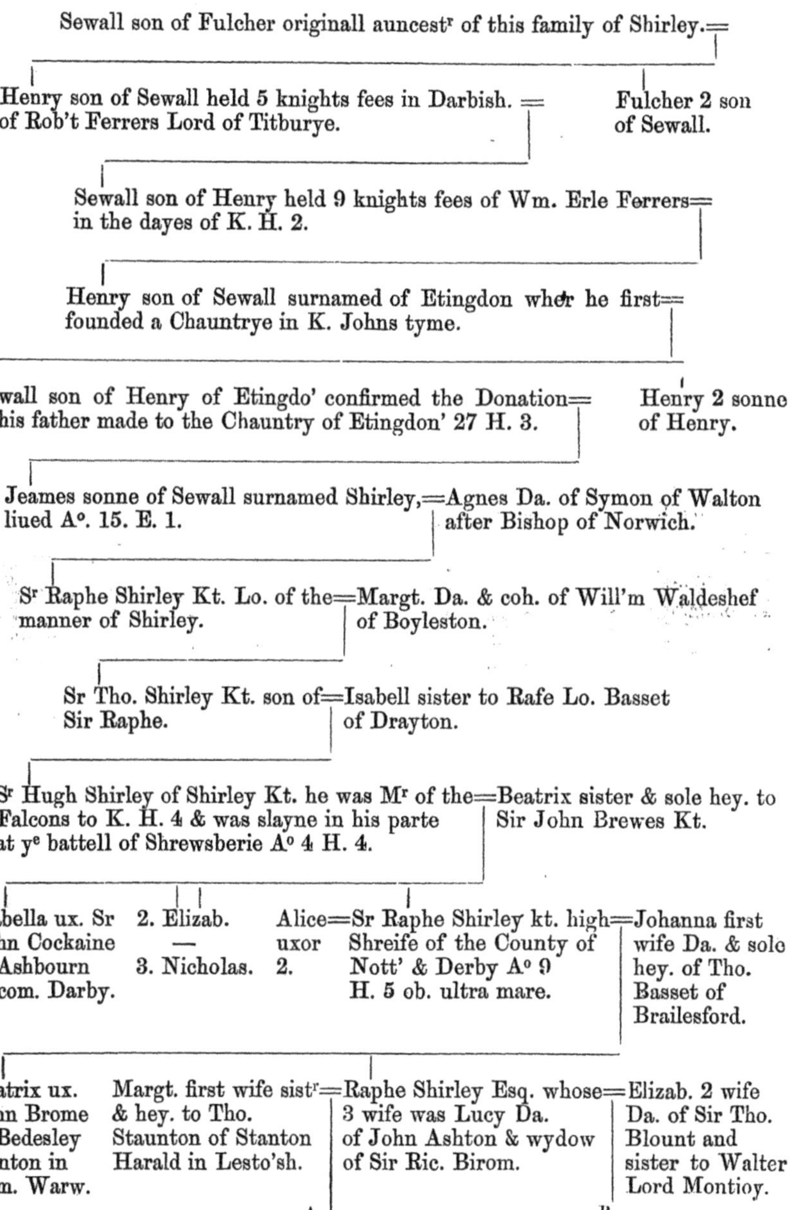

Sewall son of Fulcher originall auncest[r] of this family of Shirley.═

Henry son of Sewall held 5 knights fees in Darbish. ═
of Rob't Ferrers Lord of Titburye.

Fulcher 2 son
of Sewall.

Sewall son of Henry held 9 knights fees of Wm. Erle Ferrers═
in the dayes of K. H. 2.

Henry son of Sewall surnamed of Etingdon whe͛r he first═
founded a Chauntrye in K. Johns tyme.

ewall son of Henry of Etingdo' confirmed the Donation═
'his father made to the Chauntry of Etingdon' 27 H. 3.

Henry 2 sonne
of Henry.

Jeames sonne of Sewall surnamed Shirley,═Agnes Da. of Symon of Walton
liued A°. 15. E. 1.　　　　　　　　　　　after Bishop of Norwich.

S[r] Raphe Shirley Kt. Lo. of the═Margt. Da. & coh. of Will'm Waldeshef
manner of Shirley.　　　　　　　of Boyleston.

S[r] Tho. Shirley Kt. son of═Isabell sister to Rafe Lo. Basset
Sir Raphe.　　　　　　　　of Drayton.

S[r] Hugh Shirley of Shirley Kt. he was M[r] of the═Beatrix sister & sole hey. to
Falcons to K. H. 4 & was slayne in his parte　　Sir John Brewes Kt.
at y[e] battell of Shrewsberie A° 4 H. 4.

abella ux. S[r]　2. Elizab.　　Alice═S[r] Raphe Shirley kt. high═Johanna first
hn Cockaine　　—　　　　uxor　Shreife of the County of　wife Da. & sole
Ashbourn　　3. Nicholas.　2.　Nott' & Derby A° 9　　hey. of Tho.
com. Darby.　　　　　　　　　H. 5 ob. ultra mare.　　Basset of
　　　　　　　　　　　　　　　　　　　　　　　Brailesford.

eatrix ux.　　Margt. first wife sist[r]═Raphe Shirley Esq. whose═Elizab. 2 wife
hn Brome　　& hey. to Tho.　　　3 wife was Lucy Da.　　Da. of Sir Tho.
Bedesley　　Staunton of Stanton　of John Ashton & wydow　Blount and
inton in　　Harald in Lesto'sh.　　of Sir Ric. Birom.　　　sister to Walter
m. Warw.　　　　　　　　　　　　　　　　　　　　　　Lord Montioy.

A　　　　　　　　　　　　　　　　　　　B

A | B |

John Shirley=Elinor, Da. of   Raphe Shirley=Jane Da. of   1 Elizab.   4. Anne.
of Shirley &   Sr Hugh Wil-   of Wistenston   Tho. Bell-
Staunto' in   loughby of   in Sussex   engham of   2. Alice.   5. Margᵗ.
Com.   Woollerton   Esq. for yᵉ   Lemister in   —
Leycest'.   in Com. Nott.   body to K.   Sussex.   3 Sanche.
             H. 7.

Sr Raphe Shirley of Sherley & Stanton=Jane Da. of Sr Rob't Sheffeild Kt. 4
in Leicest' had 4 wiues.   wife after maried to Wᵐ Hastings.

Francis Shirley of Shirley & Stan-=Dorothy Da. of John Gifford of Chillingto'
ton Harold Com' Leicest'.   in Staffordsh. wydow of John Congraue.

John Shirley of Shirley=Jane Da. & sole hey. of Tho. Louet of Astwell
Leyc.   in Com. Northamp.

Fran. Da. of=George Shirley of Shirley & Stan-=Dorothie Da. of Wroughton
Hen. Lord   ton in Com' Ley. Liuing 1585   relict' Sr Hen. Umpton
Berkley.   ob. 27 April 1622.   s. p.

Henricus Shirley=Dorothia filia 2   Tho. Shirley 2 fil. miles   Georgius.   Maria
mil. Baronettus   Rob'ti Deuc-   duxit Maria' filiam Tho.   —   ob. s.p.
fil. et hær.   reux Comitis   Harper de Rushall in   Johannes
sup'stes 1622.   Essexiæ.   Com. Staff. Ar.   ob. s. p.

Leticia filia unica ætatis circa quinq' annor' 1622.

Isabell ux.   Anne Da.=Sr Richard=Elizab. 2   Tho. Shirley of   Jane ux. John
John   of John   Shirley   wife Da.   West Grinsted   Dauney of Pet-
Dawney of   Shelley of   was Lo. of   of Sr   in Sussex 2   worth in
Hampton.   Michel-   yᵉ mannor   Ric.   son mar. Eliz.   Sussex.
—   groue in   of Wist-   Guilford   Da. & coh. of   —
Beatrix ux.   Sussex   neston in   Kt. of   Marmaduke   Eliz. ux. John
Edw. Eld-   first wife.   Sussex ob.   the   of Glouces-   Lee of Fitle-
rington of   34. H. 8.   Garter.   tersh.   worthie in
Hogsto'.   Sussex.

Will'm Shirley=Mary Da.   John 2 son.   Cicely ux. John   Elizab. ux. John
of Wistenes-   of Tho.   —   Ledes.   Michell of Stamer-
ton in Com'   Isley of   Edward 3   —   ham.   —
Sussex.   Sundridg   sonne s.   Anne ux. Ric.   Alice ux. Tho. Chan-
       in Kᵗ Esq.   p'le.   Fernwold.   celer of Lindford.

C |

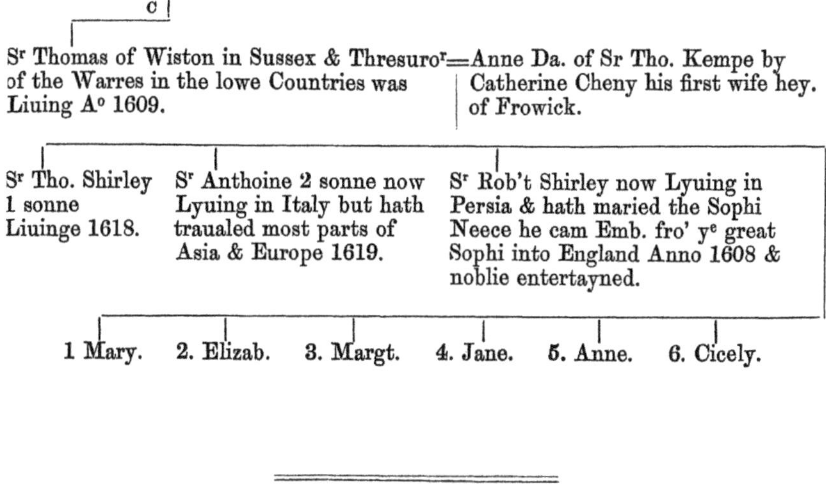

c |

Sr Thomas of Wiston in Sussex & Thresuror=Anne Da. of Sr Tho. Kempe by
of the Warres in the lowe Countries was | Catherine Cheny his first wife hey.
Liuing Aᵒ 1609. | of Frowick.

Sr Tho. Shirley	Sr Anthoine 2 sonne now	Sr Rob't Shirley now Lyuing in
1 sonne	Lyuing in Italy but hath	Persia & hath maried the Sophi
Liuinge 1618.	traualed most parts of	Neece he cam Emb. fro' yᵉ great
	Asia & Europe 1619.	Sophi into England Anno 1608 &
		noblie entertayned.

1 Mary.   2. Elizab.   3. Margt.   4. Jane.   5. Anne.   6. Cicely.

𝕷𝖆𝖜𝖗𝖊𝖓𝖈𝖊.

ARMS. *Three lozenges, each charged with a saltire (untinctured).*

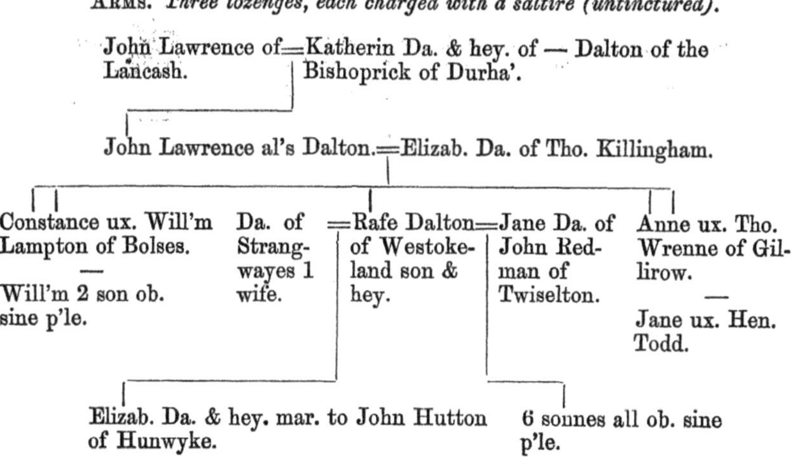

John Lawrence of=Katherin Da. & hey. of — Dalton of the
Lancash. | Bishoprick of Durha'.

John Lawrence al's Dalton.=Elizab. Da. of Tho. Killingham.

Constance ux. Will'm	Da. of	=Rafe Dalton=Jane Da. of	Anne ux. Tho.
Lampton of Bolses.	Strang-	of Westoke- John Red-	Wrenne of Gil-
—	wayes 1	land son & man of	lirow.
Will'm 2 son ob.	wife.	hey. Twiselton.	—
sine p'le.			Jane ux. Hen.
			Todd.

Elizab. Da. & hey. mar. to John Hutton   6 sonnes all ob. sine
of Hunwyke.   p'le.

Faunt.

ARMS. *Quarterly :—1. Argent, a lion rampant between five cross crosslets fitchée gules. 2. Argent, two bars, and in chief three mullets sable. Or, a saltire sable, in chief a mullet for difference.*
CREST. *A naked boy crined or, in the dexter hand a toy (paper windmill ?) of the last.*

Will'm Faunt Linially descended from yᵉ Barons == — Da. & hey. to Moyne.
Hardy in Ireland 18. R. 2.

Will'm Faunt buried at Ramsey Abbey of Wistow == — Da. to Sr Tho. Moulton.
in Huntingdo'sh.

John Faunt a Counceller of the == — Da. & hey of Tho. Claruaux.
Lawe ob. at Wistowe.

Alice ux. John Clarvaux of Senton buried at Ramsey.

John Faunt mar. the sister to Geo. Hide.

Will'm Faunt scruant to the == — Da. of Scot.
Lo. Poyninges buried at Winstow.

Tho. Faunt ob. sine p'le.

Alice uxor Draper of Essex.

Anne Da. of Sr Wm Feilding of Newna' in Com. Warw. sine p'le. == Will'm Faunt a man of Law of fosson in Com. Leic. ob. 1. Elizab. 1559 ætat. 63. == Jane of Geo. Vincent of Pecleton ob. 7. Elizab.

Anthonie Faunt 3 sonne ob. at Wistowes.

John first sonne disinherited by his father & became a Monke at Ramsey.

Mary ux. Geo. Kerkin of Hallend in Warw. sh.

Dorothy ux. Rodolph Burton of Linley.

Alice ux. Humphrie Purifoy of Barwell.

Griswold ux. John Hales of Couentrie.

Will'm Faunt ob. 1574 in Flanders in yᵉ wares ætat. 27.

Arthur 3 son ob. in Polonia 1591.

Vincent ob. sine p'le 1571.

Anthonie Faunt of fossion ob. 1588. == Elizab. Da. of Andrew Noell of Dalby.

John Faunt.

Thomas Faunt mar. Jane Da. of Tho. 3 sonne of George Vincent.

2. Henry.
—
3. Anthonie.
—
Barbara a Daught'.

Mabill ux. to Henry son & hey. of Sr Edw. Hastinges of Leicest' Abbey.

Sr Will'm Faunt of Fossion in Com' Leic' Kt. == Lucy da. of Sr James Harrington of Ridlington in Rutl.

Francis. ob. sine p'le.

Will'm Faunt.

Alice.
—
Judith.
—
Jane.

Villers.

ARMS. *Quarterly :—1. Argent, on a cross gules five escallops or. 2. Sable, a fess between three cinquefoils argent. 3. Gules, a chevron between three cross crosslets fitchée argent. 4. Per pale gules and sable, a lion rampant argent. 5. Azure, a bend (untinctured) between six stars argent. 6. Argent, a cross vert, in the first and fourth quarters an annulet of the last.*
CREST. *A lion rampant crowned (untinctured).*

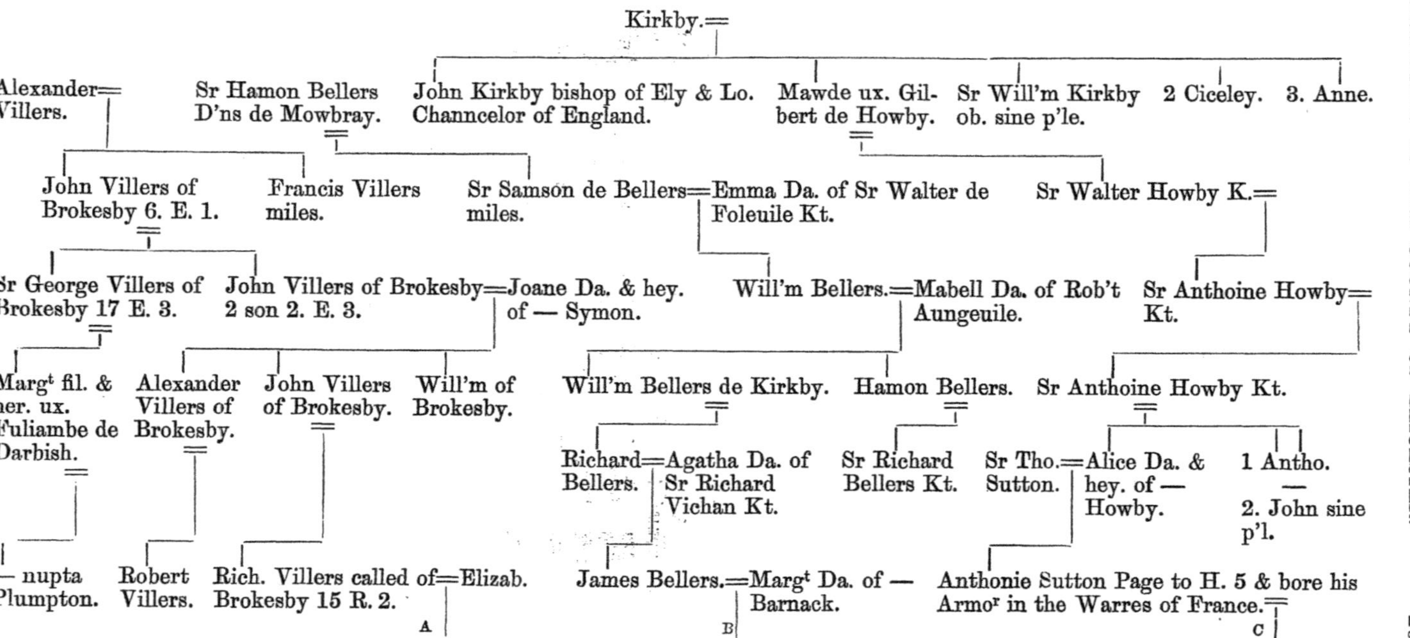

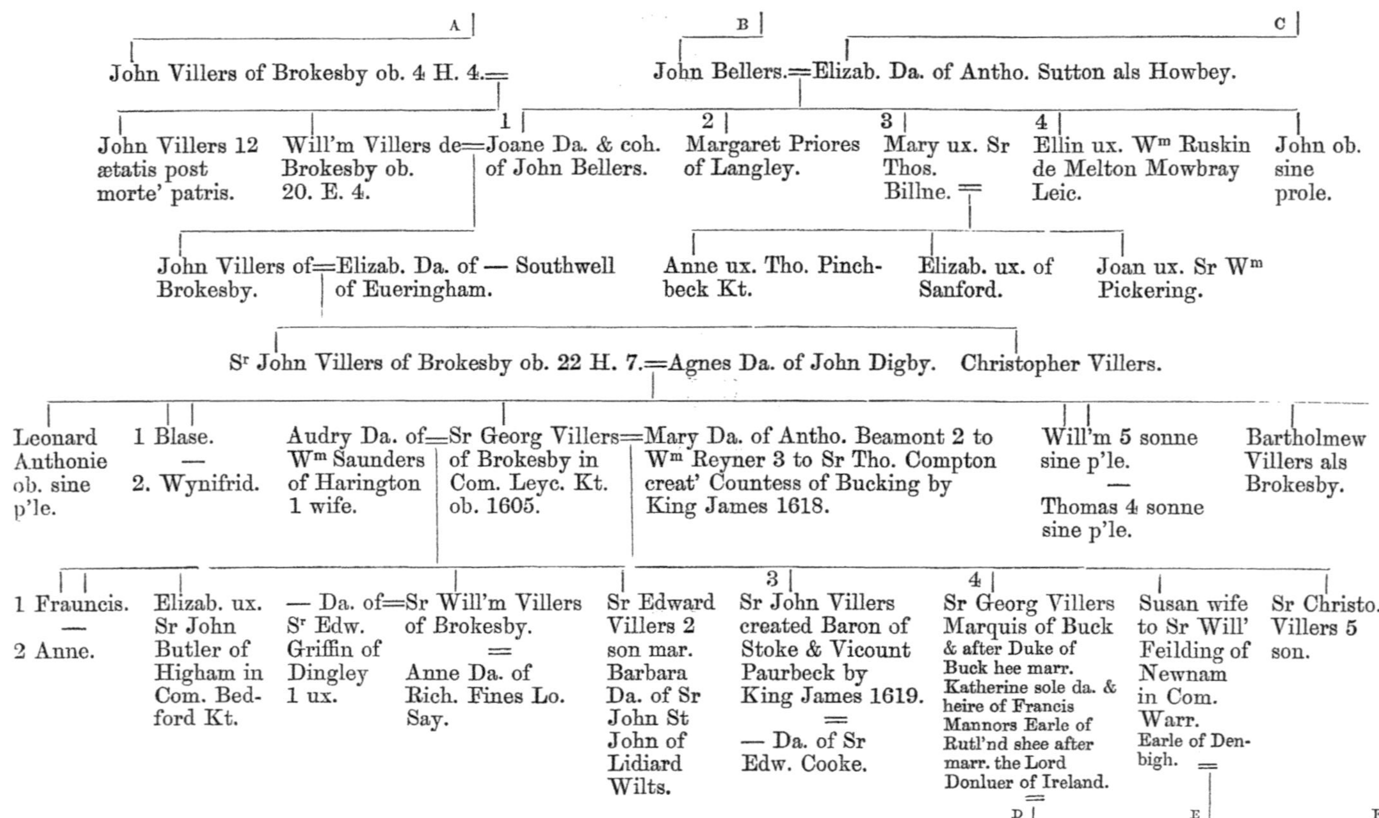
A   B   C
John Villers of Brokesby ob. 4 H. 4. =
John Bellers. = Elizab. Da. of Antho. Sutton als Howbey.
John Villers 12 ætatis post morte' patris.
1 Will'm Villers de Brokesby ob. 20. E. 4. = Joane Da. & coh. of John Bellers.
2 Margaret Priores of Langley.
3 Mary ux. Sr Thos. Billne. =
4 Ellin ux. Wm Ruskin de Melton Mowbray Leic.
John ob. sine prole.
John Villers of Brokesby. = Elizab. Da. of — Southwell of Eueringham.
Anne ux. Tho. Pinchbeck Kt.
Elizab. ux. of Sanford.
Joan ux. Sr Wm Pickering.
Sr John Villers of Brokesby ob. 22 H. 7. = Agnes Da. of John Digby.   Christopher Villers.
Leonard Anthonie ob. sine p'le.
1 Blase. —
2. Wynifrid.
Audry Da. of Wm Saunders of Harington 1 wife. = Sr Georg Villers of Brokesby in Com. Leyc. Kt. ob. 1605. = Mary Da. of Antho. Beamont 2 to Wm Reyner 3 to Sr Tho. Compton creat' Countess of Bucking by King James 1618.
Will'm 5 sonne sine p'le. — Thomas 4 sonne sine p'le.
Bartholmew Villers als Brokesby.
1 Frauncis. —
2 Anne.
Elizab. ux. Sr John Butler of Higham in Com. Bedford Kt.
— Da. of Sr Edw. Griffin of Dingley 1 ux. = Sr Will'm Villers of Brokesby. = Anne Da. of Rich. Fines Lo. Say.
Sr Edward Villers 2 son mar. Barbara Da. of Sr John St John of Lidiard Wilts.
3 Sr John Villers created Baron of Stoke & Vicount Paurbeck by King James 1619. = — Da. of Sr Edw. Cooke.
4 Sr Georg Villers Marquis of Buck & after Duke of Buck hee marr. Katherine sole da. & heire of Francis Mannors Earle of Rutl'nd shee after marr. the Lord Donluer of Ireland.
Susan wife to Sr Will' Feilding of Newnam in Com. Warr. Earle of Denbigh. =
Sr Christo. Villers 5 son.
D   E   F

D | E | F

1 | 2 |

George Villers duke of Buck liueing 1640.

Francis Lord Villers.

Mary wife of James Stuard Duke of Lenox.

Basil Fielding 1 sonne lord Feilding of Newnham Padox. = Ann da' of the Earle of Portland.

James ob. sine p'le.

George 2 sonn now Earle of Desmond in Ireland.

Mary wife of James Marquesse Hamilton Earle of Cambridge.

Ann & Elizabeth.

Georg Villers of Brokesby Kt. = Jane Da. of John Harington.

Elizab. Da. of — Wake 1 ux. = Edw. Villers 6 sonne. = Joan Da. & hey. of Tho. Roos of Dowseby m. 2 to Dauid Cicell.

John Villers Esq. of the Body. = Elizab. Da. of John Winger of London.

George Villers sine p'le.

Richard sine p'le.

Elizab. ux. Edward Waterhouse.

1 Dorothy.

2. Elizab.

Clement Villers son & hey. = Janne Da. of Tho. Saunders & sist' to Sr Edw. Saunders.

2. Will'm.   3. Rob't.   4. Blast'.

Richard ob. sine p'le.

Edw. Villers of Northampton son & hey. = Sibell Da. of — Turpin sister to Sr George Turpin Kt.

2. George.   3. Richard sine p'le.

Anthoine ux. eius Elizab. John Lane of Kettering. =

— ux. francis Browne.

Anna ux. Tho. Rigden of Chartham. =

Edward Villers ob. sine p'le.

Will'm Rigden of Dowseby.

Purifoy.

ARMS. *Quarterly :—1. Blank. 2. Argent, on a fess sable three escallops of the field. 3. Azure, three stirrups or. 4. Gules, a chevron ermine between three leopards' faces or. 5. Gules, three piles meeting in base or, on a canton sable a mullet argent. 6. Blank. 7. As second. 8. As third. 9. As fourth. 10. Quarterly, gules and or. 11. Or, on a fess gules three water bougets of the field. 12. Azure, a cross engrailed or. 13. Gules, a fess ermine between two chevrons or. 14. Paly of six or and azure. 15. Blank.*
CREST. *A dexter gauntlet erect, grasping a broken tilting spear in sinister bend (untinctured).*

Will'm Purefoy de Minsterton in Com. Leycest. 20 H. 3 1275.=

Adam Wollesborow Kt. de Wellesbrough in Com' Leic.=

Symon Purefoy de Minsterton 1277.=

Adam Wellesbrough.=

Will'm Purifoy de Minsterto' 1283.=Amis.

Thomas.=

Will'm Purifoy de Minsterton.=Mary Da. & coh. to Sr Henry Wenle of Warwicksh. Kt.

Thomas 1 filius.=   Rob't 2 fil.   3 Ric'us.   4 Rad'us.   Phillip Purifoy of Newnam in Com. Warw. 1322.=

Johannes.=

Will'm Purifoy of Newnham.=

Will'ms ob. s.p.   Katherine ux. Tho. Purifoy.

Phillip Purifoy of Shelford in comitat'=Margaret Da. & sole hey. of Symon de Shelford Warw. E. 3.   in Com' Warw.

John Wellesbrough Esqr lo' of Wellesbrough and of Phennie Draiton did giue to Tho. Purifoy all his lands of Wellesbrough and Phennie Draiton wt his Armes and a warrant to them both Ao 21 Ri. 2.

Thomas Purifoy son &=Katherin Da. & hey. of hey. 6 Ri. 2.   John Wellesborough of

Will'm Purifoy=Marian Da. & sole hey. of Allen 2 sonne.   Ayott of Shalston.

Will'm Purifoy son &= hey. 4 H. 4.

Phillip Purifoy ob.=Elizab. Da. of sine p'le.   Brome.

John Purifoy 2= sonne.

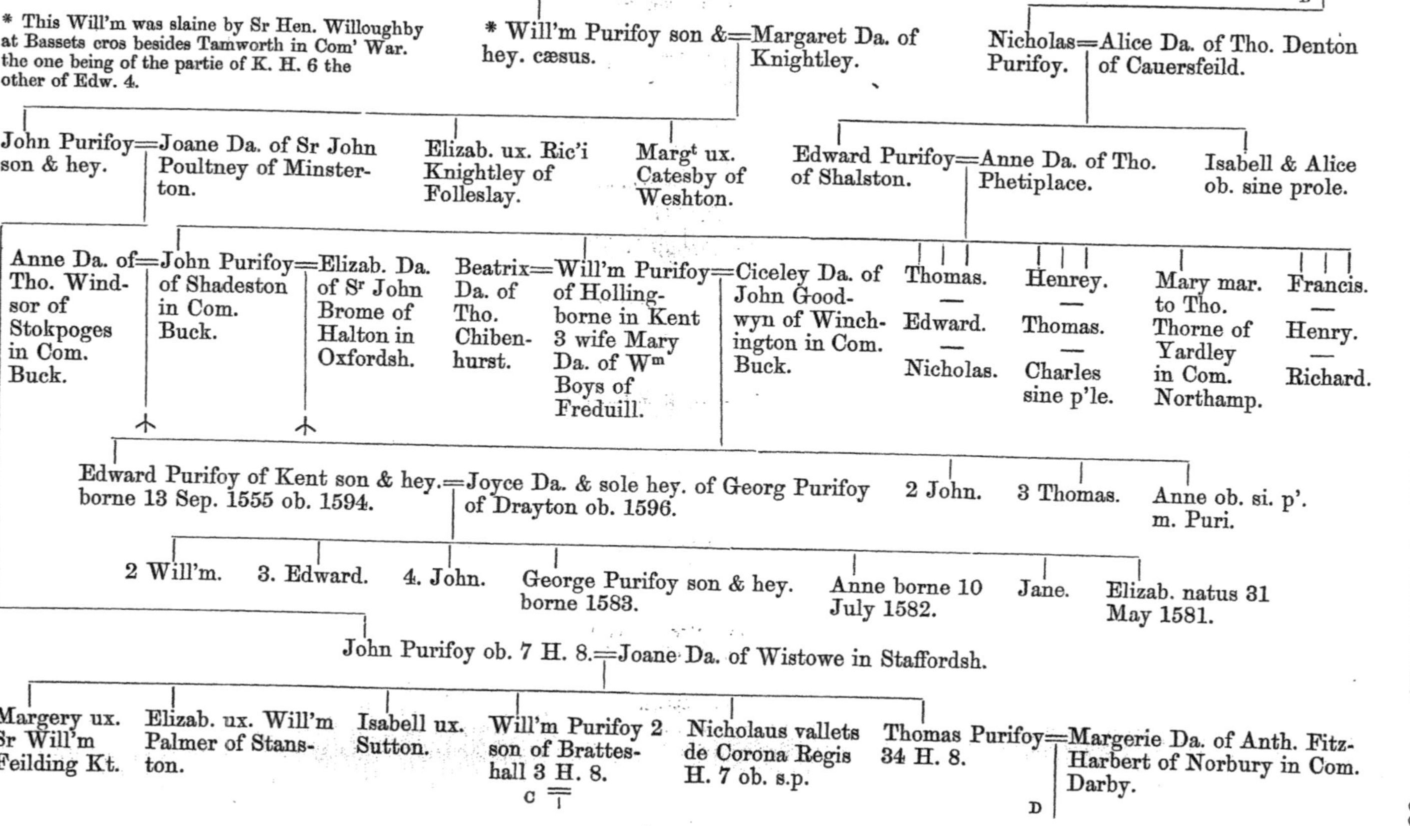

A

B

* This Will'm was slaine by Sr Hen. Willoughby at Bassets cros besides Tamworth in Com' War. the one being of the partie of K. H. 6 the other of Edw. 4.

* Will'm Purifoy son & hey. cæsus. =Margaret Da. of Knightley.

Nicholas Purifoy.=Alice Da. of Tho. Denton of Cauersfeild.

John Purifoy son & hey.=Joane Da. of Sr John Poultney of Minsterton.

Elizab. ux. Ric'i Knightley of Folleslay.

Margt ux. Catesby of Weshton.

Edward Purifoy of Shalston.=Anne Da. of Tho. Phetiplace.

Isabell & Alice ob. sine prole.

Anne Da. of Tho. Windsor of Stokpoges in Com. Buck.=John Purifoy of Shadeston in Com. Buck.=Elizab. Da. of Sr John Brome of Halton in Oxfordsh.

Beatrix Da. of Tho. Chibenhurst.=Will'm Purifoy of Hollingborne in Kent 3 wife Mary Da. of Wm Boys of Freduill.=Ciceley Da. of John Goodwyn of Winchington in Com. Buck.

Thomas. — Edward. — Nicholas.

Henrey. — Thomas. — Charles sine p'le.

Mary mar. to Tho. Thorne of Yardley in Com. Northamp.

Francis. — Henry. — Richard.

Edward Purifoy of Kent son & hey. borne 13 Sep. 1555 ob. 1594.=Joyce Da. & sole hey. of Georg Purifoy of Drayton ob. 1596.

2 John.

3 Thomas.

Anne ob. si. p'. m. Puri.

2 Will'm.

3. Edward.

4. John.

George Purifoy son & hey. borne 1583.

Anne borne 10 July 1582.

Jane.

Elizab. natus 31 May 1581.

John Purifoy ob. 7 H. 8.=Joane Da. of Wistowe in Staffordsh.

Margery ux. Sr Will'm Feilding Kt.

Elizab. ux. Will'm Palmer of Stanston.

Isabell ux. Sutton.

Will'm Purifoy 2 son of Bratteshall 3 H. 8.

C

Nicholaus vallets de Corona Regis H. 7 ob. s.p.

Thomas Purifoy 34 H. 8.=Margerie Da. of Anth. Fitz-Harbert of Norbury in Com. Darby.

D

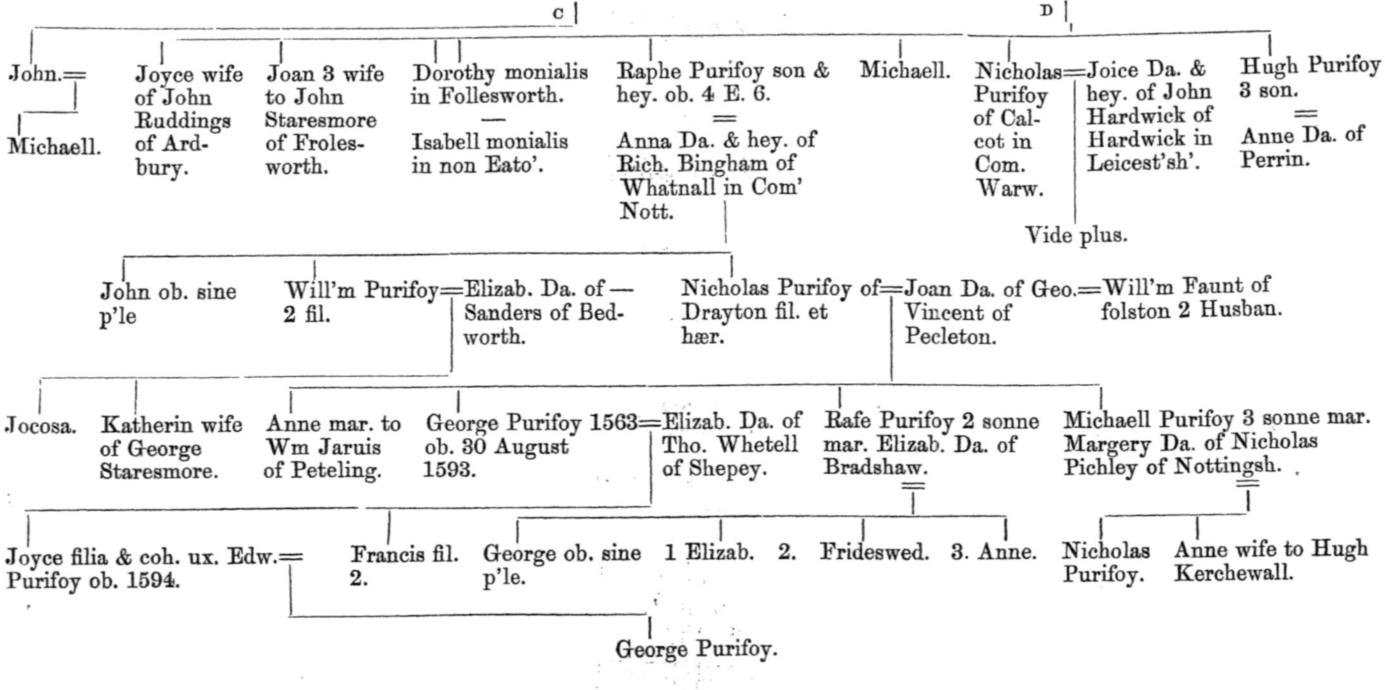

C |

D |

John.=

Michaell.

Joyce wife of John Ruddings of Ardbury.

Joan 3 wife to John Staresmore of Frolesworth.

Dorothy monialis in Follesworth.

Isabell monialis in non Eato'.

Raphe Purifoy son & hey. ob. 4 E. 6.
=
Anna Da. & hey. of Rich. Bingham of Whatnall in Com' Nott.

Michaell.

Nicholas Purifoy of Calcot in Com. Warw.
=
Joice Da. & hey. of John Hardwick of Hardwick in Leicest'sh'.

Hugh Purifoy 3 son.
=
Anne Da. of Perrin.

Vide plus.

John ob. sine p'le

Will'm Purifoy 2 fil.
=
Elizab. Da. of — Sanders of Bedworth.

Nicholas Purifoy of Drayton fil. et hær.
=
Joan Da. of Geo. Vincent of Pecleton.
=
Will'm Faunt of folston 2 Husban.

Jocosa.

Katherin wife of George Staresmore.

Anne mar. to Wm Jaruis of Peteling.

George Purifoy 1563 ob. 30 August 1593.
=
Elizab. Da. of Tho. Whetell of Shepey.

Rafe Purifoy 2 sonne mar. Elizab. Da. of Bradshaw.
=

Michaell Purifoy 3 sonne mar. Margery Da. of Nicholas Pichley of Nottingsh.

Joyce filia & coh. ux. Edw.= Purifoy ob. 1594.

Francis fil. 2.

George ob. sine p'le.

1 Elizab.   2.   Fridexwed.   3. Anne.

Nicholas Purifoy.

Anne wife to Hugh Kerchewall.

George Purifoy.

Purifoy.

Will'm Purifoy.=Marian.

John Purifoy 2 sonne. — Phillip Purifoy buried in Badesley ob. sine p'le. =Isabell Da. & hey. of John Brome of Badesley in Warw. =John Denton 2 husband.

Clemence Da. of Lidiard & Wydow of Eyre 2 wife.=Nicholas Purifoy of Shalston 3^d maried Katherin Da. of Ric. Broyesfeild.=Alice Da. of John Denton 1 wife. — Thomas Denton. — Anna wife to Sr Edward Greuill.=

Sr John Greuill. — Sr Foulk Greuill.

Simond Purefoy.=Barbara Da. of Will'm Dixwell of Churchouer. — Susan mar. to Edw. Jenney of Suff.

Martyn Purefoy.=Anne Da. of Rooke de Kent. — Elizab. wife to Will'm Ackworth of Hernhill in Kent.

2 Thomas. 3. Will'm. 4. Martin. 5. Simon. 1 Anne. 2. Elizab. 3. Jane. James Purifoy son & hey. A° 1601. 4 Joyce. 5. Ciceley.

Isabell wife to Tho. Goodwin Bishop of Bathe & Welles. — Martyn Purifoy.=Elizab. Da. of Reinold Willm's brother to the Lo. Willm's of Tame. — Francis rector Eccl'iæ de Ruckings in Kent. — Edw. Purifoy borne at Effeild 13 Januar. 1494. et ob. 1558.=Anne Da. of Ric. Phetiplace borne in p'ua Shelford 16 July 1496 et ob. 3 Aug. 1568.

A

B

A | B |

Richard ob. at Breast in Britanie.　1 Elizab.　2. Lucas.　Anne.　Diolata.

Mary wife to Tho. Thorne of Yardley Hastings.

Susan a Nunne at Syon.

Tho. Purifoy mar. the sister of Rich. Waynman ob. sine p'le

Rich. Purifoy=Da. of Pell wydow of Nich. Foxston. 5 sonne sine p'le.

Francis Purifoy=Anne Da. of Anthonie Furtho of Furtho in Com' Northa'. 4 sonne ob. 1564.

George ob. sine p'le.　Elizab.

Anne Da. of Tho.=John Purifoy 1=Da. of John Brome of Halton. Windsor 2 wife.　son ob. sine prole.

Beatrix Da. & hey. of=Will'm Purifoy 2=Ciceley Da. of John Goodwin of Winchington in Com' Buck. Tho. Cheselhurst wydow of Strelley 1 ux. sine p'le.　sonne borne 10 of March 1519 ob. 1595.

Edw. Purifoy borne 13. Sep. 1555. et ob. 1594.=Joice Da. & sole hey. of Geo. Purifoy of Drayto' ob. 1596.

John Purifoy 2 son Canonicus ædis Christiani Oxoniæ ob. sine p'le 1601.

Thomas Purifoy 3=Blendina Da. of Tho. Goodwin Bishop of Bath & Wells. son 1601.

Janill.　Elizab. nata 31 May.　Anne Borne 10 July 1582　2 Will'm.　3. Edward.　4. John.　Georg Purifoy son & hey. Borne 1583.

Purifoy.

Michaell Purifoy of Caldecot 2. son of Tho. Purifoy of Drayton.=Joice Da. & Coh. of John Hardwick of Lindley in Com' Leic.

5. Francis ux. John Smalley of Carleton Curlow.

4. Dorothy ux. Michaell Bradshaw of Moorbarne.

3. Margerie wife Rad'i Salisbury of Ullesthorp.

2. Jane ux. Christ' Wright of Hoppesford in Com. Warw.

1. Katherin ux. Tho. Wightman of Burbach in Com' Leicest'. 1601.

John Purifoy 2 son mar. Isabell Da. of Rob't Bradshaw of Moreborne.

Francis Purifoy 7 son mar' ye Da. of Langham of Coggeshall.

Robert 2 sonne.   Nicholas Purifoy.   1 Katherin.   2. Joyce.   3. Anne.

Arthur 6 son Chancelor of Worcest' ob. sine prole.

Tho. Purifoy 4 son mar. Elizab. Da. of Rob't Bradshaw of Moorborne.

Will'm Purifoy of Caldecot first son Aº 1601.=Katherin Da. of Sr Wm Wigston in Com' Warr.

John Purifoy 2 son mar. Isabell Da. of Rob't Bradshaw of Moreborne.

Katherina.

Humphrie Purifoy of Barwell 3 sonne ob. 1598 mar. Alice Da. Wm Faunt of Foston in Leicest'.

Geo. Purifoy of Woluershill 5 son mar. Jane Da. of John Dauenport.

Joyce ux. Tho. Holt.
—
Janne.

Susanna ux. Rob't Goodall.

Michaell Purifoy.

Thomas slayne at Ostend 1601.

Mary ux. Bellers of Henley.

1 Elizab.
—
2 Dorothy.

3 Will'm
—
4 Edward.

Mawdelin wife to Anth. Grey of Burbach.

Francis=Elianor Da. of John Purifoy Baskeruile of Curdof Cal-worthe in decot. Warwsh.

Will'm Purifoy 1 son.   2 Rafe.   3. Georg.   4. Francis.   5. Nathaniell.   1. Joyce.   2 Marg.

1. Henry.
2. Humfrie.

3. John.
4. Georg.

5. Will'm.
6. Thomas.

Mary ux. Hen. Pollard of Treland Cornwall.

Alice.
—
Elizab.

Margt ux. Ric. Dall of Colineston.

1. Judith.
—
2. Susan.

Gamaliel son & hey.

Woodford et Turuill.

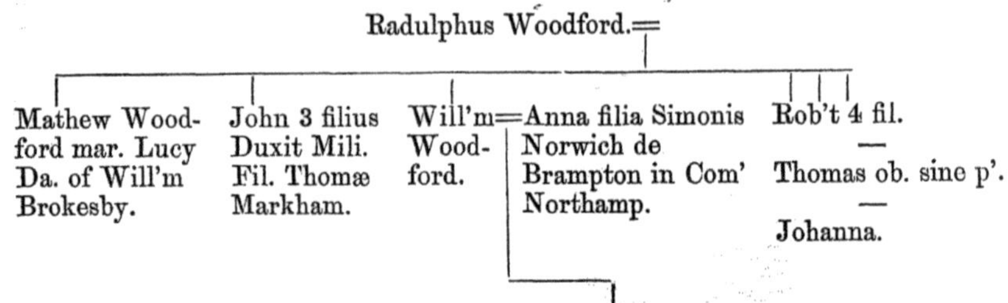

Sr Hugh.

Radulphus Woodford.=

| | | | |
| Mathew Wood-ford mar. Lucy Da. of Will'm Brokesby. | John 3 filius Duxit Mili. Fil. Thomæ Markham. | Will'm Wood-ford. | =Anna filia Simonis Norwich de Brampton in Com' Northamp. | Rob't 4 fil. — Thomas ob. sine p'. — Johanna. |

Johannes Turuill fil. et her. Johannis=Margareta fil. & her. postea uxor
Turuill de Newhall ob. ætat. 22.   Will'mi Turuill frater Johannis.

Hubert.

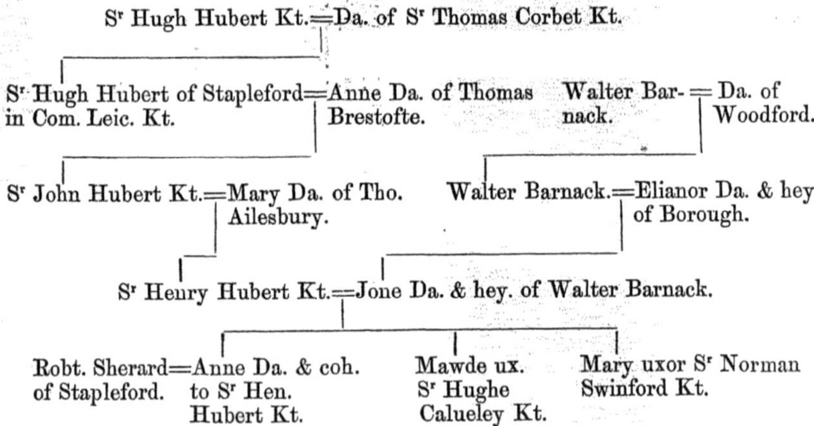

Sr Hugh Hubert Kt.=Da. of Sr Thomas Corbet Kt.

Sr Hugh Hubert of Stapleford=Anne Da. of Thomas   Walter Bar-=Da. of
in Com. Leic. Kt.   Brestofte.   nack.   Woodford.

Sr John Hubert Kt.=Mary Da. of Tho.   Walter Barnack.=Elianor Da. & hey.
        Ailesbury.   of Borough.

Sr Henry Hubert Kt.=Jone Da. & hey. of Walter Barnack.

Robt. Sherard=Anne Da. & coh.   Mawde ux.   Mary uxor Sr Norman
of Stapleford.   to Sr Hen.   Sr Hughe   Swinford Kt.
        Hubert Kt.   Calueley Kt.

Palmer et Harecourt.

ARMS. *Azure, three fleurs-de-lis argent within a bordure engrailed or.*

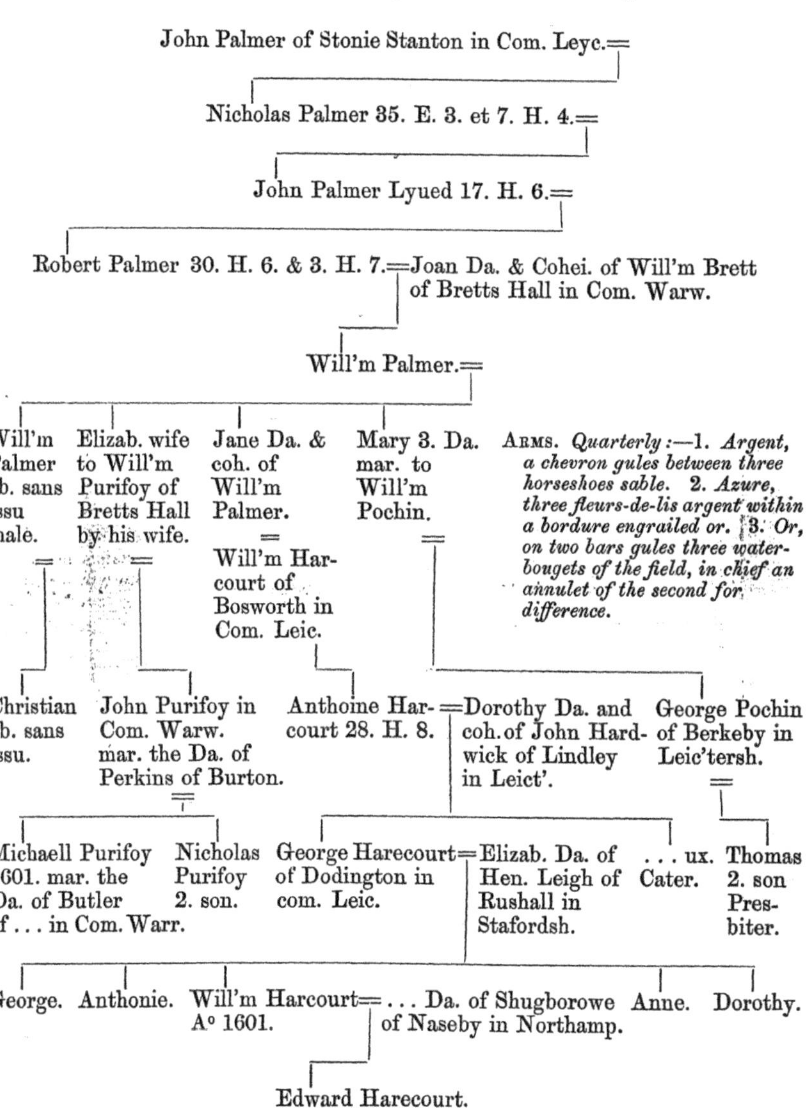

John Palmer of Stonie Stanton in Com. Leyc.=

Nicholas Palmer 35. E. 3. et 7. H. 4.=

John Palmer Lyued 17. H. 6.=

Robert Palmer 30. H. 6. & 3. H. 7.=Joan Da. & Cohei. of Will'm Brett of Bretts Hall in Com. Warw.

Will'm Palmer.=

Will'm Palmer ob. sans issu male. =

Elizab. wife to Will'm Purifoy of Bretts Hall by his wife. =

Jane Da. & coh. of Will'm Palmer. = Will'm Harcourt of Bosworth in Com. Leic.

Mary 3. Da. mar. to Will'm Pochin. =

ARMS. *Quarterly:—1. Argent, a chevron gules between three horseshoes sable. 2. Azure, three fleurs-de-lis argent within a bordure engrailed or. 3. Or, on two bars gules three water-bougets of the field, in chief an annulet of the second for difference.*

Christian ob. sans issu.

John Purifoy in Com. Warw. mar. the Da. of Perkins of Burton. =

Anthoine Har-court 28. H. 8. =Dorothy Da. and coh. of John Hard-wick of Lindley in Leict'.

George Pochin of Berkeby in Leic'tersh. =

Michaell Purifoy 1601. mar. the Da. of Butler of . . . in Com. Warr.

Nicholas Purifoy 2. son.

George Harecourt=Elizab. Da. of Hen. Leigh of Rushall in Stafordsh.

. . . ux. Cater.

Thomas 2. son Pres-biter.

of Dodington in com. Leic.

George. Anthonie. Will'm Harcourt=. . . Da. of Shugborowe of Naseby in Northamp. A° 1601.

Anne. Dorothy.

Edward Harecourt.

Digbye.

ARMS. *Quarterly :—1. Azure, a fleur-de-lis argent, in dexter chief a crescent for difference. 2. Gules, a fess ermine. 3. Argent, on a bend gules three martlets or. 4. Argent, on a fess sable three mullets of the field between as many martlets of the second. 5. Ermine, on a bend (untinctured) three chevrons (untinctured). 6. As first.*

CREST. *An ostrich argent, holding in its beak a horse-shoe (untinctured).*

Rob'tt Digby.=Jane Da. of Sr James Bellers renupta Tho. Seyton.

Sr Will'm Dauers of Chamb' ho. in Com. Oxon.=Anne Da. & hey. of John Pury. ux. . . . Drayton. Euerard Digby=Agnes Da. of John Clerk relict Rob't Seddall. . . . ux. Bowles. John Elis.= of Welby.

John Dauers of Warrestock. = Marg·t Da. of Wm Hamton of Harwell.

Symond Digby Lieutenant of the Towre temp. H. 7.=Alice Da. of John Weles or Walleys.

Euerard Digby. — Sr Libbes Digby mar. ye Da. of Hunt.

Sr John Digbye Kt.=Katherin Da. of Nicholas Griffin.

Euerard Digbye of Ketlebye.=Jaquet Da. & hey. of John Ellis of Deuonsh.

Jilian ux. Sr Euerard feilding. K.

Rowland Digby mar. Agnes Da. & hey. of John Shilton. — Sr Tho. Digby mar. Dorothy Da. & hey. of Tho. Oxenbridg.

Elizab. ux. Tho. Caue of Stanford.

Dorothy ux. Nich. Hubert of Ipsley in Com. Warr.

Anne Da. & hey. of John Dauers of Warrestock.=Reignold Digbye of Colshull.

Thomas Digby. — Will'm Digb.

Alice ux. Clifton. — . . . ux. Mich. Strelley.

Agnes uxor Wm Tracy.

Elizab. ux. Humphrie. *Hercy* Jane *= Edmund Bussy* cohvr

1 Anne. — 2. Dorothy. — 3. Alice

Symond Digby 1 son.

2 Libbes. — 3. Will'm. — 4. Thomas. — 5. Perciuall.

A   B

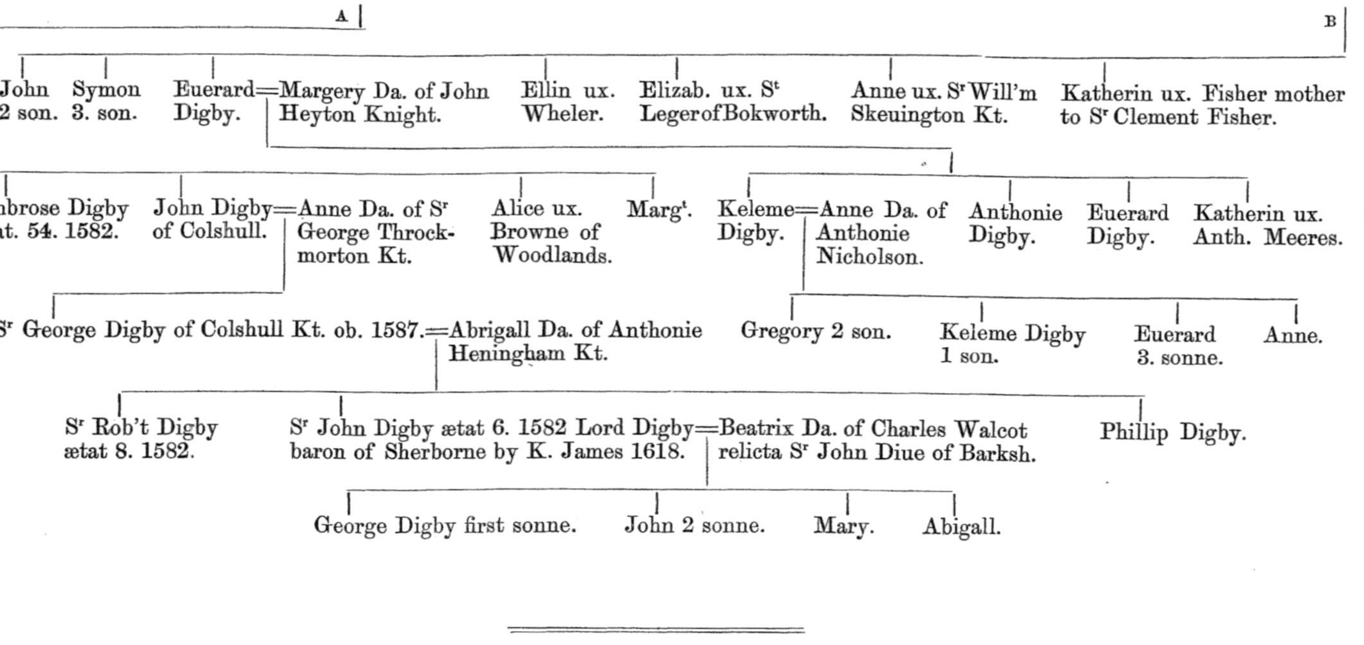
A
B
John 2 son.
Symon 3. son.
Euerard Digby.=Margery Da. of John Heyton Knight.
Ellin ux. Wheler.
Elizab. ux. St Leger of Bokworth.
Anne ux. Sr Will'm Skeuington Kt.
Katherin ux. Fisher mother to Sr Clement Fisher.
Ambrose Digby ætat. 54. 1582.
John Digby of Colshull.=Anne Da. of Sr George Throckmorton Kt.
Alice ux. Browne of Woodlands.
Margt.
Keleme Digby.=Anne Da. of Anthonie Nicholson.
Anthonie Digby.
Euerard Digby.
Katherin ux. Anth. Meeres.
Sr George Digby of Colshull Kt. ob. 1587.=Abrigall Da. of Anthonie Heningham Kt.
Gregory 2 son.
Keleme Digby 1 son.
Euerard 3. sonne.
Anne.
Sr Rob't Digby ætat 8. 1582.
Sr John Digby ætat 6. 1582 Lord Digby baron of Sherborne by K. James 1618.=Beatrix Da. of Charles Walcot relicta Sr John Diue of Barksh.
Phillip Digby.
George Digby first sonne.
John 2 sonne.
Mary.
Abigall.

(𝕮𝖆𝖎𝖓𝖙𝖊𝖗.)

ARMS. *Quarterly :—Sable, on a chevron argent between three tuns (untinctured) a chessrook azure ; and gules, a saltire engrailed argent between four mullets or.*
ANOTHER COAT. *Checquy or and sable, a fess azure. This erased, and at the top is written " Nihill."*
CREST. *A hawk close argent, holding in its dexter claw a fish erect or.*

Henry Winter of Worthington in Com' Leic.=

Rob't Winter de Worthington.=filia English.

George Winter of Northington=Anne Da. & coh. of John Hardwick of Lindesley in Com. Leicest. | in Com. Leic. by the Da. of Laughton.

Anne wife to John Bowles of Lincolnsh. | Elizabeth wife to John Crewker postea to Tho. Bradbrig. | Edward Winter=Katherine sist' of Northing-ton. | to Sr Wm. Grisley Kt. | Joyce wife to Willing-ton of Hur-ley.

Georg Winter son & hey. | Edward Basker-=Mary 1 Da. & uile of Carey-worthy. | coh. of Edw. Winter. | Anna 2 Da. wife to Winter of Worcestersh. | Ciceley uxor Rolandi Stockey de Leycest.

Ursela.   Edward Baskeruile first son.   John 2 son.   Margaret.

(𝕽𝖊𝖕𝖎𝖓𝖌𝖙𝖔𝖓.)

ARMS. *Quarterly :—1. Gules, a fess dancetty ermine between six billets or. 2. Gules, a saltire or. 3. Gules, a crescent or.*

Will'm Repington of Armington.=

Mary wife to Swinfen of Swinfen. | Anne wife to Tho. Cockin of Holland. | Francis Re-=Maudes Da. of pington of Arming-ton. | Ric. Cotton of Ridware in Com. Staff. | Katherin ux. Rob't Bur-ton of Lindley. | Edith a nun at Peles-worth.

Will'm. — Richard. | Thomas Re-=Francis Da. of pington 1601. | Wm Stanford Justice of the Common pleas. | Margaret wife to=Kendall of Smitheses in Darbsh. | Sr Clemt Fisher of Packington in Com' Warw. 2 Husband.

Humphrie 2 sonne. | Edward 3 sonne. | John Re-pington 1 sonne. | Letice. — Sr Rob't Fisher K. | Anne ux. Dilkes. | Mary ux Sr Edward Littleton of Pilling-ton Kt.

(Brasbridge.)

ARMS. *Vair argent and sable, a fess gules.*
CREST. *A staff raguly argent.*

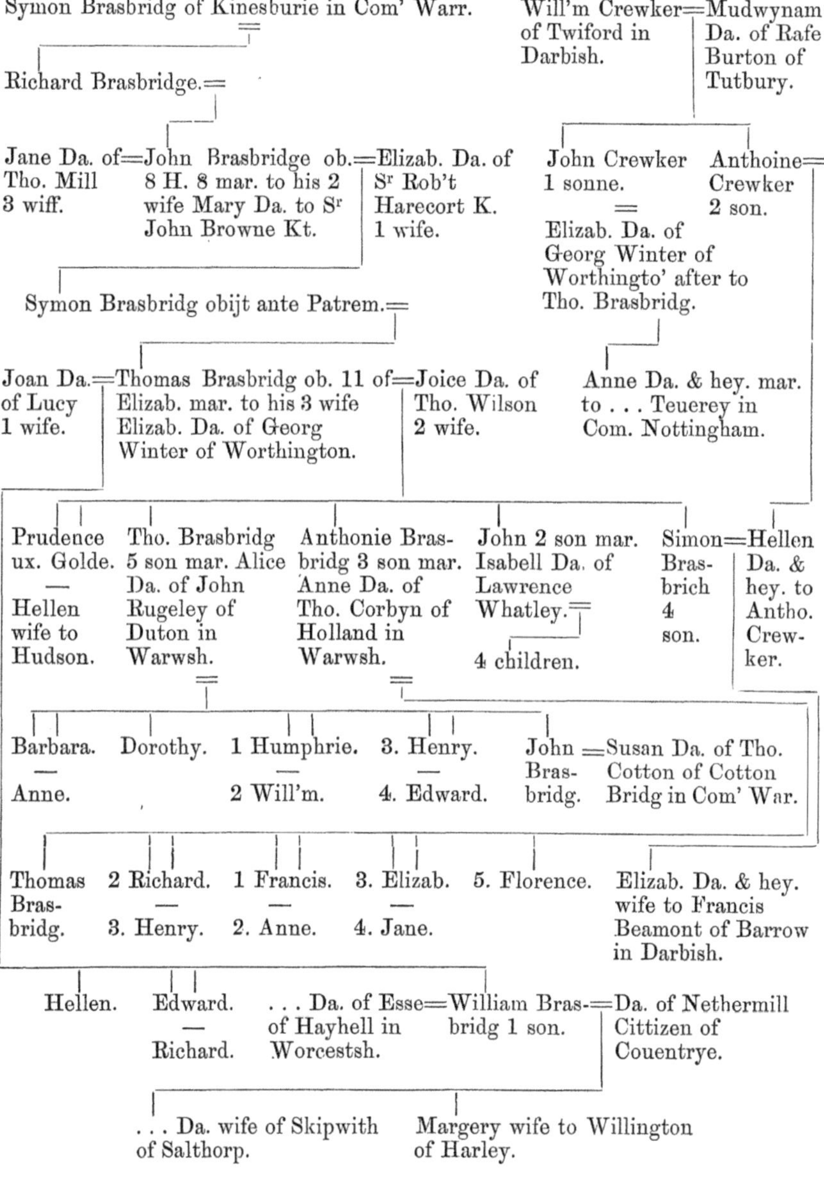

Symon Brasbridg of Kinesburie in Com' Warr. ==

Richard Brasbridge. ==

Jane Da. of=John Brasbridge ob.=Elizab. Da. of
Tho. Mill   8 H. 8 mar. to his 2   Sʳ Rob't
3 wiff.   wife Mary Da. to Sʳ   Harecort K.
            John Browne Kt.   1 wife.

Will'm Crewker=Mudwynam
of Twiford in | Da. of Rafe
Darbish. | Burton of
               | Tutbury.

John Crewker   Anthoine=
1 sonne.   Crewker
    =   2 son.
Elizab. Da. of
Georg Winter of
Worthingto' after to
Tho. Brasbridg.

Symon Brasbridg obijt ante Patrem. ==

Joan Da.=Thomas Brasbridg ob. 11 of=Joice Da. of
of Lucy Elizab. mar. to his 3 wife   Tho. Wilson
1 wife. Elizab. Da. of Georg   2 wife.
         Winter of Worthington.

Anne Da. & hey. mar.
to . . . Teuerey in
Com. Nottingham.

Prudence   Tho. Brasbridg   Anthonie Bras-   John 2 son mar.   Simon=Hellen
ux. Golde. 5 son mar. Alice   bridg 3 son mar.   Isabell Da. of   Bras- | Da. &
—   Da. of John   Anne Da. of   Lawrence   brich | hey. to
Hellen   Rugeley of   Tho. Corbyn of   Whatley.==   4 | Antho.
wife to   Duton in   Holland in | son. | Crew-
Hudson.   Warwsh.   Warwsh.   4 children. | ker.
               ==   ==

Barbara.   Dorothy.   1 Humphrie.   3. Henry.   John =Susan Da. of Tho.
—   —   Bras- Cotton of Cotton
Anne.   2 Will'm.   4. Edward.   bridg. Bridg in Com' War.

Thomas   2 Richard.   1 Francis.   3. Elizab.   5. Florence.   Elizab. Da. & hey.
Bras-   —   —   —   wife to Francis
bridg.   3. Henry.   2. Anne.   4. Jane.   Beamont of Barrow
                                                                  in Darbish.

Hellen.   Edward.   . . . Da. of Esse=William Bras-=Da. of Nethermill
           —   of Hayhell in   bridg 1 son. Cittizen of
           Richard.   Worcestsh.   Couentrye.

. . . Da. wife of Skipwith   Margery wife to Willington
of Salthorp.   of Harley.

(Bradshaw.)

ARMS. *Argent, two bends between two martlets sable.*

Hugh Bradshaw of Moorebarne in Comitat=. . . Da. of Orme.
Leicest. descended out of Lancash.

John Bradshaw=. . . Da. of   Rob't Bradshaw=Anne Da. of Glouer   Mary wife
of Orton in   Forster.   of Moreborne ,   of Baxterley in   to Arthur
Leic.   2 sonne.   Com. War.   Corbet of

Will'm 2   . . . a Da. wife to   . . . Da. ux.   George Brad-=
son.   Printoft.   Cosby.   shaw.

Richard Bradshaw.=. . . Da. of Colledg of Sted.   . . . Da. ux. Halilford.

wife to   Michaell Bradsaw   Rob't Bradshaw of   Florence ux.   Anna uxor
Wattes.   1 son mar.   Moreborne 2 son   Reines.   Symon Whethill.
       Dorothy Da. of   mar. yᵉ Da. of   —   —
       Michaell Purifoy   Gibon of Sutton in   Isabell ux.   Elizab. ux. Rafe
       & ob. sine p'le.   Colford Warwsh.   John Purifoy.   Purifoy.

George Bradshaw of=Anne Da. of Rafe Burton   Margaret mar. to
Moreborne.   of Lindesey.   Jennings.

Robert Bradshaw 1 sonne.   Dorothy.   2 Margaret.   2 Jane.

(Whethill.)

ARMS. *Quarterly* :—1. *Argent, on a fess or three mullets gules.* (WHETHILL.) 2.
Argent, a fess gules, in chief three mullets sable. (FLAUNDERS.) 3. *Azure, a
cross gules fretty argent.* (SHEPEY.)

John Whethill of Shepey in Com' Leic.=

Richard Whethill 4 H. 4 & 13=Margt. Da. & Coh. of John Flandus of
H. 6.   Flandus in Com' Warw.

Thomas Wheathill sonne & hey.=
A

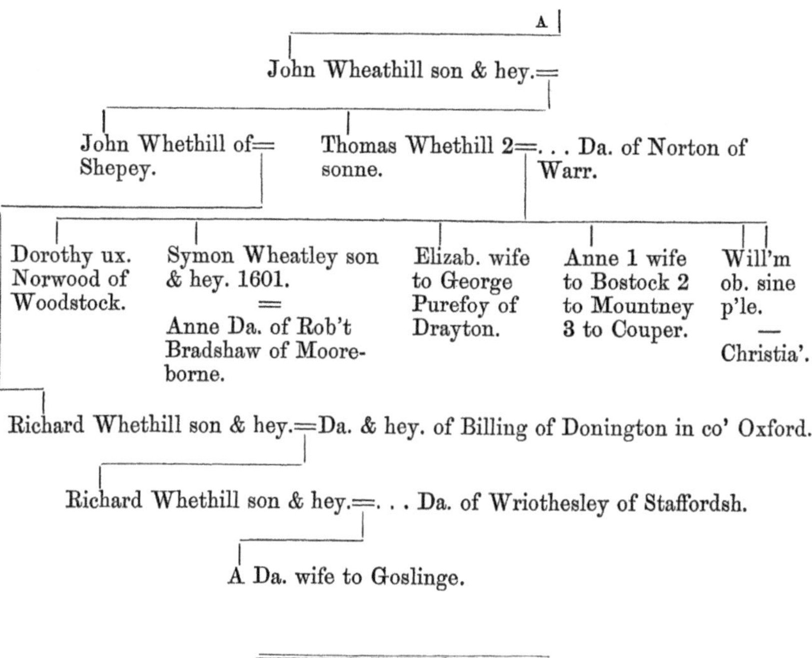

John Wheathill son & hey.═

John Whethill of═ Shepey.

Thomas Whethill 2═... Da. of Norton of sonne. Warr.

Dorothy ux. Norwood of Woodstock.

Symon Wheatley son & hey. 1601. ═ Anne Da. of Rob't Bradshaw of Mooreborne.

Elizab. wife to George Purefoy of Drayton.

Anne 1 wife to Bostock 2 to Mountney 3 to Couper.

Will'm ob. sine p'le. — Christia'.

Richard Whethill son & hey.═Da. & hey. of Billing of Donington in co' Oxford.

Richard Whethill son & hey.═... Da. of Wriothesley of Staffordsh.

A Da. wife to Goslinge.

(Neele.)

ARMS. *Quarterly :—Gules, three greyhounds' heads erased argent, collared or ; and or, a lion rampant double queuée vert.*

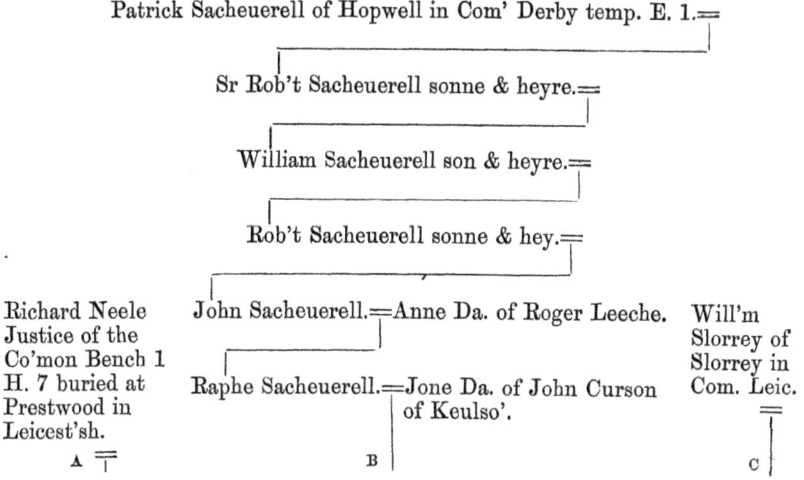

Patrick Sacheuerell of Hopwell in Com' Derby temp. E. 1.═

Sr Rob't Sacheuerell sonne & heyre.═

William Sacheuerell son & heyre.═

Rob't Sacheuerell sonne & hey.═

Richard Neele Justice of the Co'mon Bench 1 H. 7 buried at Prestwood in Leicest'sh.

John Sacheuerell.═Anne Da. of Roger Leeche.

Raphe Sacheuerell.═Jone Da. of John Curson of Keulso'.

Will'm Slorrey of Slorrey in Com. Leic.

A ═

B

C

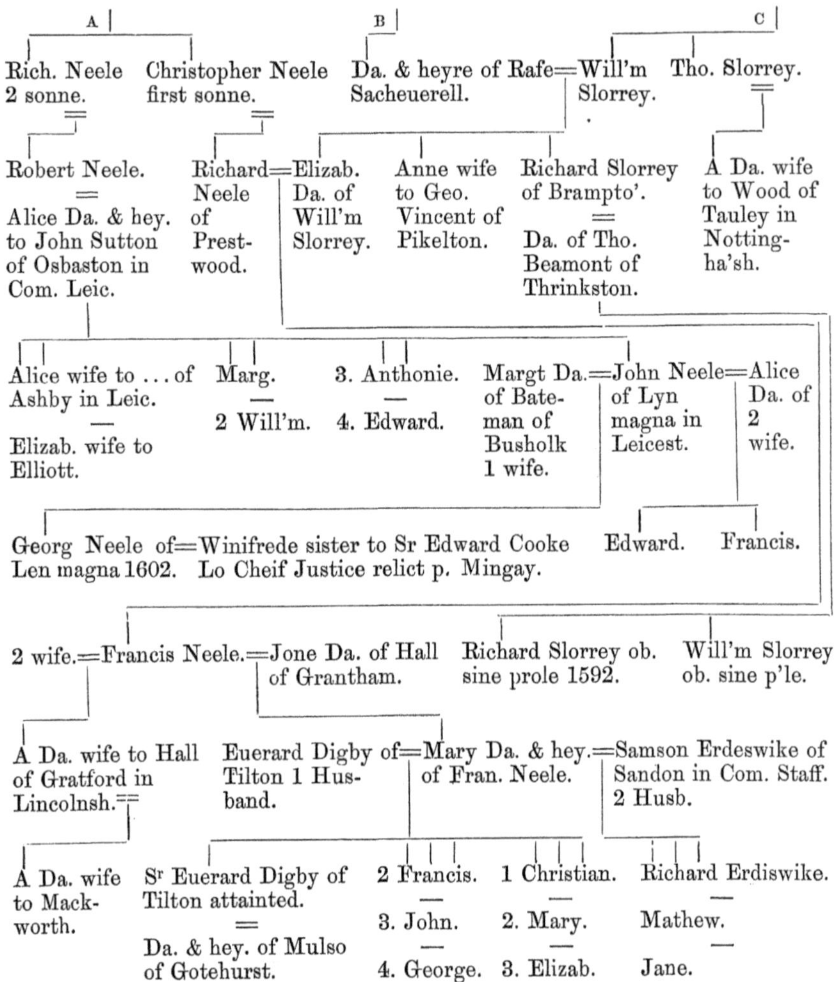

A
B
C
Rich. Neele
2 sonne.
Christopher Neele
first sonne.
Da. & heyre of Rafe=Will'm
Sacheuerell.   Slorrey.
Tho. Slorrey.

Robert Neele.
=
Alice Da. & hey.
to John Sutton
of Osbaston in
Com. Leic.
Richard=Elizab.
Neele   Da. of
of   Will'm
Prest-   Slorrey.
wood.
Anne wife
to Geo.
Vincent of
Pikelton.
Richard Slorrey
of Brampto'.
=
Da. of Tho.
Beamont of
Thrinkston.
A Da. wife
to Wood of
Tauley in
Notting-
ha'sh.

Alice wife to ... of
Ashby in Leic.
—
Elizab. wife to
Elliott.
Marg.
—
2 Will'm.
3. Anthonie.
—
4. Edward.
Margt Da.=John Neele=Alice
of Bate-   of Lyn   Da. of
man of   magna in 2
Busholk   Leicest. wife.
1 wife.

Georg Neele of=Winifrede sister to Sr Edward Cooke
Len magna 1602. Lo Cheif Justice relict p. Mingay.
Edward.   Francis.

2 wife.=Francis Neele.=Jone Da. of Hall
                       of Grantham.
Richard Slorrey ob.
sine prole 1592.
Will'm Slorrey
ob. sine p'le.

A Da. wife to Hall
of Gratford in
Lincolnsh.==
Euerard Digby of=Mary Da. & hey.=Samson Erdeswike of
Tilton 1 Hus-   of Fran. Neele. Sandon in Com. Staff.
band.   2 Husb.

A Da. wife
to Mack-
worth.
Sr Euerard Digby of
Tilton attainted.
=
Da. & hey. of Mulso
of Gotehurst.
2 Francis.
—
3. John.
—
4. George.
1 Christian.
—
2. Mary.
—
3. Elizab.
Richard Erdiswike.
—
Mathew.
—
Jane.

(Brabazon and Woodford.)

ARMS. *Gules, on a bend argent three martlets of the field.*

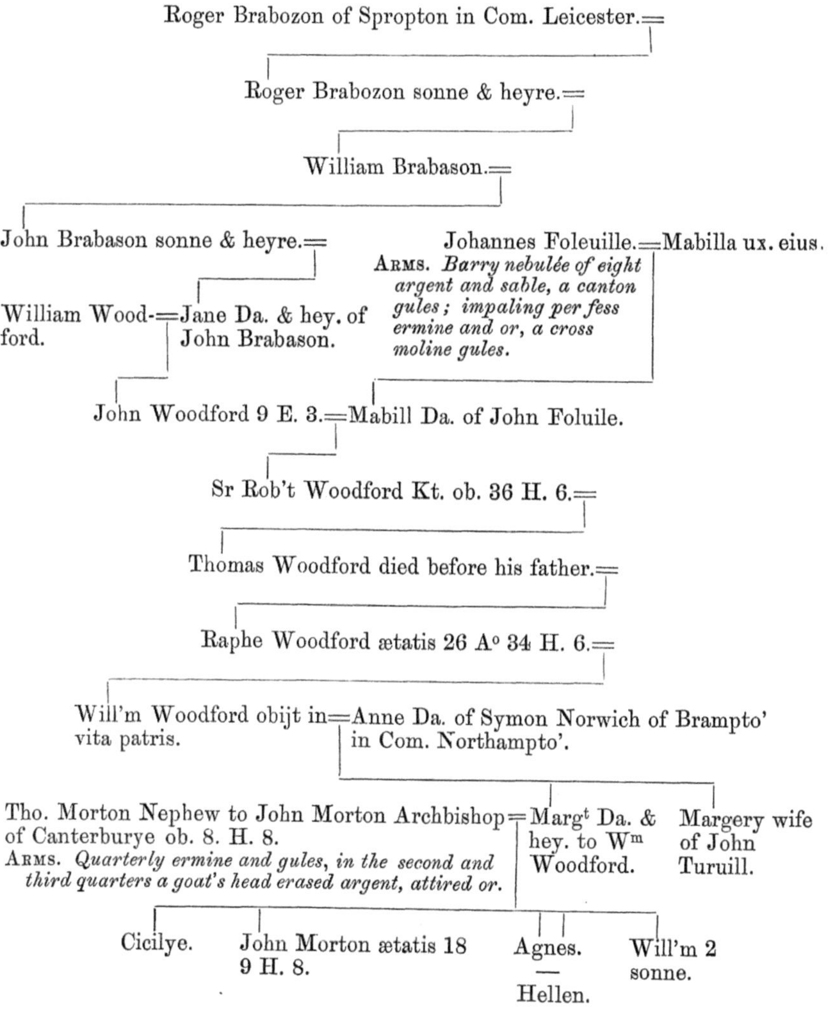

Roger Brabozon of Spropton in Com. Leicester.=

Roger Brabozon sonne & heyre.=

William Brabason.=

John Brabason sonne & heyre.=

William Wood-=Jane Da. & hey. of
ford.   John Brabason.

Johannes Foleuille.=Mabilla ux. eius.

ARMS. *Barry nebulée of eight
argent and sable, a canton
gules; impaling per fess
ermine and or, a cross
moline gules.*

John Woodford 9 E. 3.=Mabill Da. of John Foluile.

Sr Rob't Woodford Kt. ob. 36 H. 6.=

Thomas Woodford died before his father.=

Raphe Woodford ætatis 26 Aº 34 H. 6.=

Will'm Woodford obijt in=Anne Da. of Symon Norwich of Brampto'
vita patris.   in Com. Northampto'.

Tho. Morton Nephew to John Morton Archbishop=Marg^t Da. &
of Canterburye ob. 8. H. 8.   hey. to W^m
ARMS. *Quarterly ermine and gules, in the second and* Woodford.
third quarters a goat's head erased argent, attired or.

Margery wife
of John
Turuill.

Cicilye.   John Morton ætatis 18   Agnes.   Will'm 2
         9 H. 8.   —   sonne.
                           Hellen.

(Corbet.)

ARMS. *Three crows (untinctured).*

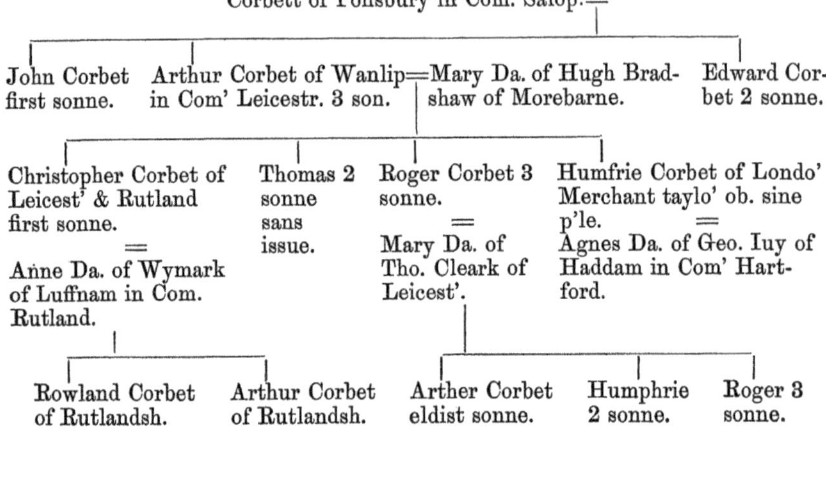

Corbett of Ponsbury in Com. Salop.==

John Corbet first sonne. — Arthur Corbet of Wanlip==Mary Da. of Hugh Bradshaw of Morebarne. in Com' Leicestr. 3 son. — Edward Corbet 2 sonne.

Christopher Corbet of Leicest' & Rutland first sonne. == Anne Da. of Wymark of Luffnam in Com. Rutland. — Thomas 2 sonne sans issue. — Roger Corbet 3 sonne. == Mary Da. of Tho. Cleark of Leicest'. — Humfrie Corbet of Londo' Merchant taylo' ob. sine p'le. == Agnes Da. of Geo. Iuy of Haddam in Com' Hartford.

Rowland Corbet of Rutlandsh. — Arthur Corbet of Rutlandsh. — Arther Corbet eldist sonne. — Humphrie 2 sonne. — Roger 3 sonne.

(Porte.)

ARMS. *Argent, two bars azure, over all a saltire gules.*

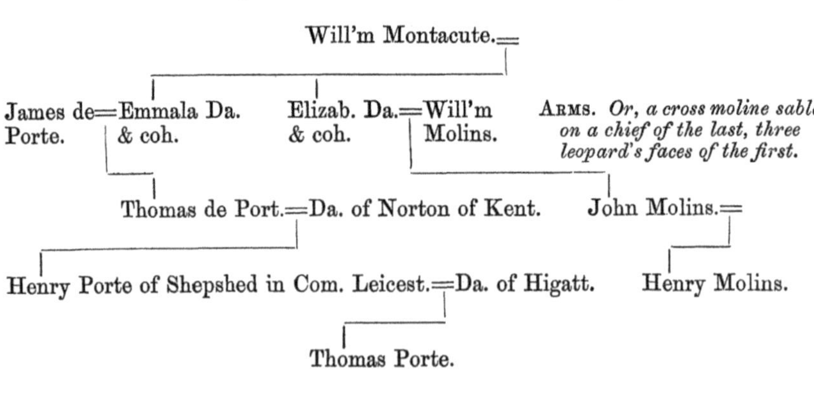

Will'm Montacute.==

James de Porte. ==Emmala Da. & coh. — Elizab. Da.==Will'm & coh. Molins. — ARMS. *Or, a cross moline sable, on a chief of the last, three leopard's faces of the first.*

Thomas de Port.==Da. of Norton of Kent. — John Molins.==

Henry Porte of Shepshed in Com. Leicest.==Da. of Higatt. — Henry Molins.

Thomas Porte.

(𝔅rokesby.)

Arms. *Quarterly:*—1. *Argent, two bars nebulée gules, on a canton of the last a mullet or, pierced.* 2. *Sable, three dovecotes argent, in chief a mullet for difference.* 3. *Gules, a fess lozengy argent.* 4. *Or, on a bend argent between three torteaux as many bars azure.* 5. *Argent, two bars gules, in chief three torteaux.* 6. *Gules, a fess lozengy or.* 7. *Gules, three arches argent, their pedestals or.* 8. *Argent, a chevron between three eagles displayed gules.* 9. *Azure, a cross flory between four martlets argent.*

Crest. *A boar's head couped at the neck gules, bristled or.*

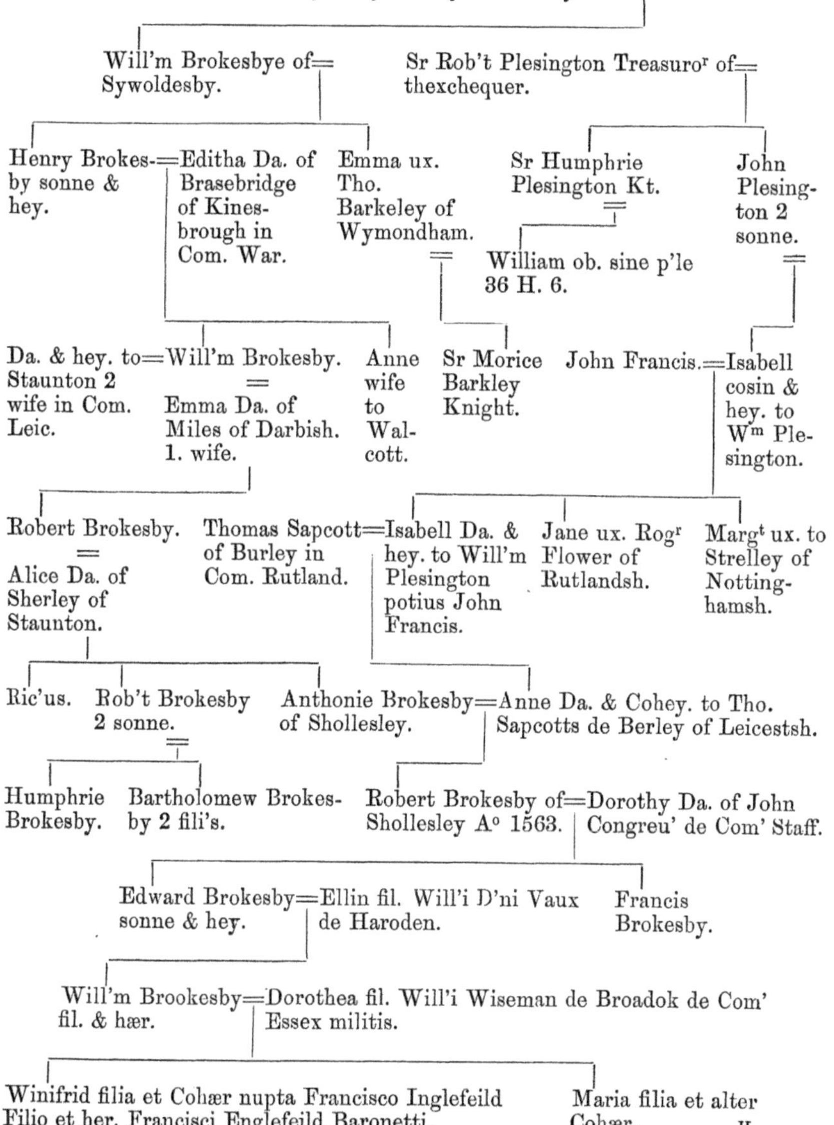

(Vincent.)

ARMS. *Quarterly* :—1. *Azure, three quatrefoils argent.* (VINCENT.)   2. *Barry nebulée of six sable and or, on a chief argent three birds of the first.* (GRIMSBY.)   3. *Argent, a chevron between three boars' heads erased sable, within a bordure engrailed gules.* (VULLIS.)   4. *Argent, a cinquefoil azure.* (MOTON.)   5. *Or, three piles meeting in base gules, a canton vair.* (BASSET.)   6. *Or, a fess gules.* (COLUILE).   7. *Or, fretty sable each of the joints charged with a cross crosslet fitcheé argent.* (CHAMPAINE.)   8. *Or, on a fess sable three water bougets argent.* (BUGGE.)

CREST. A *demi-ram rampant couped sable, attired and collared or.*

Thomas Grimsby of Dracklowe.=. . . Da. of Harecourt.

Will'm Grimsby of=Anne Da. & coh. of Reinold Dracklow 38. H. 6. Moton of Pickleton in Com' Leicest.

Elizab. wife to John Montgomory of Cubley.

Rich. Vincent of Messingham=Anne Da. & hey. to Will'm=Rich. Waterton in Com. Lincoln 20. E. 4. Grimsby of Dracklowe. 2 husband.

Anne Da.=George Vincent of=Da. of Coles of Pickleton in Com' in Com' Will'm Leic. ob. 7 Eliz. Northamp' Slorey ætat 80. mar. to 3 wife. 1 wife. his 2 wife y^e Da. of Barnard s. p'le.

Richard Waterton.=

Joane=Richard Euerard of Shenton in Com' Leic.
Da.
&   ARMS. *Argent, on a chief gules three mullets of the field, within a bordure sable bezantée.*
hey.

Peter 1 son ob. sine p'le.

Phillip =Da. of Eyre of Vincent Yorksh. relic 2 sonne. Hatfeild.

Jane wife to Francis Caue of Kelby in Com. Leic.

Rich. Euerard of Shenton 1601.   = Da. of Butler of Aston in Com. Northamp.

George Vincent.

Rob't Vincent 6 son mar. Alice Da. of Faunt & ob. sine p'le.

Anthonie 5 sonne mar. the Da. of Will'm Salisburie. =

Tho. Vincen=Da. of Forman 2 sonne. of Marston in Darbish.

Jane first mar. to Nicholas Purifoy after to Faunt of Foston.

Richard Vincent.   Rob't Vincent.   Nicholas Vincent.   Jane ux. Tho. Faunt.

A

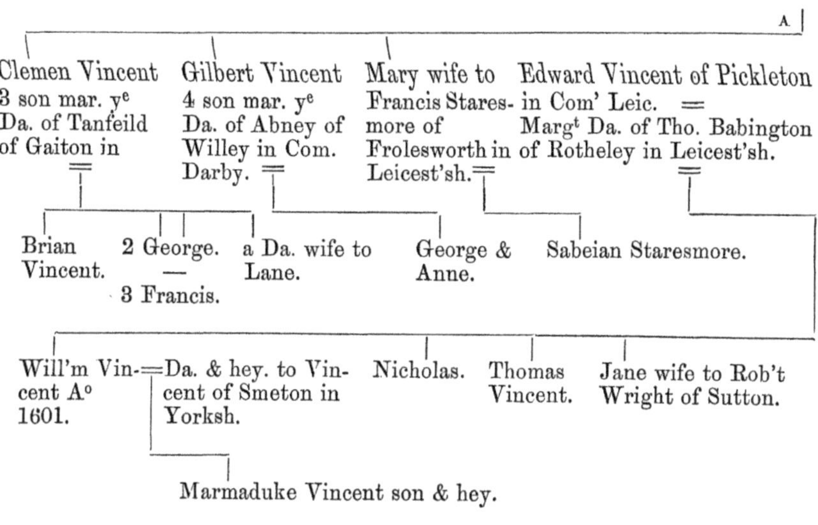

A.

Clemen Vincent	Gilbert Vincent	Mary wife to	Edward Vincent of Pickleton
3 son mar. y^e	4 son mar. y^e	Francis Stares-	in Com' Leic. =
Da. of Tanfeild	Da. of Abney of	more of	Marg^t Da. of Tho. Babington
of Gaiton in	Willey in Com.	Frolesworth in	of Rotheley in Leicest'sh.
=	Darby. =	Leicest'sh. =	

Brian	2 George.	a Da. wife to	George &	Sabeian Staresmore.
Vincent.	—	Lane.	Anne.	
	3 Francis.			

Will'm Vin-=Da. & hey. to Vin-	Nicholas.	Thomas	Jane wife to Rob't
cent A°	cent of Smeton in		Vincent.	Wright of Sutton.
1601.	Yorksh.			

Marmaduke Vincent son & hey.

Chambers.

ARMS. *Quarterly :—1. Ermine, a fess chequy or and gules. 2. Sable, guttée d'eau, on a canton argent a mullet of the first. 3. Gules, a fess between three birds or, within a bordure engrailed of the last. 4. Gules, a chevron between three towers or.*
CREST. *Out of a coronet or, three holly leaves vert.*
" WHEATLEY. *Ar. on cheif gu. 3 garbs Ar.*"

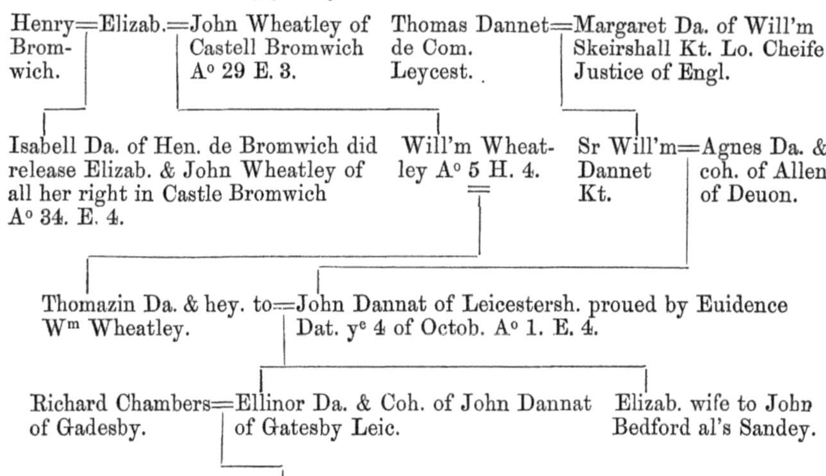

Henry=Elizab.=John Wheatley of	Thomas Dannet=Margaret Da. of Will'm
Brom-	Castell Bromwich	de Com.	Skeirshall Kt. Lo. Cheife
wich.	A° 29 E. 3.	Leycest.	Justice of Engl.

Isabell Da. of Hen. de Bromwich did	Will'm Wheat-	Sr Will'm=Agnes Da. &
release Elizab. & John Wheatley of	ley A° 5 H. 4.	Dannet	coh. of Allen
all her right in Castle Bromwich	=	Kt.	of Deuon.
A° 34. E. 4.			

| Thomazin Da. & hey. to=John Dannat of Leicestersh. proued by Euidence |
| Wm Wheatley. | Dat. y^e 4 of Octob. A° 1. E. 4. |

| Richard Chambers=Ellinor Da. & Coh. of John Dannat | Elizab. wife to John |
| of Gadesby. | of Gatesby Leic. | Bedford al's Sandey. |

| Elizab. Da. of Barthol-=Will'm Chambers mar. to his=. . . Da. of Lathberye of |
mew Villers sine	2 wife y^e Da. of Mallowe	Darbish. 3 wife.
p'le 1. wife.	of Walton s'ne p'le.	ARMS. *Barry of 6 A. b. on*
		A	*canton or, a v. sa.*

A

Rich. Chambers eldist=... Da. of Ashbie   Will'm Chambers =Barbara Da. of
son ob. sine p'le   of Leicest'sh.   of Gatesby ob.   Will'm Pochin
1558.   1558.   of Leicest'.

Will'm Chambers eldist son   John Chambers son &   Mary wife to John   Elizab.
ob. sine p'le 1564.   hey. ætat. 26. 1575. Barnes.

(Draper.)

ARMS. *Quarterly :*—1. *Argent, on a fess between three annulets gules a mullet of the field between two covered cups or.* 2. *Argent, on two chevrons sable between three escallops vert, six martlets or.* 3. *Ermine, on a chief azure three lions rampant or.* 4. *Ermine, a fess chequy sable and argent.*
CREST. *A dexter arm couped at the elbow erect, vested vert, slashed argent, holding a covered cup or.*

John Draper of Flintham in Com' Nottingh.=

Tho. Draper of=... Da. & hey. of John Agar by the Da. &
Flintham.   hey. of Urswick.

Tho. Draper of=... Da. of Kettlebye.
Flinthamp.   ARMS. *B.* × *ragule betweene* 4 (*martlets*) *Ar.*

John Draper of Mel-=... Da. of   Robert Draper 2=Elizab. Da. & Coh. to John
ton Mowbray in   Gunston.   sonne of   Fifeild al's Lowe of
Com. Leicest.   Camerwell.   Camerwell.

Mathew Draper of=Sence Da. of Black-   Benet ux. John   Elizab. uxor John
Camerwell.   well of London.   Fromond.   Boweyr.

Tho. Draper of   Will'm   Sr Christopher Draper=Margaret Da. of
Melton Mow-   Draper.   maior of London   Hen. Greene of
bray.=   =   1567. ob. 1580.   Essex.

John Draper of   Rob't   Bennet wife to Sr   Briget wife   Anne wife to Sr
Melton Mow-   Drap'.   Will'm Webbe   to Stephen   Wolstan Dixie maior
bray 1591.   maior of London   Woodroffe.   of London 1586 ob.
                        1591.   1593.

(Turbile.)

ARMS. *Quarterly :*—1. *Gules, three chevrons vair.* (TURUILL.) 2. *Argent, a maunch azure.* (FLAMUILL.) 3. *Or, on a fess sable three water bougets argent.* (BOUGGE.) 4. *Gules, three lozenges between six cross crosslets fitchée argent.* (FOUCHER.) 5. *Vair argent and sable, a canton gules.* (CHAMPAINE.) 6. *Blank.* (STANTON.)

CREST. *A dove close proper, holding in its beak a branch of olive slipped vert, fructed with three olives or.*

Turuill.=

Nicholas Turuill.

Hugo Turuill= 28 H. 3.

Adamus Turuill de Thurlaston 44. H. 3.

Rogerus Turuill.

Rad'us Turuill de Normanton 43. H. 3.

ARMS. *Gules, three chevrons vair.*

Rad'us Turuill Benefactor Abbatiæ Leicestriæ.

Ricardus Turvill= miles 20. E. 3.

Hugo Turuill 20. E. 3.

A

Flamvill.=

Henricus Flamvill.

Johannes Flamville.

Thomas Flamvill & W^ms Flamvill de Aston Testes Chartis sans date.==

Rob'tus Flamvill miles= 8 E. 3. ARMS. *Argent, a maunch azure.*

Will'm Flamvill= miles 37. E. 3.

B

Hugo de Champaine.

Nicholas de Champaine de Thurlaston.

Sr Rob't Champion Kt. 8 E. 3.=

Sr Rob't Champion de Champion Kt. 34 E. 3.=

ARMS. *Or, fretty sable each of the joints charged with a cross crosslet fitchée argent.*
CREST. *A demi-mermaid erased proper, crined argent, holding in the dexter hand a looking-glass (untinctured), and in the sinister a comb or.*

Rob't Fowcher mar. Cicelye sister to John Francis of fowark.==

Rob'tus Champion.

=Margareta fil. Rogeri St Loo D'ns de Thurlaston et Wigingston.

1. Jane.
—
2. Marion.

3 Auis.
—
4. Alice.

Edmond Fowcher of Cotton.
—
John Foucher of Eggington.

Rob't Foucher of Champion.

=Marg^t sist. & hey. to Will'm Champton.
c

Will'm ob. sine p'le.
—
Elizab. wife to Edw. Hardwick.

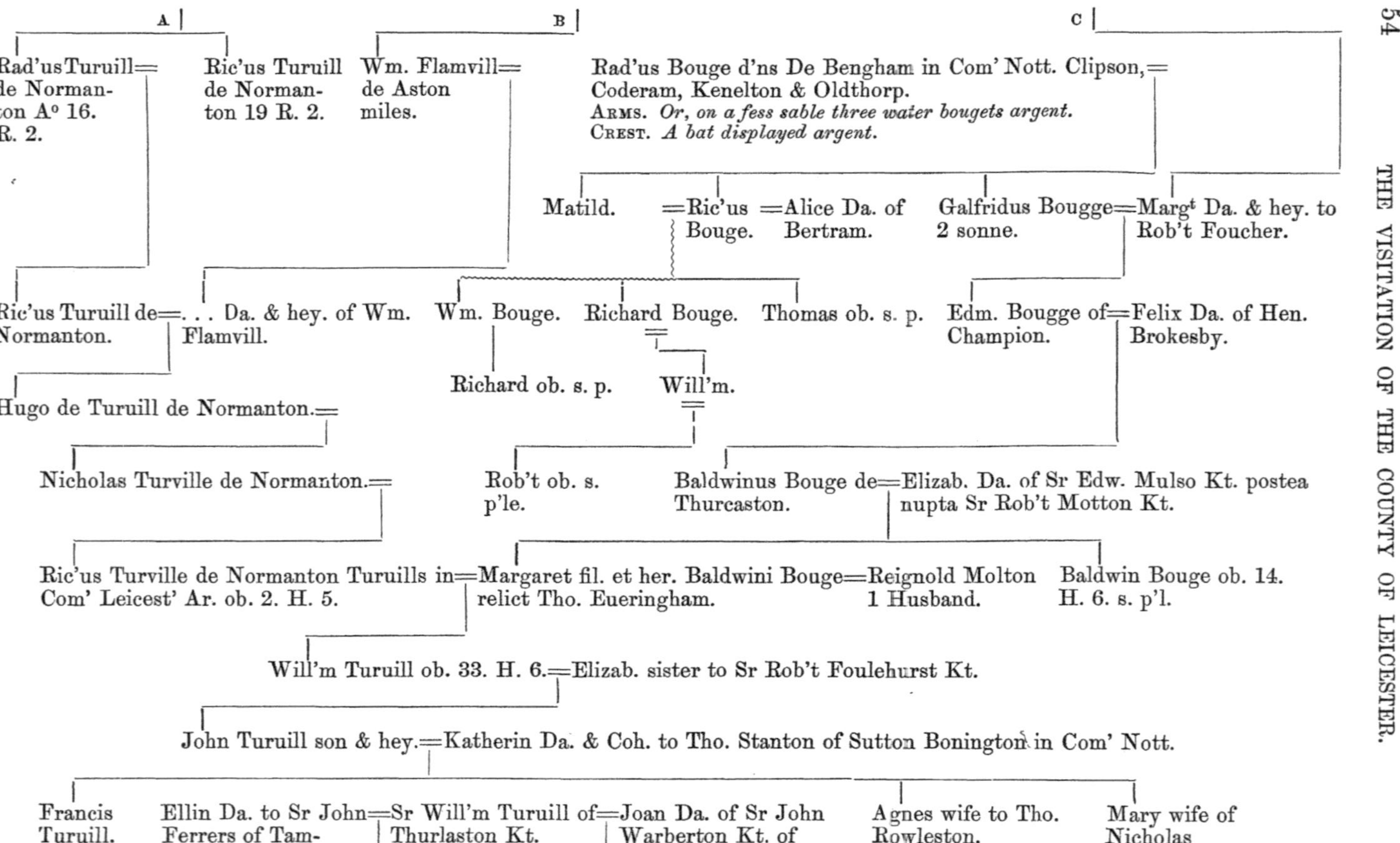

A |
B |
C |
Rad'us Turuill= de Norman-ton A° 16. R. 2.
Ric'us Turuill de Norman-ton 19 R. 2.
Wm. Flamvill= de Aston miles.
Rad'us Bouge d'ns De Bengham in Com' Nott. Clipson,= Coderam, Kenelton & Oldthorp.
ARMS. Or, on a fess sable three water bougets argent.
CREST. A bat displayed argent.
Matild.
=Ric'us Bouge.
=Alice Da. of Bertram.
Galfridus Bougge= 2 sonne.
Marg^t Da. & hey. to Rob't Foucher.
Ric'us Turuill de= Normanton.
. . . Da. & hey. of Wm. Flamvill.
Wm. Bouge.
Richard Bouge.
Thomas ob. s. p.
Edm. Bougge of= Champion.
Felix Da. of Hen. Brokesby.
Richard ob. s. p.
Will'm.
Hugo de Turuill de Normanton.=
Rob't ob. s. p'le.
Baldwinus Bouge de= Thurcaston.
Elizab. Da. of Sr Edw. Mulso Kt. postea nupta Sr Rob't Motton Kt.
Nicholas Turville de Normanton.=
Ric'us Turville de Normanton Turuills in= Com' Leicest' Ar. ob. 2. H. 5.
Margaret fil. et her. relict Tho. Eueringham.
Baldwini Bouge= 1 Husband.
Reignold Molton
Baldwin Bouge ob. 14. H. 6. s. p'l.
Will'm Turuill ob. 33. H. 6.= Elizab. sister to Sr Rob't Foulehurst Kt.
John Turuill son & hey.= Katherin Da. & Coh. to Tho. Stanton of Sutton Bonington in Com' Nott.
Francis Turuill.
Ellin Da. to Sr John Ferrers of Tam-
=Sr Will'm Turuill of Thurlaston Kt.
=Joan Da. of Sr John Warberton Kt. of
Agnes wife to Tho. Rowleston.
Mary wife of Nicholas

D | E |

John Turuill of=Mary Da. of | Will'm Turuill ob. | Mary wife to Waldron. | Anne wife | ... Da. of=Georg Turuill=Anne Da.
Thurlaston | Tho. Fendern | sine p'le. = | — | to Swil- | Hinde of | of Aston | of John
eldist sonne. | of Fendren | Elizab. Da. of Sr | Elizab. wife to Sr | lington. | Cam- | Flamuill in | Sheldon
| in Darbish. | Humphrie Brad- | Hump. Bradborne of | | bridgsh. 2 | Com' Leic. | of Shel-
| | borne Kt. | Darbish. Kt. | | wife. | | don.

Galfridus=Turuill. | Rob'tus 4 son. | Richard Turuill of Thur-=Jane Da. of Tho. | 3. Georg. | 6. Raph. | Ellin ux. | Margerie ux.
| — | laston et Normanto' | Babington of Rod- | — | — | Bicker- | Malory postea
| Jasper 5 son. | Turvile sup'stes 1563. | ley in Leict'sh. | 2. Thomas. | 7. Francis. | ton. | Cleyton.

Elizab. ux. | Frances. | Georg Turuill mar. | Mary ux. Gill. | John Turuill. | Henry Turuill=Anne Da. of | Tho. Turuill=... Da. of
| — | Elizab. Da. of | | | 1601. | Cooke of | 2 son. | Wright of
| Katherin. | Tho. Bridges. | | | | London. | | Noneaton.

Georg Turuill of Aston Flamuill.=Anne Da. & Coh. of John Martin of Poole house. | Francis.

Henry Turuill sonne & hey. | Dorothy.

ARMS. *Gules, a chevron vair between three mullets argent.*

Ambrose Turuill. | 2 Katherin. | Soward Turuill of=Ellin Da. of Hugh | John Turuill | Martha ux. Georg | Jane ux. Charles | Elizab. uxor
| — | Thurlaston in | Armestrong of | of Woluey | Blunt of Osbas- | Gunter of | Alcock of
| 3. Dorothe. | Com. Leyc. 1601. | Nottinghamsh. | 2 son. | ton. | Berksh. | Oxfordshere.

Henry Turuill 1 sonne. | Thomas ob. sine p'l. | Hugh Turuill. | Jane ux. Bate. | Margt.

(𝕶𝖊𝖇𝖊𝖑𝖑.)

ARMS. *Quarterly :—Barry nebulée of six argent and sable, on a canton gules a crescent (untinctured) ; and gules, a chevron argent between three eagles displayed (untinctured).*

CREST. *A demi-eagle with wings displayed argent, gorged with a bar gemel gules.*

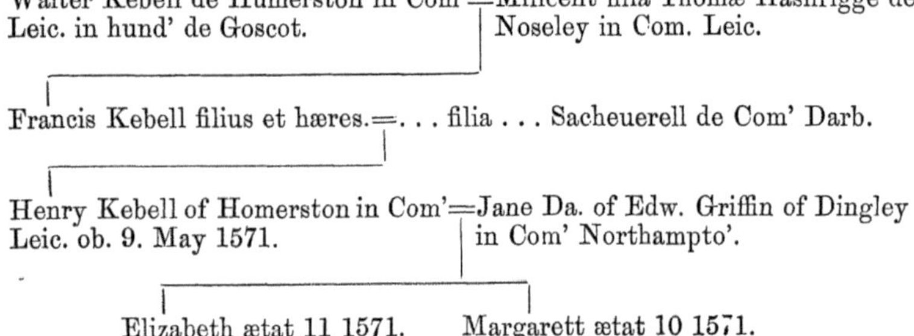

Walter Kebell de Humerston in Com'=Milicent filia Thomæ Hasilrigge de Leic. in hund' de Goscot.   Noseley in Com. Leic.

Francis Kebell filius et hæres.=. . . filia . . . Sacheuerell de Com' Darb.

Henry Kebell of Homerston in Com'=Jane Da. of Edw. Griffin of Dingley Leic. ob. 9. May 1571.   in Com' Northampto'.

Elizabeth ætat 11 1571.   Margarett ætat 10 1571.

(𝕭𝖚𝖗𝖙𝖔𝖓.)

ARMS. *Quarterly :—1. Azure, a fess between three talbots' heads erased or. 2. Or, three mullets gules pierced. 3. Argent, a bend sable between three pellets. 4. Azure, an eagle displayed or. 5. Gules, a saltire engrailed between four mullets or. 6. Or, on a chief sable three griffins' heads erased argent. 7. Or, two bends gemelles sable. 8. Argent, a fess gules, in chief three mullets sable. 9. Gules, three eagles displayed or. 10. Vair argent and sable, a chevron gules. 11. (Field untinctured) fretty, each joint charged with a cross crosslet (untinctured). 12. Gules, on a bend or, three garlands vert.*

CREST. *On a mount vert, a beacon argent, cresset sable, ladder or, inflamed proper.*

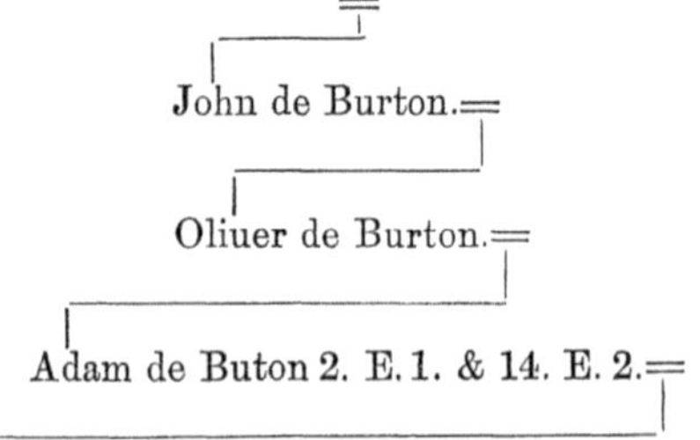

Sr James Burton of Titbury in Com. Staff. Kt. Scutifer to K. R. 1.

John de Burton.=

Oliuer de Burton.=

Adam de Buton 2. E. 1. & 14. E. 2.=

Nicholas de Burton de Titbury 14=Joan Da. of Creucure of Titbury. E. 2 & 12 E. 3.   ARMS. " *Or + unde g.*"

A

A

Will'm Burton of Titberie=Mawde sister & hey. to Tho. Curtois of Titbery.
23. E. 3 & 7. R. 2.   ARMS. *G*. 3. (*stars*) *or*.

Richard Burton of Titbery=Matild sister to Rob't   Oliuer Burton Seneshall of
7. R. 2.   Gibon of Titbury.   the honor of Titbury.

Will'm Burton vexillarius Regis=Elizab. Da. & Coh. to Tho. Cotton
39. H. 6.   of Cotton. E. 4.

Raphe Burton maried 18. E. 4=Elizab. Da. of Phillip Ockouer
buried at Titbery 3. H. 8.   of Ockouer 16. H. 8.

| Dorothy ux. Willnes of Milborne. — Mudwynne ux. William Creueker of Twiford. | Anne Da. of Bolston of Fawde 1. wife. | =James Burton of Lindesey in Com. Leic't. mar. 36. H. 8. buried at Higham. | =Elizab. Da. & coh. of John Hardwick of Lindsey 24. H. 8. | Katherin wife to Milles. — Mary wife to John Wakefeile. |

Thomas Burton   Rob't Burton of Lindesey maried 35=Kattherin Da. of Will'm
2 sonne.   H. 8 ob. 5. May buried at Higham.   Ripington of Armington.

| James died at Louayn sine p'le. | Will'm. — Thomas. | Edward sine p'le. | Raphe Burton of Lindesey mar. 14. Elizab. | =Dorothy Da. of Will'm Faunt of Foston. | Mary & Frances ob. sine p'le. |

| Will'm Burton 1 son ob. sine p'le. | George Burton 3. sonne. — Raphe 4. son. | Rob't Burton of Fawde in Com. Staff. | Anne wife to Geo. Bradshaw of Morebarne. | 1 Katherin. — 2. Mary. | 3. Elizab. — 4. Jane. |

Moton.

ARMS. *Argent, a cinquefoil azure.*

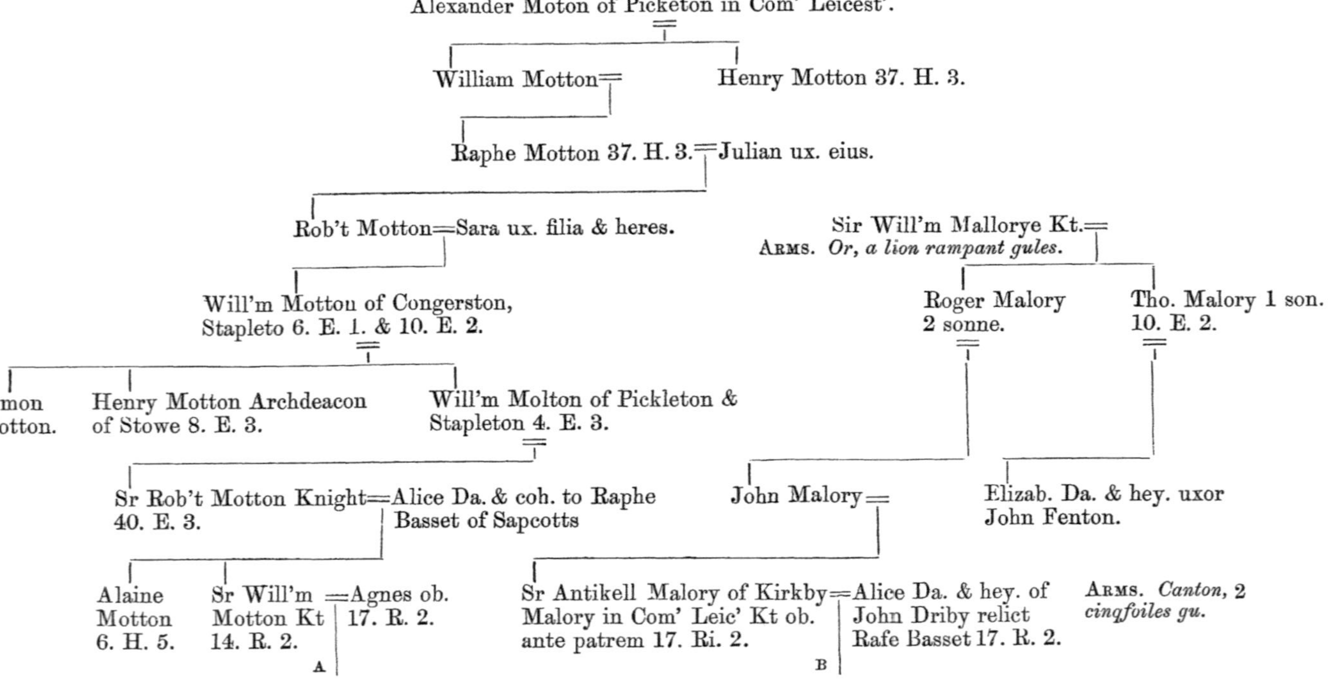

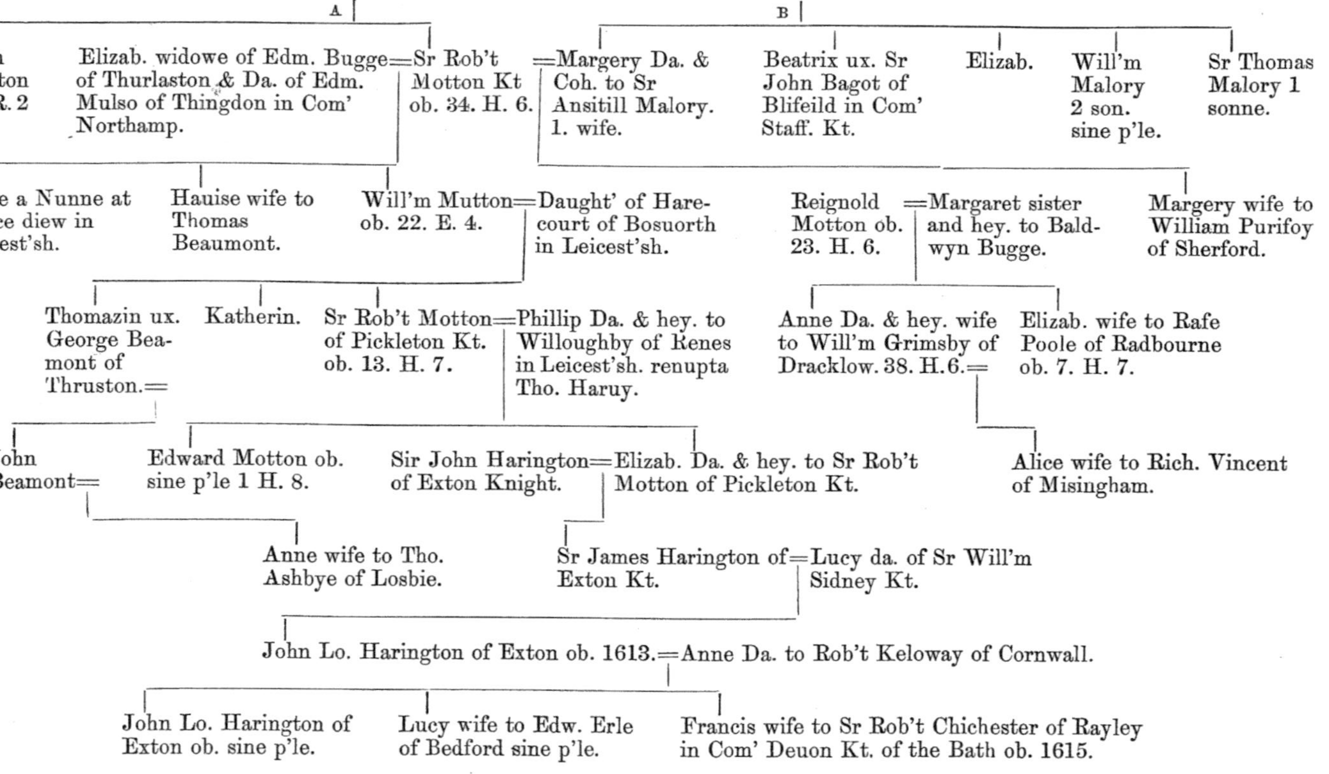

A

B

John Motton 17. R. 2

Elizab. widowe of Edm. Bugge of Thurlaston & Da. of Edm. Mulso of Thingdon in Com' Northamp. = Sr Rob't Motton Kt ob. 34. H. 6.

= Margery Da. & Coh. to Sr Ansitill Malory. 1. wife.

Beatrix ux. Sr John Bagot of Blifeild in Com' Staff. Kt.

Elizab.

Will'm Malory 2 son. sine p'le.

Sr Thomas Malory 1 sonne.

Anne a Nunne at Grace diew in Leicest'sh.

Hauise wife to Thomas Beaumont.

Will'm Mutton = ob. 22. E. 4.

Daught' of Harecourt of Bosuorth in Leicest'sh.

Reignold Motton ob. 23. H. 6. = Margaret sister and hey. to Baldwyn Bugge.

Margery wife to William Purifoy of Sherford.

Thomazin ux. George Beamont of Thruston. =

Katherin.

Sr Rob't Motton of Pickleton Kt. ob. 13. H. 7. = Phillip Da. & hey. to Willoughby of Renes in Leicest'sh. renupta Tho. Haruy.

Anne Da. & hey. wife to Will'm Grimsby of Dracklow. 38. H. 6. =

Elizab. wife to Rafe Poole of Radbourne ob. 7. H. 7.

John Beamont =

Edward Motton ob. sine p'le 1 H. 8.

Sir John Harington of Exton Knight. = Elizab. Da. & hey. to Sr Rob't Motton of Pickleton Kt.

Alice wife to Rich. Vincent of Misingham.

Anne wife to Tho. Ashbye of Losbie.

Sr James Harington of Exton Kt. = Lucy da. of Sr Will'm Sidney Kt.

John Lo. Harington of Exton ob. 1613. = Anne Da. to Rob't Keloway of Cornwall.

John Lo. Harington of Exton ob. sine p'le.

Lucy wife to Edw. Erle of Bedford sine p'le.

Francis wife to Sr Rob't Chichester of Rayley in Com' Deuon Kt. of the Bath ob. 1615.

(Beamont.)

ARMS. *Azure, a lion rampant between five fleurs-de-lis or.*
CREST. *An elephant (untinctured) trapped or, surmounted with a tower (untinctured).*

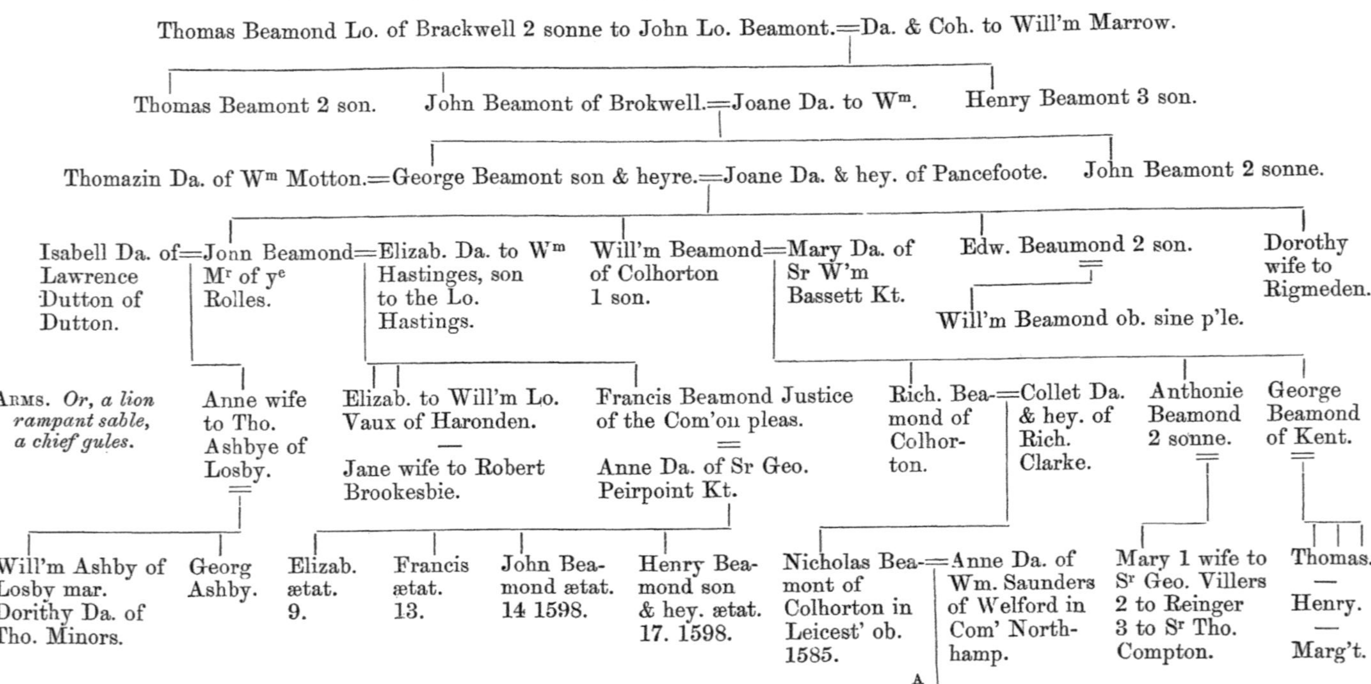

A

| Huntindon Beamont. | Francis Beamont 2 sonne. | Sʳ Henry Beamont of Colherton in Com' Ley. ob. 1607. ═ Da. & hey. of Lewis of London. | Sʳ Tho. Beamont of Staugton Kt. 3 sonne. ═ Katherin Da. & hey. of Farnham of Staugham. |

Will'm Beamont 2 sonne.

Thomas Beamont sonne & hey. Knight of Cole Orton in the countie of Leicester Aᵒ 1619 maried Elizabeth dau'r and heire to Hen. Sapcote of Elton in co. Hunt.

Mary maried to Richard Paramour de Loseby in Com. Leic.

Francis ux. Sr Wolstan Dixie Kt.

Elizab. uxo' Sr John Ashbornham Kt.

Sapcote Beaumont son & heire æt. 6.

Henry ætatis. 4.

Thomas ætatis. 2.

Robert ætatis. 1.

Thomas. — Anne.

Jane s. p.

Elizabeth. — Katherine.

Frances. — Maria.

Elianor.

Anne uxor John Dillon of fardringhay.

Isabell uxor Hugh Snowse of Belton in Yorksh.

Thomas 3 sonne.

Hen. Beamont sonne & heyre mil. duxit Elizab. fil. Willi' Turpen de Knoptoft in Com' Leic. militis.

Farnham Beautmond 2 sonne.

Elinor.

Jane uxor Wᵐ Tempell of London Merchant.

Tho. Beaumᵗ fil. et hær. æt. 11 1619.

2 Willm's æt. 9.

3. Henricus. 7.

1 Elizab. 6.

2. Fran. 4.

Humphrey.

ARMS. *Quarterly :—Gules, a cross bottonée argent quarter pierced of the field and charged in each end with three escallops sable ; and azure, a bend between four leopards' faces or, a crescent for difference.*
CREST. *A harpy, argent, crined or, with wings displayed of the last.*

Sr Peter Humphrey of Cirencester= in Com' Gloucest'.

Peter Humphrey=Elizab. widow of Gastangs of Barton of Cirencester. who gaue Barton to her son John.

John Humphrey of Barton in=Elianor Da. to Sr Will'm Vaulx. Com' Northamp. of Harendon.

Will'm Humphrie=Mawde Da. of Sr Ric. of Barton. Knightley of Fawsley.

Edward 2 sonne.

Richard 3 sonne.

Elinor 1 wife to Wm Stafford of Totton in Com' Buck. 2d to Sr Edm. Ashfield K.

Isabell Da. of Stanley ; widow to Will'm Tanfeild of Britton. =Richard Humphrie of Barton. =Jane Da. of Rob't Parsell of Bedford.

Anna uxor Tho. Pagi de Wolgraue.

Elinor mar. to Tho. Babington of Temple Rotherley in Com' Leyc.

Will'm Humphrie of Barton. =Jane Da. of Tho. Linne of Bassingboure in Com' Cantabrigiæ.

John Humphrie 2 son mar. Margaret Da. of Rous of Worcestersh.=

Audrye mar. to Ric. Haruey of Shenton in Com' Salop.

Rich. Humphrey of Barton 1 sonne. =Mary Da. of Sir Will'm Lane of Norton Kt.

Sir Tho. Humphrie of Shipson in Com' Leyc. =Mary Da. of Wm Meringe of Meringes in com' Northam.

John 1 son.
—
Edw. Humphrie.
—
Mary wife of Malorye of.

1. Anne
—
2. Theodosia.

Nathaniell Humphrie son & hey.

Zacharias 2 sonne.

Pace.

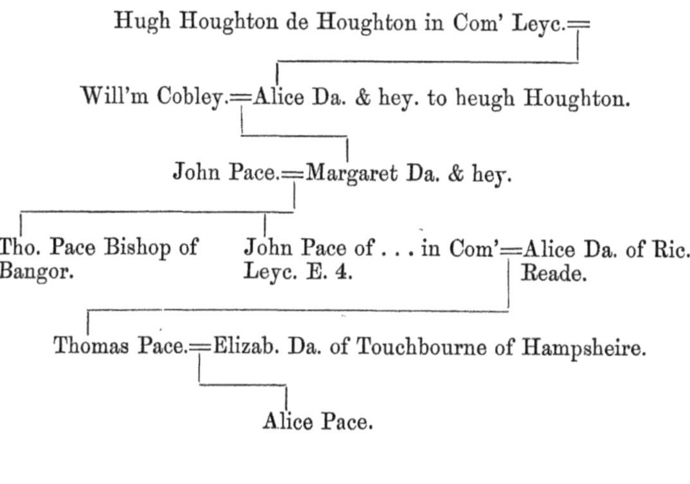

Prestwich.

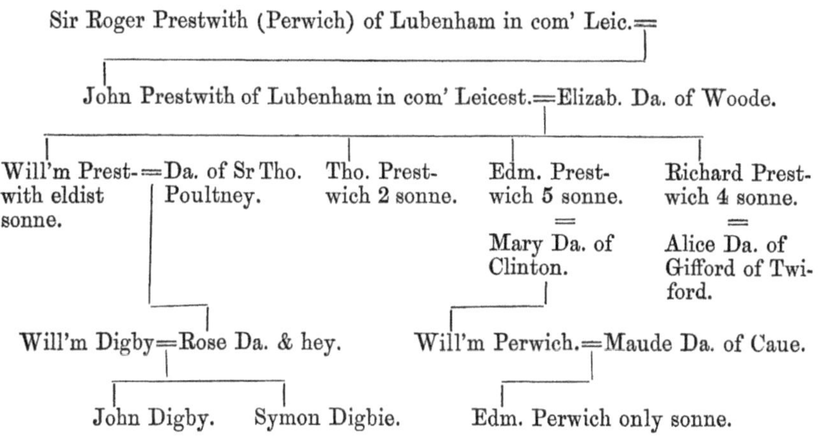

(Dannet.)

ARMS. *Quarterly :*—1. *Sable, guttée d'eau a canton ermine.* (DANNAT.)　2. *(Field untinctured) on two bars, six lions rampant (untinctured).* (DELAHAY.)　3. *Azure, on a bend cotised (untinctured) three eagles displayed argent.* (BELKNAP.)　4. *(Field untinctured) two bends gules.*　5. *Azure, three birds rising argent.* (SUDLEY.)　6. *Bendy of six or and azure.* (MONTFORT.)　7. *Gules, a fess chequy argent and sable, between six cross crosslets fitchée or.* (BUTLER.)　8. *Argent, barry of six nebulée gules, within a bordure engrailed sable, bezantée.*
CREST. *A greyhound's head erased argent, collared and ringed gules.*

Dannat.=

Sr Will'm Dannat Knight.　Richard Dannat 2 sonne.　. . . Dannat.=

Will'm Dannat.=Juliana fil. naturalis Henrici Ducis Lancastriæ.

Will'm Dannat gaue all his Landes at South Croxton to his uncle Sr Will'm Aº 33. E. 3.

Will'm Dannat.=Anne Da. of Norwood.

Mawde Da. of John Pickwell.=Rich. Dannat of West hope.=Mawde Da. of Knightley.=Tho. De la Hey 2 husb.

Rob't Dannet son of Rich.=Agnes Da. & hey. of John Peake.　Thomas Dannat 2 sonne.　Rob't 3 sonne.　John Dannet 4 sonne.=Joane Da. & sole hey. to De la hay.

Thomas Dannet.　Anne Da. & hey. of . . . Higford 1. wife.=Gerrard Dannat.=Mary Da. & coh. to Sr Edw. Belknap of Warwicksh. Knight.　Tho. Dannet 2 sonne.

Elizab. wife to John Arundell of Lanhern Cornw.　Alice mar. to Edw. Brunha'.　Sr John Dannet Knight.=Anne Da. & sole hey. of Thomas Ellingbridge.　Tho. Dannet 2 sonne. = Anne Da. of Sr Mathew Browne of Surrey Kt.　Mary wife of Georg Medley of Whitnes in Com' Warw.

Leonard Dannet.　Agnes Da. of John Belmeg 2 wife.=John Dannet son of Sr John.=Elizab. Da. of John Lenton ob. s. p.　Thomas Dannet.
—
Audley Dannatt.

(Brooke.)

ARMS. *Quarterly:—Or, a cross engrailed per pale gules and sable; and argent, a chevron sable between three bucks' heads caboshed gules, a crescent for difference.*

CREST. A *badger (untinctured), charged on the flank with a crescent for difference.*

Thomas Brooke of Leighton in Com. Cestriæ.═Anne Da. of . . . Venables.

Rob't Brooke.	Alice wife to Raph Leech of Nantwich.	Hen. Brooke Cheif Cleark of the Greencloth.	Tho. Brooke of Leighton. ═ Jane Da. of . . . Meuerell of Throwley in Com' Staff.	Margaret wife to Rog^r Maneringe. — Raph Boolke Lo. of Calleis.

John Brooke.	Raphe mar. the Da. of Fetherston.	Tho. Brooke of Leighton in Com. Cest. ═ Elizab. Da. of Hugh Starkie of Culto.	Alice wif of Georg Delues.	Anne wife to Tho. Whitney of Cowcaus.

3. Reginold. — 4. Edward.	John Brook of Leighton. ═ Margerie Da. of Charles Manwaring of Crowton.	Andrewe Brooke of Kirby in Com. Warr. ═	Elizab. wife to Richard Walker of Leigh greene.	Anne wife to Shelton.	Rich. Brooke of Norton mar. Christian Da. of John Carew of Hacomb. ═

Tho. Brooke of Leighton. ═ Alice Da. of Wm. Croxton of Rauenscroft.	Sr Bassell Brooke of Lubnam in Com' Leic.	Tho. Brooke of Norton. ═ Anne Da. of Henry Lo. Audeley.

Sr Rich. Brooke of Norton Kt.

(Peche.)

ARMS. *Azure, a lion rampant double queuée ermine, on a canton or, a mullet gules.*

John Peche of Kingsthorp & Sherowhall in Com. Leic. & Derby.

John Peche de Kingesthorp in Comitatu Leic.

Willm's Peche de Kingesthorp sup'stes 1563.═ . . . filia Will'mi Whitchestell.

Henricus Peche fil. et hæres.   Franciscus 2 filius.

Smith al's Harris.

ARMS. *Quarterly :—1. Gules, on a chevron or, between three bezants as many crosses pattée fitchée sable ; and argent, three piles meeting in base gules between twelve martlets sable, three and three in chief, and three and three in base palewise.*
CREST. *Out of a ducal coronet or, an Indian goat's head argent, eared sable, bearded and attired of the first.*

ARMS. *Gules, on a chevron or, between three bezants as many crosses pattée fitchée sable.*

John Smith al's Harris of Withcottes in Com' Leic. ob. 1546. = Dorothie Da. of Ric. Cave of Stamford in Com' Northamp. = Henry Poole Kt of ye Roodes 2 Husb.

Roger Smith of Withcooks ob. 1603. = Frances Da. of Sr Tho. Griffin of Dingley Kt.

Francis Smith 2 sonne. =

Anthonie Smith 3 son. =

Erasmus Smith of Bosworth 3 sonne. = Margaret sister to Wm Cicell Lo Burley & wydow of Roger Caue. = Da. of Baiard 1 wife relict Wye.

Briget wife to Norwich 2d to Sands.

Francis wife to Tho. Sturton of Sturton in Com' Nott.

Jane wife to John Melley of London Grocer.

Roger Smith = Da. of Woodcoook.

Francis 2 sonne. — Margaret mar to Iues.

Edward Smith 3 sonne. = Dorothy Da. of Anthonie Smith.

Henry Smith Rector Eccl'iæ de St. Clements ob. s. p.

James Smith 2 sonne.

Roger Smith 3 son ob. Bosworth. = Jane Da. of Sr Edw. Heron Knight sergiant at Lawe.

Edward Smith.

Margaret wife to Gilbert Bery of Lincolnsh.

Ambrose Smith of London 4 son. = Joane Da. of John Cooe of Coxall in Essex.

Clement Smith 5 son. — Will'm Smith 6 son.

Robert Smith of Groby 8 sonne. — Henry Smith 9 son.

Georg Smith of Withcottes 10 sonne. = Mary Da. of Will'm Allen of Marfield in Com' Leic.

Isabell 1 wife to Lowes 2 to Maynard of Hartford'sh.

Elizab. wife to Martin Calthrop of Antingham Norff.

Margar. wife to Sr Thom. Wilkes Kt. Clerk of the Counsell to Queene Eliz.

Dorothy wife to Benedict Barnham Alderma' of London after to Sr John Pagington.

Henry Smith of Withcocks in com' Leic'. = Da. of Hen. & Sister to Will'm

Francis Smith 2 son. = Da. of Taylor of London.

Sir Will'm Smith of London Kt. 1601. = Elizab. Da. of Tho. Sinner Alderman of London.

Elizab.   Joane.   Will'm.   George.   Thomas.   John.   Ambrose Smith sonne and hey.

Joyce mar. John Ingell of Essex.

Elizab. wife to John Hall of Northamp'sh.

Anne wife to Sherington Montgomerie of Sherington.

Dorothy wife to Tho. Arwaker of Essex.

Erasmus 4 filius obiit s. p.

Joh'es Smith 3 fil. ob. in Barb(uic ?) sine prole.

Rob't Smith 2 son mar. y^e Da. of Peper.

Humphrie = Anne Da. of Georg Bowles Smith of London Grocer. Alderma' of London.

George Smith eldist sonne.   2. Humphrie.   3. John.   4. Thomas Smith.

(Belgrabe.)

ARMS. *Quarterly :—1. Gules, a chevron ermine between three mascles argent. 2. Argent, three pairs of bellows sable. 3. Sable, three escallops argent. 4. Ermine, three mascles conjoined in fess sable. 5. Or, on a fess gules three fleurs-de-lis of the field, in chief as many fleurs-de-lis of the second. 6. Gules, a pelican in its piety argent.*
CREST. *A ram's head couped at the neck (untinctured).*

Johannes Belgraue fil. et hær. Ric'i = Johanna filia et unica hær. Thomæ Swyke burges of leicest'.

Georgius Belgraue filius et her. = Dorothea filia Lawrencij Sanders.

Johanna filia Rob'ti Farnham de = George Belgrave filius = Maria filia Rob'ti Querne in Com' Leic' ux. 2.   et hæres.   Chantrell ux. 1.

Rob'tus Belgraue.   2. Dorothy.   4. Francis.   6. Anna.   Rob'tus Belgraue filius et hæres sup'- stes 1563.   Ambrose 2 filius.

1. Margaret.   3. Elizabeth.   5. Margerie.   7. Maria.

(Belgraue.)

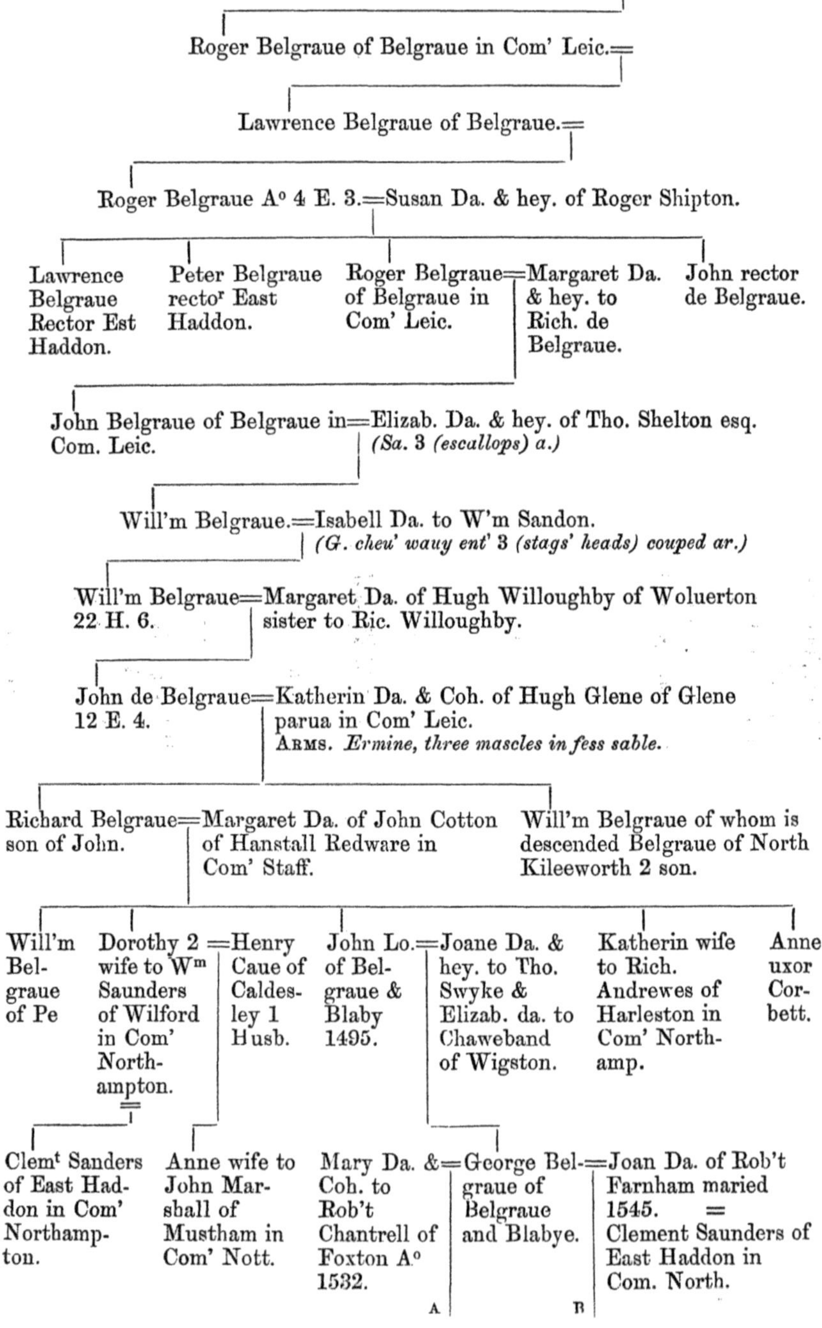

Hugh Belgraue of Belgraue in Com' Leic.=

Roger Belgraue of Belgraue in Com' Leic.=

Lawrence Belgraue of Belgraue.=

Roger Belgraue A° 4 E. 3.=Susan Da. & hey. of Roger Shipton.

| Lawrence Belgraue Rector Est Haddon. | Peter Belgraue recto^r East Haddon. | Roger Belgraue of Belgraue in Com' Leic. | =Margaret Da. & hey. to Rich. de Belgraue. | John rector de Belgraue. |

John Belgraue of Belgraue in Com. Leic.=Elizab. Da. & hey. of Tho. Shelton esq.
(Sa. 3 (escallops) a.)

Will'm Belgraue.=Isabell Da. to W'm Sandon.
(G. cheu' wauy ent' 3 (stags' heads) couped ar.)

Will'm Belgraue 22 H. 6.=Margaret Da. of Hugh Willoughby of Woluerton sister to Ric. Willoughby.

John de Belgraue 12 E. 4.=Katherin Da. & Coh. of Hugh Glene of Glene parua in Com' Leic.
ARMS. *Ermine, three mascles in fess sable.*

| Richard Belgraue son of John. | =Margaret Da. of John Cotton of Hanstall Redware in Com' Staff. | Will'm Belgraue of whom is descended Belgraue of North Kileeworth 2 son. |

| Will'm Belgraue of Pe | Dorothy 2 wife to Saunders of Wilford in Com' Northampton. | =Henry Caue of Caldesley 1 Husb. | John Lo. of Belgraue & Blaby 1495. | =Joane Da. & hey. to Tho. Swyke & Elizab. da. to Chaweband of Wigston. | Katherin wife to Rich. Andrewes of Harleston in Com' Northamp. | Anne uxor Corbett. |

| Clem^t Sanders of East Haddon in Com' Northampton. | Anne wife to John Marshall of Mustham in Com' Nott. | Mary Da. & Coh. to Rob't Chantrell of Foxton A° 1532. | =George Belgraue of Belgraue and Blabye. | =Joan Da. of Rob't Farnham maried 1545.   = Clement Saunders of East Haddon in Com. North. |

A   B

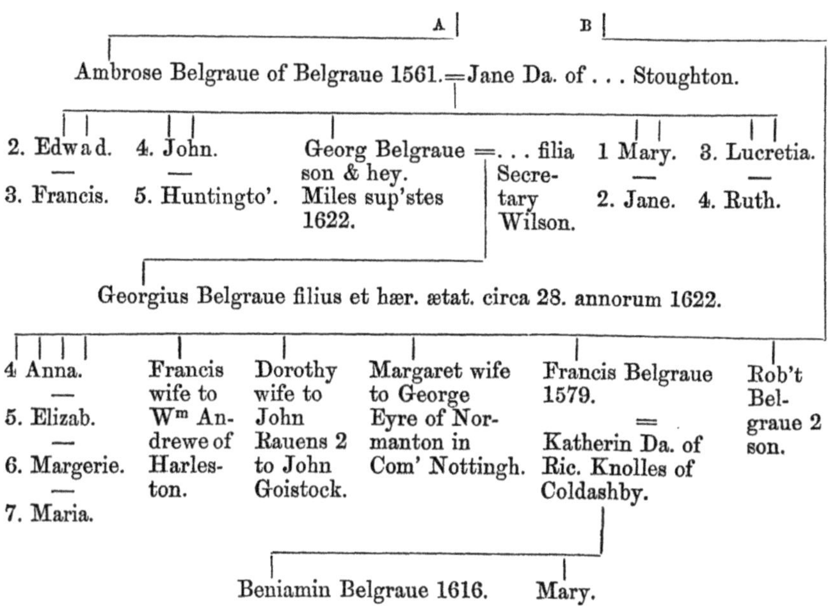

ARMS. *Quarterly :—1. Gules, on a bend argent three lions' heads erased sable.*
(TURPEN.)   *2. (Field untinctured) a fess chequy or and sable between six
cross crosslets (untinctured).* (KINSMAN.)   *3. Argent, a cross flory between four
crescents gules.* (TILLEY.)   *4. Gules, a cross flory argent.* (PAWCOE.)   *5. Quarterly or and barry of six argent and gules, within a bordure sable, charged with
ten fishes naiant of the second.* (GOBEON.)
CRESTS. 1. *A griffin passant with wings endorsed or, guttée de sang, unguled azure.*
   2. *A lion's head erased sable, ducally gorged or.*
   3. *On a wreath or and gules, a cockatrice's head couped argent, beaked, combed,
      and wattled of the second.*
   4. *A shoveller's head couped (untinctured).*

(Poultney.)

ARMS. *Quarterly :—1. Argent, a fess dancettée gules, in chief three leopards' faces sable.* (POULTNEY.) *2. Argent, a pale lozengy gules.* (WHYMALL.) *3. Quarterly gules and or, in the first quarter a lion passant argent.* (DANIELL.) *4. Barry of six argent and gules, over all a bend (untinctured). 5. Per fess crenellée azure and or, three eagles displayed counterchanged. 6. Argent, a lion rampant sable, crowned or, in dexter chief a crescent for difference. 7. Ermine, a fess between three lozenges gules. 8. Argent, a chevron between three martlets sable. 9. Field (untinctured), three bars (untinctured), on a canton (untinctured) a bend lozengy or. 10. Argent, three bends gules.*

CREST. *A lion's head erased guardant sable.*

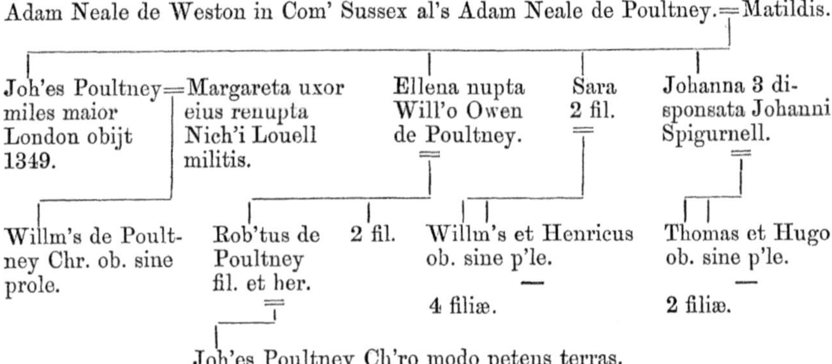

Adam Neale de Weston in Com' Sussex al's Adam Neale de Poultney.═Matildis.

Joh'es Poultney═Margareta uxor miles maior eius renupta London obijt Nich'i Louell 1349. militis.

Ellena nupta Will'o Owen de Poultney.

Sara 2 fil.

Johanna 3 disponsata Johanni Spigurnell.

Willm's de Poultney Chr. ob. sine prole.

Rob'tus de Poultney fil. et her.

2 fil.

Willm's et Henricus ob. sine p'le.

4 filiæ.

Thomas et Hugo ob. sine p'le.

2 filiæ.

Joh'es Poultney Ch'ro modo petens terras.

---

* ARMS. *Quarterly :—1. Argent, a chevron between three hazel leaves vert. 2. Argent, three squirrels séjant gules. 3. Gules, three herons argent. 4. Gules, a chevron between three martlets or. 5. Argent, a cinquefoil sable. 6. Vair, argent and sable, a canton gules. 7. Or, a bend between six martlets gules. 8. Paly of six or and gules, on a bend sable three horse-shoes argent. 9. Vair, argent and sable. 10. Sable, a lion rampant argent. 11. Argent, on a bend engrailed sable three mullets of the field. 12. Argent, a whirlpool azure. 13. Lozengy or and azure, over all a chevron gules. 14. Argent, on a chief gules three bezants. 15. Gules, a lion rampant ermine. 16. Argent, a chevron ermines between three dice azure, charged with three spots of the field.*

CREST. *On a cap of maintenance gules, turned up ermine, a man's head couped in dexter profile proper, crined and bearded or.*

These Coates were thus
Marshalled for Sr Arthur
Haselrigg Kt. & Barronett
1644.

---

* These arms tricked by Henry Parker.

(Gerueis.)

Willm's Jerueis de Thorpe Langton in Com. Leic. Aº. 37. E. 3.

Radulphus Gerueis Aº. 9. R. 2.

Thomas Gerueis.=Editha 10. E. 4.

Radulphus Gerueis Aº. 3. H. 5.

Robertus Gerueis Aº. 23. H. 6.

Robertus Gerueis= Willm's Edmundus Gerueis de Bowden parua in
Aº. 2. E. 4. Gerueis. Com' Northto' Aº. 14. E. 4.

Robertus Gerueis Aº. 3. R. 3.

Willm's Gerueis Aº. 14. H. 7.

Johannes Gerueis de Thorp=Margareta filia Tho. Goodman de
langto' Aº. 20. H. 8. Luffingham in Com' Rutland.

Thomas =Alicia fil. Willm's Gerueis de=Katherina fil. Elizabetha ux. Ric'i
Gerueis. | Holyoke. Peatling magna in | Will'i Ward Bradgate de
　　　　　　　　　Com' Leic. de Shankton. Peatling p'ua.

1. Johannes. Katherina 1 Francisca=Willm's =Anna filia Gracea 3 filia
— filia uxor filia Ric'i Gerueis Nic'i ux. Noe Ducket.
2. Thomas. Ric'i Burdet. Marson filius et Purefoy —
— ux. 2. hæres. de Dray- Anna 4 fil. ux.
Johanna 2 ton Ar. Ed'ri Ward.
fil. ux. Tho. ux. 1. —
Payne. Thomas Gerueis
2 filius.

Will'us Gerueis=Elizab. filia Shepard Georgius =Elizab. fil. et Willm's
Vicecom. Com' de Hockley in Gerueis hær. Michell Gerueis.
Leic. ob. Com' Bedf. renupta de Peat- Henshaw de
Januaru 1618 Roberto de Sutton ling in Malden in
ob. s. p. Chenell in Com' Com' Leic. Com' Sussex.
Leic. militi. 2 filius.

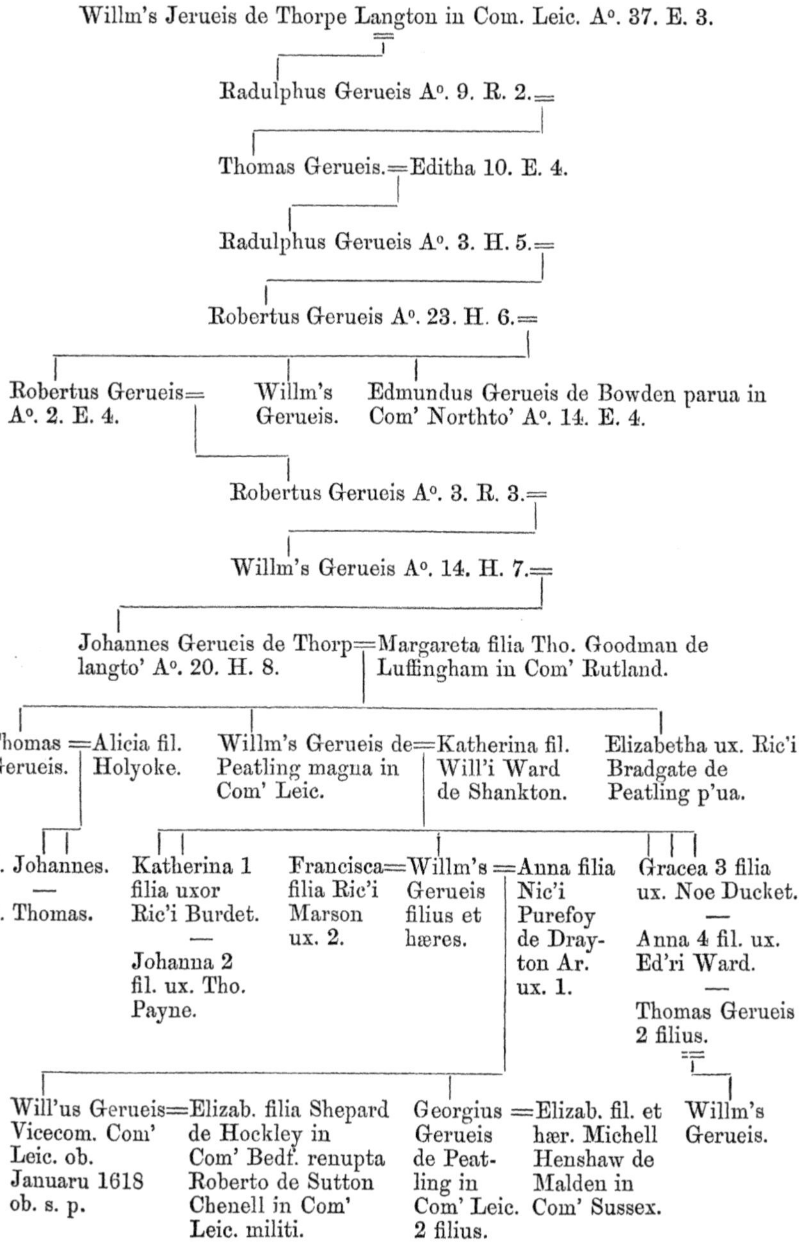

(Hastings.)

ARMS. *(The whole untinctured).* 1. *A maunch.* 2. *Per pale a saltire engrailed countercharged.* 3. *Quarterly, France ancient and England.* 4. *A saltire, in chief a label of three points.* 5. *Three lozenges in fess.* 6. *An eagle displayed.* 7. *A lion rampant between ten fleurs-de-lis, three, two, two, and three.* 8. *England within a bordure.* 9. *A fess between six cross crosslets.* 10. *Chequy, a chevron ermine.* 11. *Quarterly untinctured and a fret, over all a bend.* 12 *Three chevrons.* 13. *Two bars, in chief three roundles.* 14. *Per pale indented, over all a chevron.* 15. *Paly of six wavy.* 16. *Two bars, in chief three roundles.*

CREST. *A bull's head erased, ducally gorged (untinctured).*

Willm's D'ns Hastinges=Katherina fil. Ric'i p' Edw. 4 factus Cubicularis eiusdem regis. Neuill Com' Sarum Relicta Willi D'ni Bonvile et Harington.

D'ns Botreux =fil. Bellamont.

D'ns Hungerford=fil. et hær.

D'ns Molis=fil. et hær.

Anna uxor Geo. Comitis Salop.

Willm's Hastings 3 filius.

Ricardus Hastings 2 fil.

Edwardus D'ns Hastinges de Asby in Com' Lestriæ. =Maria neptis et hæres Rob'ti D'ni Hungerford Botreux Moelis et Molins.

Ric'us Poole=Margareta Comitissa miles Garterii. Saru' fil. et hær. Geo. Ducis Clarentiæ fratris E. 4.

Anna ux. Thomæ Stanley Comitis Derbiæ.

Georgius D'ns Hastinges Hungerford,=Anna filia Hen. Botreux, Moelis et Molins &c Comes Huntington p. R. H. 8. aº 1530. Ducis Buckingham.

Hen. Poole=Jana fil. Geo. D'ns Montegue. Newell D'mini Bergaueni.

Dorothea uxor Rici Deuereux militis. fil. et hær. Walteri Vice-Comitis Heref.

Thomas Hastinges.

Edwardus Hastinges mil. D'ns Hastinges de Loughborough in Com' Leic. Cubicularius Mariæ Reginæ ob. s. p.

Franciscus Hastinges=Katherina filia Hen. Comes Huntington 2. Poole D'ni Montifacuti.

A

Walterus
Hastinges.
=
Jocosa filia
Will'i Roper.

Elizab. ux. Edw.
Som'set Comitis
Wigorniæ.
—
Francisca ux. Hen.
D'ni Compton.

Katherina
uxor Hen.
Comitis
Lincoln.

Henricus Comes Hunt-
ington 3 ob. sine prole
1596.
=
Katherina fil. Joh'is
Ducis Northumbriæ.

Georgius
Dn's
Hastinges
2 filius et
4 Comes
Hunting-
ton.
= Dorothea
filia et Coh.
Johis Port
de Etwall
militis in
Com'
Darbiæ.

Edwardus
duxit Bar-
bara' Will'mi
Deuereux
militis et
relicta Caue.
=

Franciscus
Hast. duxit
Matilda' fil.
Ric. Long-
ford mil.
Relict Geo.
Vernon mi-
litis.

Edwardus
duxit
Barbara
fil. Wm.
Deuereux.
=

Henry
Hastings.

Franciscus
Duxit
Matild' fil.
Ri. Long-
ford.

Dorothea.
—
Katherina uxor
Ed. Umpton de-
inde Walteri Chet-
win militis.

Henricus Hastings
Duxit fil. et Coh.
fran. Willoughby
militis.
—
Edwardus Hastinges
sine prole.

Franciscus Dn's = Sara fil. Jacobi
Hastinges obijt   Harington militis
1596 sepultus   renupta Geo Kings
cum patruo.   millti postea Edw.
                   D'no Zouch.

Henry.
—
Edward.
—
Francis.
—
Walter.
—
Dorothea.

Henry.   Edward.   Francis.   Walter.   Dorothe.

Henricus Hastinges Com' = Elizab. 3 fil. et Coh. Ferdi-
Huntington sup'stes 1619.   nandi Comitis Darbiæ.

Katherina uxor Phillippi
D'ni Stanhop de Shelford.

Ferdinando D'ns
Hastings.

Henricus 2 fil.

Alicia.
—
Elizab.

L

(Gray.)

ARMS. *Quarterly:*—1. *Barry of six argent and azure, in chief three torteaux, over them a label of three points gules.* 2. *Or, a maunch gules.* 3. *Barry of ten (untinctured), an orle of eight martlets.* 4. *Azure, a cinquefoil ermine.* 5. *Vair or and gules.* 6. *Argent, a fess and canton conjoined gules.* 7. *Sable, six mullets argent, three, two, one.* 8. *Sable, a fret argent.*

Matilda filia Rad'i D'ni Basset de Blore ux. 2. = Joh'es Gray de Wilton filius Reginaldi ob. 16. E. 3. = Anna fil. D'ni Ferrers de Groby ux. 1.

Rogerus Dn's Gray de Ruthin. = Elizab. filia et hær. Joh'is Dni Hastinges de Bergauenie.

Henricus Dn's Gray de Wilto'. = Anna fil. et her. Rad'i Rockley by Isabell Da. of Will'm Clare younger son of Rob't Com' Glouc.

Reginald Dn's Gray de Ruthin. = Elinor. fil. D'ni Strange de Blackmore.

Reginaldus Dn's Gray de Wilton. = Matilda fil. et hær. Joh'is Boutort Lo. of Weley.

Margaret fil. Wm. D'ni Roos de Hamlack ux. 1. = Reginald D'ns Gray de Ruthin. = Jone fil. et hæres Will'i D'ni Astley ux. 2.

Henricus Dn's Gray de Wilton ob. 19. R. 2. = Elizab. fil. Tho. Talbot.

Johannes Dn's Gray de Ruthin Eques Garterij. = Constantia filia Johis Holland Comitis Huntington & Elizab. fil. Ducis Lancastriæ.

Edwardus Gray Miles Dn's de Groby in Com' Leic. iure uxoris. = Elizab. fil. et hæres D'ni Ferrers de Groby.

Rob'tus Gray de Whittington et Envill in Comitat. Staff. cuius posteritas in eo loco adhuc continuatur.

Edm. Dn's Gray de Ruthin primus Comes Cancij p. E. 4. = Catherina filia Hen. Percy Comitis Northumb'.

Joh'es Gray miles ob. in vita patris matris occisus apud St. Albini 1455. = Elizab. fil. Rici Wooduile Comitis Riparijs renupta Ed. 4. Regi.

Edwardus Gray Vicecomes Insulæ Jure uxoris. = Eliz. soror et hær. Tho. Talbot Vicicomitis Insulæ.

Tho. Gray Merchio Dorset D'ns de Groby et p' uxorem D'ns de Bonvile et Harington. = Cicilia filia et her. Will'i Dni Bonvile et Harington.

Joh'es Gray Vicecomes Lisley duxit Muriell fil. Tho. Ducis Norff. =

Elizab. Nupta Edm. Dudley postea Arthur Plantagenet. =

Thomas 2 Merchio Dorset D'ns de Groby = Margareta fil. Robti Wotton de Com' Cantij militis relicta Wm. Medley Ar.

Elizab. uxor Hen. Courtney Comitis Deuoniæ s. p.

Joh'es Dudley Dux Northumb'.

A

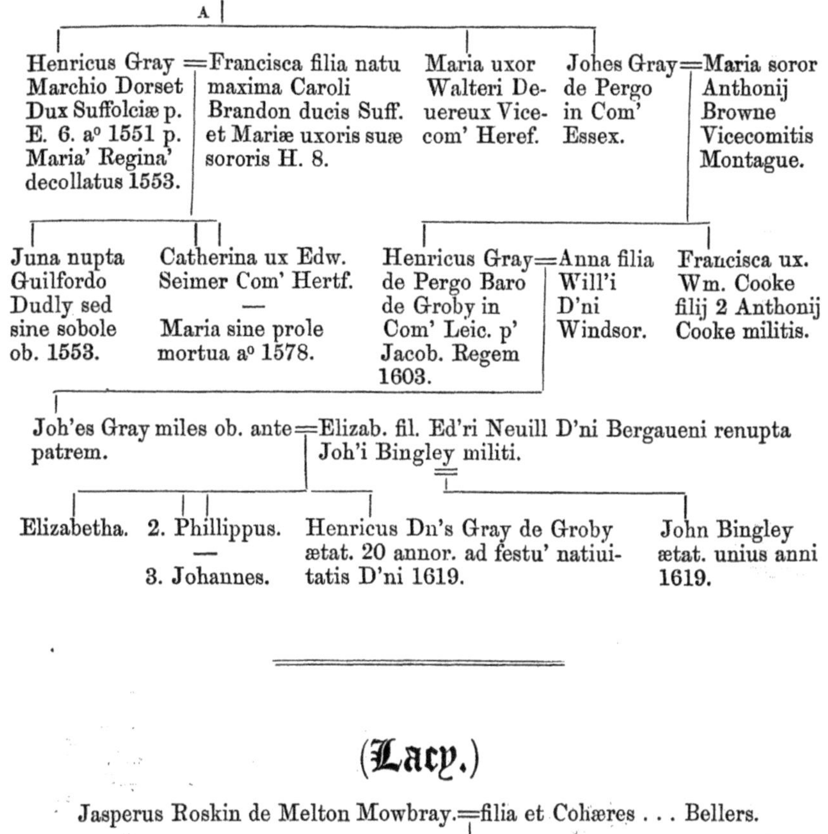

A |

Henricus Gray = Francisca filia natu	Maria uxor	Johes Gray = Maria soror
Marchio Dorset	maxima Caroli	Walteri De-	de Pergo	Anthonij
Dux Suffolciæ p.	Brandon ducis Suff.	uereux Vice-	in Com'	Browne
E. 6. aº 1551 p.	et Mariæ uxoris suæ	com' Heref.	Essex.	Vicecomitis
Maria' Regina'	sororis H. 8.			Montague.
decollatus 1553.				

Juna nupta	Catherina ux Edw.	Henricus Gray = Anna filia	Francisca ux.
Guilfordo	Seimer Com' Hertf.	de Pergo Baro	Will'i	Wm. Cooke
Dudly sed	—	de Groby in	D'ni	filij 2 Anthonij
sine sobole	Maria sine prole	Com' Leic. p'	Windsor.	Cooke militis.
ob. 1553.	mortua aº 1578.	Jacob. Regem		
		1603.		

Joh'es Gray miles ob. ante = Elizab. fil. Ed'ri Neuill D'ni Bergaueni renupta
patrem. Joh'i Bingley militi.

Elizabetha.	2. Phillippus.	Henricus Dn's Gray de Groby	John Bingley
	—	ætat. 20 annor. ad festu' natiui-	ætat. unius anni
	3. Johannes.	tatis D'ni 1619.	1619.

(Lacy.)

Jasperus Roskin de Melton Mowbray. = filia et Cohæres . . . Bellers.

Ricardus Lacy de Hallifax = Margareta filia et Coheres Jasperi Roskin
in comitat Eb. de Melton Mowbray in Com' Leic.

Leonardus Lacy 2 filius	Seth Lacy fil. = Isabella filia Hen.	Johannes Lacy 3
duxit Johanna' filia	et hæres	Fawer de	filius duxit Elizab.
. . . Muston.	Ricardi.	Halefax.	filiam Lissay.

Thomas	1 Eliza-	Seth	Elizab.	Willm's = Anna filia	Matheus	Faith.
Lacy 2	betha.	fil. et	uxor Tho.	Lacy de	Joh'is Digby	Lacy fil.	—
filius.	—	hæres.	Freareh et	Melton	de Welby in	primo-	Isabell.
	2. Maria.		postea Joh'is	Mow-	Com' Leic.	genit.	—
	—		Elwood.	bray.	liued in Aº		Modwen.
	3. Gracia.				1563.		

Johannes Lacy filius et hæres.

(𝔖mallep.)

Joh'es Smalley de Bolton dedit t'ram Rob'to Smalley de Alwaston
t'ram ib'm per Cart. dat. 8. H. 4.

* Iste Rob'tus feoffauit Hen. Dominu' Grey Joh'em Sacheuerell et alios in t'ris suis de Elweston, Bolton, Ambaston, Thurleston Barow sup' Trent, Chaddesdon, Spendon Derby p'ua, Eyton, Breydsale, Smalley et Kirkhallome in Com' Derb. 10 H. 6.

SEAL. *On a bend three roses, in sinister chief a chess-rook (untinctured).*

* Rob'tus Smalley de Alwalton=Margeria. in Com. Derby cui Abbas de la vale dedit manerium de Alwalton et Margeriæ ux. eius A° 1. H. 4 10 Octob', et cui Rob't de Hampton dedit t'ras ib'm 10. H. 5. condidit testam[t] 1 Septemb' 1444. 22. H. 6. in quo legauit Collerum suum qd habuit de liber'one H. 4. æccl'iæ de Alwisto' ad sustentationem suam.

Joh'es Smalley Ar. cui Ric's Sowre de Ambaston relaxauit= ius suum in tris suis de Bolton 36. H. 6.

Johanna 22 H. 6.

Rob'tus filius et hæres= Joh'is Smalley de Alwaston Ar. 2. R. 3.

Rob'tus Smalley fil. iunior cui frater confirmauit ius suum in t'ris suis de Alwalston Bulton, Thurlaston, Baro-Chaddesdon, Spondon, Derby parua, Eyton, Breydsale Smalley et Kirkhallom, 1. R. 3 et cui pater Joh'is dedit eiusdem t'ras 20. E. 4.

Anthonius Smalley fil. et hæres de=Alionora uxor eius 25. H. 8 superuixit Thorpe Arnold in Com' Leic. 29. H. 8.

et Condidit testam't 20 Nouemb' A° 10. Eliz.

Georgius Smalley de Stonesby in Com' Leic.
=
... filia et ... hæres Croke de Ringsted in Com' North'ton.

Maria uxor Sligh.
—
Modwina ux. Venables renupta Catesby.

John Smalley de=Francisca filia Mich'is Purefoy de Caldecot in Com' War. Ar. Thorpe Arnold in Com' Leic. et de Villa Leicest. vendidit Thorpe Arnold Tho. Hartop de Burton Lazors Yeoman. 11. Eliz.

... uxor Atkins de Pickwell in Com' Leic.
—
... uxor Gulson de Wymondham in Com' Leic.

Anthonius Smalley de Alwes-= ton in Com' Leic. et Ringhed in Northamp.

Nicholaus= filius 2.

3 Edwardus.   5. Mauritius.
—
4. Henricus.

Anthonius 2 filius.   Georgius Smalley de Alweston 1619.   Thomas filius Nich'i.

A

A

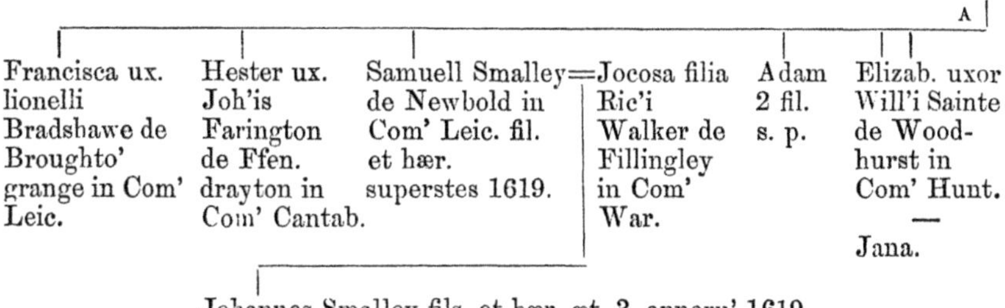

Francisca ux. lionelli Bradshawe de Broughto' grange in Com' Leic.	Hester ux. Joh'is Farington de Ffen. drayton in Com' Cantab.	Samuell Smalley de Newbold in Com' Leic. fil. et hær. superstes 1619.	=Jocosa filia Ric'i Walker de Fillingley in Com' War.	Adam 2 fil. s. p.	Elizab. uxor Will'i Sainte de Wood- hurst in Com' Hunt. — Jana.

Johannes Smalley fils. et hær. æt. 3. annoru' 1619.

(Farnham.)

ARM. *Quarterly, or and azure, in the first and second quarters a crescent counter-changed.*

Johannes Farnham miles de Querne.=
in

Robertus Farnham filius et hæres.=

Robertus Farnham filius et hæres.=

Rob'tus Farnham filius=Margareta filia et hæres Rob'ti Whatton   Thomas Farn-
Primogenitus.   de Monsorrell in Com' Leic.   ham 2 filius.

Thomas Farnham=Margareta filia Rad'i Kingston de   Johannes
filius et hæres.   Dalby in Com' Leic.   Farnham.

Robertus Farnham=Maria filia Rob'ti Lawghton de Gopsell   Thomas
filius et hæres.   in Com' Leic.   Farnham.

Francis Farnham fil. 1.   Joanna nupta   Thomas Farnham 2 fil. et   Willm's
ob. sine p'.   Geo. Bel-   hæres fratris vixit in a°   Farn-
=   graue de Com'   1563.   =   ham.
Margeria filia Tho.   Leic.   Anna fil. & hæres Hen. =
Caue de Stanford   Harrold de Boughton in
militis.   Com' Norff.

John Farnham sup'stes in a° 1563 of y[e] neither   Thomas
hall of Querne in Com' Leic.   2 filius.

(𝕻ilkington.)

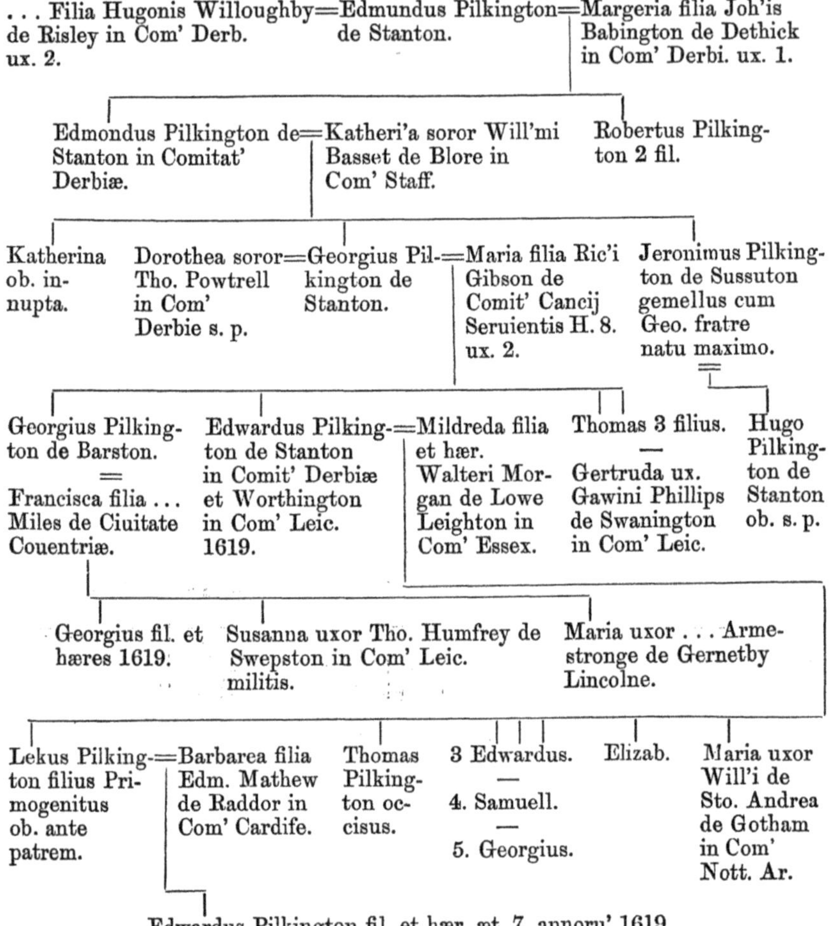

Remember to search who was father to
Tho. Pilkington that maried w^t y^e Da. &
hey. of Marmion, whose sister was mar.
to Haselwood, whether it was Sr Thomas
or not.

(𝕼incent.)

Sturgis.=

Johannes Vincent de Shepey=Johanna filia et hæres   . . . altera filia et hær.
in Com' Leic. 4. H. 7.   . . . Sturgis.   nupta Joh'i Meringe.

Rob'tus Vincent gen'==Margareta filia . . . Huet   Johannes Vincent
a° 38. H. 8.   de Calton.   clericus.

Joh'es Vincent de=Alicia filia Abell vidua   Robertus Vincent
Shepey magna.   de Lichfeild.   2 filius.

Maria filia Joh'is=Richardus=Francisca   Anna uxor Ric'i Clerke   Jocosa uxor
Bury famuli   Vincent   filia Joh'is de Wigston in Com.   Ric'i Kisse
Ducis Suffolciæ,   de   Baker de   Leic.   —   de Wither-
relicta Joh'is   Shepey   Hering-   Elizab. uxor Joh'is   ley in Com.
Bent de Cosby.   magna   worth   Midleton de Asherston   Leic.
                   1619.   uxor 1.   in Com. War.

1 Dorothea.   Willm's Vin-   Johannes Vincent=Elizab. filia   Margareta uxor
    —   cent filius 2 de Shepey   . . . Haruey.   Will'mi Mow-
2. Emma.   a't 21. annor' ætat. 30 annor'   lesley de
    —   1619.   1619.   Ansley in Com.
3. Susanna.   War.

Ricardus Vincent fil. et hær.   1 Anna.   2. Dorothea.

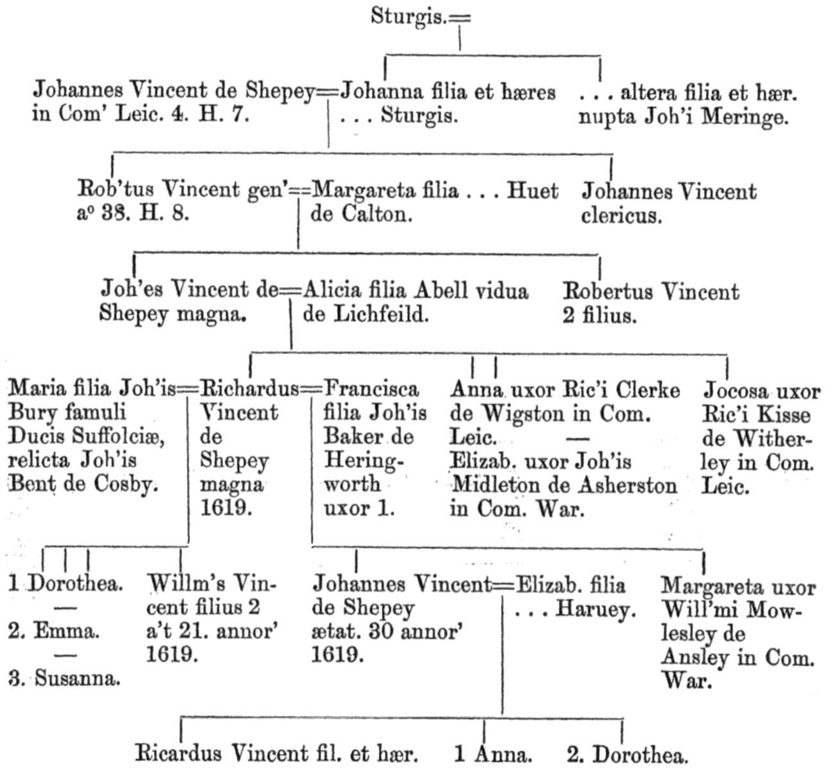

(Vincent.)

Rob'tus Mutton Miles Dn's de Peckleton in Com' Leic.=Alicia filia et coh. . . . Basset de Sapcott.

ux. 1.=Rob'tus Mutton Ar.=ux. 2.

Thomas Grimsby de Drakelow et=. . . filia . . . Harebert.
Grimsby in Com' Leic.

Reginaldus Mutton.=Anna filia et hær. Tho. Bugges.

Will'm Mutton a quo Jacobu' Harrington de Exton in Rutl.

Ric'us Vincent de Walton=fil. et hær. Wallis.
in co' Lincoln.

Willm's Grimsbie de=Anna filia & coh. Reginaldi Moton de Pickleton in Com' Leic.
Drakelow 38. H. 6.

Elizab. 2 filia et coh. nupta Rad'o Poole de Radbourne in Com' Darby.

Ricardus Vincent de Messingham in Com' Lincoln 20. E. 4.=Anna filia et heres Will'mi Grimsby =Ricardus Waterton 2 maritus.

Jane filia Ric'i Soltey vel Slorey=Georgius Vincent de Pickleton ob. 7 Eliz. ætat'=Amy filia Petri Coles de
uxor 1. de Sleford in Com' Linc. | 80. uxor 2. Ann filia R'i. Ratcliff de Com' Lanc. | Presto' de Northampto'
ux. 1. uxor 3.

Ricardus Waterton. =

Phillip Vincent duxit filia et heredem . . .
Yorksheir relicta . . . Hatfeild.

Peter ob. sp.

Jane uxor Fran. Caue de Kilby in Com' Leic.

Jana Waterton fil. et her. nupta Ric'o Euerard de Shenton in Com' Leic.=

Ricardus Euerard Duxit filiam . . . Butler de Aston in Com' Northamp.

A

| A

Gilbert Vincent duxit Maria' filiam Geo. Abney de Willesley in Com' Darb.=

Francis 6 son — Rob'tus Vincent fil. 7 Duxit Alicia' filiam Anthonij Faunt et ob. s. p.

Jana nupta Nicho' Purifoy de Draiton et postea Will'mo Faunt de Foston in Com' Leic.

Anthonius Vincent filius 5 duxit Mary fil. Hen. Salisberie de Ulesthorp.

Maria uxor Francisci Starismore de Frolsworth in Com' Leic. =

Clemᵗ 3 filius duxit Mary filiam Ro. Tanfeild de Gayton in Com'North'ton. =

Thomas Vincent 2 fil. duxit Mariam filiam Ri. Forman de Darby. fuit ille de Marston. =

Edw. Vincent filius et hær. = Margerett fil. Hum. Babington de Rothay in Com' Staff.

Georgius = Alicia filia . . . Withe de Kilby in Com' Leic. | Vincent de Thrinkeston in Com' Leic. fil. 1. 1619.

Katherina ux. Will'i Barker de Keyworth in Com' Nott. Clericus.

Elizab. ux. Xrofri Mason. — Elinora ux. Joh'is Sewell de Keyworth in Com' Nott.

Ricardus Vincent.

Sabine Staresmore filius et hæres.

Brian Vincent fil. 1. — Filia uxor Lane. — 1. Georgius. — 2. Franciscus.

Rob'tus Vincent fil. 1. — 2. Will'm. — 3. Thoma. — Jana uxor Tho. Faunt.

Sara filia primogenita æt. 18. 1619.   2. Ursula.   3. Katherina.   4. Maria.

Willm's Vincent fil. et hæres aº 1610 duxit fil. et hær. . . . Vincent de Smiton in Com' Ebor'u. =

Thomas 4 filius. — 2. Nicholas.

3. Michaell. — Franciscus s. p.

Nicholas 2 fil. de Leic. 1619. = Maria filia Brokesby.

Jana uxor Rob't Wright de Broughto' in Com' Leic.

2 Elinor uxor Hall.

Anna 1 filia. — Jane 3 fili'.

Marmaducus Vincent de Smiton = filia . . . Snowsdale de Belton. 1619 in Com' Ebor'u.

Thomas filius et hæres æt. 9 1619.

Jana æt. 11 annor' 1619.

M

(𝕭incent.)

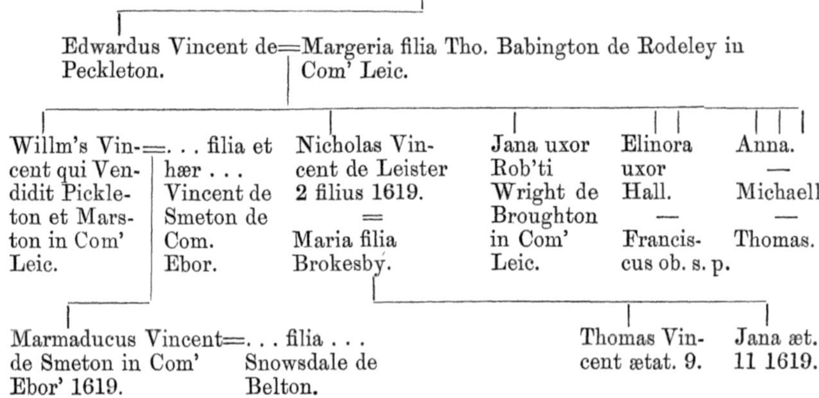

Georgius Vincent de Peckleton in Com' Leic.
=

Edwardus Vincent de=Margeria filia Tho. Babington de Rodeley in
Peckleton. | Com' Leic.

Willm's Vin-=... filia et	Nicholas Vin-	Jana uxor	Elinora	Anna.
cent qui Ven- hær ...	cent de Leister	Rob'ti	uxor	—
didit Pickle- Vincent de	2 filius 1619.	Wright de	Hall.	Michaell.
ton et Mars- Smeton de	=	Broughton	—	—
ton in Com' Com.	Maria filia	in Com'	Francis-	Thomas.
Leic. Ebor.	Brokesby.	Leic.	cus ob. s. p.	

Marmaducus Vincent=... filia ...   Thomas Vin-   Jana æt.
de Smeton in Com'   Snowsdale de   cent ætat. 9. 11 1619.
Ebor' 1619.   Belton.

(𝕾hipward.)

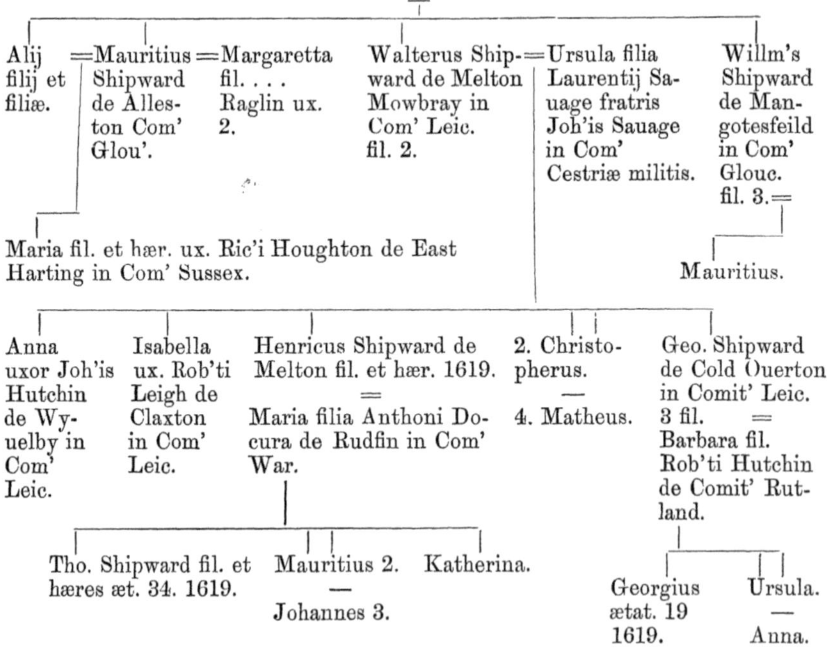

George Shipward de foresta de Dene in Com' Glouc.
=

Alij =Mauritius =Margaretta	Walterus Ship-=Ursula filia	Willm's
filij et Shipward fil. ...	ward de Melton Laurentij Sa-	Shipward
filiæ. de Alles- Raglin ux.	Mowbray in uage fratris	de Man-
ton Com' 2.	Com' Leic. Joh'is Sauage	gotesfeild
Glou'.	fil. 2. in Com'	in Com'
	Cestriæ militis.	Glouc. fil. 3.=

Maria fil. et hær. ux. Ric'i Houghton de East
Harting in Com' Sussex.   Mauritius.

Anna	Isabella	Henricus Shipward de	2. Christo-	Geo. Shipward
uxor Joh'is	ux. Rob'ti	Melton fil. et hær. 1619.	pherus.	de Cold Ouerton
Hutchin	Leigh de	=	—	in Comit' Leic.
de Wy-	Claxton	Maria filia Anthoni Do-	4. Matheus.	3 fil. =
uelby in	in Com'	cura de Rudfin in Com'		Barbara fil.
Com'	Leic.	War.		Rob'ti Hutchin
Leic.				de Comit' Rut-
				land.

Tho. Shipward fil. et   Mauritius 2.   Katherina.   Georgius   Ursula.
hæres æt. 34. 1619.   —   ætat. 19   —
                         Johannes 3.   1619.   Anna.

(𝖂𝖆𝖗𝖉.)

ARMS. *Azure, a cross flory between four annulets or.*

Warde de Carlton Curlew.=

Theobaldus Ward de Carlton Curlew=Anna filia . . . Cheselden vide in Com' Leic. ob. 25. H. 6. | Pat. 20. H. 6. pl. 2. m. 30.

Thomas Warde de=Felicia filia Joh'is Frisby Carlton Curley. | de Carlton.

Margareta uxor Joh'is Dansey.

Johannes Warde de Carlton Curlew.=. . . filia Allen de Markfeild in Com' Leic.

Johannes Warde de Carlton Curlew in Com' Leic.=Elizab. filia Rob'ti Ashby de Quenby in Com' Leic. Ar.

Willm's Ward de=filia . . . Burton Ouerey | Weston in Com' Leic. | de fil. 3. | Carlton.

Johannes Ward=filia . . . Cham-famulus Abba-| berlaine de tis Leic. 1619. | Newton in filius 5. | Com' Leic.

Georgius Ward de Frisby in Com' Leic. filius 2. =

Thomas Ward=Alicia filia Will'i de Carlton | Barton de Curlew fil. et | Bramston in hæres. | Com' Rutland.

Robertus Ward de Frisby in Com' Leic. filius 4.=

Isabella uxor Bartho-lomei Woodward de Burton.

Anna uxor Fran-cisci Hodges de Burton.

Johanna uxor Petri Aston de Burton.

Elizab. fil. et her. uxor Tho. Allen de Whes-ton in Com' Leic.

Amicia fil. et Coh. uxor Alexandri Coles de Kingston in Com' Leic.

Christiana filia et heres uxor Joh'is de Walcot in Com' Leic.

1
Georgius Ward=Jana filia et hæres de Carlton | Joh'is White de Curlew et de | Marston Trussell Marston | in Com' North'-Trussell 1619. | ton.

2
Johannes Ward de London 1619.
=
Maria soror Rogeri Halton de Carlton in Com' Lincoln milit.

3
Tho. Warde de=Martha filia Abington in | . . . Lan-Com' Cantab. | caster in famulus | Com' Norff. Comitis North'ton.

4
Willm s Warde de Hospitio Graisen fil. 4. 1619.

Johanna uxor Joh'is Capet de Gretford in Com' Lincolne.

Johannes Jacobus.

Johannes fil. et hæres æt. 20. annoru' 1619.

1 Francisca.

2. Elizabetha.

3. Maria.

Alexander Ward ætat. 16 annoru' 1619.

Thomas Ward ætatis 3 annor' 1619.

Alicia.

(Goodman.)

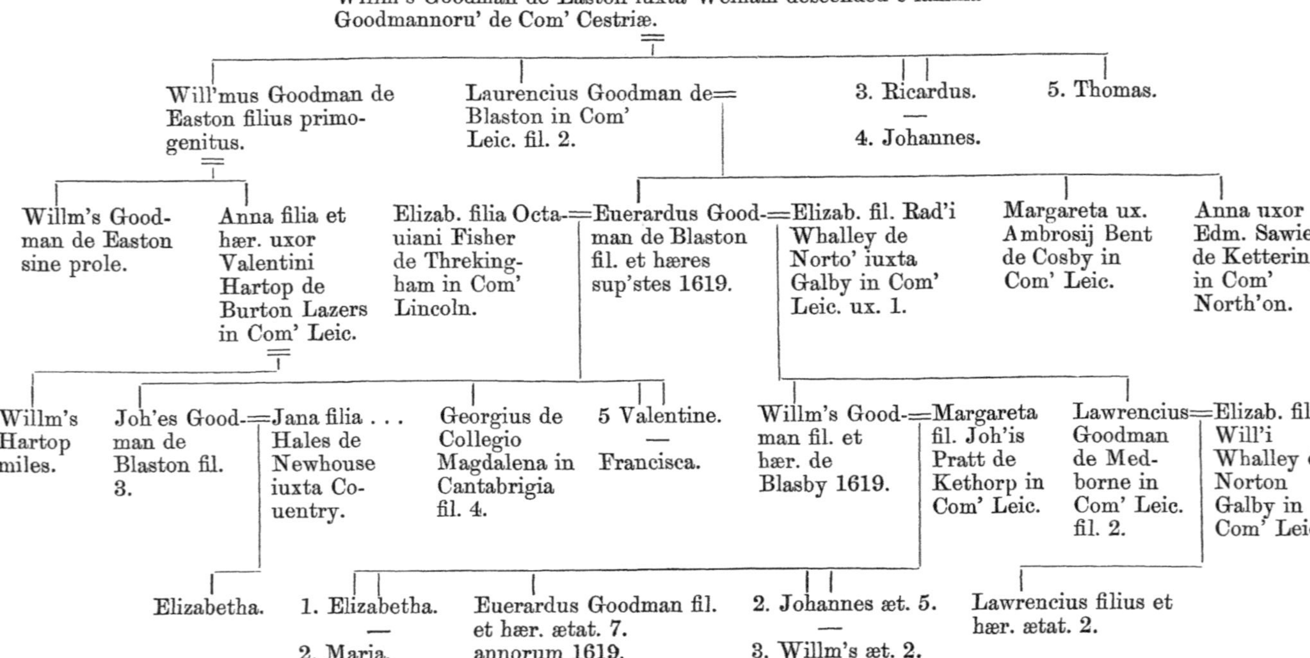

Willm's Goodman de Easton iuxta Welham descended e familia Goodmannoru' de Com' Cestriæ.

Will'mus Goodman de Easton filius primogenitus.

Laurencius Goodman de Blaston in Com' Leic. fil. 2.

3. Ricardus.

4. Johannes.

5. Thomas.

Willm's Goodman de Easton sine prole.

Anna filia et hær. uxor Valentini Hartop de Burton Lazers in Com' Leic.

Elizab. filia Octauiani Fisher de Threkingham in Com' Lincoln. = Euerardus Goodman de Blaston fil. et hæres sup'stes 1619. = Elizab. fil. Rad'i Whalley de Norto' iuxta Galby in Com' Leic. ux. 1.

Margareta ux. Ambrosij Bent de Cosby in Com' Leic.

Anna uxor Edm. Sawier de Kettering in Com' North'on.

Willm's Hartop miles.

Joh'es Goodman de Blaston fil. 3. = Jana filia . . . Hales de Newhouse iuxta Couentry.

Georgius de Collegio Magdalena in Cantabrigia fil. 4.

5 Valentine.

—

Francisca.

Willm's Goodman fil. et hær. de Blasby 1619. = Margareta fil. Joh'is Pratt de Kethorp in Com' Leic.

Lawrencius Goodman de Medborne in Com' Leic. fil. 2. = Elizab. filia Will'i Whalley de Norton Galby in Com' Leic.

Elizabetha.

1. Elizabetha.

—

2. Maria.

Euerardus Goodman fil. et hær. ætat. 7. annorum 1619.

2. Johannes æt. 5.

—

3. Willm's æt. 2.

Lawrencius filius et hær. ætat. 2.

(Gore.)

Johannes Gore de Kimbalton in Com' Hunt. == . . . filia . . . Sabin de Irtlingburgh.

Edwardus Elkington 4 filius. == Joh'es Elkington mercator London.

1 Thomas. — 3. Henricus.

Dorothea.

Grissell da. of Lathum 2 to Aston of . . . 2 wife. == Thomas Gore de Lutterworth in Com' Leic. filius et hæres 1619. == Margareta filia . . . Bletsho de Rushden in Com' North't.

Tho. Marshall de Sheresby. == Gracea filia et hæres Ed'ri Elkington de Cathorp in Com' Leic.

Hugh Aston. == Eliz. da' of Tookey of Galby in Com' Leicest.

Anthony Gore of Lutterworth in Com' Leic.

Johanna uxor Joh'is Pratt de Wellingburgh.

Thomas Gore de Ullesthorpe in Com' Leic. fil. et hæres 1619. ob. 1625. == Francisca filia et hæres Thoma' Marshall de Sheresby in Com' Leic.

Tho. — Ann.

Thomas Pratt ob. s. p'le. — Henry ob. s. p.

John liuing 1645 mar. Ellen da' of Aston.

Hugh.

Eliz. wife Obediah Brooksby of Stow Goulden in Com' Leicester.

Ann wife of Jo. Dison.

Thomas. — Mathias. — Beniame. — Sarah & Sarah ob. s. p. — John. — Joseph. — Patience. — Eliz. — Ruth. — Hanna. — Esther.

Thomas Gore fil. et hæres æt. 7. annoru'. ob. 1645. == . . . da' of . . . Bailes in Com' Leic.

Edwardus 2 filius æt. 6 ob. sine p'le.

marr. dau'r of . . . Chapman. == Johannes 3. fil. 3. Hebdomadoru'.

Maria 1. ob.

Gracia 3. ob. — Francisca 2.

Henry. — Eliz.

Charles 4 marr. Eliz. da' of Cardwell of Stony Stratford.

Thomas. — Jonathan. — John.

Thomas.

(𝔇anbers.)

ARMS. *Quarterly :—1. Argent, on a bend gules three martlets or, in sinister chief a trefoil slipped (untinctured). 2. Argent, on a cross formée azure five fleurs-de-lis or. 3. Argent, a lion rampant gules. 4. Gules, two bars argent, in chief two stags' heads caboshed of the last.*

CREST. *A parrot vert, holding in its beak a slip of oak proper, fructed with three acorns or.*

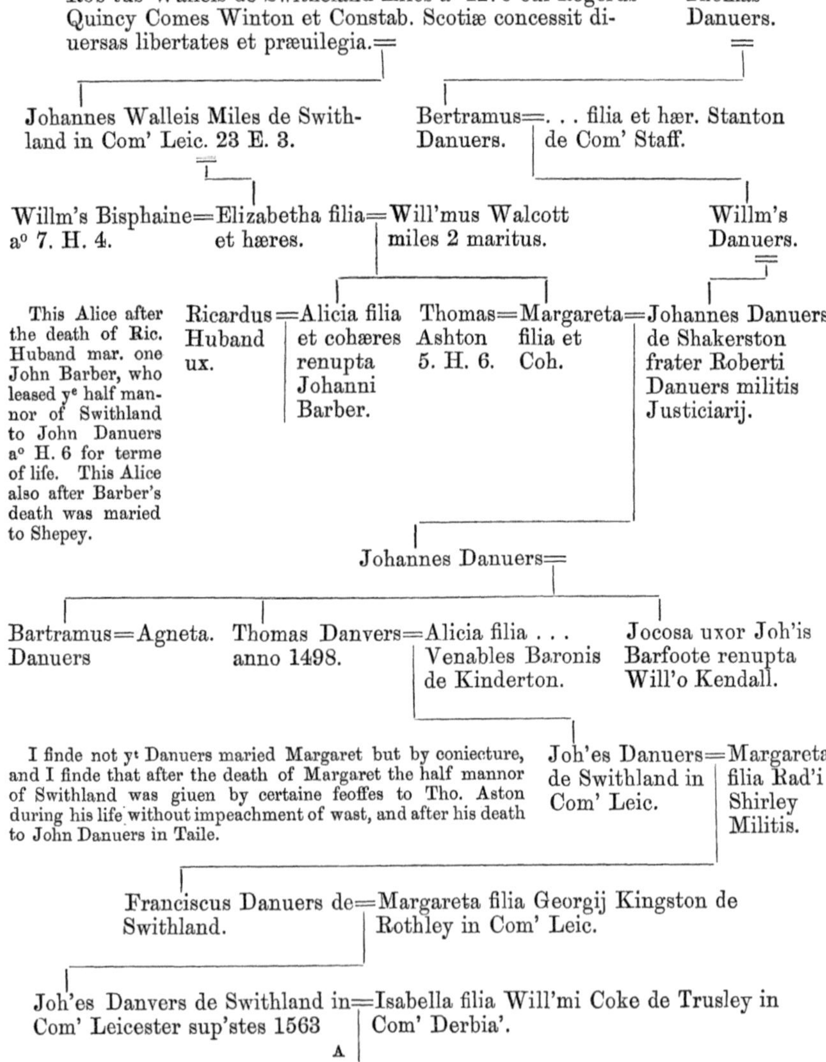

A |

| Dorothea uxor Arthur Barford de Shakerston in com' Leic. | Brigetta filia . . .=Werley relicta Arthuri Barford de Shakerston. | Franciscus Dan-=uers de Swithland in Com' Leic. superstes 1619. | Elizab. filia Joh'is Skeffington de . . . Fisherwick in Com' Staff. ux. 1. | Anna uxor Francisci Mulsho de Turwell in Com' Northamp. |

| Johannes Danuers 2 filius. | Will'mus Danvers de Roth-=ley in Com' Leic. filius et hær. ætatis 28 annoru' 1619. | Elizab. filia Tho. Babington de Rothley in Com' Leic. | Elizabetha filia unica. |

(𝕯𝖎𝖌𝖇𝖞.)

ARMS. *A fleur-de-lis, in dexter chief a mullet for difference (untinctured).*

Henry Digby=Margareta uxor eius.

| Thomas Digby. | Joh'es Digby fil. et=hær. | Ursula Halfehead de London. | Henricus Digbie. |

Thomas Digbie de Rauenston in Com'=Maria filia Rad'i Gegge de Bradley in Leic. Com' Chest'.

| Henry Digbie. | John Digbie. | Elizab. Digbie. |

(𝕮𝖆𝖗𝖉𝖊.)

ARMS. *Azure, a cross flory between four annulets or.*

Warde of Carlton Curlew in Com' Leic. ent' in the Visitac'on of Cambridgsh. 1619.

Thomas Warde of Abbington=Martha filia Hugonis Lancastre de Wetherfeild in in Com' Cantabrig. 1619. Com' Norff.
3 fil. *Ar. 2 barres Gu. on canton G. lion pass't or.*

| Thomas filius et hær. et. 3. | Dorothea. |

(Sherrard.)

ARMS. *Quarterly:—1. Argent, a chevron gules between three torteaux. 2. Argent, on a bend sable three trefoils or. 3. Ermine, a fess gules. 4. Argent, on a saltire sable five swans of the field. 5. Argent, three leopards' faces jessant-de-lis sable. 6. Ermine, a talbot passant sable. 7. Gules, on a bend or, three martlets sable. 8. Per fess ermine and or, a cross moline gules.*

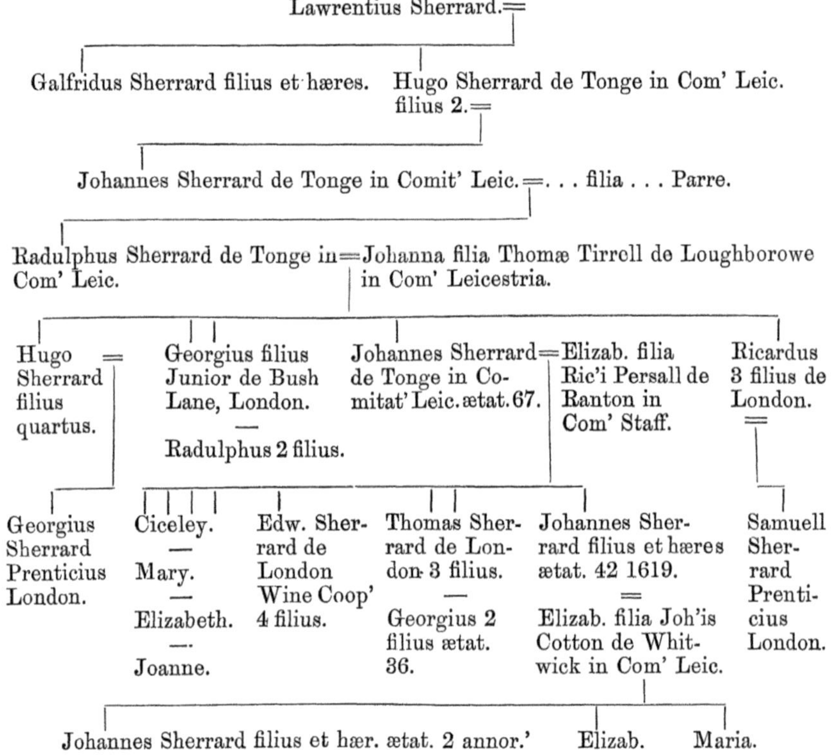

(Dethick.)

(Pate.)

ARMS. *Argent, three text R's sable, in chief a crescent gules for difference.*

Pate.=

Edwardus Pate de Kettleby in Com' Leic. fil. et hæres.

Joh'es Pate de Brin in Comit' Leic. filius 2.=Hellena filia Thoma' Saltmarsh de Eppin in Com' Essex.

Edwardus Pate de Brin in Com' Leic.=Anna filia Will'mi Blount de Osbaston in Com' Leic.

Tho. Pate 2 filius duxit Mariam filiam . . . Neuill de Groe in Com' Nott.=

Henricus Pate fil. et hæres Mr. Artium in Academia Oxoniæ ætat. 27 1619.=Jana filia . . . Hidson de Com' Warr.

Edmondus Pate filius et hæres.

Alter filius.

1. Ellena.
—
2. Rebecca.
—
3. Anna.
—
4. Elizab.

Ricardus 5 filius Prenticius apud Breminsham æt. 18. 1619.

Timotheus 4. filius æt. 20.

Edwardus 3 fil. de London ætat. 22.

Thomas 2 filius de Londo' ætat. 23.

(Sharpe.)

ARMS. *Azure, a pheon argent within a bordure of the last, charged with eight torteaux, in dexter chief a crescent for difference.*
CREST. *On a ducal coronet or a peacock sitting proper, in the beak an ear of wheat of the first, charged on the breast with a crescent for difference.*

This is the Armes and Creast of Will'm Sharpe of Rolston in Com' Leic. descended of a younger brother of the Sharpes of Baydon in the county of Cumberland.

Ric. St. George Norroy
Kinge of Armes.

Joh'es Sharpe de Baydon in Cumb'land.=

Hugo Sharpe de Baydon in Cumb'.=

Willm's Sharpe de Winge.=. . . filia Burton de Braunston.

Eustachius Sharpe de Winge in Com' Rutland fil. et hær.=Margeria filia Ric'i Dixon de Rolleston in Com' Leic.

Willm's Sharpe de Rolleston in Comit' Leic. iam cælebs et ætatis 37 annoru' 1619.

(Cooper.)

Willm's Cooper de Sapcott in Com' Leic. whose auncesto[r] cam out of Chesheire or Lankesheir.

Willm's Cooper de Stonie Stanton in Com' Leicest.=Margeria filia Will'i Denston de West Sutton in Com' Leic.

Johannes Cooper fil. et hær. duxit Elizab. fil. Will'mi Gilbert de Stonie Stanton ætat. 57.

Edmundus Coper de Sapcott in Com' Leic. 3. fil. ætat. 42.=Jana filia Will'mi Staresmore de Frolesworth in Com' Leic.

Willm's Cooper 2 fil. ætat. 49 duxit Joanna' filiam Ric'i Dawson de Walton in Com' Northamp.

Willm's Cooper filius et hæres ætat. 24.

Gilbertus Cooper 2 filius.=Elizab. filia Rob'ti Frier de Wigston cum duobus Penaculis in Com' Leic.

1 Alicia.
—
2. Gracia.

3 Johannes 20.
—
4. Edmondus 14.
—
5. Matheus 9.

2 Johannes æt. 18.
—
3. Georgius æt. 8.
—
4. Franciscus æt. 7.
—
5. Samuell æt. 7.

Willm's Cooper fil. et hæres ætat. 19. 1619.

1 Elizabeth. 17.
—
2. Christian. 13.
—
3. Kathein. 10.

4. Maria. 9.
—
5. Lidia. 6.

Daniell Cooper fil. et hæres ætat. 24.

Willm's 2 filius ætat. 16.

3. Edmundus æt. 10.
—
4. Galfridus æt. 4.

1 Emmot. 19.
—
2. Jone. 12.

3. Grace. 5.

(Kendall.)

ARMS. *Gules, a fess chequy or and azure between three eagles displayed of the second.*

Bartholmeus Kendall de Twicresse in Comit' Leic.=. . . filia et hær. . . . Shepee de

Willm's Kendall fil. et hær. de Smithson in Com' Darbiæ.=

Christopherus Kendall de Smithsby in Comit' Darbiæ.=

A   B

A | B |

Georgius Kendall=... filia   Johannes Kendall de=Margeria filia ...
filius et hæres. | Jenninges.   Smithsby ob. 1615. | Sadler de Com' War.

Henricus Kendall fil. et hæres.=

Henricus=... filia Gabrieli   Susanna filia ...=Humphridus=Marg^ta fil.
Kendall | Armestronge de   Leeson de Com'   Kendall de | August' Sway-
filius et | Thorp in Comit'   Northam' relicta   Blaby in | feild de Branson
hæres. | Notting.   Willmi Sauill de   Com' Leic. | in Com' Rutland
           Blaby ux. 2. | ux. 1.

Henricus filius et   Henricus Kendall filius   1. Catherina 20.   2. Margareta 17.
hæres ætat. 9 1619.   et hæres æt. 18. 1619.

(Yarde.)

ARMS. *Quarterly :—Argent, a chevron gules between three water bougets sable ;
and or, on a bend sable three horse-shoes argent.*

Gilbert Yarde of Bradley=filia ... Wadham de Merifeild   quere if Yarde matched
in Com' Deuon. | in Com' Som'.   wt Wadham.

Rogerus Yarde de Bradley in=... filia ... Halse de Kenedon
Com' Deuon. | in Com' Deuon.

Ric'us Yarde de Bradley in=Margareta filia Walteri Bamfeild de
Com' Deuon. | Poultmore in Com' Deuon.

Elizab. filia John Luson=Thomas Yarde=Johanna filia Will'mi Hurst ciuis et
uxor. 1. de Com' War. | de Bradley. | Marcator Exeter uxor 2.

Edwardus Yarde fil. et hær.   Will'mus Yarde de=Elizab. fil. Tho. Walton de
duxit Agnis filiam Will'm   Cosby in Com' | Bushby in Com' Leicest.
Stroude de Comit' Deuon.   Leic. 3 filius. | relicta Joh'is Bent.

Elizab. nupta Thobiæ   Margeria 2 filia uxor Ed'ri   Elinora 3. filia nupta Johi
Herick filio Rob'ti   Hill filij Joh'is Hill de   Cotes filio Alexandri Cotes de
Herick de Leicest'.   parua pipe in Com' Staff.   Knighton in Com' Leic.

Willm's Hill   Maria unica   2 Johannes. æt. 8.   4. Edward's   Alexander
filius et hæres   filia æt.   —   æt. 2.   Cotes fils. et
ætat. 10.   5.   3. Thomas æt. 6.   hær. æt. 1.

Will'mus Herick fil.   Maria unica   2 Johannes æt. 8.   3. Franciscus æt. 2.

(Whiting.)

ARMS. *Per saltire azure and ermine, a leopard's face or, in chief three bezants.*

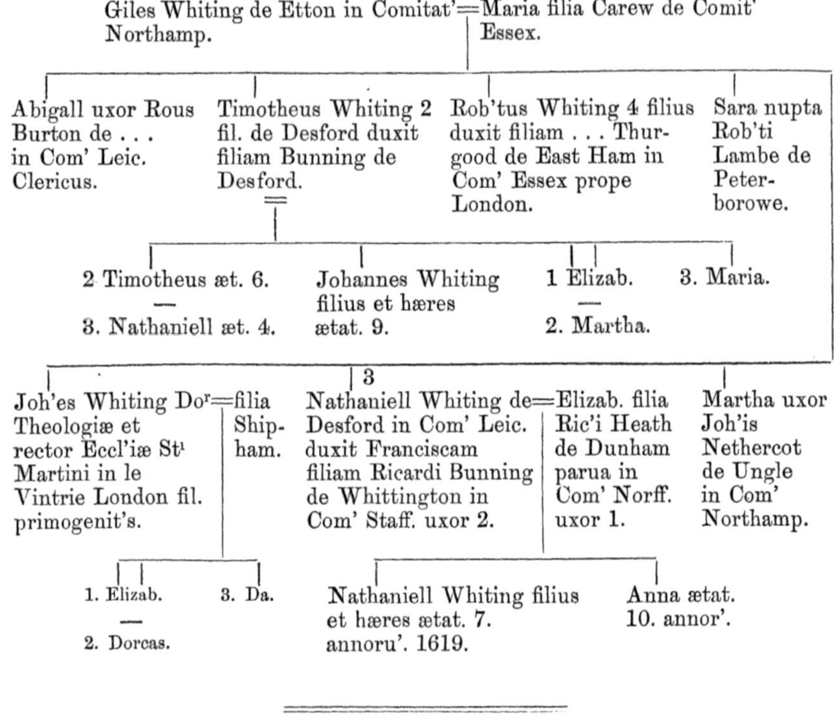

(Roos.)

(𝕾𝖆𝖇𝖎𝖑𝖑.)

ARMS. *Quarterly :—Argent, on a bend sable three owls of the field, in sinister chief a trefoil ; and per pale or and azure, two piles meeting in base counterchanged, on a canton argent, a mullet gules.*

CREST. *An owl argent, membered or, charged on the breast with a trefoil for difference.*

Thomas Sauill, fitz Juniee de la Maison de Howlow=Katherina filia & hæres in la Conte de Yorke, venue et Demoure a Blaby | Hugonis de Blaby in en la Conte de Leic't. temps. H. 6. | Com' Leic.

Ricardus Sauill filius et hæres.

Will'mus Sauill de Blaby in Com' Leic.=Martha filia . . . Villers.

. . . filia . . . Corbet de=Johannes Sauill de=Ell'no‍ᴿ filia . . . Astell Misterton in Com' | Blaby in Com' | de Comit' War. ux. 1. Leicest' 2. uxor. | Leic.

Rob'tus Sauill Elinora Nicholaus Sauill de Blaby fil.=Anna filia Simonis de Blaby 2 fil. filia. et hæres sup'st 1563. | Pigeon de Com' Warr.

Jana Will͏m's Sauill=Susanna filia Edwardus Sauill de Blaby=Elizab. fil. — de Blaby in Tho. Leeson 2. fil. This Edw. Sauill Simonis Kathe- Com' Leic. de Soulgraue had the com'aund of 200 Rogers filij rina. in Com' footemen in the warres of Ric'i Rogers Northamp. Sweden under Charles 9 mil'is. kinge of Sweden in aᵒ 1609.

Elizab. ætat. 13. Jana nupta 2. Will'mus æt. 20. Tho. Sauill=Anna filia — Ric'o Bridges — fil. et Ed'ri Anna uxor Va- de Com' 3. Humphrids æt. 19. hæres ætat. Heron lentini Allen de Ebor'um. — 30. 1619. militis Com' Northamp. 4. Anthonius æt. 17. Baronis — Scaccarij. 5. Georgius æt. 10.

Georgius Sauill filius et hæres ætat dimidij anni. 1619.

Nicholaus Sauill filius primogenitus ætat. 18.   Lauinia ætat. 12.

(Cotes.)

ARMS. *Argent, a fret azure, on a canton or, a lion rampant sable.*
CREST. *A cock or, wattled gules.*

Alexander Cotes de Withington in Com' Staff.=

=Franciscus Cotes de Withington filius et hæres.

Johannes Cotes de Elson=Agneta filia Rob'ti Sterkie de Sutton supra
in Com' Leic. 2. filius. | le monte in Com' Derbiæ.

Franciscus Cotes filius et hæres æt. 34.

Elizab. uxor Thomæ Linfeild de Houghton in Com' Leic. postea ux. Fabiani Andrewes de Stretton in Com' Leic.

Katherina nupta Rogero Roe de Auport in Com' Derbiæ. postea Nic'i Foxley de Basset house in Com' Leicest.

Joh'es Cotes=Anna fil.
de Elson in Comit' Leic. 3. filius ætat. 46. 1619.

Anna uxor Ric'i Swinfen de Sutton Cheyney.

Rogerus Cotes 4 filius Duxit Hellenam filiam Rob'ti Gillett de Leicest.=

Alexander=Anna fil.
Cotes de Knighton in Com' Leic. ætat. 52. | Johannis Warde de Knighton in Com' Leic.

Tho. Cotes=Anna fil.
de Belgrang in Com' Derbiæ fil. 2. ætat. 48.

Rob'tus 3. fil. ætat. 4.

Joh'es Cotes fil. et hæres ætat. 10. Annor'. 1619.

Alexander Cotes 2. fil. ætat. 8.

Anna unica filia etat. 5.

Rob'tus Cotes fil. et hær. æt. 10.

Johannes Cotes=Ellena filia Will'mi
fil. et hæres æt. 26. 1619. | Yarde de Cosbie in Com' Leic. who cam out of Deuonsh.

Thomas Cotes 2 fil. ætat. 13.

Ricardus Cotes fil. et hær. ætat. 23.

Alexander fil. et hæres ætat. dimidiu' anni 1619.

(𝕿urner.)

ARMS. *Quarterly :—Argent, a fer de moline sable ; and ermine, a chevron azure between three garbs or ; impaling or, a fess indented gules, in chief three boars' heads sable.*

Ricardus Turner de Sutton Colfeid in Com' Warr Barrest' de medio Templo London. = Maria filia . . . Masterson de Com' Cestriæ et soror et coh. Joh'is Masterson.

Will'mus Turner de Sutton Coldfield in Com' War. = Margereta filia Christopheri Breton de Tecon in Com' Northampton.

Jocosa uxor Ed'ri Hunne de Marson Trussell in Comitat' Northamp.

Edwardus Turner de Leicester filius et hæres. = Jocosa filia Libei Chamberlaine de Leicester.

Ric'us Turner 2. filius.

Johannes 3. filius.

Willm's Turner filius primogenitus ætat. 8.

Edwardus 2 fil. ætat. 2.

1. Elizabetha.

2. Francisca.

(𝕭elgrabe.)

ARMS. *Quarterly :—1. Gules, a chevron ermine between three mascles argent. 2. Argent, three pairs of bellows sable. 3. Sable, three escallops argent. 4. Ermine, three mascles conjoined in fess sable.*

Hugonis Belgraue de Belgraue in Com' Leic. =

Rogerus Belgraue de Belgraue in Com' Leic. =

Laurencius Belgraue de Belgraue in Com' Leic. =

Rogerus Belgraue de Belgraue aº 4. E. 3. = Susanna fil. et hær. Rogeri Shipton.

Rogerus Belgraue de Belgraue in Com' Leic. = Margaret fil. et hær. Ric'i de Belgraue.

Peter de Belgraue rector eccl'iæ est Haddon.

Johannes rector de Belgraue.

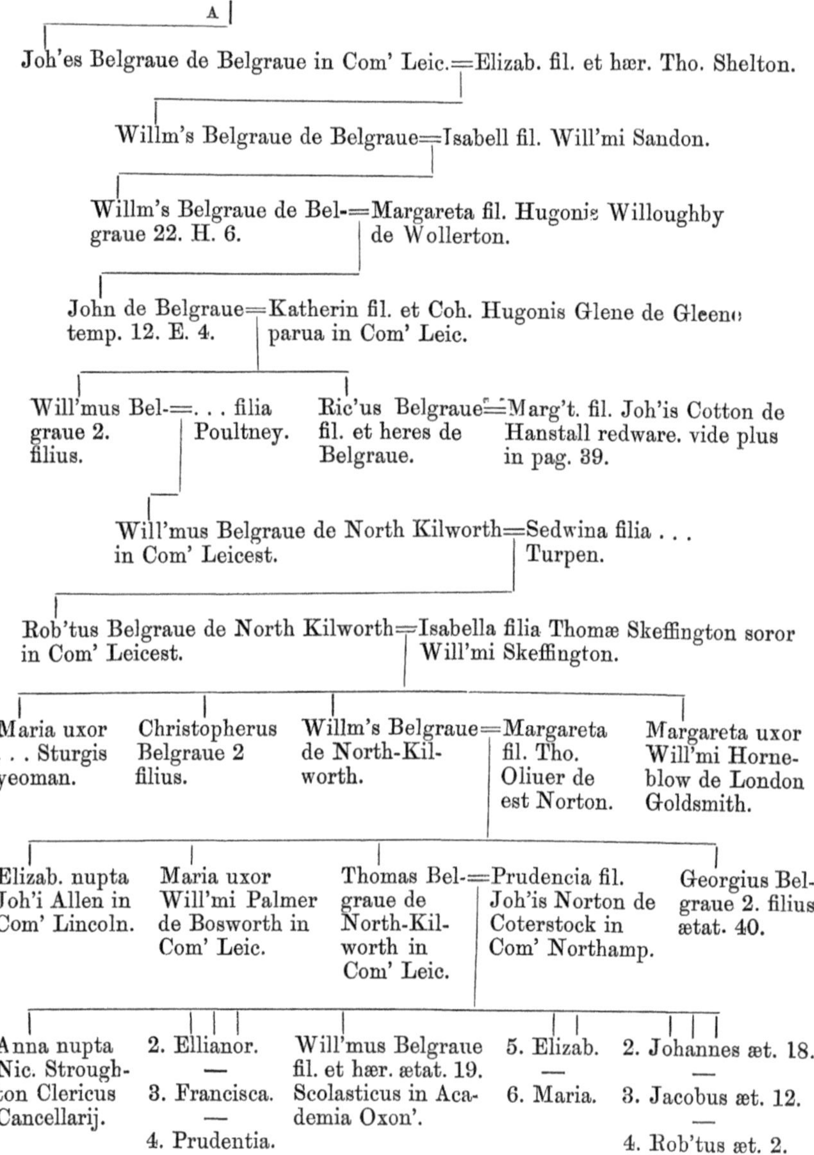

A

Joh'es Belgraue de Belgraue in Com' Leic.=Elizab. fil. et hær. Tho. Shelton.

Willm's Belgraue de Belgraue=Isabell fil. Will'mi Sandon.

Willm's Belgraue de Bel-=Margareta fil. Hugonis Willoughby
graue 22. H. 6.　　　　de Wollerton.

John de Belgraue=Katherin fil. et Coh. Hugonis Glene de Gleene
temp. 12. E. 4.　　parua in Com' Leic.

Will'mus Bel-=. . . filia　　　Ric'us Belgraue=Marg't. fil. Joh'is Cotton de
graue 2.　　　Poultney.　　　fil. et heres de　　Hanstall redware. vide plus
filius.　　　　　　　　　　　Belgraue.　　　　in pag. 39.

Will'mus Belgraue de North Kilworth=Sedwina filia . . .
in Com' Leicest.　　　　　　　　　　　Turpen.

Rob'tus Belgraue de North Kilworth=Isabella filia Thomæ Skeffington soror
in Com' Leicest.　　　　　　　　　　Will'mi Skeffington.

| Maria uxor . . . Sturgis yeoman. | Christopherus Belgraue 2 filius. | Willm's Belgraue de North-Kilworth. =Margareta fil. Tho. Oliuer de est Norton. | Margareta uxor Will'mi Horne-blow de London Goldsmith. |

| Elizab. nupta Joh'i Allen in Com' Lincoln. | Maria uxor Will'mi Palmer de Bosworth in Com' Leic. | Thomas Bel-graue de North-Kilworth in Com' Leic. =Prudencia fil. Joh'is Norton de Coterstock in Com' Northamp. | Georgius Belgraue 2. filius ætat. 40. |

| Anna nupta Nic. Strough-ton Clericus Cancellarij. | 2. Ellianor. — 3. Francisca. — 4. Prudentia. | Will'mus Belgraue fil. et hær. ætat. 19. Scolasticus in Academia Oxon'. | 5. Elizab. — 6. Maria. | 2. Johannes æt. 18. — 3. Jacobus æt. 12. — 4. Rob'tus æt. 2. |

(𝕮𝖚𝖎𝖌𝖑𝖊𝖞.)

ARMS. *Paly of six embattled argent and sable.*
CREST. *Out of flames proper a tiger's head argent, maned sable, gorged with a collar embattled gules.*

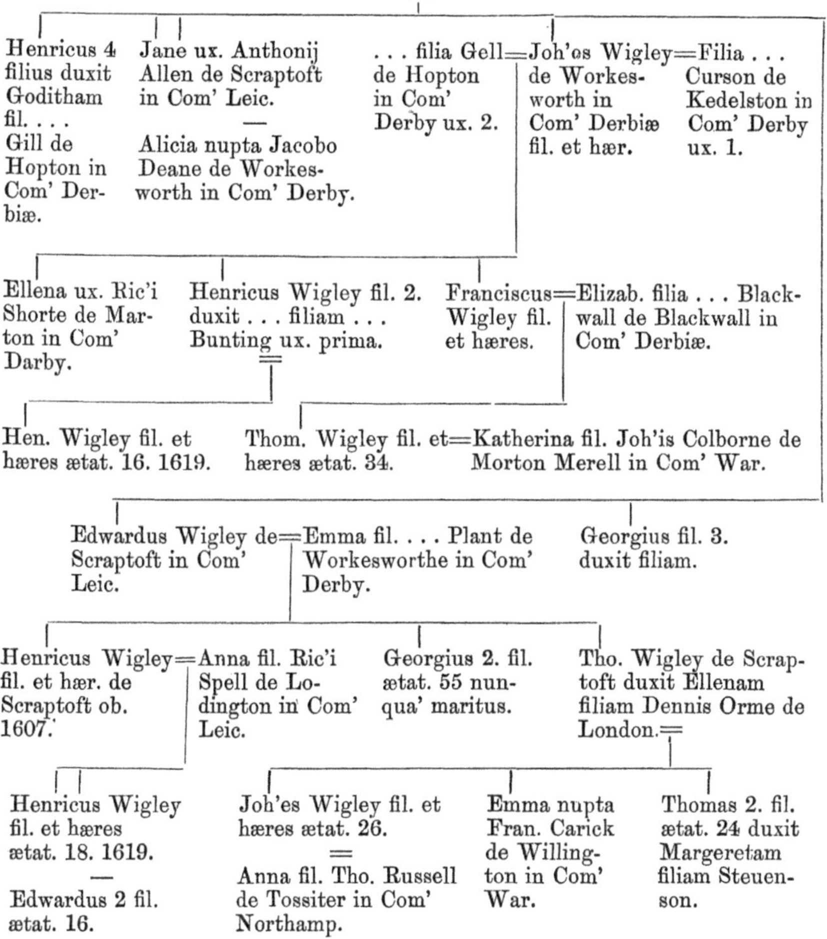

Henricus Wigley de Workesworth in Com' Derbiæ.

Henricus 4 filius duxit Goditham fil. . . . Gill de Hopton in Com' Derbiæ.

Jane ux. Anthonij Allen de Scraptoft in Com' Leic.

Alicia nupta Jacobo Deane de Workesworth in Com' Derby.

. . . filia Gell de Hopton in Com' Derby ux. 2.

Joh'es Wigley de Workesworth in Com' Derbiæ fil. et hær.

Filia . . . Curson de Kedelston in Com' Derby ux. 1.

Ellena ux. Ric'i Shorte de Marton in Com' Darby.

Henricus Wigley fil. 2. duxit . . . filiam . . . Bunting ux. prima.

Franciscus Wigley fil. et hæres.

Elizab. filia . . . Blackwall de Blackwall in Com' Derbiæ.

Hen. Wigley fil. et hæres ætat. 16. 1619.

Thom. Wigley fil. et hæres ætat. 34.

Katherina fil. Joh'is Colborne de Morton Merell in Com' War.

Edwardus Wigley de Scraptoft in Com' Leic.

Emma fil. . . . Plant de Workesworthe in Com' Derby.

Georgius fil. 3. duxit filiam.

Henricus Wigley fil. et hær. de Scraptoft ob. 1607.

Anna fil. Ric'i Spell de Lodington in Com' Leic.

Georgius 2. fil. ætat. 55 nunqua' maritus.

Tho. Wigley de Scraptoft duxit Ellenam filiam Dennis Orme de London.

Henricus Wigley fil. et hæres ætat. 18. 1619.

Edwardus 2 fil. ætat. 16.

Joh'es Wigley fil. et hæres ætat. 26.

Anna fil. Tho. Russell de Tossiter in Com' Northamp.

Emma nupta Fran. Carick de Willington in Com' War.

Thomas 2. fil. ætat. 24 duxit Margeretam filiam Steuenson.

(𝕯𝖆𝖜𝖊𝖘.)

ARMS. *Argent, on a bend azure cotised gules between six battle-axes sable, three swans or.*

CREST. *A demi-battle-axe erect, staff or, and blade argent, on the point a dragon volant with tail nowed sable, bezantée.*

Johannes Dawes de Stapleton in Com' Leicest.

Ric'us Dawes de Staple-=Ellena filia	Isack Dawes=Charitie fil.	Daniell et Eliza-
ton fil. et hær. duxit ... Seller	de Staple- Jacobi	beth ob. sans
Margaretam filiam de Com'	ton 2. fil. Lightfoote	issue.
Vernam de Quarn in Staff. uxor	et hær. de Ashford	—
Com' Leicest. uxor 1. 2. sine	fratris. in Com'	Beatrix ux.
sans issue. prole.	Kent.	Tho. Woode.

Joseph Dawes 2 fil. ætat. 32. duxit   Joh'es Dawes fil.=Elizab. fil. Geo. Gerueis
Mariam fil. . . . Saunders rector   et hæres ætat.   de Peteling magna in
Eccl'iæ de Ausley in Com' War.   35 1619.   Com' Leic.

Johannes 3 filius   Gerueis Dawes fil. et hæres   Willm's 2 filius ætat.
ætat. 4.   ætat. 6 annor' 1619.   3. annoru'.

(𝖂𝖍𝖎𝖙𝖆𝖕𝖍.)

Willm's Whitaph de Reresby in Com' Leic. Bacalarius=Margareta filia Ric'i
Theologiæ et rector Eccl'iæ de Reresby obijt 1617.   Catiell de Rerisby.

Maria nupta	Anna uxor	Willm's Whi-=Anna filia Fran-	Thomas	Alicia
Tho. Steuens	W'mi Mussen	taph fil. et hær. cisci Sacheuerell	2. fil.	filia
de Glen parua	de Ratherby	ætat. 25. 1619. de Reresby in	ætat. 13.	Juni-
in Com' Leic.	in Com' Leic.	Com' Leic.		ora.

Maria fil. 1. ætat. 3.   Rachell ætat. 6. menses. 15 Septemb' 1619.

(𝔖taresmore.)

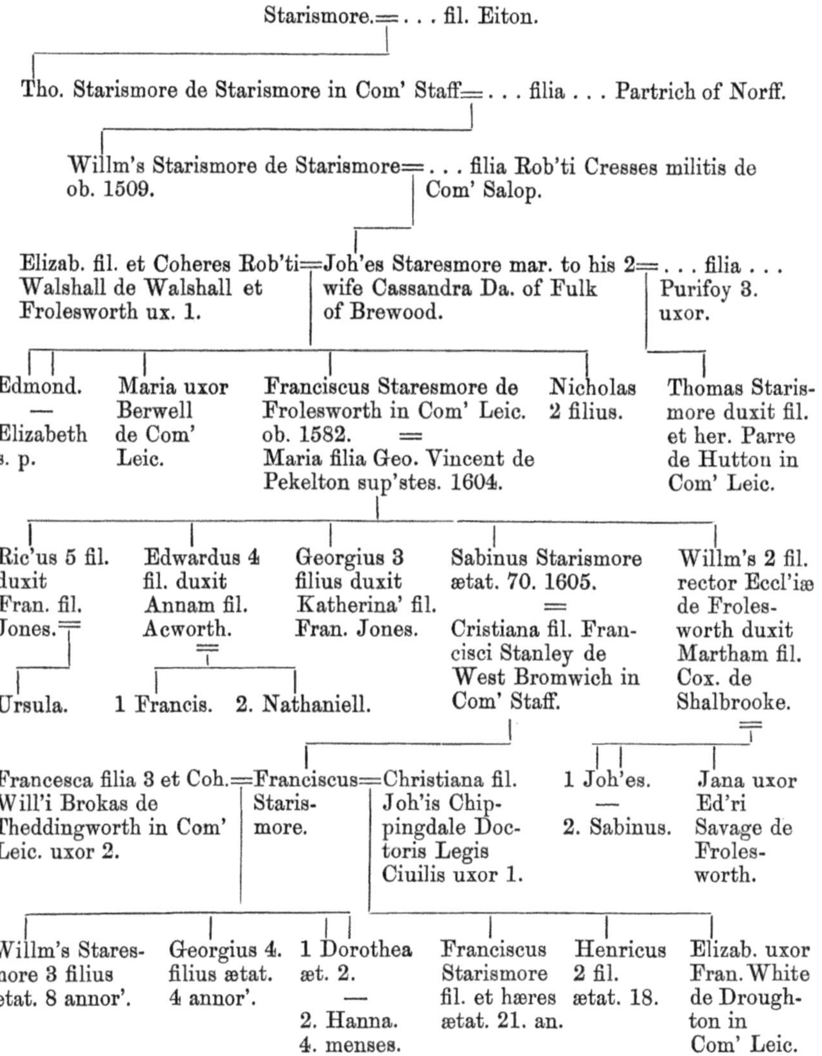

Starismore.=... fil. Eiton.

Tho. Starismore de Starismore in Com' Staff=... filia ... Partrich of Norff.

Willm's Starismore de Starismore=... filia Rob'ti Cresses militis de
ob. 1509.   Com' Salop.

Elizab. fil. et Coheres Rob'ti=Joh'es Staresmore mar. to his 2=... filia ...
Walshall de Walshall et   wife Cassandra Da. of Fulk   Purifoy 3.
Frolesworth ux. 1.   of Brewood.   uxor.

Edmond.   Maria uxor   Franciscus Staresmore de   Nicholas   Thomas Staris-
—   Berwell   Frolesworth in Com' Leic.   2 filius.   more duxit fil.
Elizabeth   de Com'   ob. 1582.   =   et her. Parre
s. p.   Leic.   Maria filia Geo. Vincent de   de Hutton in
                            Pekelton sup'stes. 1604.   Com' Leic.

Ric'us 5 fil.   Edwardus 4   Georgius 3   Sabinus Starismore   Willm's 2 fil.
duxit   fil. duxit   filius duxit   ætat. 70. 1605.   rector Eccl'iæ
Fran. fil.   Annam fil.   Katherina' fil.   =   de Froles-
Jones.=   Acworth.   Fran. Jones.   Cristiana fil. Fran- worth duxit
                    =   cisci Stanley de   Martham fil.
                                              West Bromwich in   Cox. de
Ursula.   1 Francis.   2. Nathaniell.   Com' Staff.   Shalbrooke.
                                                                         =

Francesca filia 3 et Coh.=Franciscus=Christiana fil.   1 Joh'es.   Jana uxor
Will'i Brokas de   Staris-   Joh'is Chip-   —   Ed'ri
Theddingworth in Com'   more.   pingdale Doc-   2. Sabinus. Savage de
Leic. uxor 2.   toris Legis   Froles-
                                     Ciuilis uxor 1.   worth.

Willm's Stares-   Georgius 4.   1 Dorothea   Franciscus   Henricus   Elizab. uxor
more 3 filius   filius ætat. æt. 2.   Starismore   2 fil.   Fran. White
ætat. 8 annor'.   4 annor'.   —   fil. et hæres ætat. 18. de Drough-
                                2. Hanna.   ætat. 21. an.   ton in
                                4. menses.   Com' Leic.

(𝕹𝖊𝖊𝖉𝖍𝖆𝖒.)

ARMS. *Argent, on a bend engrailed azure between two bucks' heads caboshed sable, a crescent for difference.*

CREST. *On a mount vert a buck lodged sable, attired or, charged with a crescent for difference.*

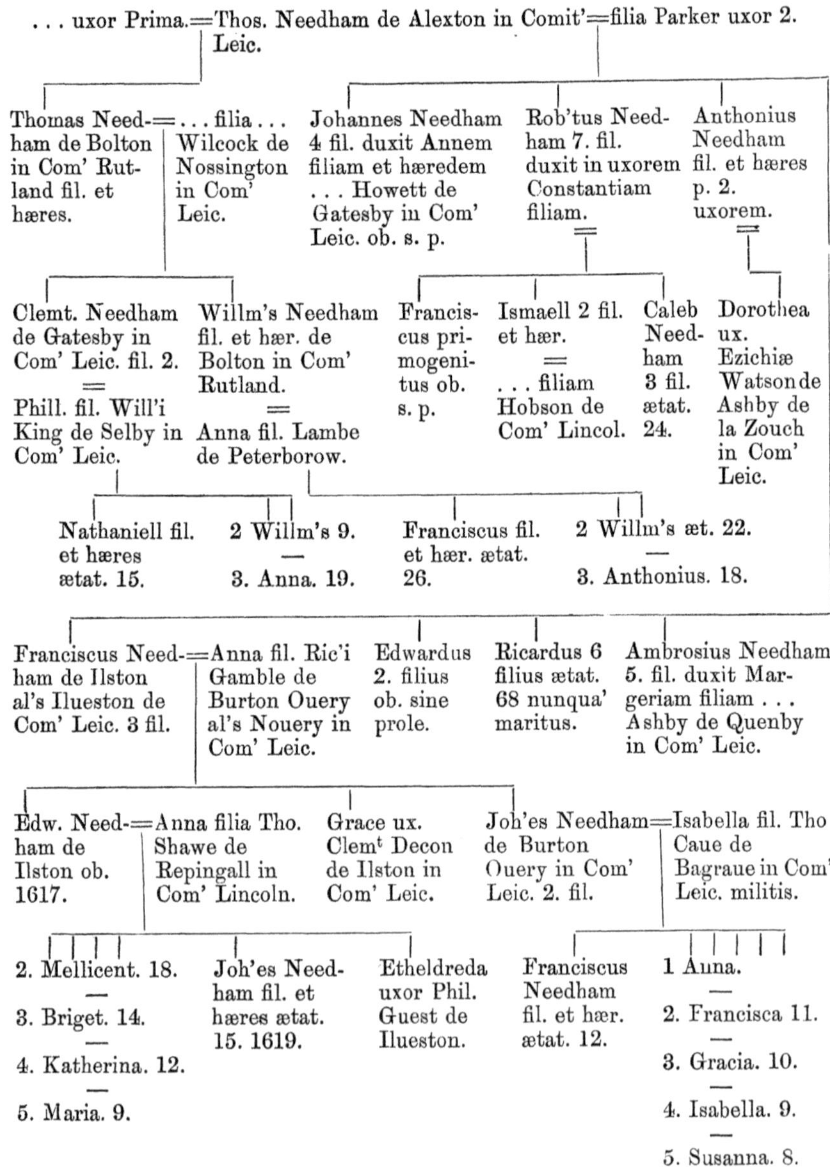

... uxor Prima.══Thos. Needham de Alexton in Comit'══filia Parker uxor 2.
Leic.

Thomas Need-══... filia ... Wilcock de Nossington in Com' Leic. — **ham de Bolton in Com' Rutland fil. et hæres.**

Johannes Needham 4 fil. duxit Annem filiam et hæredem ... Howett de Gatesby in Com' Leic. ob. s. p.

Rob'tus Needham 7. fil. duxit in uxorem Constantiam filiam.

Anthonius Needham fil. et hæres p. 2. uxorem.

Clemt. Needham de Gatesby in Com' Leic. fil. 2. ══ Phill. fil. Will'i King de Selby in Com' Leic.

Willm's Needham fil. et hær. de Bolton in Com' Rutland. ══ Anna fil. Lambe de Peterborow.

Franciscus primogenitus ob. s. p.

Ismaell 2 fil. et hær. ══ ... filiam Hobson de Com' Lincol.

Caleb Needham 3 fil. ætat. 24.

Dorothea ux. Ezichiæ Watson de Ashby de la Zouch in Com' Leic.

Nathaniell fil. et hæres ætat. 15.

2 Willm's 9.
—
3. Anna. 19.

Franciscus fil. et hær. ætat. 26.

2 Willm's æt. 22.
—
3. Anthonius. 18.

Franciscus Need-══Anna fil. Ric'i Gamble de Burton Ouery al's Nouery in Com' Leic. — **ham de Ilston al's Ilueston de Com' Leic. 3 fil.**

Edwardus 2. filius ob. sine prole.

Ricardus 6 filius ætat. 68 nunqua' maritus.

Ambrosius Needham 5. fil. duxit Margeriam filiam ... Ashby de Quenby in Com' Leic.

Edw. Need-══Anna filia Tho. Shawe de Repingall in Com' Lincoln. — **ham de Ilston ob. 1617.**

Grace ux. Clemt Decon de Ilston in Com' Leic.

Joh'es Needham de Burton Ouery in Com' Leic. 2. fil. ══ Isabella fil. Tho Caue de Bagraue in Com' Leic. militis.

2. Mellicent. 18.
—
3. Briget. 14.
—
4. Katherina. 12.
—
5. Maria. 9.

Joh'es Needham fil. et hæres ætat. 15. 1619.

Etheldreda uxor Phil. Guest de Ilueston.

Franciscus Needham fil. et hær. ætat. 12.

1 Anna.
—
2. Francisca 11.
—
3. Gracia. 10.
—
4. Isabella. 9.
—
5. Susanna. 8.

Marstone.

Arms. *Sable, a fess indented ermine between three fleurs-de-lis argent.*

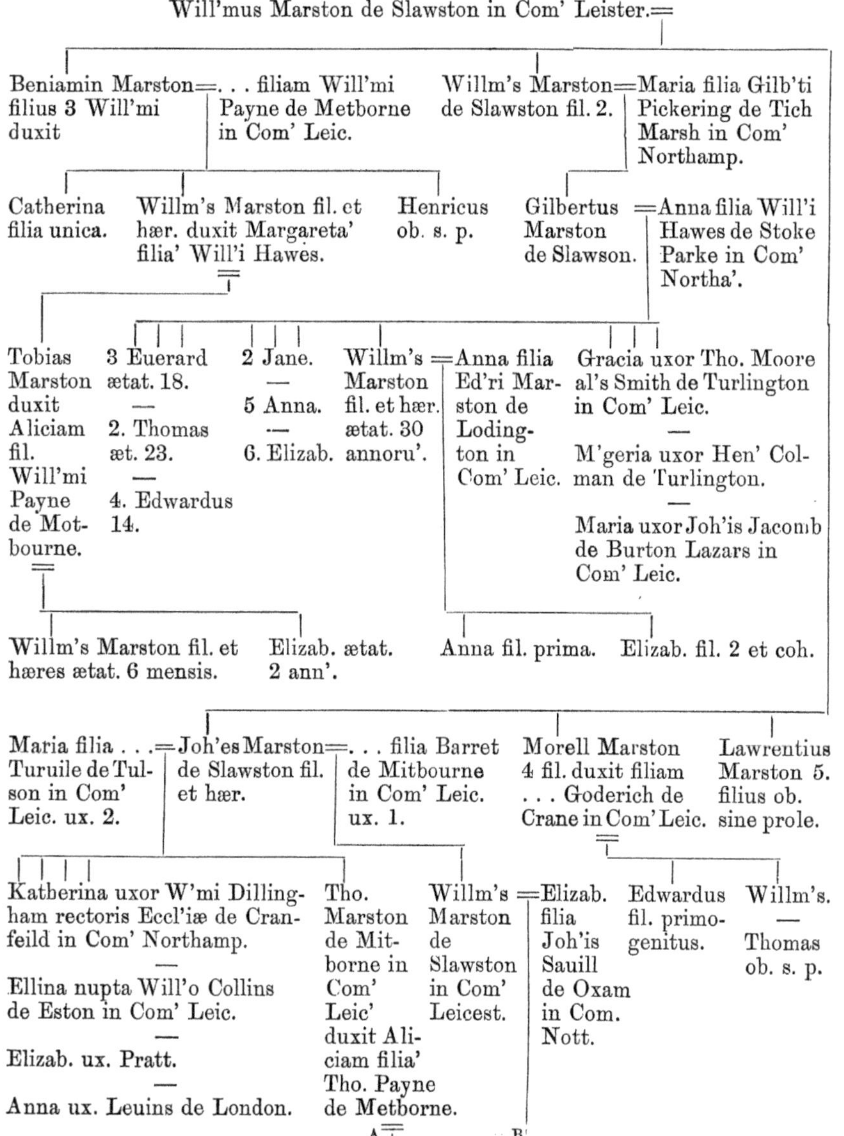

A | B |

1 Will'mus.   Johanna.   Willm's Mars-=Johanna filia et hær. Zacheriæ   Johannes
—   —   ton fil. et hær. Bowman de Marston Trussell   Marston
2. Johannes. Katherina   ætat. 26.   in Com' Northamp.   2 filius
                                                                           ætat. 24.

Johannes Marston filius et   Tobias 2. fil. ætat. 1 anni.   Willm's ob. infantulu'.
hæres ætat. 4. 1619.

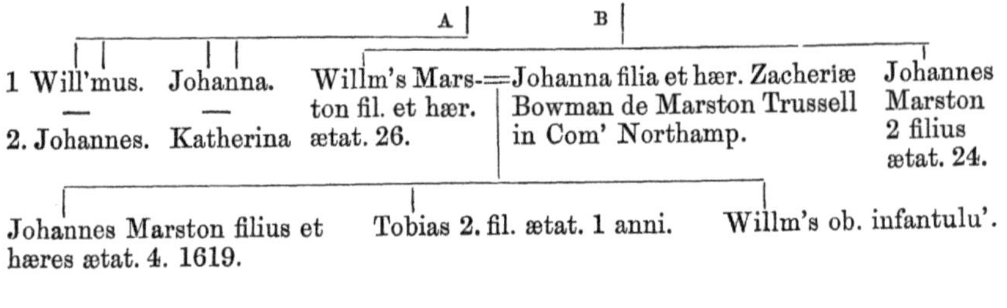

(Lawrence.)

. . . Lawrence de longe Whatton in Com' Leic.═

Johannes   Tho. Lawrence=Jana filia   Elizab. nupta   Willm's   Rob'tus 3. fil.
Lawrence   de Longe   Rob'ti   Crispe de   ob. s. p. duxit Elizab.
fil. et hær. Whatton in   Parsons   Belton in   filia' . . . Wright
ob. s. p.   Com' Leic.   de Longe   Com' Leic.   de Shepsted in
                            Whatton.   Com' Leic.
                                                                        ═

Thomas=Isabella filia   Edwardus   Rob'tus   Will'mus =Elizab. fil.   Thomas Law-
Law-   Launcelott   Lawrence   2. filius Lawrence Joh'is   rence duxit
rence Baroden de   3. filius. ob. s. p. de Longe Litherland   Isabellam
4. filius. Sileby in   Whatton. de Belton   filiam . . .
       Com' Leicest.   in Com'   Hayes.
                                                         Leic.   ═

4 Anna.   1 Elizabetha.   Willm's Law-   Thomas   Tho. Lawrence fil. et
—   —   rence fil. et   2 fil.   hæres ætat. 24. nunc in
5. Rebecca. 2. Maria.   hæres. ætatis   ætat. 6. Hib'nia et ibi nuptus.
             —   20. 1619.   mensis.
             3. Sara.

Sara uxor   Anna nupta   Elizab. uxor   Tho. Law=Ellina filia . . .   Maria uxor
Joh'is   Joh'i Chet-   Joh'is Cran-   rence fil. Denham de Com'   Geo. Sar-
Barnby   wood de   well de   et hæres Nott. qui duxit   son de
de Com'   Asby in   Loughborow   æt. 28.   filiam Joh'is   Loughbroug
Nott.   Com' Leic.   in Com' Leic.   1619.   Hersie Militis.   in Com' Leic.

Will'mus Lawrence fil. & hær. ætat. 4.   Elizabetha siue Ellinora.

𝔐arshall.

Thomas Marshall de Worthington in Com' Leic.=. . . filia
whose auncesters cam out of y^e north. Smith de

Willm's Marshall de Whitwick in Com' Leic. fil. et hæres.=

Geo. Marshall de Diceworth in Com' Leic. 2. filius.=Margareta filia Rolandi Milborne de Diceworth.

Franciscus Marshall 3. filius.=Isabella filia Rolandi Milborne soror Margaretæ prædictæ.

Jacobus Marshall filius et hæres.=

Sibilla fil. Rad'i Claxston de London uxor 2.=Georgius Marshall de Diceworth in Com' Leic. ætat. 41. 1619.=Katherina filia Joh'is Champion de Castle Dunington in Com' Leic. ux. 1.

Tho. Marshall fil. et hær. ætat. 40. annoru' 1619.

Johannes Marshall fil. et hær.

3 Willm's æt. 7.
—
4. Francis æt. 4.
—
5. Rowland æt. 2.

1 Sara æt. 6.
—
2. Sibilla æt. 5.

Georgius Marshall fil. et hær. ætat. 12. 1619.

Johannes 2. filius ætat. 10.

(𝔓eper.)

ARMS. *Quarterly :*—1. *Gules, on a chevron argent, between three demi-lions rampant, couped or, as many sickles sable, in chief an annulet for difference.* 2. *Or, on a fess sable three water bougets argent.* 3. *Argent, a chevron between three garbs gules, in chief a martlet for difference.*

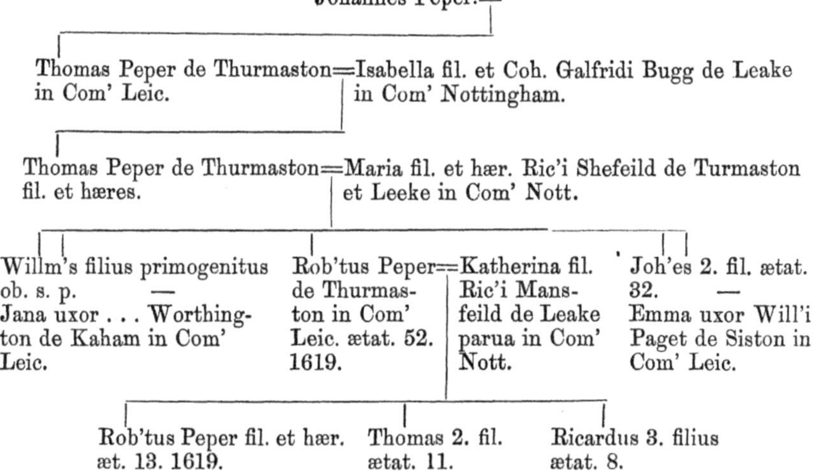

Johannes Peper.=

Thomas Peper de Thurmaston in Com' Leic.=Isabella fil. et Coh. Galfridi Bugg de Leake in Com' Nottingham.

Thomas Peper de Thurmaston fil. et hæres.=Maria fil. et hær. Ric'i Shefeild de Turmaston et Leeke in Com' Nott.

Willm's filius primogenitus ob. s. p. — Jana uxor . . . Worthington de Kaham in Com' Leic.

Rob'tus Peper de Thurmaston in Com' Leic. ætat. 52. 1619.=Katherina fil. Ric'i Mansfeild de Leake parua in Com' Nott.

Joh'es 2. fil. ætat. 32. — Emma uxor Will'i Paget de Siston in Com' Leic.

Rob'tus Peper fil. et hær. æt. 13. 1619.

Thomas 2. fil. ætat. 11.

Ricardus 3. filius ætat. 8.

(𝕽𝖚𝖉𝖎𝖓𝖌.)

ARMS. *Quarterly :—*1. *Argent, on a bend between two lions rampant sable, a dragon extended of the field, a crescent for difference.* 2. *Argent, on two bars sable three plates.* 3. *Sable, three fleurs-de-lis between seven cross crosslets fitchée argent, three, three, one, a canton ermine.*
CREST. *A dragon's head couped, collared, and chained, in the mouth a lion's gamb, erased (untinctured).*

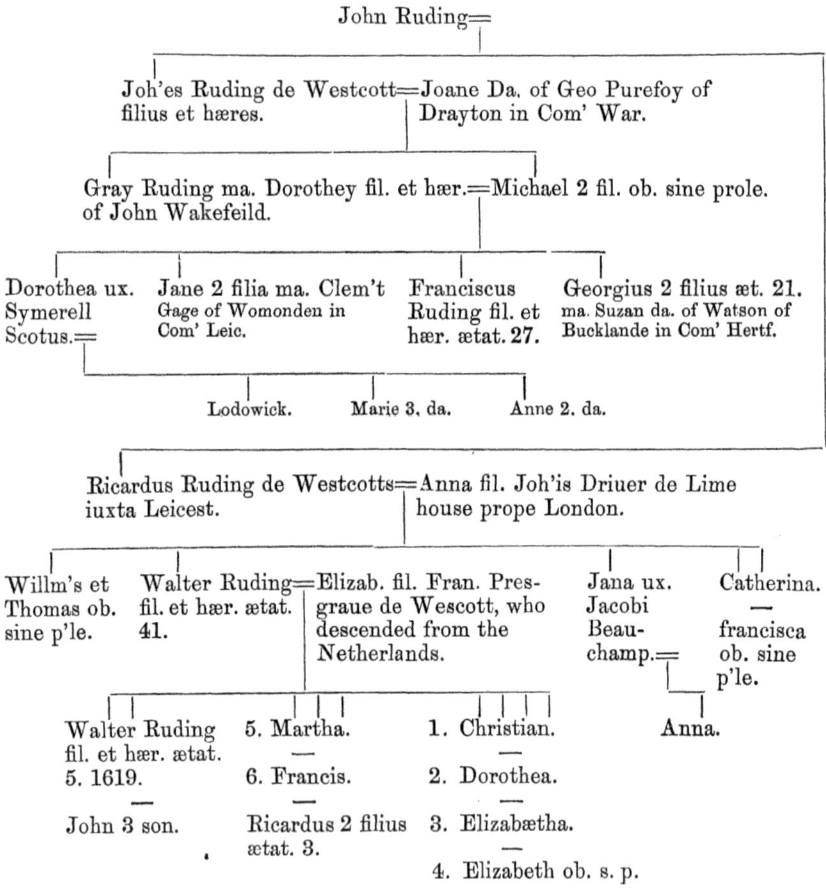

(Alsop.)

ARMS. *Sable, on a chevron between three doves or, a mullet for difference.*

Humphredus Alsop de Alsop in Com' Derbiæ
Steward to Edward last Duke of Buck.

Willm's Alsop de Alsop=Isabella filia Joh'is Warner de Marke-
in Com' Derbiæ. | feild in Com' Leic.

Carolus Alsop de=Maria fil. Will'i | Joh'es Alsop rector | Willm's Alsop
Markefeild in | Cooper de Thur- | Eccl'iæ de Beeby in | 4. filius ob.
Com' Leic. 3. fil. | maston in Com' | Com' Leic. 2. fil. | s. p.
| Leic. |

Jana 2. filia. | Humphredus=Katherina | 2. Willm's ætat. 28. | Nicholas 5
— | Alsop fil. et | fil. . . . | — | filius ætat.
Maria nupta | hær. ætat. | Allen de | 3. Georgius æt. 25. | 17.
Ric'o Spencer | 30. | Com' Rut- | —
de Onlippe in | | land. | 4. Johannes æt. 21.
Com' Leic. |

Willm's Alsop fil. et hæres. | Maria 2. septimano' 15.
ætat. 3. 1619. | Septemb' 1619.

Dorothea fil.=Humphredus Alsop=Elizaab. fil. Welsh | Georgius Alsop 5
Moleneux | fil. et hæres de | who maried the | filius de Leicester
de Carlton | Putterley Hall in | Da. of Judg South- | duxit Anna' fil. Geo.
in Com' | Com' Darbiæ. | cott uxor. 1. | Agar de Newborow
Nott. ux. 2. | | | in Com' Staff.

. . . fil. p' uxore' 2. | Humphredus Alsop fil. et | Maria ætat. 19.
| hær. ætat. 15. 1619.

(Pochin.)

ARMS. *Quarterly :—1. Argent, a chevron gules between three horse-shoes sable. 2. Or, on two bars gules three water bougets argent, in chief an annulet for difference. 3. Argent, on a cross azure five mullets or. 4. Blank. 5. Azure, three fleurs-de-lis argent within a bordure engrailed or. 6. Gules, a fess indented between six billets or.*

CREST. *A harpy (untinctured).*

Walter Power de Barkby in Com' Leic.=

Peter Lincolne de Barkby in Comitat'=Anna fil. et hæres
Leic. temp. E. 3. Walteri Power.

Will'mus Willoughby de Barkby in Com' Leic.=Anna fil. et hæres Petri Lincolne.

Ricardus Pochin de Barkby in Com' Leic.=Alicia fil. et hæres Will'i Willoughby.

Johannes Pochin de Barkby in Com' Leic.=

Thomas Pochin de Barkby.=Elizab. filia . . . Sherley.

Willm's Pochin de=Maria fil. et Coh. Will'mi Palmer de Stonie
Barkby. Stanton in Com' Leic.

Barbara uxor Ric'i Chambers de Gatisby in Com' Leic.	Georgius Pochin de Barkby sup'stes 1563.=Katherina fil. Thomas Skevington de Skevington.	Willm's 2 filius cuius proles ob. sine sobole.=Alicia filia Edw. Brokesby.

Will'm. — John. — Mary. — Elizab.	Dorothea ux. Will'i Cogan de Insula Axome in Com' Lincoln.	Ellina uxor Ric'i Harrington de Bagworth in Com' Leic. — Willm's filius 1.	Matheus Pochin de Barkby in Com' Leic. = Katherina fil. . . . Blewett.	Maria nupta Rob'to Moore de Knighton in Com' Nott.	Edward. — Georg. — Valentine.

1 Alicia æt. 18. — 2. Dorothea. 17. — 3. Katherina. 16.	4. Gracia. — 5. Pasca. — 6. Maria. — 7. Margaret.	2 Johannes æt. 21. — 3. Franciscus æt. 19. — 4. Rob'tus æt. 16. — 5. Matheus æt. 12.	Georgius Pochin fil. et hær. ætat. 24. = . . . filia Doctoris Doue Episcopi Peterborowe.

Tho. Pochin fil. et hæres ætat. 6 menses 1619.

(Barret.)

ARMS. *Per pale argent and gules, a fess counterchanged.*

Ric'us Barret de Wimsole in Com' Leic. qui vienne del Contie d'Essex.

Willm's Barret de Wimsole in Com' Leic.

Willm's Barret de Wimsole in Com' Leic.=Anna filia Leake.

Thomas Barret de Wimsole in=Margareta fil. Hen. Laser de
Com' Leic.　　　　　　　　　Winsole in Com' Leic.

Willm's Barret de Winsole in=Juditha fil. et Coher. Edwardi Bowier de
Com' Leic.　　　　　　　　　Shepshed in Com' Leic.

| Dorothea nupta Rob'to Reynes filio Nic'i Reynes. | Margareta ux. Hugonis Bothum de Leicest'. | Will'mus Barret fil. et hæres ætat. 28. 1619. | =Jocosa fil. Nicholaij Reynes de Stanford in Com' Nott. | Elizabetha nupta Rob'to Fox de Wimsole. |

| Rob'tus 2 filius ætat. 4. | Willm's Barret fil. et hæres ætat. 6. 1619. | Judith ætat. 3. | Dorothea ætat. 2. |

(Cheseldon.)

Johannes Cheseldon de Weldon in Com' Northam.

Ric'us Cheselden de Weldon in Com' Northamp.=

Joh'es Cheseldon de Weldon in Comit' Northamp.=Johanna fil.

Jocosa filia . . . Barsby=Ric'us Cheseldon de Weldon=Anna fil. Will'mi Stacy de
de Thorp ux. 2.　　　　　in Com' Northamp.　　　　Thorpe in Com' Leic. ux. 1.

1 Elizab.	3 Ricardus.	Willm's 2 fil. ætat. 20.	Johannes Cheseldon fil. et hæres ætat. 30. 1619.	1 Jocosa.
2. Anna.	4. Thomas. 10.			2. Johanna.
3. Francisca.	5. Georgius 6.			

(Cooke.)

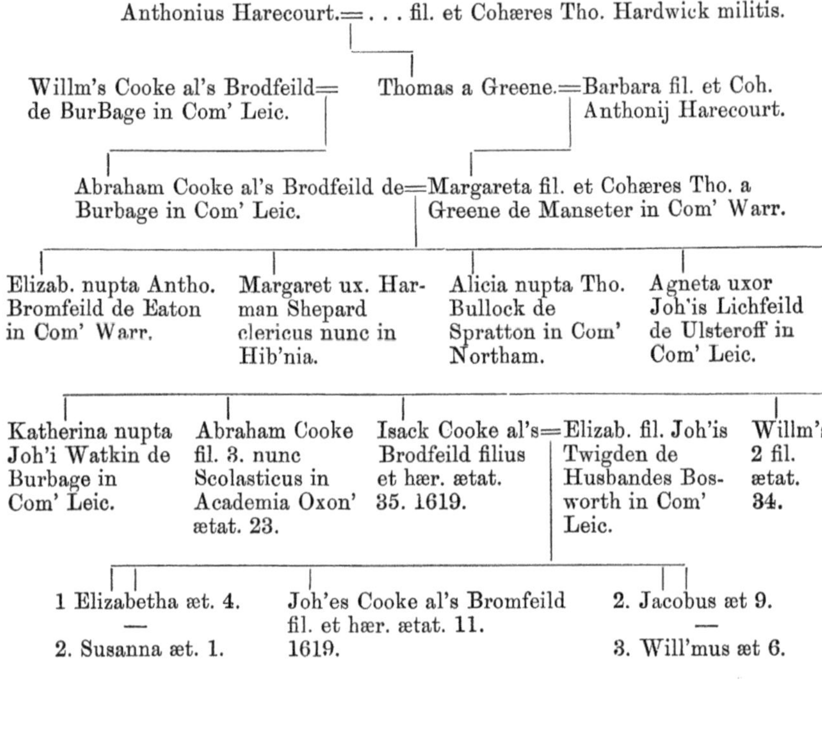

Anthonius Harecourt.=... fil. et Cohæres Tho. Hardwick militis.

Willm's Cooke al's Brodfeild= de BurBage in Com' Leic.

Thomas a Greene.=Barbara fil. et Coh. Anthonij Harecourt.

Abraham Cooke al's Brodfeild de=Margareta fil. et Cohæres Tho. a Burbage in Com' Leic. Greene de Manseter in Com' Warr.

Elizab. nupta Antho. Bromfeild de Eaton in Com' Warr.

Margaret ux. Harman Shepard clericus nunc in Hib'nia.

Alicia nupta Tho. Bullock de Spratton in Com' Northam.

Agneta uxor Joh'is Lichfeild de Ulsteroff in Com' Leic.

Katherina nupta Joh'i Watkin de Burbage in Com' Leic.

Abraham Cooke fil. 3. nunc Scolasticus in Academia Oxon' ætat. 23.

Isack Cooke al's=Elizab. fil. Joh'is Brodfeild filius et hær. ætat. 35. 1619.

Elizab. fil. Joh'is Twigden de Husbandes Bosworth in Com' Leic.

Willm's 2 fil. ætat. 34.

1 Elizabetha æt. 4.
—
2. Susanna æt. 1.

Joh'es Cooke al's Bromfeild fil. et hær. ætat. 11. 1619.

2. Jacobus æt 9.
—
3. Will'mus æt 6.

(Arms and Seals of Leicester.)

ARMS. 1. *A cinquefoil pierced ermine.*
CREST. *A dragon with wings displayed and tail nowed ermine.*
2. *England, in chief a label of three points, the shield surmounted by a ducal coronet.*
SEALS.—1. *A cinquefoil pierced ermine.*
  Legend.—✠ SIGILLUM : COMMUNITATIS : LEYRCESTRIE.
  2. *Issuant from clouds a sheaf of three arrows, points downwards, one in pale and two in saltire, on the dexter side a scroll, inscribed thereon "IN ANTITRINITARIOS," on the sinister a cinquefoil pierced ermine.*
  Legend.—✠ SIGILL : HOSPITALIS : S'CTÆ : TRINITATIS : IN : NOVO : OPERE.
  3. *A cinquefoil pierced ermine.*
  Legend.—✠ SIGILLUM : STATUT : BURGI : LLICESTRIE.
  4. *A cinquefoil pierced ermine.*
  Legend.—✠ VILLA . LEIC . TARLAT.

5. *The Virgin crowned, holding a sceptre in the dexter hand and nude child in sinister arm, seated under a canopy with finials, below them on a small shield, a cinquefoil pierced ermine.*
Legend.—SIGILL : MAIORATUS . VISTE : LEICESTRIE.

These are the Armes and towne Seales used by the Maior & Burgesses of the Borough of Leicester, wch now is incorporated by the name of Maior Bailiffes and Burgesses of the sayd Borough of Leicester, and inabled with many great priuileges and large immunities by many the auncient Kinges of England, and sithens confirmed & enlarged by Kinge James that now is.   Of which sayd Borough at the tyme of this present Visitac'on. videl't 23. Septemb. 1619. Nicholas Gillott was Maior, Will'm Morton Will'm Iue, Tho. Erick & Rowland Pusey Justices of the Peace w^thin the sayd Borough, John Wilne & Will'm Hunt Bailiffes, John Freman Steward John Tatam & John Norrice Chamberlaines and Fran Haruy Esq. Sergeant at Lawe Recorder of the sayd Borough.

(Allen.)

ARMS. *Per pale argent and sable, a chevron between three talbots passant, all counterchanged, the talbots collared or.*

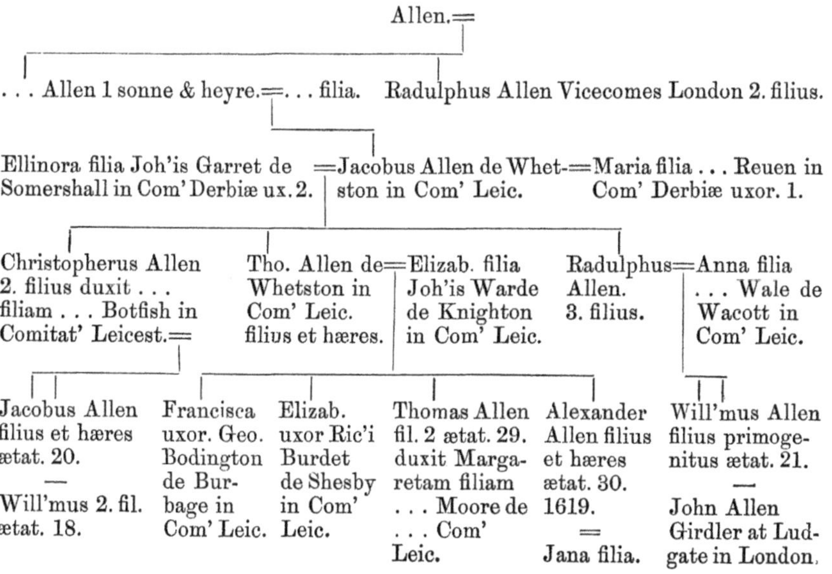

(Skeffington.)

Galfridus Skeffington de Skeffington in Com' Leic.=

Simon Skeffington miles=

Joh'es Skeffington Miles temp. H. 3.=Petronilla.

Sr. Rob't Skeffington Miles temp. E. 1.=

Galfridus Skeffington Miles.=Mabilla.

Willm's Skeffington de Skeffington.=

Will's Cambridg al's Clark.=Jone fil. et hær. Brian Deane.=Thomas Roose 2 Maritus.

Rob'tus Skeffington de Skeffington miles.=

Willm's Oldbeefe.=Matilda fil. et hær. Will'miCambridg.

Sr Rob't Roose Kt. ob. s. p.

Ri'cus Skeffington de Skeffington in Com' Leic.=Isabella ux. eius.

Willm's Oldbeefe=Margareta fil. et hær. Will'mi English.

Stanhop.=

Joh'es Skeffington de Skeffington.=Margareta fil. et hær. Will'mi Oldbeffe.

Johannes Stanhop.=   1. Thomas.   2. Michaell.

Tho. Skeffington de Skeffington in Com' Leic.=

A |

Hen Stanhop 2 fil.=Johanna filia et hær. Hen. Rochford D'us de Stoke in Com' Lincoln.

B |

Anna filia Euerard Digby de Dristoke militis=Willm's Skeffington Miles Prorex=Anna filia John Digby Edmondus=Alicia
et D'ns de Tilton in Com' Leic. ux. 1. Hib'niæ temp. H. 8. de Kettleby. Stanhop. | Flie.

Thomas Skeffing-=Margareta filia Katherina uxor 2. Anna. Joh'es Skeffing-=filia et hæres . . . Tho. Skeffiington
ton de Skeffing- et hæres Edm. Anthonij Colley — ton de London Peck. 3. filius duxit . . .
ton. Stanhop Miles. de Glason or 3. Isabella. Miles 2 filius Or, 3. eagles disp. sa. filiam . . . Hasil-
  Glowson. ob. s. p. rigge.=

Elizab. uxor Willm's Skeffing-=Johanna filia Jacobi Leueson ARMS. Quarterly :—1. Argent, three bulls' heads erased sable, armed
Geo. Griffith ton de Com' Ar. renupta Will'o Foulke et or. 2. Azure, a bend cotised between six mullets or. 3. Sable,
de Wichmore Salop. postea uxor Edwardi Gifford three garbs argent. 4. Azure, on a bend or, in dexter chief point
in Com' Staff. Ar. illa ob. 1572. an annulet gules for difference. 5. Ermine, on a chief indented
militis. gules three escallops or. 6. Or, a pale azure, a chief vert. 7. Ermine, a bend azure. 8. Or, three eagles displayed gules.

Joh'es Skeffington de Fisher-=Alicia filia Thomæ Caue de Stan- Thomas Skeffington 1. Elizabetha. 2. Ursula.
wick in Com' Staff. ford in Com' Northamp. Legum Doctor 3. fil.

Will'mus Skeffington de Fisher-=Elizab. filia Ric'i Deering de Elizab. uxor Francisci Danuers de
wick in Com' Staff. 1619. Pluckley in Com' Cantij. Swithland in Com' Leic.

Joh'es Skeffington filius et hæres=Ursula soror et cohær. Joh'is Elizab. nupta Will'i Jetter de
ætat. 30. 1619. Skeffington de Skeffington. Skeffington in Com' Leic.

Elizab. filia Dan-=Jacobus Skef-=. . . filia Bradley de London re- Georgius Skeffington fil. 3. duxit Ric'us Skeffington de Lon-
uers relicta Tho. fington 2. licta Will'i Cockeram de Hamp- Goditham filiam Tho. Ros de don Justiciar' ad pacem 4.
Caue. filius. sted in Com' Midd. Lutterworth in Com' Leicest. filius.

A | B

A | B

. . . filia monialis apud Sempringha'.

Jocosa ux. . . . Ingarsby de Kibworth in Com' Leic.

Maria uxor Ouerey de Iueston in Com' leic. renupta . . . Kingston.

2. Leonardus.
—
4. Matheus.

3. Anthonius Presbiter.

7. Jocosa uxor Tho. Bendage de Burrington in Com' Cantab.
—
8. Maria uxor Rob. Monke de Kirkby in.

5. Elizab. ux. Ri. Egleby de Estcot in Com' War.
—
6. Lucia uxor . . . Bell.

3. Katherina uxor Georgij Pochin de Barkby in Com' Leic.
4. Dorothea uxor Tho. Hunt de Aston sup' Trent in Com' Nott.

2. Anthonius s. p.
—
3. Edwardus.
—
4. Georgius s. p.
—
5. Franciscus sup'stes 1563.

1. Isabella uxor Rob'ti Belgraue de Kilworth in Com' Northamp.
—
2. Anna uxor Tho. Ludford de Anseley in Com' War.

Will'mus Skeffington de Skeffington sup'stes 1563. = Maria filia Tho. Caue de Stanford in Com' Northamp. mils.

4
Alicia uxor Bandon de Kibworth in Com' Leic.

Agneta 3. filia.

Margaret 1 filia.
—
2. Elizab. uxor . . . Browne de Com' War.

Henricus 2. filius.

Thomas Skeffington de Skeffington in Com' Leic. Ar. ob. 1600. = Isabella filia Joh'is Biron de Newsted in Com' Nott militis.

Elizab. soror et Coh. uxor Will'i Jettour de Warwick.
—
Ursula soror et Coh. uxor Joh'is Skeffingto' de Fisherwick in Com' Staff.

Maria soror et Coher uxor Will'mi St Andrew de Gotham in Com' Nott.=

Katherina soror et hær. uxor Will'mi Brome de Woodlow in Com. Warr. ar.

Joh'es Skeffington frater et hæres Will'i occisus in Hospitio Graies Inne London p' Mich'em Bray sine prole.

Willm's Skeffington de Skeffington miles ætat. 20. Aº. 1600 ob. s. p. = Katherina filia Ric'i Chetwood de Woodhull in Com' Bedf. mil. = Michaell Bray 2 maritus occisus in hospitio Grayes Inne London per Joh'em Skeffington.

Joh'es de St Andrew.

Guliellmus de St Andrew
2 filius.

Jana.

Barbara.

Ric'us Bray 1 filius.

Egidius 2 filius.

Anna ob. 16. July 1618.

(Noel.)

ARMS. *Or, fretty gules, a chief azure.*

Noelus Lo. of Elenhall in Com' Staff. of whome═
this posterity tooke their surname.

Rob't Noell Lo. of Elenhall first founder═Alicia   Ricardus 2
of the Monastrie of Ranton in Com' Staff.   ux. eius.   filius Noeli.
according to yᵉ Rule of Haghmon Abbey.

Phillippus   Ric'us Harcourt   Thomas fil. Rob'ti fil. Noeli 1. fil.═Margareta soror
Noell 2.   de Stanton in   Dn's de Elenhall et Ranton et   Guidonis le Strang
filius.   Com' Oxon.   patronus eiusdem prioratus.   de Com' Salop.

Rob'tus ═Joan filia . . .   Willm's Har-═Alicia filia   Willm's   ═Johanna fil.
Noell fil.│ Acton miles.   Court de   │ et Coh. vixit Duston.   │ et coh. vixit
Phillippi.│ (*Ar. B. quarterly* Stanton │ 11. Regis   ("*G. 3 bucks'* │ 11. Joh'is
          │ *p. fes endented.*)   miles. │ Joh'is.   *heades ca-*   │ fuit D'na de
          │   │   *bosed or.*")   │ Ranton.

Phillippus Noell de Cest-═   Ric'us Harcourt miles   Roisia fil. et hær. fuit D'na
forde superstes 52. H. 3.│   D'ns de Stanton.   de Ranton et nupta Joh'i
                                                      Doiley et habuit exitum.

Phillippus Noell de Cestford et Newbold.═

Phillippus Noell obijt ante patrem.═Cicilia, ouer liued her husband
                                    │ and was a widow. 12. E. 2.

Thomas Noell fil. et hæres.═Alicia fil. et hær. Henrici de Wiuerston.

Willm's Noell de Newbold.═

Ricardus Noell de Newbold.═

Jana filia . . .═Thomas Noell═Jana filia Rogeri Dracott   Rob'tus Noell 2. filius
Sonde uxor   │ de Newbold. │ de Painsley in Com' Staff.   superstes 28. H. 6.
prima.   ux. 2.

Isabella uxor Tho. Chet-   Rob'tus Noell de Hilcott in═Matilda filia Breerton.
wood sup'stes. 6. E. 4.   Comit' Staff. 6. E. 4.

A

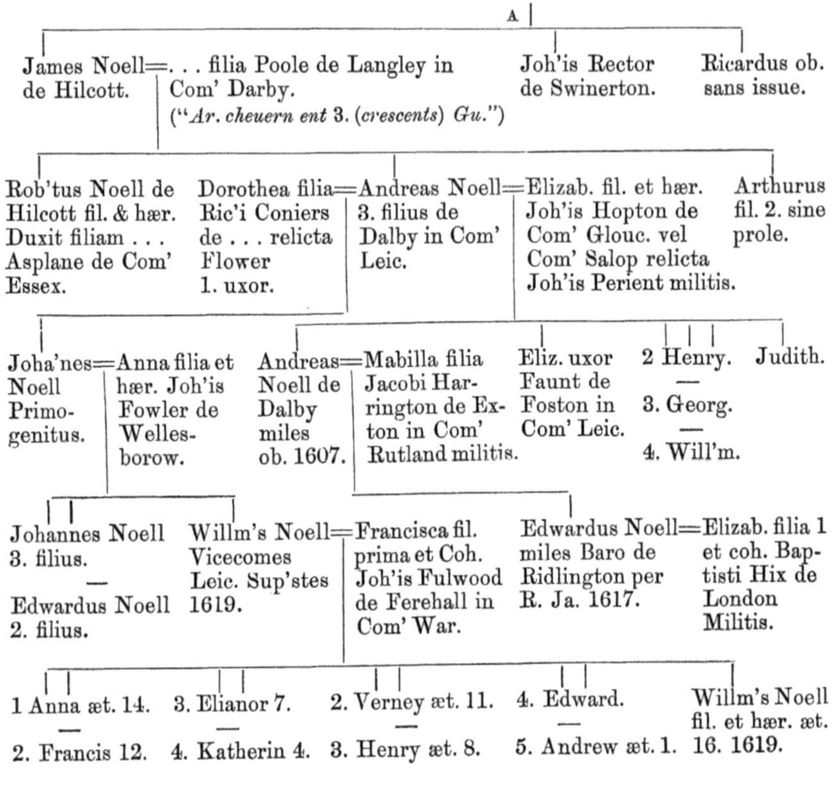

A

James Noell=... filia Poole de Langley in Com' Darby. ("*Ar. cheuern ent* 3. (*crescents*) *Gu.*") de Hilcott.　　Joh'is Rector de Swinerton.　　Ricardus ob. sans issue.

Rob'tus Noell de Hilcott fil. & hær. Duxit filiam ... Asplane de Com' Essex.

Dorothea filia=Andreas Noell=Elizab. fil. et hær. Joh'is Hopton de Com' Glouc. vel Com' Salop relicta Joh'is Perient militis. Ric'i Coniers de ... relicta Flower 1. uxor. 3. filius de Dalby in Com' Leic.

Arthurus fil. 2. sine prole.

Joha'nes Noell Primogenitus.=Anna filia et hær. Joh'is Fowler de Wellesborow.

Andreas Noell de Dalby miles ob. 1607.=Mabilla filia Jacobi Harrington de Exton in Com' Rutland militis.

Eliz. uxor Faunt de Foston in Com' Leic.　　2 Henry. — 3. Georg. — 4. Will'm.　　Judith.

Johannes Noell 3. filius. — Edwardus Noell 2. filius.

Willm's Noell Vicecomes Leic. Sup'stes 1619.=Francisca fil. prima et Coh. Joh'is Fulwood de Ferehall in Com' War.

Edwardus Noell miles Baro de Ridlington per R. Ja. 1617.=Elizab. filia 1 et coh. Baptisti Hix de London Militis.

1 Anna æt. 14. — 2. Francis 12.　　3. Elianor 7. — 4. Katherin 4.　　2. Verney æt. 11. — 3. Henry æt. 8.　　4. Edward. — 5. Andrew æt. 1.　　Willm's Noell fil. et hær. æt. 16. 1619.

(𝕹𝖔𝖇𝖑𝖊.)

ARMS. *Quarterly :—1. Argent, on a chief gules a lion passant or.　2. Barry of six argent and sable, on a canton gules a crescent or.　3. Argent, on a bend sable five bezants.　4. Gules, a chevron ermine between three eagles displayed or.*
CREST. *An eagle displayed or.*

Will'mus Noble de Rushington in Com' Leic.=Elizab. soror et Coh. Joh'is Kebell de Reresby in Com' Leic.

Georgius Noble de Reresby in Com' Leic.=Katherina filia Hen. Hoode de Boston in Com' Lincoln.

Tho. Noble de Thrussington in Com' Leic. 2. fil.=... filia Will'i Webster de Thrussington.

A

B

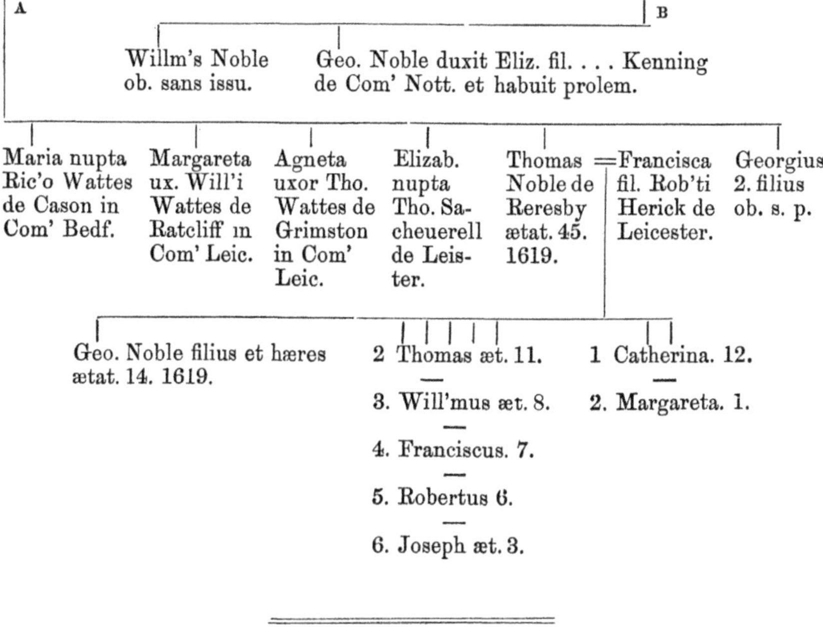

Sᵣ Beamount Dixsey.

† ARMS. *Quarterly:*—1. *Azure, a lion rampant and chief or.* 2. *Argent, a saltire engrailed between four escallops sable.* 3. *Argent, on a saltire gules five cross crosslets or.* 4. *Sable, a chevron between three mullets argent.* 5. *Sable, a bend between six étoiles or.* 6. *Argent, on a saltire engrailed gules a mullet or.* 7. *Azure, a lion rampant between five fleurs-de-lis or.* 8. *Azure, three garbs or.* 9. *Gules, seven mascles conjoined or.* 10. *Gules, a cinquefoil ermine.* 11. *Gules, a pale or.* 12. *Azure, a lion rampant argent, crowned or.* 13. *Argent, an inescutcheon within a tressure flory counterflory gules.* 14. *Gules, a saltire argent.* 15. *Azure, a wolf's head erased argent, langued gules.* 16. *Gules, a lion rampant vair.* 17. *Azure, a fess argent between three cinquefoils or.* 18. *Argent, a maunch sable, in chief a crescent for difference. (The Ulster badge.)* *Impaling quarterly:*—1. *Or, on two bars gules three water bougets of the field.* 2. *Vert, three stags trippant proper.* 3. *Gules, three bars argent.* 4. *Argent, a chevron engrailed between three trefoils slipped sable.* 5. *Sable, a saltire engrailed between four cross crosslets or.* 6. *Ermine, on a fess gules three annulets or.* 7. *Paly of six, argent and azure.* 8. *Argent, a mullet sable.* 9. *Argent, on a bend (untinctured) between six martlets gules three bezants.*

CREST. *An ounce séjant proper, ducally gorged or.*

"Two Atcheivmᵗˢ to be by monday morning
Early into the Country. Ell square."

---

† This does not form part of the Visitation, but has been inserted.

(𝔇ixie.)

ARMS. *Quarterly :—Azure, a lion rampant and a chief or; and argent, a saltire engrailed between four escallops sable.*
CREST. *An ounce séjant proper, ducally gorged or.*
MOTTO. *Quod dixi, dixi.*

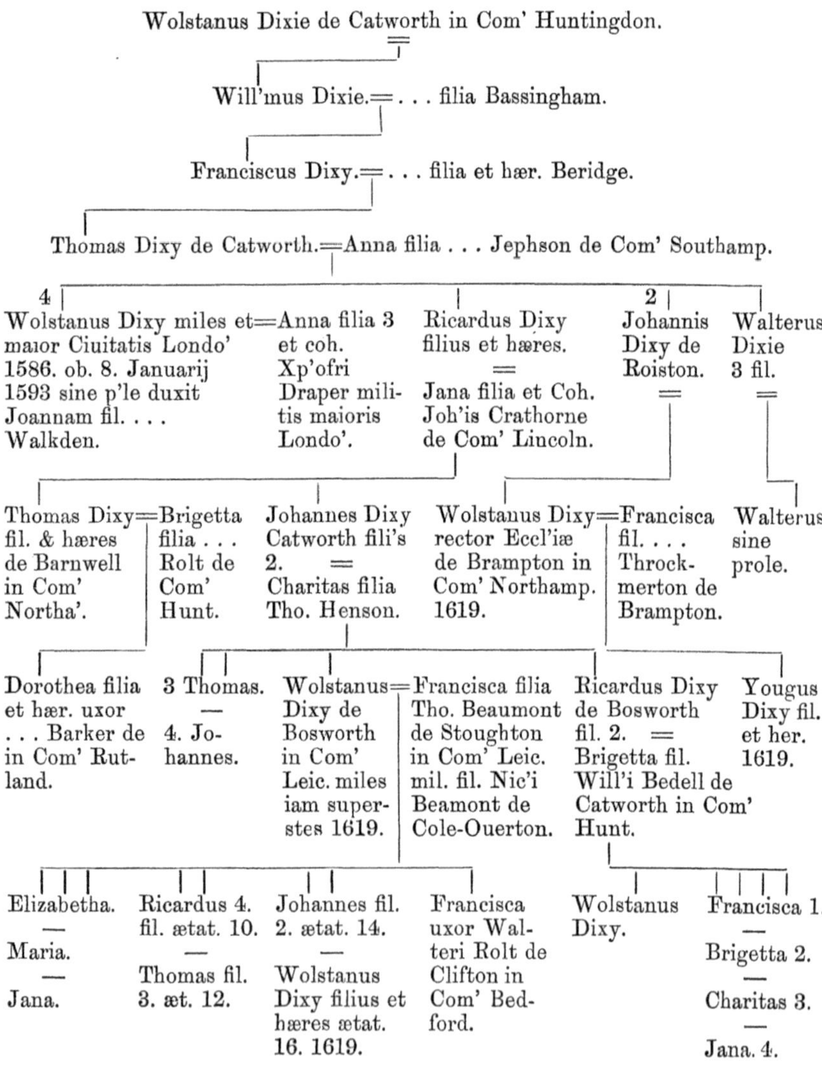

(Robertes.)

ARMS. *Per pale argent and gules, a lion rampant sable.*
CREST. *An heraldic antelope's head erased per fess argent and gules.*

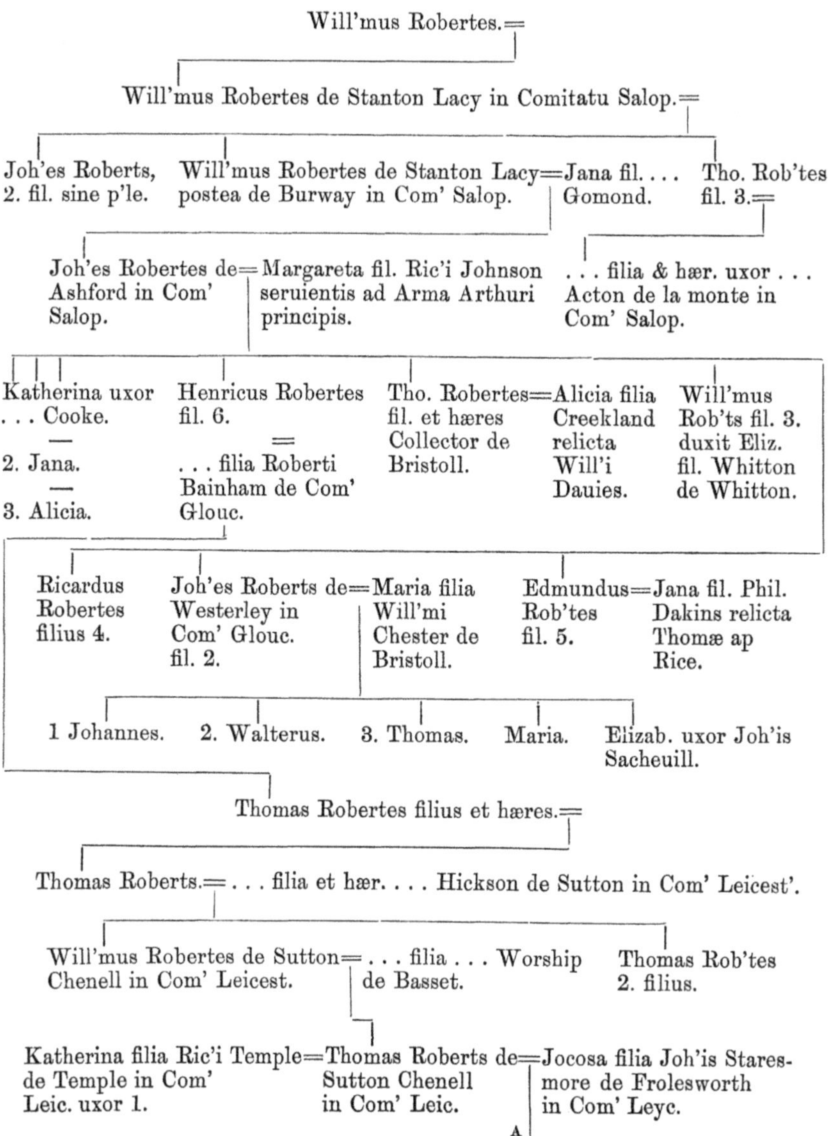

A

A |

3 | Ricardus=Dorothea filia | 1 | Will'mus Robertes=Katherina fil. Ric'i | 2 Michaell

Ricardus=Dorothea filia | Will'mus Robertes=Katherina fil. Ric'i | 2 Michaell
Roberts | Will'i Gerueis | de Sutton Chenell | Elkington de Sha- | Rob'ts 2
de Sutton | de Petling in | in Com' Leic. | well in Com' Leic. | filius ob.
Chenell | Com' Leict'. | miles. Vicecomes | relicta Rob'ti | sine prole.
in Com' | Ar. | Comitatus | Gerueis de Thorpe
Leyc. | | Leicestriæ A° | Langton in Com'
| | 1619. | Leic.

Will'mus Roberts=Francisca filia | Thomas | Geruasius | Jocosa uxor Edm.
filius et hæres | Georgij Bale de | Rob'ts 2 | 3. fil. ob. | Bale de Sading-
ætat. 24. 1619. | Carlton Curlew | fil. ætat. | s. prole. | ton in Com'
| in Com' Leyc. | 22. | | Leic.

Will'mus Rob'ts | 2 Johannes. | 3. Georgius. | 1 Elizabetha.
filius et hæres. | — | — | —
| 4. Ricardus. | 5. Thomas. | 2. Katherina.

4 Georgius | 5 Johannes | 6 Thomas | Jana uxor | Anna uxor | Lucia uxor
Robertes 4 | Robertes 5 | Robertes de | Nic'i Geary | Tho. Perkins | Tho. Acres,
filius. | filius. | Brigstock | de Barles- | de Marston | renupta
== | == | in Com' | ton. — | Jabbets in | Tho.
Elianor fil. | Dorothea filia | North'm. | Elizab. uxor | Com' War. | Chancy al's
Gilberti | . . . Lawn | == | Will'i | | Giles de
Diglin de | de London. | . . . relicta | Wright de | | Bosworth.
Couentry. | | Dudley. | Sutton.

1 Will'mus. | 1 Katherina. | 4. Elinora. | 1 Johannes. | 1 Jocosa. | Will'mus
— | — | — | — | — | Robertes.
2 Ricardus. | 2. Jocosa. | 5. Dorothea. | 2. Petrus. | 2. Dorothea.
| — | | —
| 3. Anna. | | 3. Willmus.

(𝔖turton.)

ARMS. *Quarterly:*—1. *Sable, on a bend or between six fountains, in dexter chief a mullet for difference* (STURTON). 2. *Gules, three bends engrailed or* (COWLEY, STAFFORDSH.). 3. *Gules, on a chevron between three bezants as many crosses pattée fitchée sable* (SMITH, LEICEST'SH).

CREST. *A demi friar, vested russett, skirted gules, cowled proper, in the dexter hand a discipline of three thongs, and in the sinister a church or.*

ANOTHER CREST. *An arm, couped at the elbow, erect, vested per pale or and gules, in the hand proper a griffin's head erased azure.*

Certified under the hand & seale of Sr. W. Segar Garter & confirmed to John and Edward Sturton Brothers A° 1616.

Thomas Sturton de Sturton in Comitat' Nottingham.

Thomas Sturton de Sturton in Com' Nottingh. = Dorothea filia . . . Colteclough de Com. Staff.

Georgius Stur-ton de Sturton sine prole. = . . . filia Floker de Whitwell in Com' Rutl.

Tho. Stur-ton de Sturton in Com' Nott. = Francisca filia et una hæredum Rogeri Smith de Withcock in Com' Leic.

Johannes Sturton.

Elizab. uxor Will'i Ap John de Collingham Longa in Com' Nott.

Rogerus Stur-ton de Sturton in Com' Nott. fil. et hæres. = Ellena filia notha Will'i Knyueton de Bradley in Com' Derb. ar.

Gartruda uxor Francisci Knyueton de Woodthorp in Com' Derby.

Tho. Stur-ton de Hibernia A° 1619 fil. 2. = Anna fil. Ed'ri North de Walkeringham in Com' Nott.

Elizabetha fil. & heres in custodia' Regis A° 1619.

Edwardus Sturton.

Thomas fil. 2.

Johannes Sturton de London Haberdasher 3 fil. 1619. = Margareta fil. Joh'is Climpeston de London Hosier.

Edw. Sturton de Narborowe in Com' Leic. fil. 4. iam sup'stes 1619. = Maria filia et hær. Tho. Sanderson de Wheston in Com' Leic. 1 maritus Willm's Beck de Narborowe.

Franciscus Sturton 5. filius.

—

Georgius ob. sine prole.

Humphridus Sturton fil. et hær.

—

Francisca.

—

Sara.

Erasmus Sturton filius et hæres 16. annoru' 1619.

Francisca nupta Francisco Armestronge de Corbie in Com' Lincoln Arm.

Katherina sine prole.

—

Elizab. ætat. 13. annoru'.

(Caue.)

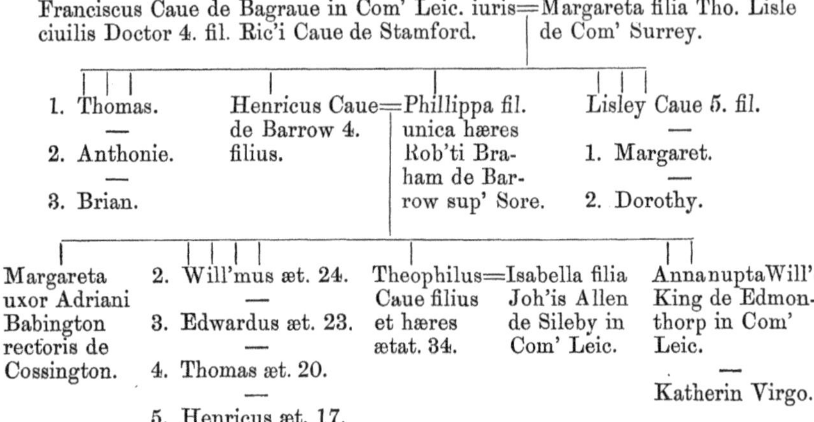

Tutbury in Com' Staff. opidum antiqui nominis floruit sub regno Saxonu' positum sub ripam fluminis Doue quod Willm's Conquestor rex Angliæ dedit Henrico de Ferrarijs qui Castrum elegans et monasterium ibidem fundauit. Hoc oppidum præbuit sedes multis familijs, inter alias familia de Burton cuius ædes ibidem dictæ Burton hall, et terræ vicinæ Burton Bache, Burton More Burton Holme, Burton hill, et Burton scheild. Ex hac familia Jacobus de Burton miles officio Scutiferi functus est regi Ric'o primo in bello Sacro et alibi, hunc Joh'es Rex fecit magistrum fofestarum quam donac'onem Henricus rex tertius confirmauit. Adhæsit hæc familia Lancastrensi et filius eius Oliuerus factus est Seneschallus honoris de Tutbury sub Johanne Gandauo D. Lancast' contra quem Ducem Ric'us Burton frater dicti Oliueri arrauiauit assisam Nonce desseisinæ filius tamen eius Willmus Burton partes Lancast'r sequutus est, atq' creatus fuit ab Henrico 6. rege Vexillarius eius. Diu habitauerunt illi apud Tutbury et Falde vicinum ubi multa priuilegia et tenuras habuere, inter quas tenura de Morton nunc Alcock de Coton Com' Stafford qui tenuit terram suam in Coton de Burton, per fidelitatem et vi⁸ viii^d annui redditus et reddendo ad obitum cuiuslibet hæredis optimum talum inuasorium, quod nuper præstitum fuit. Locus sepulturæ fuit in Capella Sc'i Stephani in monasteria beatæ Mariæ de Tutbury; Willm's Burton Vexillarius Hen. 6 regis struxit ædes apud Falde, ibidemq' habitauit Rad'us filius eius transtulit sedem ad Mafeild iuxta Okeouer in Com' Staff.; Jacobus fili's Radi ducens in uxorem Elizabetham filiam natu maximam et cohæredem Joh'is Hardwick de Lindley in Com' Leic. a° 3. H. 8. tunc mutauit sedem suam ad Lindley ubi iam a° 1619. Radulphus eius ex filio Roberto nepos movatur, et Will'mus Burton filius dicti Rad'i nunc a° 1619. inhabitat apud Falde prædictum.

ARMS. *Quarterly :—1. Azure, a fess between three talbots' heads erased or. 2. Or, three stars gules pierced of the field. 3. Azure, on a chevron argent three catharine wheels gules. 4. Azure, an eagle displayed argent, armed or. 5. Gules, a saltire engrailed argent between four mullets or. 6. Azure, semée of cinquefoils (untinctured). 7. Or, two bends cotised azure. 8. Argent, a fess gules, in chief three mullets sable. 9. Gules, three eagles displayed or. 10. Vair (untinctured), a chevron (untinctured). 11. Or, fretty sable, each joint charged with a cross crosslet fitchée argent. 12. Gules, on a bend or, three garlands vert.*

CRESTS. *First, a beacon argent, ladder or, inflamed proper. Second, out of a ducal coronet a cypress-tree vert, semée of cinquefoils or.*

(𝔓lumbe.)

ARMS. *Ermine, a bend vair, cotised sable ; impaling a bend engrailed, cotised (untinctured).*

CREST. *On a mount vert a greyhound séjant argent, collared gules.*

Walterus Plumbe de Aldeburgh in Com' Norff.

Johannes Plumbe filius Walteri.

Johannes Plumbe=Margareta filia . . . Lindsey   . . . uxor Redham de Redfilius Johannis. | de Horham in Suff.   ham in Com' Norff.

Alicia fil. Will'mi Fawnt de =Johannes Plumbe, qui per-=Maria fil. Tho. Duport
Foston in Com' Leic. relicta   quisiuit manerium de   de Shepeshed in Com'
Humfri Purifoy de Barwell   Marston in Com' Leic.   Leic. ux. 1.
in Com' Leic. uxor 2.   obijt 6. Aug. a° 1616.

Will'mus 3 filius.   Johannes   Thomas Plumbe de Marston=Elizabetha filia
—   Plumbe.   in Com' Leic. fil. & hær.   Joh'is Fortescue de
Anna.   2 filius.   superstes 1619.   Fabians in Essex.

2. Will'mus.   4. Radulphus.   Johannes Plumbe fil.   Maria.   Elizab.
—   —   et hæres ætat. 22   —   —
3. Thomas.   5. Walterus.   annoru' 1619.   Judith.   Alicia.

Katherina uxor   Margareta ux.   Maria uxor   Cornelia ux. Tho.
Joh'is Stafford   Johannis Lloyd   Rogeri Pugh   Smith de Crofts
de Huncote in   de Oswaldestrie.   renupta Ed'ri   in Com' Leyc.
Com' Leic.   Thornes.

(𝕮𝖆𝖛𝖊.)

ARMS. *Quarterly :—1. Azure, fretty argent.   2. Ermine, on a bend sable three fishes' heads erased argent.   3. Argent, a chevron between three birds vert.*
CREST. *A greyhound courant sable, collar (untinctured).*
ARMS OF SAMPSON. *Sable, a cross flory between four escallops sable.*

Ricardus Caue de Stamford in Com' Northamp.

Franciscus Caue fil. 4. de Bagraue═Margareta filia Thomæ
in Com' Leic. iuris Ciuilis Docto' │ Lisle de Com' Surrey.

Maria filia Rob'ti═Lisley Caue de Horspoole Grange═Juditha filia 2 et coh.
Sampson de │ in parochia de Thornton in Com' │ Will'mi Porter de
Carsey in Com' │ Leic. fil. 5. iam superstes. 1619. │ Escote in Com' Warr.
Suff. uxor. 1. │ │ uxor 2.

Francisca uxor Arthuri Shuger de London gent.
—
Ursula uxor Will'i Dauenport de Com' Nott.

Maria.
—
Elizabetha.
gemellæ.

Johannes Caue fil. et hær. æt. 7. annoru' 1619.
—
Lisley Caue 2. filius.

1. Rutha.
—
2. Martha.
—
3. Juditha.
—
4. Susanna.

(𝕮𝖍𝖆𝖗𝖓𝖊𝖑𝖑𝖘.)

ARMS. *Quarterly :—1. Azure, a cross engrailed or.   2. Argent, three fleurs-de-lis between six cross crosslets fitchée sable, three, one and two.   3. Argent, three garbs azure.   4. Argent, three eagles displayed gules within a bordure engrailed sable.*
CREST. *Out of a coronet (untinctured) a demi-plover or, with wings displayed argent; against it is written " a puet."*

Will'mus Charnells.═

ARMS. *A cross engrailed (untinctured).*

Nicholas Charnelles de Elmesthorp, Beulton, Swepston et Merwe in Com' Leic. Warr, et Surrey miles fil. et hæres.   ═
Cicilia.

Will'mus Charnells═Petronilla
de Snarkeston in │ fil. et hær.
Com' Leic. miles. │ Simonis
ARMS. *A cross en-* │ Bereford
grailed (untinc- │ de Snar-
tured), in chief a │ keston.
label of five points
gules.

Radulphus Charnelles filius 3.
ARMS. *A cross engrailed (untinctured), in first and second quarters a mullet (untinctured).*

Will'mus Charnelles.

Will'mus Charnelles de Snarkeston.

A═

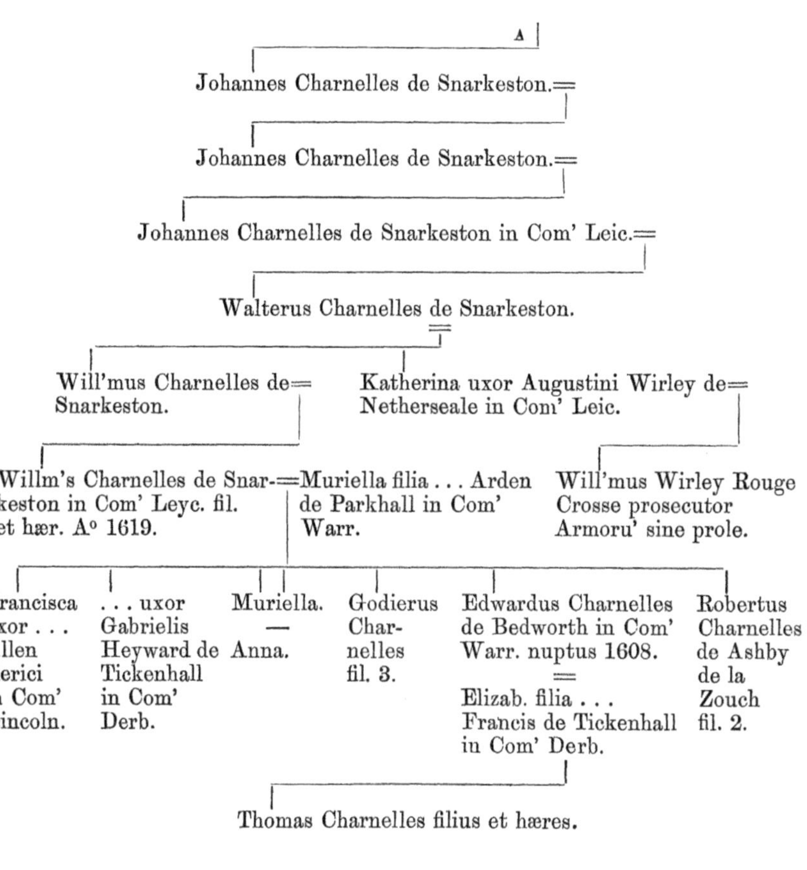

(Duport.)

ARMS. *Quarterly :—Per chevron embattled a crescent in dexter and a mullet in sinister chief, in base a lion rampant, within a bordure (all untinctured) ; and argent, three fusils in fess gules between three pellets.*

CREST. *On a rock argent guttée de sang, a falcon* proper, beaked gules ; against the wings is written "blowish."*

MOTTO. *Invitis ventis.*

"Guillaume Segar, Jartiere Roy principall d'Armes."

ANOTHER. *Per chevron embattled azure and sable, in dexter chief a crescent argent, and in sinister a mullet or, in base a lion rampant of the last, within a bordure gules.*

CREST. *On a rock vert a falcon proper.*

SUPPORTERS. *On mounts two savages wreathed about the middle with leaves all proper, each brandishing in the dexter hand a spiked club argent.*

---

* Arms tricked by Nicholas Charles, Lancaster Herald (Harl. MSS. 1113, fo. 10). "Henricus Du Porte de Shepeshed" gives the crest thus : upon a rock "a halcion" proper, in its beak a scroll inscribed "Invitis ventis," and beneath the shield a second motto, "Portum Teneo."

La Genealogie Armories et Supporteurs fort anciens de Monsieur Duport iadys demourant aupres La Riuiere au port de Caen en Normandie de la quelle ilz pvint leur nom et astheure sont resiant en le Comté de Lecestre en Angleterre.

Ces deux Sauuages defendant leur testes auec leur Bastons furent donnez a l'Ancestre du dict Guillaume a son retour en Normandie auec Guillaume le Conquerant apres la conquest d'Angleterre come ill appert par ung viel Genealogie.

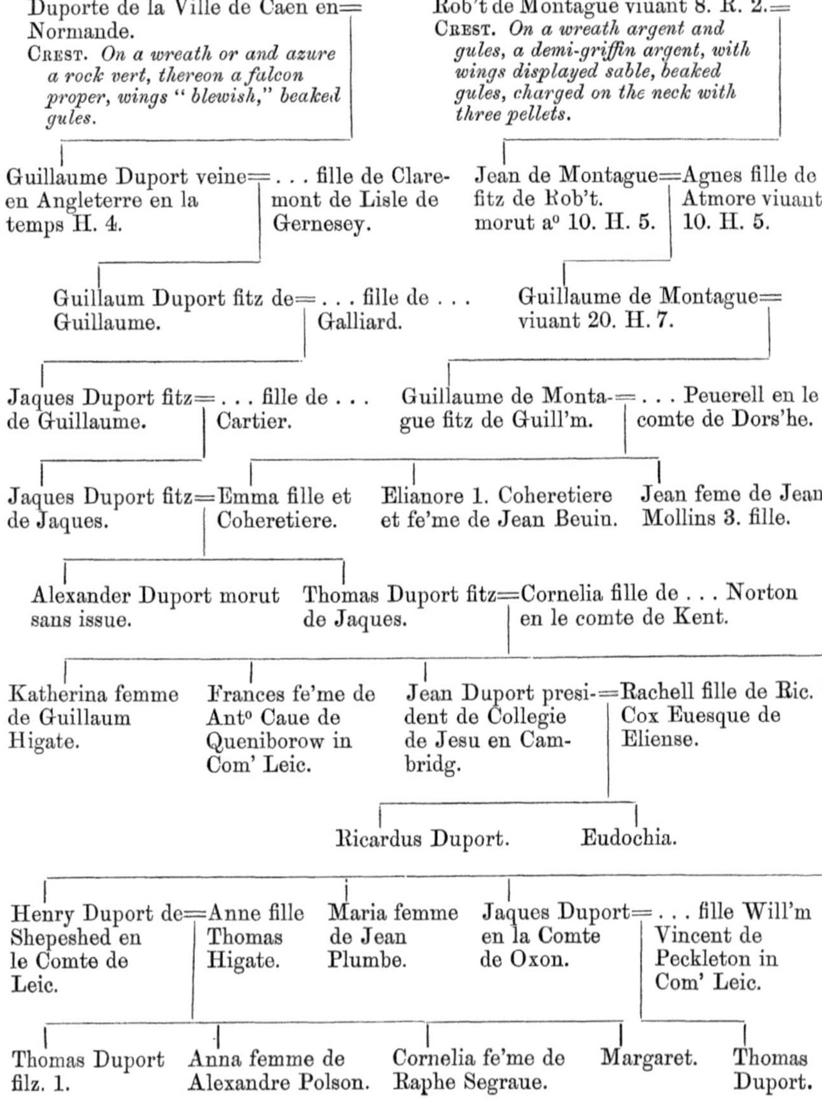

(Cave.)

Sr Alexander Caue Lo. of South Caue.=Matilda fil. Petri Maldacu' Lo. of Lockington in Com' Leic.

Piers Caue Esq. fil. et hær.=Anna filia Sr Simon Warde Knight.

Sr Alexander Caue Knight.=Amfilicia filia Galfridi Hotham militis.

Johannes Caue miles.=Maria filia et hæres Petri Genill al's Gilliott.

Sr Alexander Caue Knight.=Catherina filia Rogeri Someruile de Grindall militis. — 2 Thomas. — 3. John. — 3 Peirs. — Maria uxor Piers de See.

Sr Alexander Caue fil. et hær.=Constance filia Rogeri Leedes. — Anna uxor Gilb'ti Stapleton militis Domini de Baiton. — Piers Caue 2. filius=Anna filia Radi Ingolby. Alexandri Caue. — Johannes 3. filius. — Catherina uxor Joh'is More de Kingfeild mil. — Grace monialis.

Sr Alexander Lounde Kt. Lord of Lownd hall & Caue.=Maria fil. et hæres Alexandri Caue militis. — Pierce Caue filius=Maria filia Burdet et hær. de Bowell. — Johannes 2. filius Abbas de Selby. — Alexander 3. filius.

Rob'tus Sheffeld de Butterwick in Com' Lincoln a quo Dn's Shefeild.=... filia et unica hæres Alexandri Lownd mil. — Rob'tus Caue fil. et hæres.=Elizab. filia. Johannis Constable de Flambrough militis. — Johannes 2. fil. Vicarius de Stamford. — Beatrix.

A

A |

Radulphus Caue 2. filius. — Thomas Caue de Stamford filius et hæres.=... filia ... Passemer de Com' Essex. — Anna monialis.

Elizab. filia ... Maruin de Church=Ric'us Caue de Stamford in Com' Northamp. =Margareta filia Tho. Saxby de Com' Northamp. ux. 2. — Henricus Caue=... filia ... Belgraue. 2. filius.
Lawford in Com' Staff.

Margareta uxor Edwardi Saunders de Harrington. — Edwardus Caue a quo =Dorothea fil. et hær. Nic'i Malorie de Com' Staff. Andrewe et Boughton. — Anna filia et hæres uxor ... Marshall de Com' Nottingham.

Katherina ux. Tho. Andrewes militis. — Margeria fil. et coh. uxor Tho. Boughton de Com' War.

Tho. Caue de Stanford in Com' Northamp. miles filius 2. ob. 1558.
=
Elizab. filia 2. et coh. Johannis Danuers militis.

Anthonius Caue de Chicheley in Com' Buck. fil. 3 mercator. =Elizab. filia Tho. Louet de Astwell.

Franciscus Caue de Bagraue in Com' Leic. iuris Ciuilis Doctor. fil. 4. =Margareta fil. Thomæ Lisle de Com' Surr'.

Clement Caue fil. 6. Duxit filia' Malorie sine prole.

Ambrosius Caue mil. Cancellarius Ducatus Lancastriæ fil. 5. =Margareta fil. et coh. Will'i Willington.

Elizab. uxor Will'i Wirley de Hondesworth in Com' Staff.

Juditha fil. 1 et una heredu', uxor Will'mi filij et hæredis Will'i Chester militis maioris ciuitatis London.

Anna uxor Griffith Hampden.

Martha ux. Joh'is Newdigate.

Maria uxor Jeronimi Weston.

Margareta filia et hæres uxor Hen. filij et her. Fran. Knolles militis.

B | C |

B |

c

Katherina fil. et cohær. Tho. Colt. uxor 1. = Tho. Caue de Bagraue in Com' Leic. fil. et hær. duxit Isabella' filia' . . . Wake. = Anna filia . . . Lany uxor. 3.

Margareta filia 1. uxor. Humfredi Babington. — Dorothea 2. filia nupta Joh'i Barnard.

Lisleus Caue filius 5. a quo vide antea.

Anthonius Caue 2. fil. de Queniborow in Com' Leic. = Francisca filia Tho. Duport.

Brianus Caue 3. filius. = . . . filia Cliffe de Com' Essex.

Henricus Caue 4. fil. de Barrow. = Phillippa fil. unica et hær. Rob'ti Braham de Barrow sup' Sore.

Will'mus Caue filius sextus. = Margareta fil. et her. Georgij Clermont de Frampton in Com' Lincoln.

Alexander Caue de Bagraue et Rotherby in Com' Leic. 1619. = Anna fil. et Coheres Johis Broket Militis de Com' Hartf.

Franciscus Caue filius 2. de Barradon in Com' Rutl. = Anna soror et coh. Gregorij Durant de Barrowden in Com' Rutl.

Isabella ux. Tobiæ Chippingdall.

Tho. Caue fil. 3. de Thorpe Sacheuill in Com' Leyc. 1619. = Agnes filia Tobiæ Houghton de Kilthorp in Rutland.

Brigetta uxor Jacobi Bury de Easton in Com' Linc. — Anna ux. Tho Hunsto' de Walpoole in Norff. — Katherina uxor xroferi Cheyney de Grantham. — Dorothea uxor Arthuri Euans.

Thomas Caue fil. et hæres. — Margareta ux. Gilb'ti Bury de Easton in Com' Lincoln.

Theophilus Caue de Barrow in Com' Leic. fil. & hæres iam sup'stes 1619. Duxit Isabellam filiam Joh'is Allen de Sileby in Com' Leicest'.

Margareta uxor Adriani Babington rectoris Eccl'iæ de Cossington. — Anna uxor Will'i Kinge de Edmondesthorp in Com' Lincoln.

Willm's 2. ætat. 24. — Edwardus 3. ætat. 23. — Thomas 4. ætat. 20. — Henricus 5. ætat. 17.

Thomas Caue fil. et hæres.

Anna fil. & coh. ux. . . . Smith de Bowdon in Com' Leic.

Francisca fil. et coh. uxor . . . Jenkenson.

3. Elizab. et 4 Temperans.

Will'mus Caue fil. et hæres ætat. 10. an. 1619.

2 Tobias. — 3. Johannes.

c

c

Ricardus Caue=Barbara filia de Pickwell in Com' Leic. filius 7. | Will'i Feilding de Newenham militis.

Augustin's fil. 9.

Dorothea ux. Will'i Smith al's Harris de Withcock in Com' Leic.

Prudencia uxor Joh'is Crooke al's Blount unus sex Clericorum Cancellariæ.

Brianus Caue=Margareta filia de Ingarsby in Com' Leic. fil. 8. | Geo. Throckmorto' militis.

Brigetta uxor Francisci Tanfeild de Gaiton in Com' Northamp.

Willm's Caue de Pickwell in Com' Leyc. Duxit Elizab. fil. ... Burnell de Wingburn in Com' Nott.=Elianora filia Tho. Gray de Enuill in Com' Staff. uxor 1.

Rosa uxor Harecourt renupta ... Hunnings.

Anthonius Caue de London fil. 2. Duxit ... filiam.

3. Mathew. — 4. Ambrosius sine p'l.

Edw. Caue fil. et hær. ob. sine p'le. = Barbara fil. et coh. Will'i Deuereux militis.

1 Francisca. — 2. Maria.

Henricus=Elizab. filia Caue de Ingarsby in Com' Leic. 2. fil. et hæres. | Geo. Isham de Pitchley in Com' Northamp.

Franciscus=Margareta filia Caue fil. 3. de Clebrooke in Com' Leic. a° 1619. | Joh'is Trussell de Billesley in Com' Warr. relicta Georgij Cope.

Edwardus Caue fil. 4.

Elizab. filia et coh. Pauli Ewart de Geddington in Com' Northamp. =Johannes Caue de Pickwell in Com' Leic. sup'stes a° 1619 fil. 2.=Magdalena Bartholomei Armine de Osgoodby in Com' Lincol uxor 1.

Ricardus Caue fil. et hær. non Compos mentis a°1619.

Tho. Caue fil. 5. Clericus. = Elizab. fil. Catlin.

Anna uxor Joh'is Sherman de Leicester. — Maria uxor Steph'i Peck de Knossington in Com' Leic. — Dorothea uxor Humfr'i Gray de Basset house in Com' Leic.

Will'mus Caue fil. et hæres.

Elizabetha.

Marcia.

Will'mus Caue fil. et hæres a° 1619.=Maria filia et coh. Joh'is White de Southwick in Com' South.

2 Johannes.

3. Thomas. — 4. Franciscus.

Johannes Caue fil. et hæres.

Will'mus Caue æt. 1. anni. Maria. Anna 1. s. p.

Ex Chartis Thomæ Hasilrigge de Nowesley in Com' Leicestriæ militis.

Sciant præsentes et futuri quod ego Herbertus de Karleton rector Eccl'iæ de parua Boughton dedi D'no Anketino de Martiuall et Agneti uxori suæ et hæredibus &c. totum clameum &c. in situ unius molendini quem emi de Roberto de Tokeby in campo de Ilueston una cum molendino ibidem constructo. Hijs testibus Rad'o de Martiuall Rad'o de Medbourne, Rob'to de Tokeby, Roberto de Karleton Waltero de Billesdon et alijs.

valde antiqua.

Uniuersis hoc scriptum visuris vel audituris Rob'tus de Martiuall de Haluton et Rad'us de Martiuall salutem, Noueritis nos pro D'no Joh'e Engærie teneri D'no Anketino de Martiuall in 40 marcis soluendis eidem aut suo atturnato apud Nouesley &c. ad terminos subscriptos &c.; ita quod uterq' n'rum tenetur in solidum. Et ad istam soluc'oem loco et terminis præd'cis fideliter et plenariè faciendam obligamus nos et hæredes, et omnia bona nostra mobilia et immobilia ubicunq' existentia districtioni Vicecomitis Leicestriæ vel Balliuorum Comitatis Leicestriæ qui pro tempore fuerint siue districtioni eiusdem D'ni Anketini vel cuiuscunq' voluerit balliui, In cuius rei testimonium &c.

sanz Date.

(Martiuall.)

ARMS. *Argent, a cinquefoil sable.*

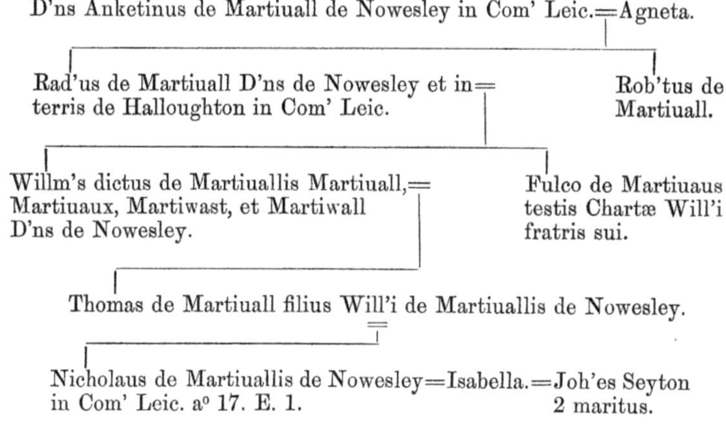

(Thame.)

ARMS. *Gules, on a chevron between three martlets or as many mullets sable, on a chief of the second three mascles of the field.*

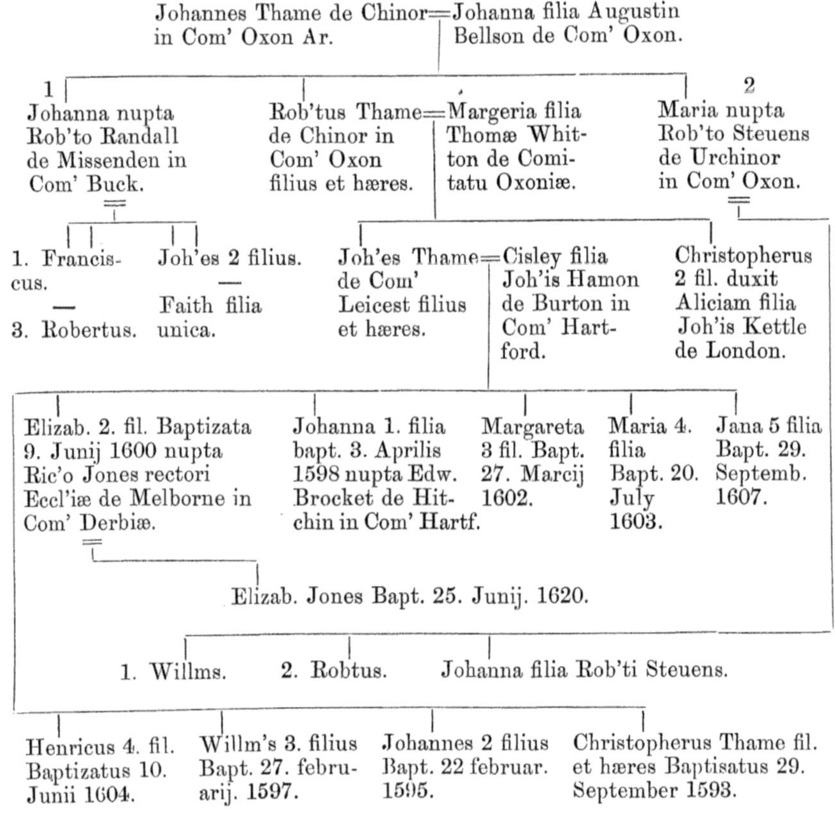

(Carrington *alias* Smith.)

ARMS. *Quarterly :—1. Argent, a cross gules between four peacocks azure. 2. Quarterly, argent and sable, in the first quarter a fleur-de-lis gules, and in the fourth, an ermine spot. 3. Argent, on a fess wavy sable three hares' heads erased or. 4. Quarterly gules and ermine, in the first and fourth quarters a goat's head erased argent. 5. Sable, three leopards' faces reversed gules, jessant-de-lis argent. 6. Ermine, a talbot passant sable. 7. Gules, on a bend or, three martlets sable.* 8. *Barry nebulée of six argent and sable, a canton gules.* 9. *Per fess ermine and or, a cross moline gules.* 10. *Or, a fess azure between two bars gemelles (untinctured).* 11. *Sable, ten bezants four, three, two, one, on a chief ermine three lozenges gules.* 12. *Gules, a fess nebulée or.*

CREST. *A peacock's head, erased azure, ducally gorged or.*

Sr Will'm Car-=Anna fil. et hær Edmundi
rington. | Farnell militis.

Sr Will'm Car-=Katherin soror Will'i Montague
rington. | Comitis Sarum.

Sr Thomas Carrington made Knight=Margaret Da. of
by the black prince ob. 4. R. 2. | Sr Rob't Rosse.

Joh'es Carrington who named=Millicent filia et hæres
himself Smith. 1446. | Rob'ti Laynham.

Tho. Smith de Riuenhall in Com' Essex. = Isabell fil. et hær. Will'i Toft de parua Baden in Essex.

Hugo Smith= 3 filius Joh'is Smith al's Carrington.

Rob'tus 2 fil.

Tho. Morton=Margareta filia nepos Joh'is | unica et hæres Morton | Will'i Wood-Archiep'i | ford de Wood-Eboru' ob. | forby et Bran-25. Decemb. | tingby. 8. H. 8.

filia et =Johannes Smith=Agneta sola fil et hær.
Cohær. | miles Baro | Joh'is Harewell de
Woode. | Scaccarij. | Wotton in Com' Warr.

(1)

|1500—
Joh'es Mor-=Hellena filia
ton Ar. fil. | . . . Roper de
et hær. | Eltham Kent.

Tho. Smith de Cres-=Maria filia et hær.
sing Temple in | Thomæ Neuill de
Com' Essex. | Holt in Com'
| Leict^r mil.

Franciscus Smith Ar.=Jana filia
filius et hæres de | et hæres
Wotton sup'stes | Joh'is
1602. | Morton.

Georgius Smith de Ashby=Anna filia Thomæ Gifford de
Foluile in Com' Leic. | Chillington in Com' Staff.

Georgius Smith=Maria filia
fil. 2 de Quene- | Ed'ri Holt
borow in Com' | de Dud-
Leyc. 1619. | deston in
| Com' War.

Tho. Smith=. . . filia
fil. 3. de | Samso-
. . . in Com' | nis Er-
Staff. 1619. | deswicke
| de San-
| don Ar.

Maria uxor
Ed'ri Man-
feild de
White place
militis.

Dorothia ux.
Cuthb'ti
Clifton de
Lithernhall
in Com'
Lanc. militis.

Anna.

Georgius fil. et hæres ætat. 5.

Edmund's æt. 4. — Robertus æt. 3.

Johannes fil. & hæres.

Franciscus .2 filius.

A

A

Franciscus Smith=Anna filia	Nicholaus.	Elizab. uxor	Anna.
miles de Ashby	Tho. Mark-	—	Tho. Haw-	—
Foluill in Com'	ham de	4. Johannes.	kins Militis	Ursula.
Leic. et Wotton	Allerton in	—	de Nash in	
in Com' Warr. aº	Com' Nott.	5. Robertus.	Com' Kent.	
1619.		—		
		6. Edward's.		

1. Maria.   4. Anna.   2. Thomas.   5. Elizabeth.   8. Dorothea.
—   —   —   —   —
2. Lucia.   Carolus Smith   3. Francis.   6. Francisca.   9. Martha.
—   miles fil. & hær.   —   —
3. Alathea. ætat. 21. annoru'   4. John.   7. Ursula.
             1619.

(Ashby.)

ARMS. *Quarterly :—Azure, a chevron ermine between three leopard's faces or ; and gules, three mallets argent.*
CREST. *Out of a mural coronet argent, a leopard's face or.*

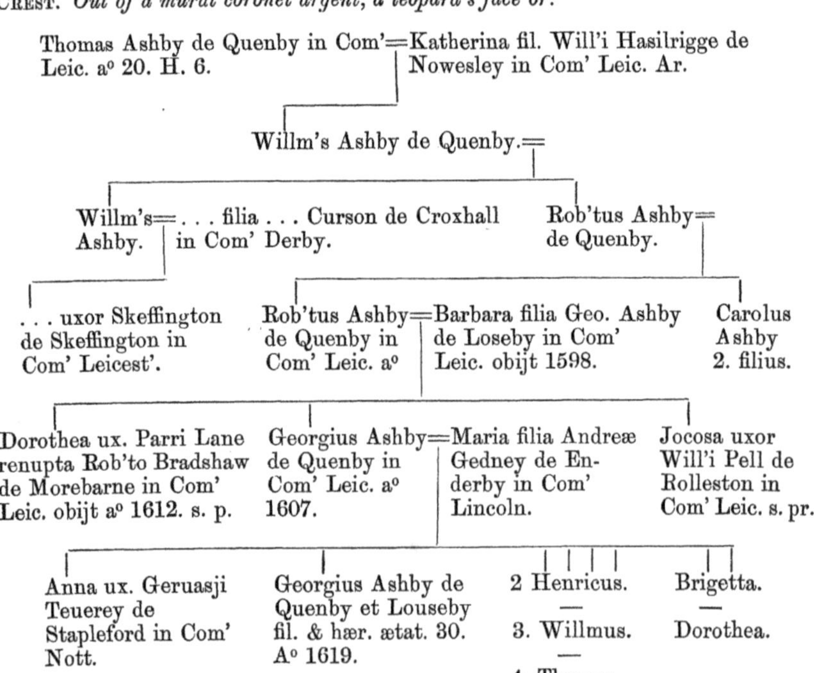

Thomas Ashby de Quenby in Com'=Katherina fil. Will'i Hasilrigge de
Leic. aº 20. H. 6.   Nowesley in Com' Leic. Ar.

Willm's Ashby de Quenby.=

Willm's=. . . filia . . . Curson de Croxhall   Rob'tus Ashby=
Ashby. | in Com' Derby.   de Quenby.

. . . uxor Skeffington   Rob'tus Ashby=Barbara filia Geo. Ashby   Carolus
de Skeffington in   de Quenby in | de Loseby in Com'   Ashby
Com' Leicest'.   Com' Leic. aº | Leic. obijt 1598.   2. filius.

Dorothea ux. Parri Lane   Georgius Ashby=Maria filia Andreæ   Jocosa uxor
renupta Rob'to Bradshaw   de Quenby in | Gedney de En-   Will'i Pell de
de Morebarne in Com'   Com' Leic. aº | derby in Com'   Rolleston in
Leic. obijt aº 1612. s. p. 1607. | Lincoln.   Com' Leic. s. pr.

Anna ux. Geruasji   Georgius Ashby de   2 Henricus.   Brigetta.
Teuerey de   Quenby et Louseby   —   —
Stapleford in Com'   fil. & hær. ætat. 30. 3. Willmus.   Dorothea.
Nott.   Aº 1619.   —
                                            4. Thomas.

(Cave.)

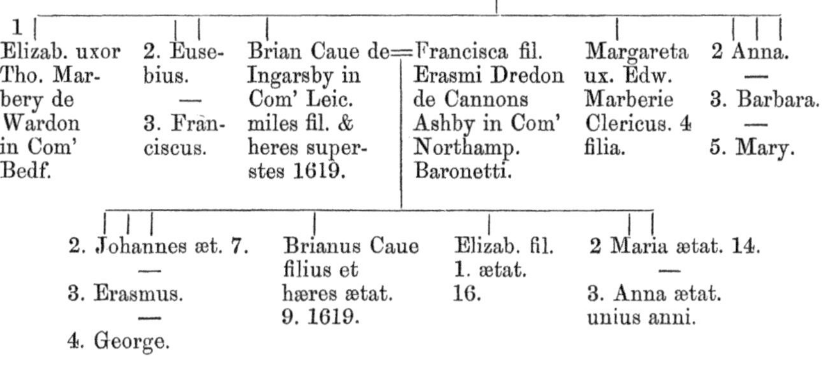

Henry Caue de Ingarsby son of Brian Caue de==Elizab. fil. Gregorij Isham de
Insgarsby. 8. son of Rich. Caue of Stanford. | Pitchley in Com' Northamp.

1			
Elizab. uxor Tho. Marbery de Wardon in Com' Bedf.	2. Eusebius. — 3. Franciscus.	Brian Caue de==Francisca fil. Erasmi Dredon Ingarsby in Com' Leic. miles fil. & heres superstes 1619.	de Cannons Ashby in Com' Northamp. Baronetti.	Margareta ux. Edw. Marberie Clericus. 4 filia.	2 Anna. — 3. Barbara. — 5. Mary.

2. Johannes æt. 7.
—
3. Erasmus.
—
4. George.

Brianus Caue filius et hæres ætat. 9. 1619.

Elizab. fil. 1. ætat. 16.

2 Maria ætat. 14.
—
3. Anna ætat. unius anni.

Ex Chartis Ric'i Swinfin de Swinfen in Com' Stafford gen' 14. September. 1619.

H. 5. Henricus dei gra' Rex Angliæ, Franciæ et D'ns Hib'niæ omnibus &c.;
Sciatis quod de gra' n'ra sp'iali de assensu D'nor spiritualium et temporalium ac ad requisic'onem com'unitatu' regni n'ri Angliæ in parliamento n'ro apud Westm' aº regni n'ri 2º tento existentium pardonauimus et relaxauimus Thomæ Swinfeen alias dicto Thomæ Lichfeld quocunq' nomine censeatur omnimodas transgressiones, offensas, misprisiones, Contemptus et impetic'ones &c. Teste meipso apud Westm' 10 die Aprilis anno regni n'ri quarto.

sub magno sigillo Angliæ.

Irrotulatur in memorand' S'ccarij aº 5. H. 5. inter recorda de termino Paschæ
ex parte rememoratoris Thesaurarij.

Sciant præsentes et futuri quod ego Joh'es de Swynfen d'ns de Swynfen dedi &c D'nis Joh'i Jones et Thomæ de Freford Capellanis, hæredibus et assignatis suis omnia t'ras et ten'ta, prata &c in villis et ham'elettis de Swynfen, Freford, et Whitinton &c Hijs testibus Rad'o de Thikbrom, Henrico Gardiner de Weford, Will'o de Bromley de Whitinton, Thomæ Menell de Hyntes et alijs. Dat. in vigilia natiuitatis S'ci Joh'is Baptistæ aº 43. E. 3.

Charta Joh'is de Swynfen in Swynfen data. aº 49. E. 3.

Ric'us 2. Ricardus dei gra' Rex Angliæ et Franciæ et D'ns Hiberniæ omnibus
balliuis &c Sciatis quod pordonauimus Rogero Lichfeld de Wigorn alias dicto Rogero Swynfen omnimoda escapia felonum catalla felonum et fugitiuor' fines amerciamenta &c. Ac insuper cum ad parliamentum n'rum apud Westm' primo die octobris aº regni n'ri decimo tentum Thomas nuper Dux Glouc' et Ric'us nuper Com' Arundell attrahentes sibi regiam potestatem fieri fecerint quandam Commissionem sub magno sigillo n'ro sibi ipsis et alijs ad eorum denominac'oem directum ad gubernac'oem n'ri et regni n'ri habendam et d'ca commissione usi fuerint iurisdictionem regiam inde super eos capientes quæ quidem Commissio præiudicialis fuit et derogatio nobis et Coronæ n'ræ ac usurpatio n'ræ regaliæ et regiæ potestatis, et super hoc præd'ci Dux et Comes eorum iniquum propsitum et regiam potestatem Colore, d'ca com'issionis continuantes attraxerint eis Thomam Comitem Warr et ipsi tres insimul manu fortè modo Guerrino cum magna potes-

tate et multitudine lig'or n'ror, insurrexerint, et apud Haringsey et alibi se congregauerint, et sic cum tali vi ad n'ram præsentiam in palacio n'ro Westm' venerint &c.   Nos Volentes ex regia n'ra benignitate gr'am facere in hac parte pardonauimus eidem Rogero fectam pacis n'ræ &c occasione d'cæ Com'issionis ac congregac'onis insurrectionis &c Teste meipso apud Westm' 26. octob. aº regni n'ri 22.

Sub magno sigillo Angliæ.

Nouerint uniu'si per præsentes me Will'um de Lichefeld alias d'cum Will'um Tauerner Armigeru' relaxasse Thomæ de Swinfen de Swynfen totum ius in quodam curtilagio iacente in Frogge Lane &c.   Hijs testibus Will'o Newport c'hr Rob'to de Swynfen et Will'o Forster de Strethay et alijs Dat. aº 12. H. 4.

SEAL. *Per chevron, in chief three leopard's faces.*
       Legend. SIGILLUM WILLIMI LICHFELD.

Sciant præsentes et futuri quod nos Will'm Swynfen et Alianora uxor mea dedimus Edmundo Crowcest de Ashby de la Zouch omnia t'ras et ten'ta n'ra quæ habemus in villis de Sutton et Cateby et alibi nobis spectantibus in Com' Leic. &c Data aº 16. E. 4.

(𝔖𝔴𝔶𝔫𝔣𝔢𝔫.)

ARMS. *Per chevron sable and argent, in chief three leopard's faces counterchanged.*
CREST. *A boar's head erased azure, charged with a crescent for difference.*

Will'mus Swynfen de Sutton temp. E. 4. aº 16.═Elianora fil. . . . Leech de

Will'mus Swynfen de Sutton Chenell═ . . . filia . . . Leeson de
in Com' Leic.   Packington.

Tho. Swynfen de Sutton Chenell.═ . . . filia . . . Geerie.

Will'mus Swynfen de═Elizab. filia . . . Cox de Sutton Chenell
Sutton Chenell.   in Com' Leic.

| Elizab. ux. . . . Farrian. | 3. Jone ux. Joh'is Fresby de Coton in Com' Leic. | 2 — Anna uxor Will'mi Cox de Darlington in Com' Leic. | 1 — Alicia nupta Joh'i Shepee de Whittington in Com' Warr. |

Richardus Swynfen═Anna filia Joh'is
de Sutton   Cotes de Elson
Chenell in Com'   in Com' Leic.
Leic.

Thomas 2. fil. Duxit
Anna' filiam . . .
Goodall de Pickleton
in Com' Leic.

Will'mus
Swynfen
3. filius.

| Katherina uxor Geo. Morris de Burbage in Com' Leic. | Johannes Swynfen fil. & hæres ætat. 24. 1619. | Anna uxor Tho. Ormeston de Thornton in Com' Leicest'. | Elizab. nupta Joh'i Elkington de Shawell in Com' Leic. |

(Wilcockes.)

Rob'tus Nowers de Knossinton in Comitatu Leicestriæ miles.

Rob'tus Nowers, fil. Roberti.

Rad'us Nowers filius Rob'ti filij Rob'ti Nowers militis fuit seisitus de diuersis terris et ten'tis cum pertinent in Knossington al's Cnossing in Com' Leic. in Dm'co suo ut de feodo, et sic inde seisitus per Cartam suam que Dat est die mercurij in vigillia assentionis a° regni Regis filij regis Ed'ri dedit feoffauit et concessit om'ia præd'ca messuag' terr' et ten't et cetera præmiss' cum pertine'n cuidam Will'o Buckland rectori Eccl'iæ de Bletherwicke habend' et tenend' &c. Et sic inde seisitus postea per Cartam suam que dat est pridie Idus feb anno regni Regis Edw. filij regis Ed'ri 12. dedit et concessit om'ia prædicta m'es terras et ten'tes et cætera præmissor' cum pert'nen' præfato Rad'o Nowers et cuidam Margeriæ filiæ prædicti Will'i Buckland ad tunc ux'i eiusdam Rad'i habend' et tenend' om'ia prædicta, m'es terras et ten'ta et cetera præmissoru' cum pertin' præfato Rad'o et Margeriæ &c. Et sic inde sæsitus idem Rad'us ob. sine exitu masculo, et habuer' exit' inter eos quendam Margeriam Nowers, Margeria ips'm superuixit et se tenuit intus p' ius hered' et inde sola fuit seisit in Dm'co suo ut de feodo, et sic inde sesit circa annu' 2. regni Regis Ric'i 2. cepit in virum quenda' Will'm Wilcockes al's dict' Hopkins virtute cuius eidem Will's Wilcocks et Margeria inde seisit' fuerunt in Dominico suo ut de feodo, et in iure ipsius Margeriæ, et sic seisitus de p'dicis terris et ten'tis habuerunt exitus inter eos quendam Will'm Willcockes &c. et postea idem Willm's vir ipsius Margeriæ obijt, post cuius mortem idem Willm's Willcockes filius prædic' Will'i et Margeriæ ut fil. et hæres propinquior ip'ius Margeriæ intrauit in omnia præde'a præmiss' &c. et sic inde seisitus obijt post cuius mortem Willm's Willcockes filius et hæres p'dici Willi in præde'is terris ten'tis cum pertin' intrauit, et inde fuit seisit &c. et postea sic seisit', obijt post cuius mortem Rob'tus Wilcockes fil's et hær. prædicti Willi in om'ia præde'a messuag' terris et ten'tis cum pertinent' intrauit &c. Et sic inde seisit obijt post mor'tem cuius Thomas Wilcockes fil. et hær. prædicti Rob'ti in om'ibus præd'cis terris et ten'tis cum pertinent' post mortem ip'ius Rob'ti intrauit et inde fuit seis' &c. Et sic Inde seisit' obijt, post cuius mortem Rob'tus Wilcockes fil. et hær. prædicti Thomæ modo tenens de om'ibus præd'cis &c. Et sil't Comptum est p' easdem euidenc' q^d prædict' ten' et tent' cum pert'ent tenent' de manerio de Knossington prædicto. &c. Et prædict' Rob'tus sic inde seisit obijt post cuius mortem Rogerus Wilcockes fil. et hær. prædicti Rob'ti in om'ibus prædict' terris et ten'tis intrauit et seisitus in D'mco suo obijt post cuius mortem Willm's Wilcockes fil. et her. prædicti Rogeri in om'ibus prædictis terris et ten'tis intrauit, et inde seisitus in prædictis terris et ten'tis pro quadam pecuniæ sum'a Galfrido Wilcockes fratri Juniori præfati Rogeri Auunculo suo per Cartam vendidit qui Galfridus sic inde seisitus in D'mco suo ut de feodo obijt post cuius mortem Thomas Wilcockes fil. et hæres præde'i Galfridi intrauit et est modo tenens.

Radulphus de Nowers de==Margeria filia Will'mi de Buckland filia et hæres.
Knossington in Com' Leic. 11. E. 2.
ARMS. *Per fess chequy or and gules, and ermine.*

Will'mus Wilcockes de==Margeria fil. & hæres Radulphi de Nowers A° 2. R. 2.
Knossington in Com' Leic.

Will'mus Wilcockes de Knossington.

Will'mus Wilcockes fil. et hæres Will'mi.

Rob'tus Wilcockes fil. & hæres Will'mi.

Thomas Wilcockes fil. et hæres Rob'ti.

A

A

Rob'tus Wilcockes de Knossington fil. & hær.

Rogerus Wilcockes fil. & hæres.

Tho. Wilcockes 2. filius Principall of Barnards Inne in London ob. sine prole.

Galfridus Wilcockes de Knossington 3. fil. et postea hæres.=Susanna 1 filia Will'mi Burton de Branson in Com' Rutl.

Willm's fil. et hæres.

Anna uxor Christop. Malson de Eagleton in Com' Rutland.

Sense nupta Joh'i Bell de Com' Bedf.

Alicia uxor Rad'i Welles de Thrumesto in Com' Leic.

Maria nupta Thomæ Rudkin de Whitsendine in Com' Rutl.

Dorothea youngest Daughter unmaried ætat. 22. 1619.

Ric'us 4. fil. ætat. 26. 1619.

Edw. 3. filius ætat. 32.

Thomas Wilcockes de Knossington fil. & her.=Maria fil. Rob'ti Woode de Warw.

Rob'tus Wilcockes 2 fil. ætat. 35.=Maria fil. Edw. Rosse de Ashwell in Com' Rutl.

(Staveley.)

Thomas Staueley de Bignell in Com' Oxon.=Margeria filia Arthuri Brooke de Okeley.

3. Elizabetha.
—
4. Temperance.

Katherina ux. Tho. Rolt de Moulton ernest in Com' Bedf.

Anna nupta Tho. Stanford de Barkby in Com' Leic.

Arthurus Staueley fil. et hæres ætat. 30. 1619.=Lucia fil. et hæres Ric'i Estwick de Wotton Bornend in Com' Bedf.

2. Thomas ætat. 28.
—
3. Eusebius æt. 26 in hib'nia.

4. Willmus æt. 23 in Oxon'.
—
5. Carolus æt. 17.

Margeria ætat. 1. mensis 14. Septemb'. 1619.

(Walker.)

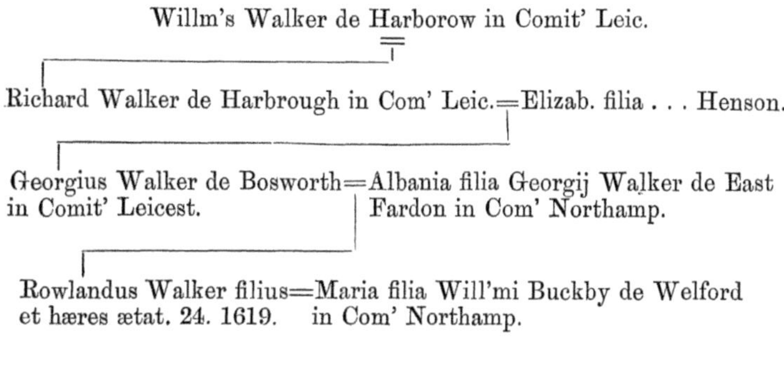

Willm's Walker de Harborow in Comit' Leic.

Richard Walker de Harbrough in Com' Leic.=Elizab. filia . . . Henson.

Georgius Walker de Bosworth=Albania filia Georgij Walker de East
in Comit' Leicest.   Fardon in Com' Northamp.

Rowlandus Walker filius=Maria filia Will'mi Buckby de Welford
et hæres ætat. 24. 1619.   in Com' Northamp.

(Chamberlaine.)

ARMS. *(Gules), on a chevron between three escallops (or) a mullet for difference.*

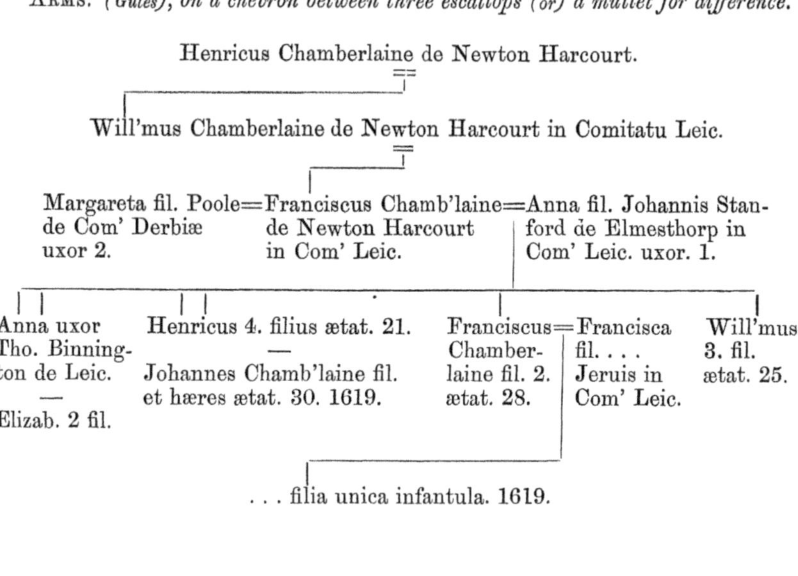

Henricus Chamberlaine de Newton Harcourt.

Will'mus Chamberlaine de Newton Harcourt in Comitatu Leic.

Margareta fil. Poole=Franciscus Chamb'laine=Anna fil. Johannis Stan-
de Com' Derbiæ   de Newton Harcourt   ford de Elmesthorp in
uxor 2.   in Com' Leic.   Com' Leic. uxor. 1.

| | | | | |
Anna uxor   Henricus 4. filius ætat. 21.   Franciscus=Francisca   Will'mus
Tho. Binning-   —   Chamber-   fil. . . .   3. fil.
ton de Leic.   Johannes Chamb'laine fil.   laine fil. 2. Jeruis in   ætat. 25.
    —   et hæres ætat. 30. 1619.   ætat. 28.   Com' Leic.
Elizab. 2 fil.

. . . filia unica infantula. 1619.

(Cutler.)

ARMS. *Argent, three dragons' heads erased gules.*

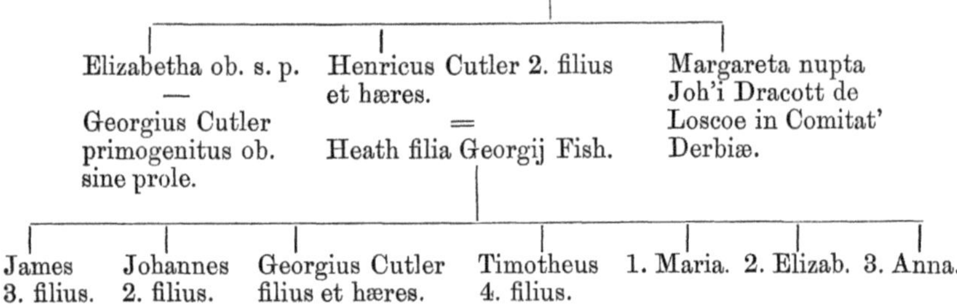

Arthurus Cutler de Bloherby in Com' Leic.=Margareta filia Henrici Herne.

Elizabetha ob. s. p.	Henricus Cutler 2. filius et hæres.	Margareta nupta Joh'i Dracott de Loscoe in Comitat' Derbiæ.
Georgius Cutler primogenitus ob. sine prole.	Heath filia Georgij Fish.	

James 3. filius.	Johannes 2. filius.	Georgius Cutler filius et hæres.	Timotheus 4. filius.	1. Maria. 2. Elizab. 3. Anna.

(Chester.)

ARMS. *Ermine, on a chief sable a griffin passant with wings endorsed argent.*

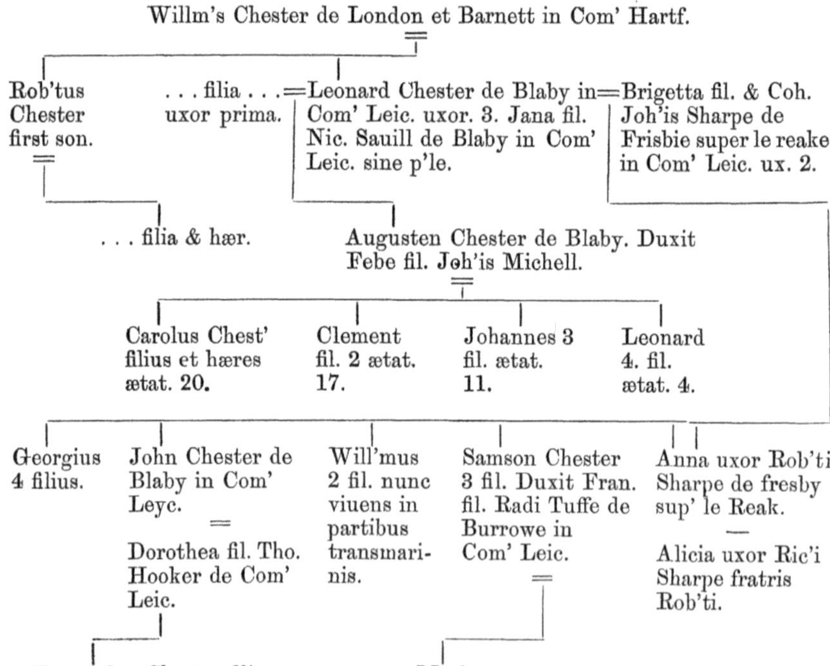

Willm's Chester de London et Barnett in Com' Hartf.

Rob'tus Chester first son.

... filia ... =Leonard Chester de Blaby in=Brigetta fil. & Coh. uxor prima. | Com' Leic. uxor. 3. Jana fil. | Joh'is Sharpe de Nic. Sauill de Blaby in Com' | Frisbie super le reake Leic. sine p'le. | in Com' Leic. ux. 2.

... filia & hær.

Augusten Chester de Blaby. Duxit Febe fil. Joh'is Michell.

Carolus Chest' filius et hæres ætat. 20.	Clement fil. 2 ætat. 17.	Johannes 3 fil. ætat. 11.	Leonard 4. fil. ætat. 4.

Georgius 4 filius.	John Chester de Blaby in Com' Leyc.	Will'mus 2 fil. nunc viuens in partibus transmarinis.	Samson Chester 3 fil. Duxit Fran. fil. Radi Tuffe de Burrowe in Com' Leic.	Anna uxor Rob'ti Sharpe de fresby sup' le Reak.
	Dorothea fil. Tho. Hooker de Com' Leic.			Alicia uxor Ric'i Sharpe fratris Rob'ti.

Leonardus Chester filius et hæres ætat. 10. 1619.

Maria.

(Grey.)

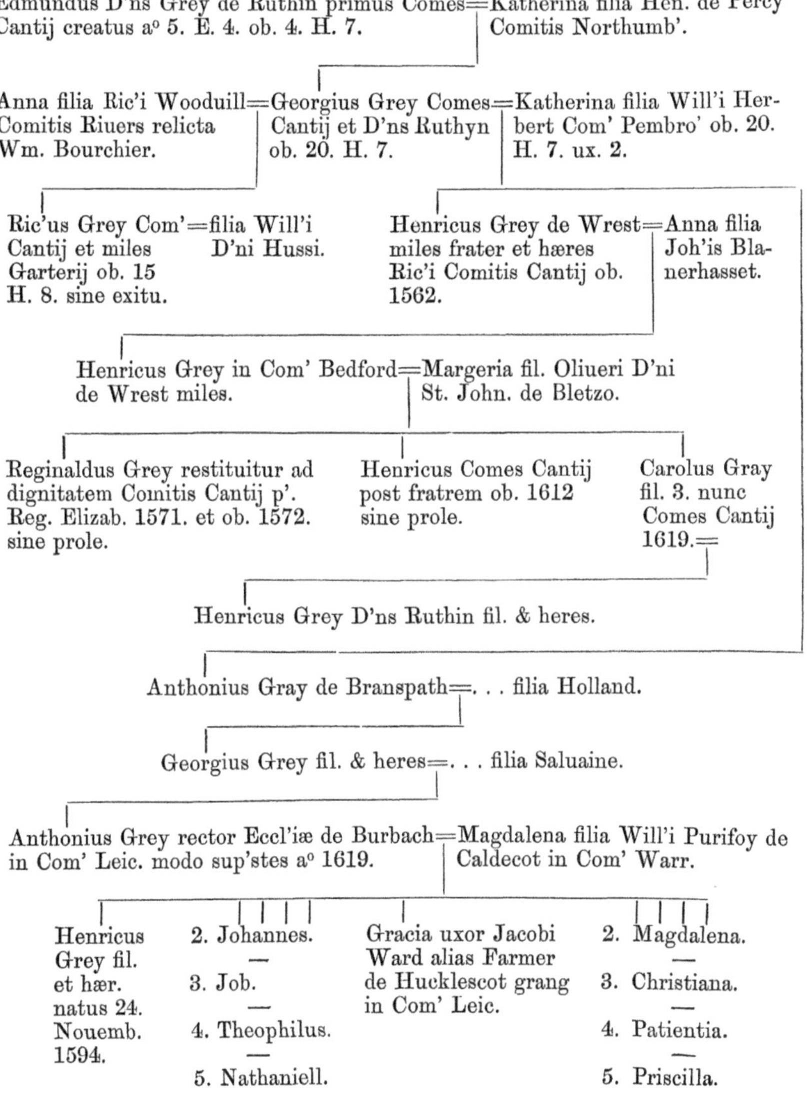

Edmundus D'ns Grey de Ruthin primus Comes=Katherina filia Hen. de Percy
Cantij creatus aᵒ 5. E. 4. ob. 4. H. 7. | Comitis Northumb'.

Anna filia Ric'i Wooduill=Georgius Grey Comes=Katherina filia Will'i Her-
Comitis Riuers relicta | Cantij et D'ns Ruthyn | bert Com' Pembro' ob. 20.
Wm. Bourchier. | ob. 20. H. 7. | H. 7. ux. 2.

Ric'us Grey Com'=filia Will'i   Henricus Grey de Wrest=Anna filia
Cantij et miles   D'ni Hussi.   miles frater et hæres | Joh'is Bla-
Garterij ob. 15   Ric'i Comitis Cantij ob. | nerhasset.
H. 8. sine exitu.   1562.

Henricus Grey in Com' Bedford=Margeria fil. Oliueri D'ni
de Wrest miles. | St. John. de Bletzo.

Reginaldus Grey restituitur ad   Henricus Comes Cantij   Carolus Gray
dignitatem Comitis Cantij p'.   post fratrem ob. 1612   fil. 3. nunc
Reg. Elizab. 1571. et ob. 1572.   sine prole.   Comes Cantij
sine prole.   1619.=

Henricus Grey D'ns Ruthin fil. & heres.

Anthonius Gray de Branspath=. . . filia Holland.

Georgius Grey fil. & heres=. . . filia Saluaine.

Anthonius Grey rector Eccl'iæ de Burbach=Magdalena filia Will'i Purifoy de
in Com' Leic. modo sup'stes aᵒ 1619. | Caldecot in Com' Warr.

Henricus Grey fil. et hær. natus 24. Nouemb. 1594.	2. Johannes. — 3. Job. — 4. Theophilus. — 5. Nathaniell.	Gracia uxor Jacobi Ward alias Farmer de Hucklescot grang in Com' Leic.	2. Magdalena. — 3. Christiana. — 4. Patientia. — 5. Priscilla.

(Croft.)

ARMS. *Quarterly :—1. Lozengy argent and azure.   2. Or, a chevron between three leopards' faces gules.   3. Azure, on two bars or three martlets gules.   4. Or, on two bars gules three water bougets argent, in chief an annulet for difference.*
CREST. *A wyvern's head couped (untinctured).*

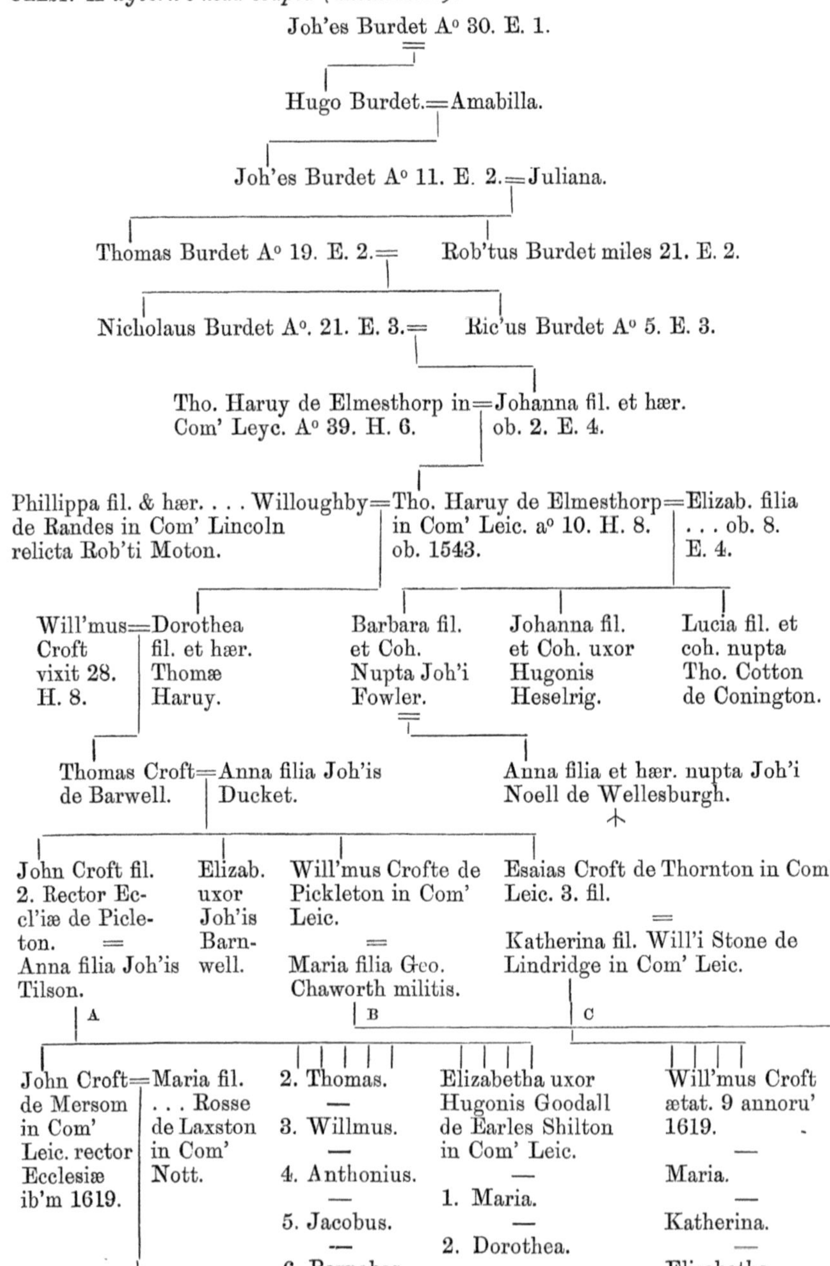

B

| Will'mus Croft fil. primogenitus obijt ante patrem 14 Nouemb' 1612 sine prole. | Thomas Croft de=Pickleton in Com' Leic. iam sup'stes 1619. | Susanna filia Tho. Wright de Snelson in Com' Darb. | Dorothea ux. Tho. Wightman de Hinkley in Com' Leic. | Gracia uxor Tho. Auerey de Fleckney in Com' Leic. clerici. |

| Anna uxor. Hen. Meade de Narborow in Com' Leic. | Maria uxor Ric'i Burdet de Mousley in Com' Leic. | Elizab. uxor Hugonis Goodall de Erle Shilton in Com' Leic. | Georgius. — Georgius. | Henricus. — Katherina sine prole. |

(Bale.)

ARMS. *Quarterly :—Per pale vert and gules, an eagle displayed argent, armed or ; and azure, three spears in bend argent, staffs or.*
CREST. *A demi-lion rampant, couped gules, grasping the handle of a broken spear erect or.*

Signed by W[m] Segar Garter to S[r] John Bale of Curlew.

Joh'es Bale de Carlton Curlew in Com' Leic.

| Joh'es Bale de Carlton Curlew in Com' Leic. s. p. | =Johanna filia . . . Pettie. | Rob'tus Bale de Carleton Curlew filius 2. | =Joanna fil. . . . Gamble de Burton Ouerey in Com' Leic. |

| Edwardus Bale filius primogenit's s. p. | Joh'es Bale de Carleton Curlew et Sadington in Com' Leic. miles iam sup'stes. 1619. | =Francisca filia Barnardi Brocas de Com' South. | Katherina ux. Tho. Sanderson de Wheston in Com' Leic. |

| Edmundus Bale de Sadington in Com' Leic. fil. 5. 1619. | =Jocosa filia Ric'i Robertes de Sutton Chenell in Com' Leic. | Franciscus Bale de London Marcator. fil. 4. a° 1619. | =Margareta fil. Joh'is Manning de London mercatoris. | Johannes Bale de Sadington fil. 3. |

| 1 Elizabetha. — 2. Francisca. | 3. Dorothea. — 4. Jocosa. | Will'mus Bale filius 1. ætat. 9. annorum. | 2 Johannes. — 3. Ricardus. | Anthonius Bale filius et hæres. | Filia. |

| Georgius Bale de Carlton in Com' Leic. fil. primogenitus. | =Elizab. filia Valentini Hartop de Burton Lazers in Com' Leic. | Rob'tus Bale de Carlton in Com' Leic. 2 filius s. p. | =Alicia filia . . . Couper de Thromaston in Com' Leic. |

A

A |

| Francisca uxor Will'i Roberts de Barwell in Com' Leic. | Johannes Bale de Carleton Curlew filius et hær. iam super-stes 1619. | =Emma filia . . . Will'i Halford de Wellam in Com' Leic. | Valentinus Bale de Humbers-ton in Com' Leic. fil. 2. 1619. | =Elizab. filia et hæres Tobiæ Chipindale filij et hæredis Johannis Chipindale Doct. iuris Ciuilis. |

| Johannes Bale ætat. 2. anno-ru' 1619. | Will'mus 2. fil. æt. 1. anni. | Georgius 3. fil. ætat. 2. annoru' 1622. | Franciscus 4. filius æt. dimidij anni. | Johannes 1. — Elizab. 2. | 2 Emma 3. men-sis. |

(Everard.)

ARMS.   *Quarterly :—1. Gules, on a fess between three étoiles argent as many mullets sable.   2. Argent, on a chief sable three mullets of the field within a bordure of the second bezantée.   3. Argent, on a fess between three bears' heads erased sable, muzzled or, as many bezants.*
CREST.   *A man's head couped at the shoulders proper, crined sable, having on his head a cap or, charged with three bars wavy of the second.*

Rob'tus Euerard de Shenton in=Margareta filia Tho. Woluerston de
Com' Leic.   Wood in Com' Staff.

| Will'mus Euerard de Newbold Verdon in Com' Leic. fil. 2. | =Elianora filia Will'i Latham de Noneaton in Com' Warr. | Samsonus Euerard filius tertius. | John Euerard de Pickleton in Com' Leic. fil. 4. modo superstes 1619. | =Jana filia . . . Madock de Noneaton in Com' War. |

| Johannes Euer-ard de Barleston in parochia de Bosworth fil. & hær. 1619. | =Elizab. soror Tho. Cockaine de Lon-don mi-litis. | Christopherus Euer-ard de Deane in Com' Northamp. 2 filius. = Elizab. filia . . . Palladay. | Marmaducus Euerard de Barleston in Com' Leic. Duxit Margt Maruin. = | Stephanus Euer-ard.   — Anna uxor Ric'i Webster de Stanton subter Barden in Com' Leic. |

| Anna uxor Tho. Mercy de Glapthorn in Com' Northamp. | 2 Jacobus. — 3. Petrus. | Johanne Euerard Doctor Theologiæ. | 1 Johannes. — 2. Ricardus. |

| Jana uxor Nichi Gorston de Thur-kaston in Com' Leic. renupta Gabrieli Rarwick in Com' Nott. | Maria ux. Joh'is Snelling de London. | Joh'es Euer-ard de Pickleton fil. et hær. 1619. | =Anna filia Walteri Aston de Lougdon in Com' Staff. | Thomas Euer-ard de Pickleton in Com' Leic. filius 2. | =Maria filia . . . Rocke de Lon-don. |

Hester fil. unica ætat. 3. annoru'
et dimid' 1619.

Maria unica filia ætat. 4
annoru'.

(𝔅𝔯𝔲𝔡𝔫𝔢𝔩𝔩.)

ARMS. *Quarterly :*—1. *Argent, a chevron gules between three morions azure.* 2. *Ermine, on a chevron gules three escallops argent.* 3. *Gyronny of eight or and sable.* 4. *Azure, a bend cotised between six cross crosslets fitchée or.* 5. *Sable, a stag's head caboshed argent, attired or, between the attires a cross pattée fitchée of the last, in its mouth an arrow barwise azure, barbed of the second.* 6. *Paly of six argent and azure, on a chief sable two swords in saltire of the first, hilted and pomelled or.* 7. *Sable, three fusils in fess argent.* 8. *Argent, on a bend engrailed sable three mullets of the field.*

CRESTS. *First. A sea-horse with tail nowed, charged on the breast with a crescent for difference (untinctured). Second. A talbot statant, ducally gorged (untinctured). Third. An arm couped at the shoulder, embowed vert, the hand proper, holding a spiked club with sling attached or.*

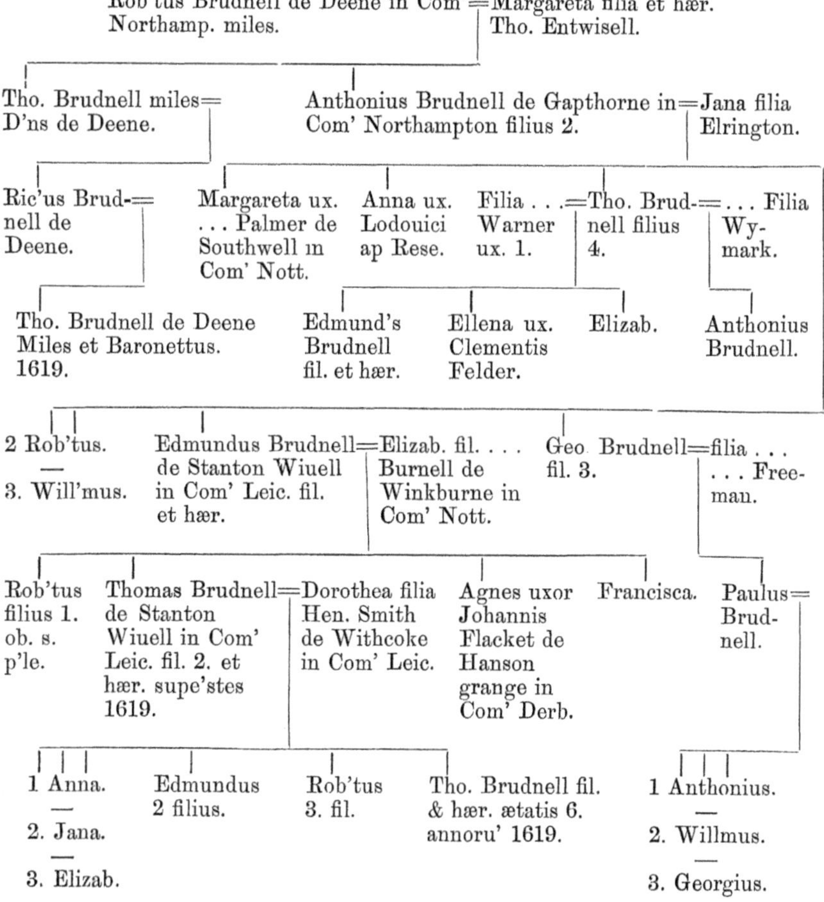

(Halford.)

Halford.=

Ricardu' Halford de Chepston in Com' North'ton.=   Will'mus Halford.=

Andreas Halford de Wistow in Com' Leic. fil. et hær. duxit Johannam filiam ... Barret de Medburne in Com' Leic. s. p.

Edwardus Halford filius 2.=Dionisia fil. ... Bury de Com' Rutland.

... filia uxor Rob'ti Henson de Slapton in Com' North'ton.

Rogerus Halford.=

Ric'us Halford de Wistow in Com' Leic. filius et hæres 1619.
=
Isabella filia Geo. Bowman de Medburne in Com' Leic.

Johannes Halford de Kebworth in Com' Leic. fil. 2. 1619.
=
Johanna filia ... Coleman de Turlangton in Com' Leic.

3. Andrea.
—
4. Willmus.

Dionisia uxor ... Sprigge de Langton in Com' Leic.
—
Elizab.
—
Agnes uxor Tho. Fauson de little Bowden in Comit' North'ton.

Willm's Halford de Wellam superstes 1619.

Andreas fil. et hæres æt. 16. annoru'.

Georgius 2 fil. æt. 12.

Johanna.

Johannes fil. primogenitus.

Ricardus ætat. 2.

(Halford.)

Willm's Halford.=

Rogerus Halford filius Will'mi.=Gracia filia Brodgate.

Willm's Halford de Wellam in Com' Leic. fil. et hæres superstes 1619.=Jana filia Nichi Foxley de Blakesley in Comitatu Northa'.

Ricardus Halford de Edithweston a quo vide Rutland. =

Emma uxor Joh'is Bale de Carleton Curlew in Com' Leic.

Edwardus Halford 2. filius.

Anthonius Halford de Lilbourne in Com' Northamp' fil. 3. 1619.=

Rogerus Halford de London Mercator fil. 6.

Gracia uxor Milonis Bussie de Hether in Com' Lincoln.

Henricus Halford de London Mercator fil. 4.

Emma.   Edwardus fil. et hær.   Nicholaus.

A |

| Elizab. fil. Edm. Bussy de Hether in Com' Lincoln mil. quæ ob. sine p'le. | Willm's Halford de Wellam filius et hær. superstes 1619. | Elizab. fil. Tho. Elmes de Greenes-norton in Comitat' Northamp. ux. 2. | Joh'es Hal-ford de Shankton in Com' Leic. fil. 5. | Jana filia . . . Mathei Saunders de Shankton militis. |

Jana.   Willm's Halford filius et hær. ætat. 4. annoru' 1619.   Thomas fil. 2.

(Carrington *alias* Smith.)

ARMS. *Quarterly :—1. Argent, a cross gules between four peacocks azure. 2. Quarterly argent and sable, in the first quarter a fleur-de-lis gules, and in the fourth an ermine spot. 3. Gules, a saltire ermine. 4. Lozengy or and gules, on a canton per pale (untinctured) a . . . ? 5. Gules, billetée a lion rampant or. 6. Bendy of six, over all a chevron (untinctured). 7. Or, two bars nebulée sable, a canton ermine. 8. Azure, a fleur-de-lis ermine. 9. Bendy of six gules and vert, a chevron ermine. 10. Bendy of six or and azure, a canton ermine. 11. Or, a chevron gules, a chief indented vert. 12. Lozengy or and sable.*

S'r Michaell Carrington Standard bearer═ to King R. the first obijt in terra sancta.

. . . Carrington sonne of S'r Michaell.═

S'r Will'm Carrington Knight by E. 1.═Anna filia et hæres Edmundi Farnell militis.

| Edm. Carington was at the Battell of Striuelin in Scotl. 1333. | Katherin fil. et coh. Tho. Heriell mil. | S'r Will'm Carrington fil. et hær. 1340. at the Battell of Sluce. | Katherina soror Will'mi Montague Comitis Sarum. |

| Sir Tho. Carrington made Kt.═Margaret fil. by the black prince ob. 4. R. 2. Rob'ti Rosse sepultus black friers London. militis. | | Michaell. 2. fil. taken prisoner in a fight at sea before Rochell & caried into Spaine where he died. |

| Edm. Carington═Jana filia 1. son. ob. 21. Joh'is Ferrus R. 2. 1397. militis. | | John Carrington who named═Millicent filia himself Smith 1446. Sepult. et hær. Robti apud Riuenhall. Laynham. |

| Tho. Smith of Riuenhall in Com' Essex 1. fil. ob. 1504 sepultus apud Riuenhall. | Isabella fil. et hær. Will'mi Toft de Little Badew in Com' Essex. | Hugo Smith 3. filius. | Robertus Smith 2. filius. | Joh'es Smith 4. filius. |

A | U

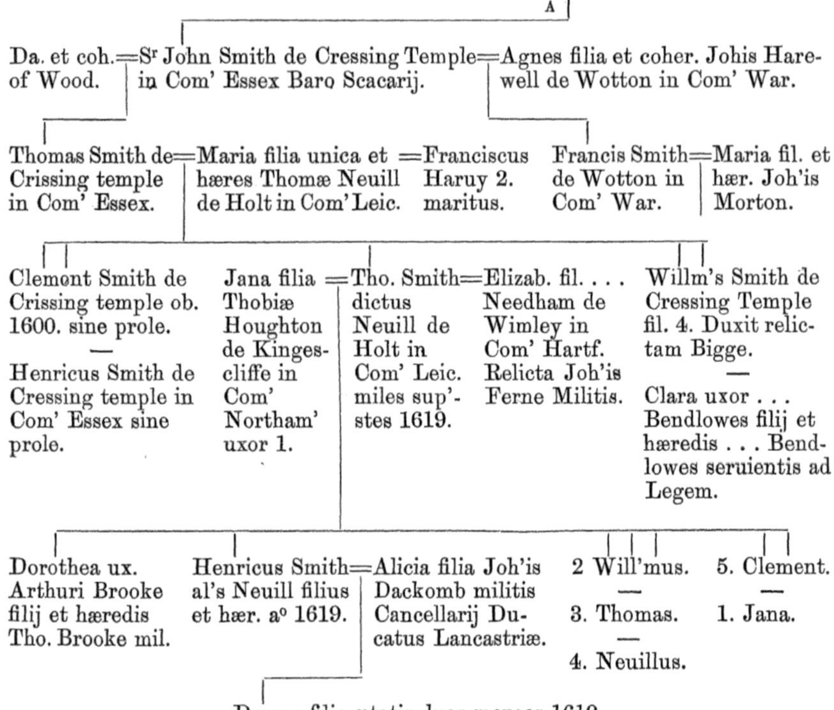

A

Da. et coh. = Sr John Smith de Cressing Temple = Agnes filia et coher. Johis Hare-
of Wood. | in Com' Essex Baro Scacarij. | well de Wotton in Com' War.

Thomas Smith de = Maria filia unica et = Franciscus   Francis Smith = Maria fil. et
Crissing temple | hæres Thomæ Neuill   Haruy 2.   de Wotton in | hær. Joh'is
in Com' Essex. | de Holt in Com' Leic. maritus.   Com' War. | Morton.

Clemont Smith de   Jana filia = Tho. Smith = Elizab. fil. . . .   Willm's Smith de
Crissing temple ob.   Thobiæ   dictus   Needham de   Cressing Temple
1600. sine prole.   Houghton   Neuill de   Wimley in   fil. 4. Duxit relic-
—   de Kinges- Holt in   Com' Hartf.   tam Bigge.
Henricus Smith de   cliffe in   Com' Leic. Relicta Joh'is   —
Cressing temple in   Com'   miles sup'- Ferne Militis.   Clara uxor . . .
Com' Essex sine   Northam'   stes 1619.   Bendlowes filij et
prole.   uxor 1.   hæredis . . . Bend-
                                  lowes seruientis ad
                                  Legem.

Dorothea ux.   Henricus Smith = Alicia filia Joh'is   2 Will'mus.   5. Clement.
Arthuri Brooke   al's Neuill filius | Dackomb militis   —   —
filij et hæredis   et hær. aº 1619. | Cancellarij Du-   3. Thomas.   1. Jana.
Tho. Brooke mil. | catus Lancastriæ.   —
                              4. Neuillus.

Dorcas filia ætatis duas menses 1619.

(Peck.)

Ric'us Peck de Wakefield. = Margareta filia et hær. . . . Haselden.

Ric'us Peck obijt   Joh'es Peck iurisperitus = Isabella filia Joh'is   Tho. Peck
in teneris.   filius 2. | Lacy.   3. filius.

Margareta ux.   Jana ux.   Ric'us Peck = Johanna filia   Rob'tus 2   Katherina
Morton.   Ric'i   filius et | Joh'is Har-   filius.   ux. Scar-
          Iorton.   hæres. | rington Ar.   gill.

A

A

3. Johanna.　　　Ric'us Peck fil.=Alicia fil. . . . Middleton　　1 Elizabetha.
　　　　　　　　　et hæres.　　de Stokeld.
4. Margareta.　　　　　　　　　　　　　　　　　　　　2. Isabella.

1 Isabella.　　　Johanne Peck de=Jana fil. Joh'is Anne　　3 Anna.
　　　　　　　　Wakefeild in　　de Freckley in
2. Margareta.　　Com' Ebor'.　　Com' Ebor'.　　　　　4. Elizab.

Ric'us Peck filius et hæres de=Anna filia Joh'is　　4 Will'mus.　　3. Thomas.
Wakefeild in Com' Ebor'.　　Hotham militis.

1 Johannes.　　　Ricardus Peck=Katherina fil. Will'i　　Elizab. uxor Rad'i
　　　　　　　　3. fil. et hæres.　Vauasour militis.　　Vauasor filius 2.
2. Thomas s p.　　　　　　　　　　　　　　　　　Will'mi Vauasour.

Joh'es Peck de Aston=. . . filia　　Nicholaus Peck de=Alicia filia　　Franciscus
in Com' Rutland　　Kirke.　　Topcliff in Com'　　Briani　　filius 6.
fil. 2.　　　　　　　　　　　Eboru'.　　Bradford.

Joh'es　　Willm's　　Ric'us Peck de=. . .　　Jasperus　2 Ricardus.　4. Johannes.
Peck de　3. fil.　　Ridlington in　　filia　　fil. et
Ridling-　　　　　Com' Rut-　　Seuens.　her.　　3. Nicho-　1. Dorothea.
ton.　　　　　　land fil. 2.　　　　　　　　　laus.

Eustacius　　　Johannes Peck de Ridlington in=Margeria filia . . . Passon de
Peck.　　　　Com' Rutland fil. 2.　　　Stanford.

Johannes Peck de=　　Prudencia ux. Will'i　　Will'mus Peck de=Elizab. fil.
Bourne in Com'　　Nedham de Hickling　　villa Leic. fil.　　Hugonis
Lincolne fil. et　　in Com' Nott.　　3 superstes　　Hunter de
hæres.　　　　　　　　　　　　1619.　　　Leic.

Reginaldus.　Johannes filius　　Richard filius 2.　　Hugo Peck filius et　　Elizabeth
　　　　　　et hæres.　　ob. sine p.　　hær. æt. 8 annor'.　　ætatis 12.

Stephanus Peck de　Juditha　　Rebecca uxor　　Margeria　Alicia uxor　Anne ux.
Knossington in Com'　ux. Joh'is　Rob't Smith　　ux. Will'i　Tho. Turuey　Will'
Leic. fil. 2. superstes　Lowth de　de Barlithorp　　Musson　　de Collis-　Wigbett
1619.　　=　　Twiford　in Com'　　de Scal-　weston in　de Stan-
Maria filia Will'i　in Com'　Leic.　　　　ford in　　Com'　　ford in
Caue de Pickwell in　Leic.　　　　　　　Com'　　Northamp.　Com'
Com' Leic.　　　　　　　　　　　　Leic.　　　　　　Lincon.

B

B

Willms Peck de Nottingham fil. primogenitus. = ... filia Will'i Peck de Spickesford in Com' Norff.

Elizab. uxor Hen. Dixson de Barston in le Vale in Com' Leic.

2 Johannes. — 3. Stephanus. — 4. Simon Peck a minister. = Joane Pope of Deping in Com' lincon.

5 Franciscus. — 6. Thomas.

Anna Maria. } ux. Wil'i Harrison of Kegworth in com' leicest'.

Phillippa. — Blanchea.

Thomas fil. et hær. æt. 2 ob. sine pr.

Will'mus æt. 2 filius hæres.

3 John. — Thomas.

Simon æta. 5. 1635.

Stephen æta. 2. 1635.

Marie. — Elizabeth.

Joane.

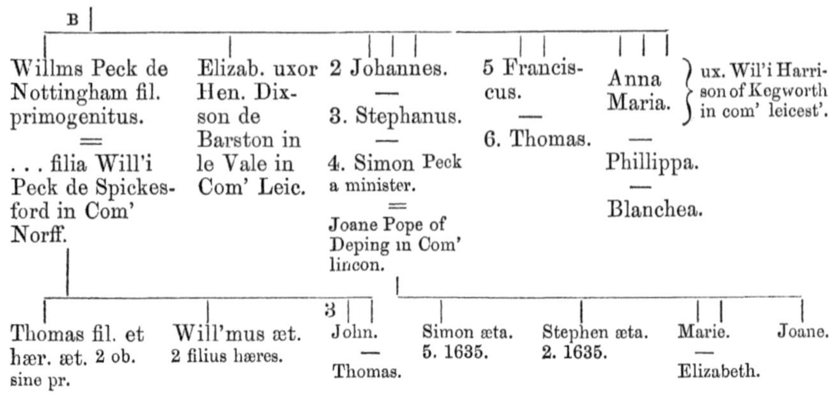

(Whalley.)

ARMS. *Argent, three whales' heads erased sable.*
CREST. *A whale's head erased sable.*

=Rob'tus Whalley de Bunney in Com' Nott.=

Rad'us Whalley de Norton iuxta Galby in Com' Leic. 2 fil. =Elizab. fil. et hær. Joh'is Welsh de Earles Shilton in Com' Leic.

Tho. Whaley de Bradmore in Com' Nottingh. =Elizab. fil. et hær. Will'i Glossop de Workesworth in Com' Derby.

Galfridus Whaley de Bradmore in Com' Nott. =Margareta fil. Will'i Coke de Trusley in Com' Derby.

Tho. Whaley de Norton iuxta Dalby in Com' Leic. fil. 2. superstes 1619.

Francisca fil. 3. et hær. Rad'i Whaley de Norton iuxta Galby in Com' Leic. =Willm's Whaly de Norton iuxta Galby in Com' Leic. fil. & hær. sup'stes 1619.

Elizab. ux. Rob'ti Garton de Willoughby in Com' Nott.

Dorothea uxor Rob'ti Abbot de Bradmore in Com' Nott.

Margareta uxor Rob'ti Bromley de Cotgraue in Com' Nott.

Will'mus filius 2.

Radulphus Whaley de Norton filius et hær. 1619. = Milicenta fil. Ed'ri Saunders de Brickesworth in Com' Northa'.

Maria uxor Joh'is Norris de Leicester.

Elizab. uxor Will'i Fisher de Threkingha' in Com' Lincoln.

Francisca ux. Ric'i Bushby de Barbisthorp in Com' Rutl.

Margaret. — Rachell. — Jana.

(𝔉𝔬𝔵.)

ARMS. *Argent, on a chevron between three foxes' head erased gules, a mullet for dif-*
ference.

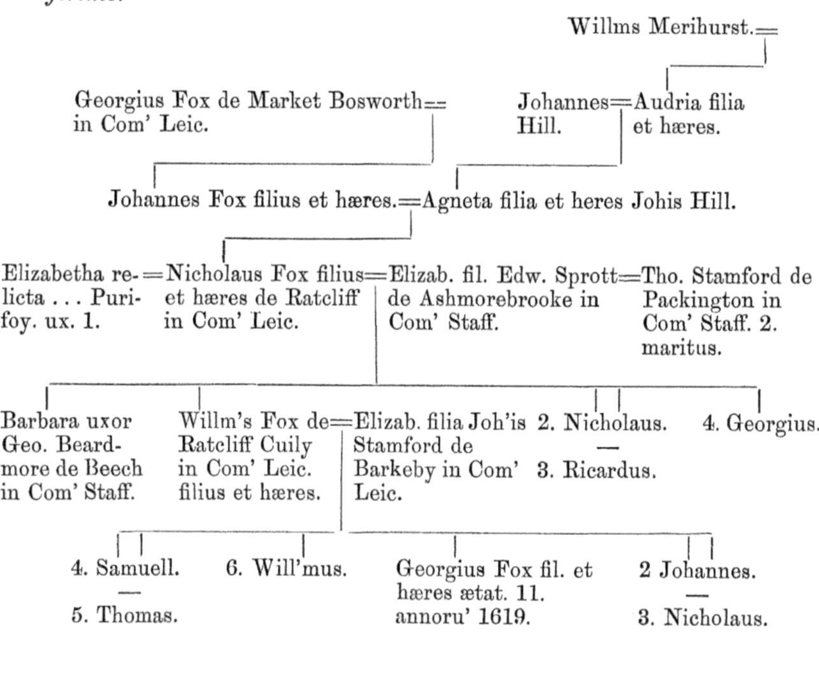

(𝔠𝔯𝔞𝔡𝔬𝔠𝔨.)

(𝕭𝖆𝖓𝖐𝖊𝖘.)

Henricus Octauus dei gra'. Angliæ, Franciæ et Hib'niæ Rex &c. Omnibus &c. Sciatis quod dedimus et concessimus dilecto seruiento n'ro Will'mo Bankes locum siue officium unius vibrellatoru' n'ror' infra Turrim n'ram London, et ulterius dedimus præfato Will'o pro exercitio officij præd'ci vad' et feodum sex denariorum sterlingoru' per diem &c. Habend' pro vita &c. Teste meipso apud Westm' nono die Februarij anno regui n'ri tricesimo quarto.

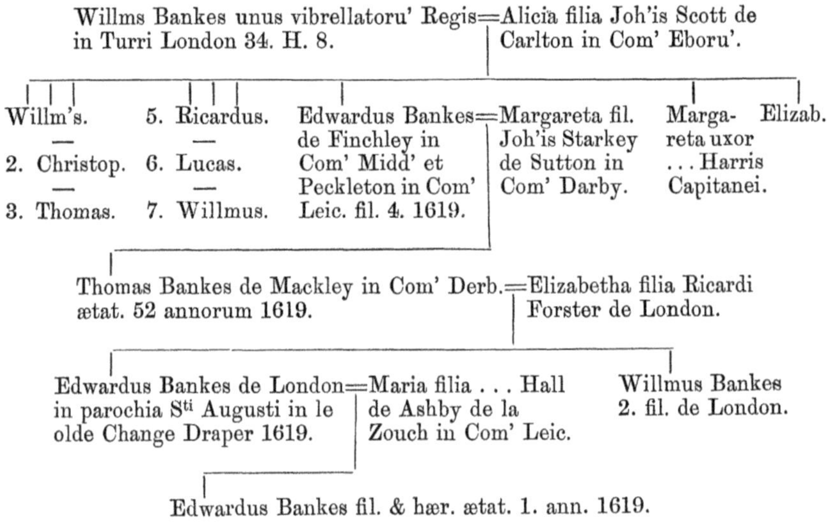

Willms Bankes unus vibrellatoru' Regis=Alicia filia Joh'is Scott de in Turri London 34. H. 8. | Carlton in Com' Eboru'.

Willm's. | 5. Ricardus. | Edwardus Bankes=Margareta fil. | Marga- Elizab.
— | — | de Finchley in | Joh'is Starkey | reta uxor
2. Christop. | 6. Lucas. | Com' Midd' et | de Sutton in | ...Harris
— | — | Peckleton in Com' | Com' Darby. | Capitanei.
3. Thomas. | 7. Willmus. | Leic. fil. 4. 1619. | |

Thomas Bankes de Mackley in Com' Derb.=Elizabetha filia Ricardi ætat. 52 annorum 1619. | Forster de London.

Edwardus Bankes de London=Maria filia ... Hall | Willmus Bankes in parochia Sti Augusti in le | de Ashby de la | 2. fil. de London. olde Change Draper 1619. | Zouch in Com' Leic.

Edwardus Bankes fil. & hær. ætat. 1. ann. 1619.

(𝕭𝖆𝖌𝖍𝖔𝖙.)

ARMS. *Ermine, on a bend gules three eagles displayed or, in chief a martlet for difference ; impaling vert, a chevron between three eagles displayed crowned or.*
CREST. *A stag's head caboshed sable, between the attires a greyhound courant argent, collared gules.*

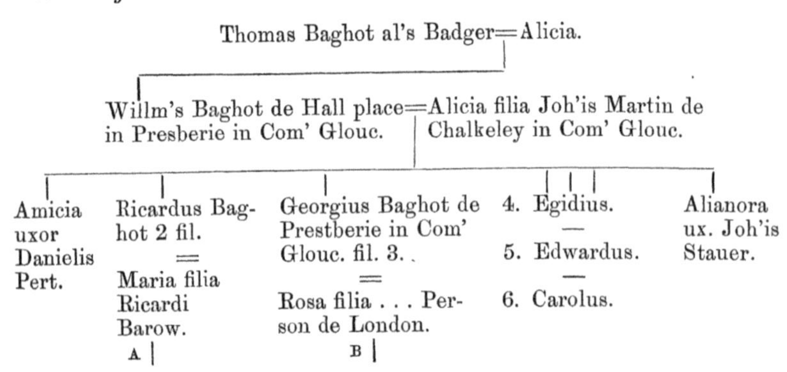

Thomas Baghot al's Badger=Alicia.

Willm's Baghot de Hall place=Alicia filia Joh'is Martin de in Presberie in Com' Glouc. | Chalkeley in Com' Glouc.

Amicia | Ricardus Bag- | Georgius Baghot de | 4. Egidius. | Alianora
uxor | hot 2 fil. | Prestberie in Com' | — | ux. Joh'is
Danielis | = | Glouc. fil. 3. | 5. Edwardus. | Stauer.
Pert. | Maria filia | = | — |
Ricardi	Rosa filia ... Per-	6. Carolus.
Barow.	son de London.	
A	B	

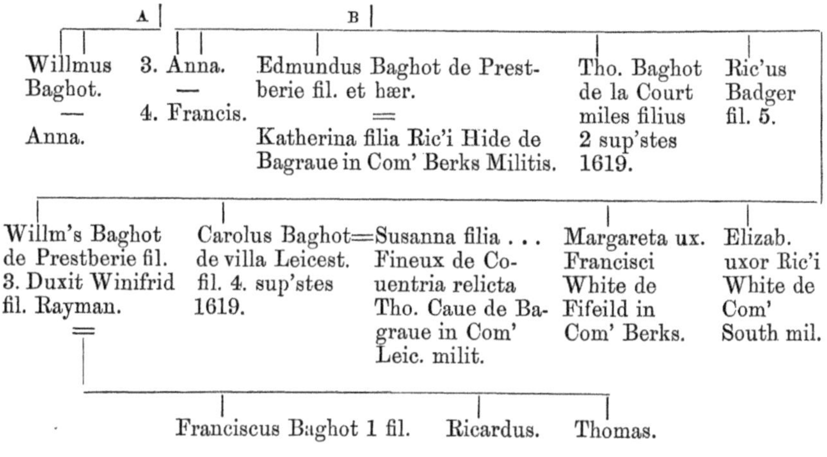

A |

Willmus Baghot.
—
Anna.

3. Anna.
—
4. Francis.

B |

Edmundus Baghot de Prestberie fil. et hær.
=
Katherina filia Ric'i Hide de Bagraue in Com' Berks Militis.

Tho. Baghot de la Court miles filius 2 sup'stes 1619.

Ric'us Badger fil. 5.

Willm's Baghot de Prestberie fil. 3. Duxit Winifrid fil. Rayman.
=

Carolus Baghot de villa Leicest. fil. 4. sup'stes 1619.
=
Susanna filia . . . Fineux de Couentria relicta Tho. Caue de Bagraue in Com' Leic. milit.

Margareta ux. Francisci White de Fifeild in Com' Berks.

Elizab. uxor Ric'i White de Com' South mil.

Franciscus Baghot 1 fil.　　Ricardus.　　Thomas.

(𝕸𝖊𝖆𝖉𝖊.)

ARMS. *Sable, a chevron between three pelicans with wings endorsed vulning themselves or.*

Willms Meade de Gretton in parochia de Horton in Com' Staff.
=
. . . filia . . . Wedgwood de Com' Staff.

Willm's Meade de Gretton hall filius et hæres.
=

Jacobus Meade de Narborowe al's Northborowe in Com' Leic.
=
Maria fil. . . . Rodes de villa Leicestriæ.

Jocosa ux. Hugonis Weston de Carlton Curlew in Com' Leic. Clericus.

Maria uxor Adriani Bent de Enderby in Com' Leic.
—
Agneta ux. Thom. Gilbert de Narborow in Com' Leic.

Henricus Meade de Narborowe filius et hær. superstes 1619.
=
Anna filia Will'i Croftes de Peckleton in Com' Leic.

Johannes.
—
3. Jacobus.
—
4. Willm's.
—
Hugo.

Marg^t.
—
Jacob.
—
Elizab.

Willmus Meade filius et hær. ætat. 9 annoru' 1619.

Henricus fil. 2. ob. in pueritia.

Maria.

(Cowper.)

ARMS. *Argent, on a bend engrailed between two lions rampant sable three plates.*
CREST. *A cockatrice's head erased argent pelletée, beaked combed and wattled gules.*

Thomas Cowper de Arthingworth=Susanna soror Pinchpooli in Com' Northamp. Clericus in artibus magist'. | Louet de Weston iuxta Weedon in Com' Northamp.

Georgius 1 filius ob. s. p'le.

Henricus Cowper de Neither Shukbrough in Com' War. = Elizab. filia Tho. Phillipps de Wormhull in Com' Oxon.

Willms Couper de Arthingworth in Com' Northamp. 1619. = Agneta filia . . . Luffe de Lidington in Rutland.

Tho. Cowper de Norton in Com' Warr. Baccalarius in artibus. = Margeria fil. Tho. Caue de Ketteringe in Com' Northa'.

Susanna.
—
Agnes.

1. Will'mus.
2. Thomas.

3. Johannes.
4. Edmundus.
5. Jonathan.

1. Anthonius.
—
2. Franciscus.

Robertus Cowper de Lubbenham in Com' Leic. fil. 5. superstes 1619. = Elizab. filia Fran. Gramer de Kenelworth in Com' War.

Susanna uxor Will'i Becke de Fresley in Com' Ward.

Agnes uxor Ric'i Glover de Hellidon in Com' Nor'.

Katherina uxor Joh'is Pollard de Wicken in Com' Buck.

(Wright.)

Rogerus Wright de Sutton in Com' Leic.

Willm's Wright de Sutton in Com' Leic.

Tho. Wright de Sutton in Com' Leic. =. . . filia Broadgate de Peatling parua in Com' Leic.

Ricardus Wright de Sutton in Com' Leic. = Katherina filia . . . Guest relicta Ric'i Breton de London in red cros streat.

Ro'btus Wright de Sutton 2 fil. = Jana filia . . . Vincent de Marston in Com' Leic.

Alicia uxor Rob'ti Breton de Barwell in Com Leic.

Edwardus Wright de Sutton in Com' Leicest. filius et hær. superstes 1619. = Maria filia Rob'ti Berrey de Ludlow in Com' Salop.

Thomas Wright.

Samuell Wright fil. et hær. ætatis 4. annoru' 1619.

1. Winifride.
2. Maria.
3. Katherin.

(Abney.)

ARMS. *Or, on a chief gules a lion passant argent.*

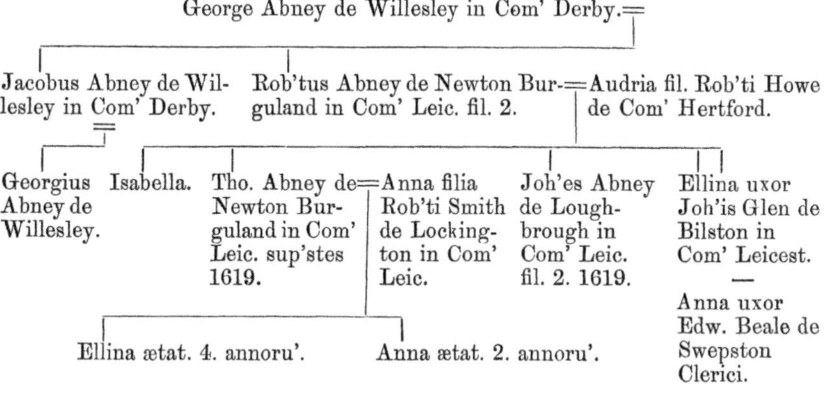

George Abney de Willesley in Com' Derby.=

Jacobus Abney de Willesley in Com' Derby.

Rob'tus Abney de Newton Burguland in Com' Leic. fil. 2.=Audria fil. Rob'ti Howe de Com' Hertford.

Georgius Abney de Willesley.

Isabella.

Tho. Abney de Newton Burguland in Com' Leic. sup'stes 1619.=Anna filia Rob'ti Smith de Lockington in Com' Leic.

Joh'es Abney de Loughbrough in Com' Leic. fil. 2. 1619.

Ellina uxor Joh'is Glen de Bilston in Com' Leicest.

—

Anna uxor Edw. Beale de Swepston Clerici.

Ellina ætat. 4. annoru'.

Anna ætat. 2. annoru'.

(Elkington.)

ARMS. *Gules, six cross crosslets or, three in chief and three in base, between two flaunches argent.*

CREST. *Out of a mural coronet chequy or and sable, embattled of the first, a demi-griffin ségreant argent, winged gules, holding in the dexter foot a gold ring, gem of the second.*

To Tho. Elkington of London Gent son of Humphrie Elkington son of Richard Elkington, son of Richard Elkington of Shawell in Com' Leic. Gent. Descended from y^e family of Elkington of Elkington in Com' Northt. & confirmed to the said Thom. & his Uncles Hen. Thomas & Edw. Elkington & their issues 22. Octob' 1608. 6. Jacobi p' Wm Camden Clarenceux.

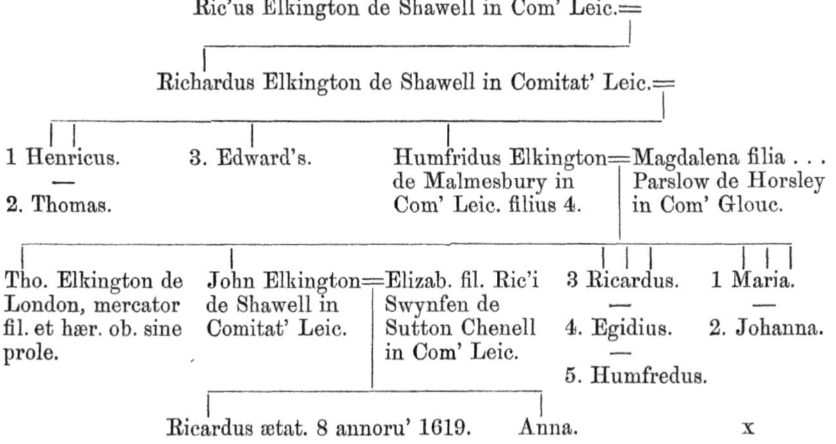

Ric'us Elkington de Shawell in Com' Leic.=

Richardus Elkington de Shawell in Comitat' Leic.=

1 Henricus.

—

2. Thomas.

3. Edward's.

Humfridus Elkington de Malmesbury in Com' Leic. filius 4.=Magdalena filia . . . Parslow de Horsley in Com' Glouc.

Tho. Elkington de London, mercator fil. et hær. ob. sine prole.

John Elkington de Shawell in Comitat' Leic.=Elizab. fil. Ric'i Swynfen de Sutton Chenell in Com' Leic.

3 Ricardus.

—

4. Egidius.

—

5. Humfredus.

1 Maria.

—

2. Johanna.

Ricardus ætat. 8 annoru' 1619.   Anna.   x

(Abney.)

ARMS. *Or, on a chief gules a lion passant argent, a mullet for difference.*

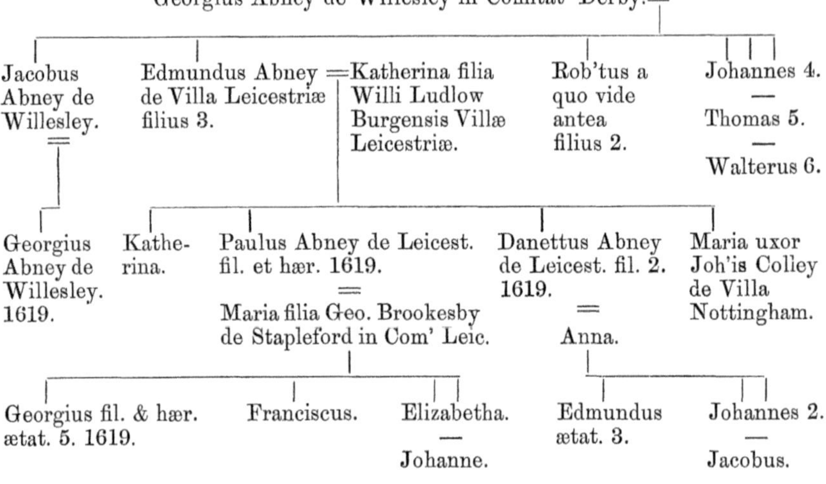

Georgius Abney de Willesley in Comitat' Derby.=

Jacobus Abney de Willesley. =

Edmundus Abney de Villa Leicestriæ filius 3. =Katherina filia Willi Ludlow Burgensis Villæ Leicestriæ.

Rob'tus a quo vide antea filius 2.

Johannes 4.
—
Thomas 5.
—
Walterus 6.

Georgius Abney de Willesley. 1619.

Katherina.

Paulus Abney de Leicest. fil. et hær. 1619.
=
Maria filia Geo. Brookesby de Stapleford in Com' Leic.

Danettus Abney de Leicest. fil. 2. 1619.
=
Anna.

Maria uxor Joh'is Colley de Villa Nottingham.

Georgius fil. & hær. ætat. 5. 1619.

Franciscus.

Elizabetha.
—
Johanne.

Edmundus ætat. 3.

Johannes 2.
—
Jacobus.

Sciant præsentes et futuri quod ego Joh'es filius Ric'i filij Nigelli de Abkettleby dedi et concessi Hugoni Bernard de Abkettleby &c. Hijs testibus Will'o de Londam, Johe Cl'ico, Henrico de Crucem Ric'o Repin & alijs.

(Hodges.)

ARMS. *Gules, a chevron ermine between three talbots' heads or, each issuing out of a mural coronet azure, in chief a mullet for difference.*
CREST. *A talbot's head couped or, guttée-de-sang, collared and ringed gules.*
MOTTO. *Fundamentum Gloriæ humilitas.*

Thomas Hodgis de Com' Dorset. =Dorothea filia Michaelis Poultney de Misterton in Com' Leic. Ar. amita Joh'is Poultney militis.

Franciscus Hodgis de Burton, Nouery alias Ouery in Com' Leic. fil. et hæres a° 1619. =Anna filia Will'i Warde de Knighton in Com' Leic.

Johannes Hodgis 2. filius.

Franciscus Hodgis de Sison in Com' Leic. fil. et hær. ætat. 31 annoru' 1619. =Martha filia Tho. Teakey de Carlile in Com' Cumbriæ.

Phœbe uxor Anth'i Thornton de Newton Harcourt in Com' Leic.

Anna uxor Steph'i May de Couentry.

Tho. Hodgis filius et hæres 1. anni et dimid. 1619.

(Lascelles.)

ARMS. *Quarterly :—1. Argent, three garlands gules. 2. Azure, on two bars or, six martlets gules. 3. Argent, a chevron between three talbots' heads erased gules.*
CREST. *Out of a ducal coronet or, a griffin's head vert, beaked of the first.*

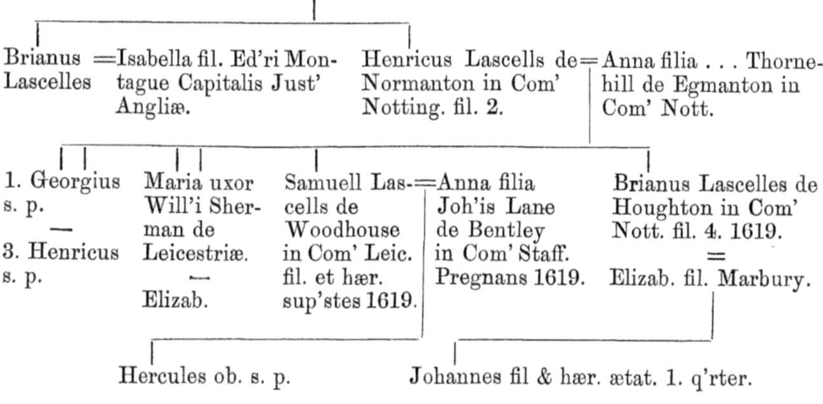

(Mulsho.)

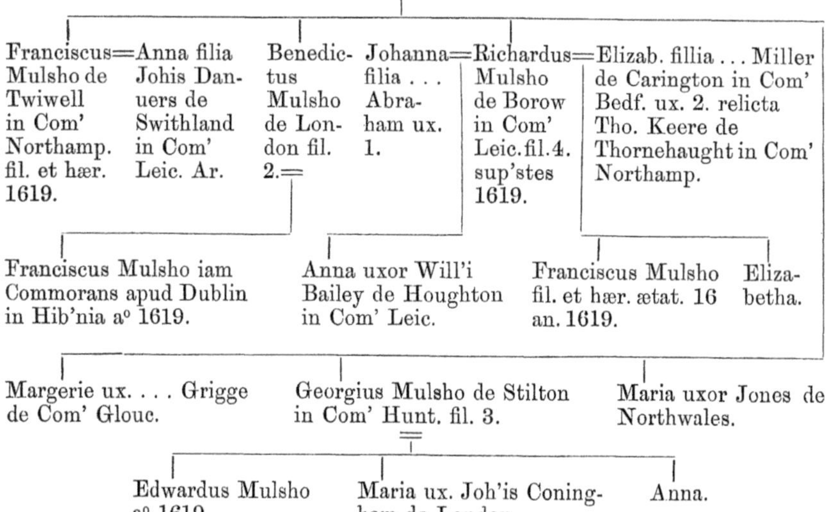

(Wincoll.)

ARMS. *Ermine, a chevron quarterly per chevron or and sable, between three crescents gules.*

CREST. *An arm couped at the shoulder, embowed and erect from the elbow in armour, holding a spear (untinctured).*

John Wincoll de Walding-=. . . filia . . . Syday
feild in Com' Suff.　　　　de Burts in Com' Suff.

Willm's Wincoll=. . . filia　Rob'tus　. . . uxor Cage　Alicia uxor . . . Spencer
de Lanham in　　Vaughan.　Wincoll　de Berrey in　Mater Joh'is Spencer
Com Suff. fil. 4.　　　　　s. p.　Com' Suff.　mil. Aldermanni Londo'.

Anna filia & Coh. uxor Leonardi Holliday militis　　Margareta fil. & Coh. uxor
Maioris London, renupta Hen. Montague　　　　Joh'is Spencer de Boxford
militi Capitali Justiciarij Angliæ.　　　　　　in Com' Suff.

Rogerus Wincoll=Anna filia Joh'is　John Wincoll de=. . . Filia . . .
de Waldingfield　Gourdon de　Waldingfeild in　Groome de
in Com' Suff. fil.　Waldingfeild.　Com' Suff. filius　Ratlesden in
2.　　　　　　　　et hær. s. p.　Com' Suff.

Joh'es Wincoll de Villa=Anna fil.　Willm's 5.　Rogerus Win-=. . . filia . . .
Leicest' fil. 8. et de medio　Joh'is Bower　—　coll de Wal-　Bantock de
Templo London Consi-　de villa　Ric'us 6.　dingfeild fil.　Hitcham in
liarius ad Legem 1619.　Gloucest'.　　et hæres.　Com' Suff.

Rogerus Wincoll fil.　Elizab.　Johannes Wincoll de=. . . filia . . . Chaplin
et hæres æt. 15.　　　Waldingfeild in Com'　de Lindsey in Com'
annoru' 1619.　　　　Suff. fil. et hær. 1619.　Suff.

Rob'tus Wincoll de　Joh'es　Thom's Wincoll de Caxston in　Maria uxor
London fil. 3. duxit　Wincoll　Comitat' Cantab' fil. 4. Duxit　Tho Hudeson
Annam fil. . . .　2. fil.　Susanna' filiam . . . Madock de　de London.
Crouch de London.　　　Ipswich in Com' Suff.
=　　　　　　　　　　　　=

Maria.　　　　　　　　Thomas Wincoll 1619.

(Chippingdale.)

ARMS. *Azure, semée of fleur-de-lis or, two lions' gambs erect and erased paleways argent.*
CREST. *A lion's gamb erect argent, erased gules, grasping a fleur-de-lis or.*

Giuen by Sr Will'm Dethick Garter 16. May. 36. Eliz. 1594.

Maria = Georgius Chippingdale == Johanna ... uxor Henrici Sapcot
uxor 2. | natus apud Crauen in | de Elton in Com' Hunt a
Com' Eboru'. | quo Beamont.

Edmundus | Elizab. fil. = Johannes Chippingdale de = Francisca filia | Edwardus
Chipping- | Garbrand | Humberston et de Villa | ... Oliuer de | Chipping-
dale ob. in- | Harkes de | Leicestriæ iuris Ciuilis | Houghton in | dale.
nuptus. | Oxford | Docto^r et unus Cancel- | Com' Nott.
ux. 1. | lariæ Magistroru' sup'stes
1619.

Christiana uxor Fran- | Elizab. uxor | Katherina uxor Joh'is | Willm's Chipping-
cisci Staresmore de | Ric'i Mere- | Walker de Barton | dale Mercator oc-
Frollesworth in | dith Decanus | subter Needwood in | cisus ab Hispanis.
Com' Leic. | Wellensis. | Com' Staff.

Tobias Chipping- = Isabella. fil. | Johannes Chipping- = Maria fil. et | Henricus.
dale fil. primo- | Tho. Caue | dale de Blackenhall | hær. Will'i | —
genitus de medio | de Bagraue | in Com' Staff. fil. | Garret de | Henricus.
Templo London | in Com' | 2. 1619. | Highamton | —
ob. ante patrem. | Leicest. Mil. | | in p'ochia de | Elizab.
| | | Washingburgh | —
| | | in Com' Lin- | Maria.
| | | coln.

Elizab. fil. et hær. ux. Valentini
Bale de Humberston in Com'
Leic.

Will'mus fil. et | Elizabetha. | Katherina.
hær. ætat. 9. | —
1619. | Johannes.

(Bent.)

Thomas Bent de Enderby in Com' Leic.=Alicia filia . . . Willmer de Enderby.

Willmus Bent de Enderby in Com' Leic. fil. primus. = Johanna fil. Tho. Bennet de Quineybarow.

Anna ux. Rob'ti Sauage de Newton in le Thistles. — Thomas Bent fil. 5.

Ric'us Bent filius 2. = Ric'us Bent.

Nicholaus Bent fil. 3. s. p.

Johannes Bent de Stony Stanton in Com' Leic. fil. 4. = Elizab. filia Tho. Blakesley de Couentry.

Willm's Bent. | Johannes fil. 2.

Thomas=. . . filia Johannis Cater. | Bent fil's 1.

Ricardus. — Lucia.

Rob'tus Bent de Gumley in Com' Leicest. Duxit filiam Jurdan.=

Valentinus Bent fil. 1.

Edm. Bent de=filia . . . Villa Leicest. Camerarius de eiusdem villæ. | Blower de Loughborow in Com' Leic.

Johannes. | Thomas. — Robertus.

Johannes Bent de Enderby in Com' Leic. = Agneta filia Joh'is Marsh de Enderby in Com' Leic.

Tho. Bent de Enderby fil. 4. = Alicia fil. Rogeri Read de Enderby.

Ric'us Bent de Stony Stanton in Com' Leicest. 2. fil. = Alicia fil. et hær. Will'mi Tackhell de Sapcot in Com' Leyc.

Nicholas Bent de Sapcot in Com' Leic. fil. 3. 1619. = Gracia fil. et coh. Will'mi Tackhell de Sapcott.

Stephanus Bent de Narborow in Com' Leic. = Gracia filia Tho. Otefeild de Narborow.

Adrianus Bent de Narborow 1619. = Maria fil. Jacobi Meade de Narborow.

Willms Bent de Enderby fil. & hær. sup'stes 1619. = Elizab. fil. Tho. Bingley de Croft in Com' Leic.

Margeria ux. Nich'i Grunday de Thornton in Com' Leic. — Alicia uxor Tho. Kendall de Houghton in Com' Leic. — Petronilla ux. Will'i Ward de Exton in Com' Rutl.

Ric'us Bent de Enderby in Com' Leic. 1619. = Filia Joh'is Goddard de Cleybrooke in Com' Leic.

Nicholaus. — Audianus. — Stephanus. — Thomas.

Willm's Bent fil. 1. Duxit Aliciam fil. Tho. Samson de Hinckley. — 2 Robertus. — 3. Richardus. — 4. Johannes.

Will'mus Bent fil. et hæres.

Thomas Bent aº 1619.

Willm's Bent fil. et hæres ætat. 13. 1619. — Jocosa. — Maria.

1 Johannes.   4. Johannes ob. s. p.   Josephus ætat. 8. 1619.   Willm's 5. m. ætat. 6.   Maria.   Anna.   Ellena.   Brigetta.   Elizab. s. p.

Rogerus Bent de Frollesworth in Com' Leic. filius ætate minimus=Agneta filia et hær. Will'mi Clarke de Frolesworth.

Margareta ux. Ric'i Perkins de Copston in Com' War. — Elizab. ux. Nich'i Smith de Barwell in Com' Leic.

Ursula ux. Tho. Hewett de Strettaston in Com' Wor. — Alicia uxor John Champion de Kirkeby Monachous in Com' Leic.

Margeria ux. Tho. Fletcher de Leicester. — Goditha uxor Hugonis Lowe de Billesdon in Com' Leic.

Georgius. — Ambrosius ob. s. p.

Willm's Bent de Billesdon in Com' Leic. fil. et hær. sup'stes 1619. = Anna fil. Rob'ti Parkenall de Glaston in Com' Rutl.

Will'm Bent de Cosby in Com' Leic.=

Thomas Bent de Cosby in Com' Leic.=

Joh'is Bent de Cosby=Elizab. filia filius 1. ob. s. p.   . . . Walton.

Ric'us Bent de=Amicia fil. Cosby. fil. 2.   . . . Jay.

Tho. Bent de Cosby in Com' Leic. fil. 3.

Willm's Bent de Cosby duxit fil. Gunston filius 4.

Rob'tus Bent de Cosby fil. 5.

. . . ux. Thomas Parker. — Agnes uxor Willi Estwell.

Elizab. uxor Willi Ward. — Alicia uxor Ric'i Miles.

Ambrosius=Margareta fil. Bent de   Lawrencij Good- Cosby fil.   man de Blaston et hær.   in Com' Leic.

Richard. — Thomas. — Will'm.

Joh'es Bent de Cosby Duxit Maria' filia' Berrey.=

1. Ricardus. — 2. Johannes.

3. Thomas. — 4. Willms 1619.

1. Ricardus. — 2. Johannes sine p'le.

Ricardus Bent fil.=Anna fil. Will'i Morton 3. de Cosby in   Archidia. Noui Castri Com' Leic.   super Tynam.

Thomas 4. — Willm's 5.

Alicia ux. Joh'is Freeman de Cosby in Com' Leic.

Elizab.

Elizab. — Maria.

Willm's ætat. 1. anni et dimid. 1619.

(𝕾𝖙𝖆𝖓𝖋𝖔𝖗𝖉.)

ARMS. *Argent, three bars azure, on a canton or a fess, and in chief three mascles sable, in chief a mullet charged with a mullet for difference.*
CREST. *A dexter gauntlet in bend or, grasping a broken sword erect argent, hilted and pomelled sable.*

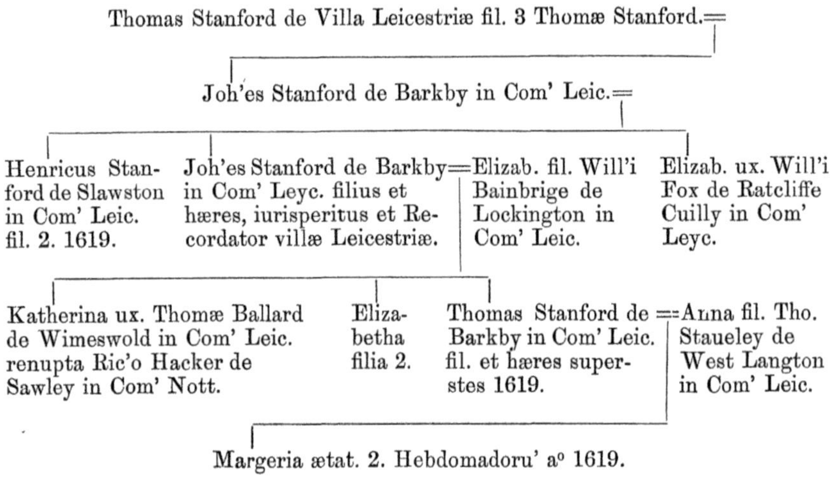

Thomas Stanford de Villa Leicestriæ fil. 3 Thomæ Stanford.══

Joh'es Stanford de Barkby in Com' Leic.══

| Henricus Stanford de Slawston in Com' Leic. fil. 2. 1619. | Joh'es Stanford de Barkby in Com' Leyc. filius et hæres, iurisperitus et Recordator villæ Leicestriæ.══ | Elizab. fil. Will'i Bainbrige de Lockington in Com' Leic. | Elizab. ux. Will'i Fox de Ratcliffe Cuilly in Com' Leyc. |

| Katherina ux. Thomæ Ballard de Wimeswold in Com' Leic. renupta Ric'o Hacker de Sawley in Com' Nott. | Elizabetha filia 2. | Thomas Stanford de Barkby in Com' Leic. fil. et hæres superstes 1619.══ | Anna fil. Tho. Staueley de West Langton in Com' Leic. |

Margeria ætat. 2. Hebdomadoru' aº 1619.

(𝕭𝖚𝖗𝖙𝖔𝖓.)

ARMS. *Sable, a chevron between three owls argent, crowned or.*

Willm's Burton de Branson in Com' Rutland.══Alicia filia Ric'i Peck.

| Bartin Burton filius 2. duxit Abigall filiam . . . Chomley. | Joh'es Burton filius et hæres.══Anna filia et hær. Thomæ Digby de Cotes in |

| Anna filia Rob'ti Reinolds de Londo' mercatoris ux. 2. ══ | Sʳ Thomas Burton de Stockerston in Com' Leic. miles et baronettus sup'stes 1619. ══ | Phillippa fil. Henrici Cobham al's Brooke de Com' Cantij uxor 1. |

| Jone ætat. dimidij Anni. | Joh'es Burton fil. & hæres ætat. 2. annoru'. | Anna. 11. ætat. | Elizab. 8. | Francis. 6. |

(𝔅𝔯𝔢𝔱𝔬𝔫.)

ARMS. *Azure, on a bend between six stars pierced or, in dexter chief a mullet for difference.*
CREST. *A lion's gamb erased erect azure, charged with a chevron or, between six billets argent.*

Willm's Breton de London.=Elizab. filia Dacon.

Ric'us Breton de=Katherina fil. Edwardi Guest de Com' Worc'.   London.

Nic'us Breton de London 2. fil.

Maria uxor Edw. Newton de Com' Leict'.

Rob'tus Breton de Barwell in Com' Leic.=Alicia fil. Ric'i Wright de Sutton iuxta Broughton in Com' Leic.

Elizab. ux. Francisci Ducket de Broughton in Com' Leic.

5. Rob'tus æt. 8.
—
6. John æt. 6.
—
7 Thom. æt. 5.

Katherina æt. 14.
—
Maria æt. 4.

Ric'us Breton fil. et hær. æt. 20. 1619.

2 Daniell etat. 19.
—
4. Francis etat. 12.

Will'm fil. 3. ætat. 16. nunc Schollasticus in Academia Cantab'.

(𝔅𝔯𝔞𝔡𝔰𝔥𝔞𝔴.)

ARMS. *Argent, two bends between two martlets sable.*
CREST. *On a mount a stag statant, under a vine-tree, all proper.*

Hugo Bradshaw de Moore Barne in Com' Leic.=... filia ... Orme.
descended out of Lankesheir.

Joh'es Bradshaw=... filia Forster.
de Orton in Com' Leic. fil. 1.

Rob'tus Bradshaw de=Anna filia Morebarne in Com' Leic. 2. fil.=Glouer de Baxterley.

Maria uxor Arthuri Corbet de Com' Rutland.

Georgius= Bradshaw.

Dorothea filia Rob'ti Ashby de Quenby 2. uxor.=Rob'tus Bradshaw de Moorebarne in Com' Leic. Ar.=Margareta filia ... Gibbons de Sutton Colfeeld in Com' War. uxor. 1.

Ric'us Bradshaw.

Rob'tus Bradshaw fil. & hær. duxit filia' Purifoy et ob. sine prole.

Georgius Bradshaw=Anna filia Rad'i de Moorebarne in Com' Leic.=Burton de Lindeley in Com' Leic.

Margareta uxor Jenninges.

A

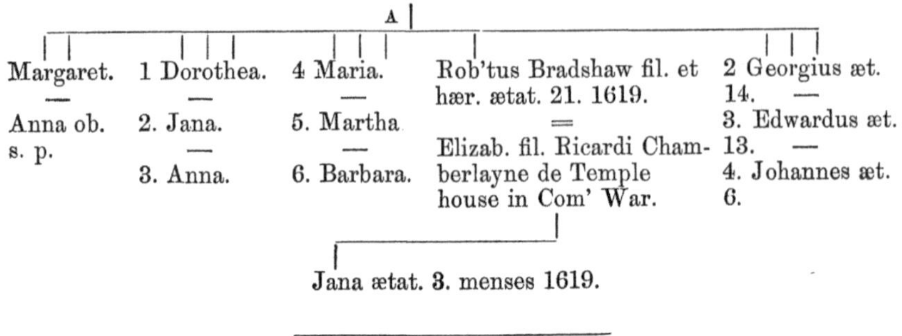

Sciant præsentes et futuri quod ego Joh'es, filius Ric'i filij Nigelli de Abkettleby dedi et concessi Hugoni Bernard de Abkettleby et Elenæ filiæ eius et hæredibus d'ci Hugonis de corpore suo Legitime procreatis quatuor acras t'ræ cum pertinentijs in Campis de Abkettleby, quarum una roda iacet &c. Hijs testibus Will'o de Loudham, Joh'e Cl'ico Henrico ad Crucem, Ric'o Repin, Will'o de Lenton et alijs. Dat' apud Abbekettlebye die omniu' Scantorum a° regni regis Edw. 1. tricessimo primo.

Alia Charta eiusdem Joh'is filij Ric'i, filij Nigelli de Abkettleby Data a° 32. E. primi.

Sciant præsent' et futuri q^d ego Joh'es filius Henrici Atte Crosse de Abkettleby dedi concessi et hac præsenti Carta mea Confirmaui Ric'o Neale de Abkettleby tres acras et dimid' terræ arrab' cum pertinentijs in Abkettleby &c. dedi etiam eidem Ric'o om'ia bona mea mobilia et immobilia in prædictis tribus acris terræ et dimid' existent'. In cuius rei testimonium præsentibus sigillu' meum apposui. Hijs testibus &c. Dat' apud Abkettleby die Sabbathi prox' post festu' S'ci Mich'is Ap'li A° regni regis Ed. tertij post conquestu' 2.

Sciant præsentes et futuri q^d ego Willm's Neele de Abkettleby dedi Concessi et hac præsenti Carta mea Confirmaui Joh'i Neele de Melton Mowbray et Robto Kirketon de Thornton super Wale Capellano omnia terras, ten'ta et rditus mea cum edificiis, pratis, et pasturis cum om'ibus suis pertinent' &c. In cuius rei testimonium sigillu' meum apposui. Hijs testibus Will'o Latham Ric'o Rinell, Joh'i de Ripon, Will'o Spencer, Ric'o de Holwell, et alijs. Dat' apud Abkettleby die dominica prox' post festu' S'cæ Luciæ virginis Anno regni regis Ed'ri tercij post conquestum Angliæ quadrigesimo sc'do.

Sciant præsent' et futuri q'd ego Willm's de Latton Capellanus didi Concessi et hac præsenti Carta mea confirmaui Joh'i filio Willm'i Neele de Abkettleby &c. In cuius rei testimonium huic præsenti Cartæ sigillum meum apposui. Hijs testibus Will'o Neele, Will'o Lawrence Joh'i de Thorpe et alijs. Dat' apud Abkettleby die martis in festo Sti Lawrencij martiris anno regni Regis Ric'i secundi post Conquestu' tertio decimo.

Sciant præsent' et futuri q'd nos Will'mus Bollers Capellanus et Thomas Michelson de Guipton dedimus, concessimus et hac præsenti Carta n'ra confirmauimus Will'o Neele filio Joh'is Neele de Abkettleby illud Capitale mesuagium in Abkettleby cum tribus bouatis terræ, q'd quidem messuagium cum præd'cis tribus bouatis terræ ha'mus ex dono et concessione prædic' Joh'is Neele quondam patris præd'ci Will'mi Neele habend' et tenend' prædictu' messuagium cum præd'cis tribus bouatis terræ præfato Will'o Neele et hæredibus de se legittime procreatis &c. In cuius rei testimonium &c. Hijs testibus &c. Dat' apud Abkettleby in festo Seancti Jeronimi A° regni regis Henrici quarti a conquesto quinto.

Hac Indentura testatur q^d ego Joh'es Neele de Abkettleby feoffauit Guill'm Bellers Capellanu' et Tho. Michelson hæredes et assignatos suos in feodo simplici, in om'ibus t'ris et ten'tis suis in Abkettleby et Holwell cum om'bus pertinent' suis &c. Conditio istius feoffamenti talis est q'd præd'cus Tho. et Willm's refeoffauerunt prædictu' Joh'em Neell, et heredes et executores suos si superstes sit &c.

Et si contingit q'd præd'm Joh'em Neale obiere, refeoffament' dcaru' terraru' q'd p'd'cs Willm's et Tho. feoffauerunt Will'm filium præd'ci Joh'is Neell sibi et hæredibus de se legittime procreatis. Et si contingat præd'cum Will'm sine hærede de se legittime proc'reat obire q'd prædicta terra et ten'ta Johannæ Sorori suæ uxori Ric'i Prate &c. In cuius rei testimoniu' &c. Dat' apud Abkettle in festo Apostoloru' Phillippi et Jacobi anno regni regis. H. 4. post Conquestu' 4.

Nouerint uniu'si per p'ntes me Thomam Spicer de Hesell in Com' Eboru' remisisse, relaxasse et omnino pro me hæred' et executores meos imperpetuu' quietu' clamasse Will'o Neele de Abkettleby in Com' Leic. & Sigillo meo Sigillat. dat. 2. die Junij anno regni Regis Hen. sexti post conq. vicesimo secundo.

Nouerint uniu'si p' p'ntes me Joh'em Derby filiu' et hæredem Will'i Derby Junioris remisisse relaxasse et omnino pro me et hæredibus meis imperpetuu' quetu' clamasse Will'o Neele totu' ius et clameam &c. In cuius rei testimoniu' &c. Dat. apud Abkettleby in festo translationis Sti Thomæ martiris A° Regni Edw. 4 post conq' Angliæ tertio.

(Neale.)

Nigellus de Abbekettleby in Com' Leic.

Ric'us filius Nigelli.

Johannes filius Ricardi A° 31. E. 1.

Ric'us Neele de Abbekettleby in Com' Leic. 2. E. 3. et 22.

Willm's Neale de Abkettleby 42. E. 3.

| Johannes Neale de Abkettleby
13. R. 2. et 4. H. 4. | Joanna nupta
Ric'o Prate. |

Willm's Neale de Abkettleby in Com' Leic. a° 5. H. 4.

Willm's Neale de Abkettleby agricola a° 22. H. 6.

Will'm Neale de Abkettleby a° 3. E. 4.

Rich. Neale de Abkettleby a° 16. H. 7. et 24.

A

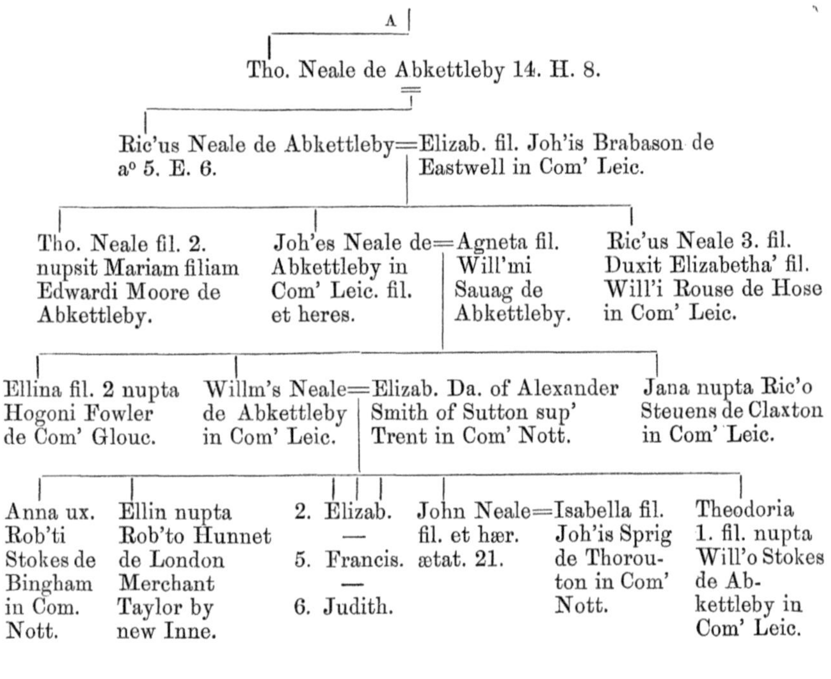

A

Tho. Neale de Abkettleby 14. H. 8.

Ric'us Neale de Abkettleby=Elizab. fil. Joh'is Brabason de
a° 5. E. 6.   Eastwell in Com' Leic.

Tho. Neale fil. 2. | Joh'es Neale de=Agneta fil. | Ric'us Neale 3. fil.
nupsit Mariam filiam | Abkettleby in | Will'mi | Duxit Elizabetha' fil.
Edwardi Moore de | Com' Leic. fil. | Sauag de | Will'i Rouse de Hose
Abkettleby. | et heres. | Abkettleby. | in Com' Leic.

Ellina fil. 2 nupta | Willm's Neale=Elizab. Da. of Alexander | Jana nupta Ric'o
Hogoni Fowler | de Abkettleby | Smith of Sutton sup' | Steuens de Claxton
de Com' Glouc. | in Com' Leic. | Trent in Com' Nott. | in Com' Leic.

Anna ux. | Ellin nupta | 2. Elizab. | John Neale=Isabella fil. | Theodoria
Rob'ti | Rob'to Hunnet | — | fil. et hær. | Joh'is Sprig | 1. fil. nupta
Stokes de | de London | 5. Francis. | ætat. 21. | de Thorou- | Will'o Stokes
Bingham | Merchant | — | | ton in Com' | de Ab-
in Com. | Taylor by | 6. Judith. | | Nott. | kettleby in
Nott. | new Inne. | | | | Com' Leic.

(𝕭𝖆𝖓𝖎𝖘𝖙𝖊𝖗.)

ARMS. *Quarterly:*—1. *Argent, a cross flory sable within a bordure gules bezantée.*
2. *Argent, on a fess gules three escallops or.*   3. *Argent, a chief vair gules and
or, over all a bend engrailed sable.*   4. *Argent, on a chief azure two mullets or,
over them a label of three points ermine.*   5. *Paly of six or and gules, on a bend
azure, three horseshoes of the first.*   6. *Argent, six lions rampant sable, three,
two, and one.*   7. *Vair, argent and sable.*   8. *Sable, a lion rampant argent.*
CREST. *A peacock sitting (untinctured), gorged with a collar gules charged with three
bezants.*

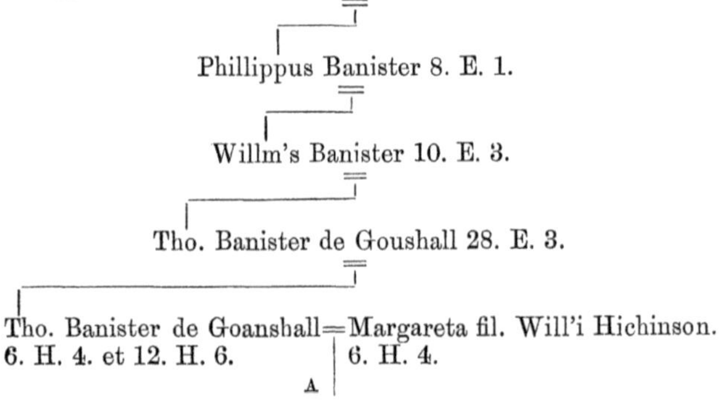

Phillippus Banister de Guonshall. 4 mille passus a Staffordia.

Phillippus Banister 8. E. 1.

Willm's Banister 10. E. 3.

Tho. Banister de Goushall 28. E. 3.

Tho. Banister de Goanshall=Margareta fil. Will'i Hichinson.
6. H. 4. et 12. H. 6.   6. H. 4.

A

A |

Willm's Banister de Guon-=Hellen 6.=Tho. Cotes de Cotes in Com'
shall 7. E. 4.   H. 7.   Staff. 2 marit's.

Joh'es Banister de Bosworth=Elizab. fil. et Coh. Rob'ti
in Com' Leic. 6. H. 7.   Jaques 16. H. 7.

Dorothea fil. Joh'is Hardwick de Linley=Tho. Banister=Anna filia et Coh.
in Com' Leic. et vidua Anthonij Har-   de Upton iure   Nic. Fitz Harbert
court de Bosworth ob. 1593.   uxoris.   uxor 1.

Nicholas Banister obijt sine prole.   Daniell Banister=Anna filia Tho. Cox
                                de Upton obijt   de Nelson in Com'
                                1608.   Leic.

Tho. Banister de Upton=Anna filia Rob'ti Hall de Ratcliff
modo superstes 1619.   super Trent in Com' Nott.

Thomas   Anna ux.   Elizab. fil. Edmondi=Henricus Banister=Anna filia Radi
2. filius   W'mi Geary   Temple de Temple   filius et hæres   Barton de
ætat. 16.   de Barleston   Hall in parochia de   ætat. 30. annoru'   Lindley in
         in Com' Leic.   Wallesbrooke in   1619.   Com' Leic.
                    Com' Leic. ux. 2.   uxor 1.

Tho. Banister fil. et. hær. ætat. 1. anni.   Elizab. ætat. 3. annoru'.

Elizab. uxor Rob'ti Stretford   Jana uxor Roberti
de Non Eaton in Com' Warr.   Corbett.

(𝕭𝖔𝖙𝖍𝖔𝖒.)

Johannes Bothom de Losipdale=Alicia fil. Rogeri Wolowe de
in Com' Derbiæ.   Wolowe in Com' Darbiæ.

Grace filia Jackson=Hugo Bothom de=Margareta fil. Willmi Barret
uxor prima.   Leicestriæ. modo   de Wemsall in Com' Leic.
              superstes 1619.   uxor 2.

(𝔏𝔞𝔠𝔶.)

Hugh Lacye who cam out of Yorksh. & liued═Elizab. fil. . . . Noell de
at Melton Mowbray in Com' Leic. | Ilcott in Com' Staff.

Andrew Lacy de Melton Mowbray═Elizab. fil. Ric'i Wilcockes de
in Com' Leic. | Barswell in Com' Leic.

2. Jana.	3. Maria.	Willm's Lacy fil. et hæres ætat. 16. 1619.	Hen. Lacye fil. 2. ætat. 7.	Elizab. uxor Joh'is Stanbridg de Com' Mid.
— 3. Agnes.				

(ℌ𝔞𝔯𝔠𝔬𝔲𝔯𝔱.)

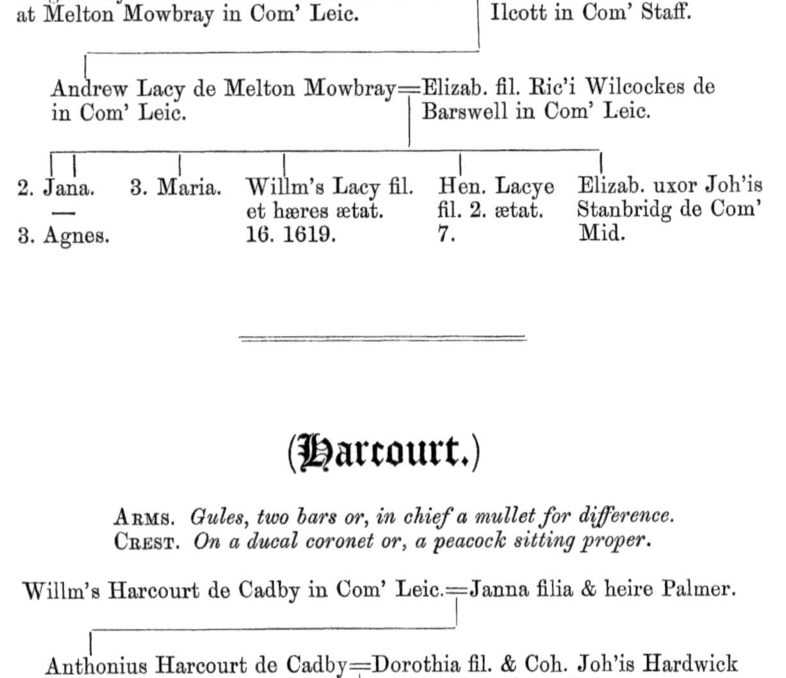

ARMS. *Gules, two bars or, in chief a mullet for difference.*
CREST. *On a ducal coronet or, a peacock sitting proper.*

Willm's Harcourt de Cadby in Com' Leic.═Janna filia & heire Palmer.

Anthonius Harcourt de Cadby═Dorothia fil. & Coh. Joh'is Hardwick
in Com' Leic. | de Linlick in Com' Leic.

Georgius Harecourt de═Elizab. fil. Henrici Leigh   Franciscus Harcourt
Dadlington in Com' | de Russel in Com'   occisus apud Hauer
Leic. | Staff.   de grace.

Willm's Harecourt de Dad-═Margareta filia Joh'is Shukbrough   Georgius Hare-
lington in Com' Leic. | de Naseby in Com' Northamp.   court fil. 2.

Jone nupta Joh'i Tew de Com' Warr.	Maria æt. 18. — Elizab. æt. 17.	Hanna æt. 14. — Margt æt. 8.	Edwardus Hare- court filius et hæres ætat. 22. annoru' 1619.	Georgius Harecourt filius 2. ætat 20.

(Temple.)

ARMS. *Quarterly:—Sable, a chevron ermine between three martlets argent; and azure, a fess ermine between six sea mews' heads erased argent.*
CREST. *A talbot séjant sable, collared and ringed or, charged on the shoulder with a mullet argent for difference.*

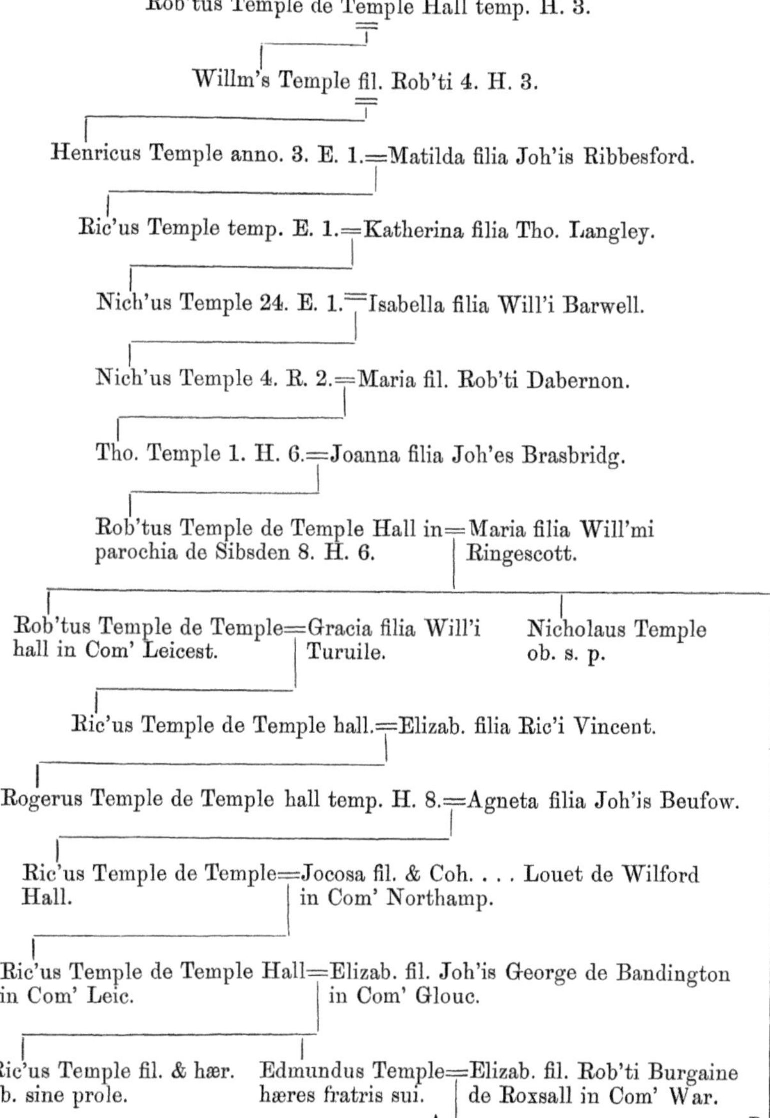

Rob'tus Temple de Temple Hall temp. H. 3.

Willm's Temple fil. Rob'ti 4. H. 3.

Henricus Temple anno. 3. E. 1.=Matilda filia Joh'is Ribbesford.

Ric'us Temple temp. E. 1.=Katherina filia Tho. Langley.

Nich'us Temple 24. E. 1.=Isabella filia Will'i Barwell.

Nich'us Temple 4. R. 2.=Maria fil. Rob'ti Dabernon.

Tho. Temple 1. H. 6.=Joanna filia Joh'es Brasbridg.

Rob'tus Temple de Temple Hall in=Maria filia Will'mi
parochia de Sibsden 8. H. 6. | Ringescott.

Rob'tus Temple de Temple=Gracia filia Will'i
hall in Com' Leicest. | Turuile.　　　　Nicholaus Temple
　　　　　　　　　　　　　　　　　　　　ob. s. p.

Ric'us Temple de Temple hall.=Elizab. filia Ric'i Vincent.

Rogerus Temple de Temple hall temp. H. 8.=Agneta filia Joh'is Beufow.

Ric'us Temple de Temple=Jocosa fil. & Coh. . . . Louet de Wilford
Hall. | in Com' Northamp.

Ric'us Temple de Temple Hall=Elizab. fil. Joh'is George de Bandington
in Com' Leic. | in Com' Glouc.

Ric'us Temple fil. & hær.　　　Edmundus Temple=Elizab. fil. Rob'ti Burgaine
ob. sine prole.　　　　　　　　hæres fratris sui. | de Roxsall in Com' War.
　　　　　　　　　　　　　　　　　　　　　A |　　　　　　　　　　　　　B

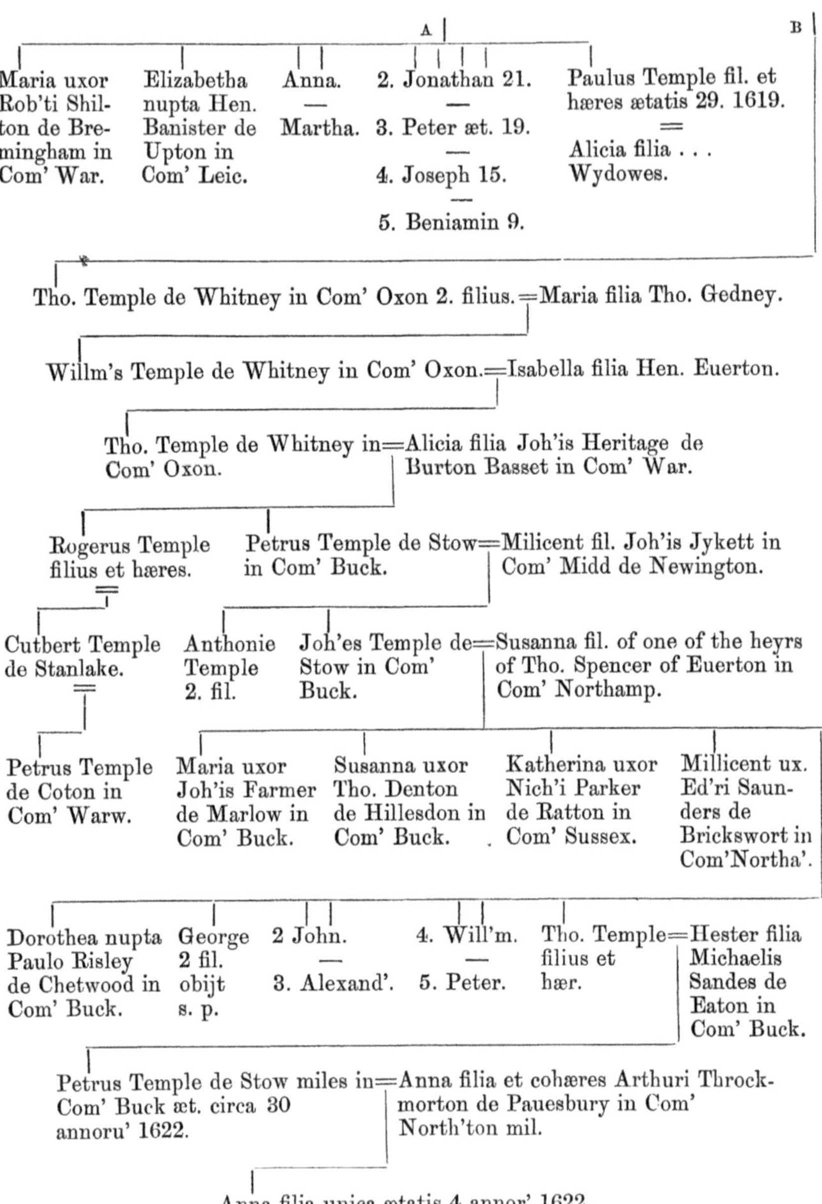

A
B
Maria uxor Rob'ti Shilton de Bremingham in Com' War.
Elizabetha nupta Hen. Banister de Upton in Com' Leic.
Anna. — Martha.
2. Jonathan 21. — 3. Peter æt. 19. — 4. Joseph 15. — 5. Beniamin 9.
Paulus Temple fil. et hæres ætatis 29. 1619. = Alicia filia . . . Wydowes.
Tho. Temple de Whitney in Com' Oxon 2. filius. = Maria filia Tho. Gedney.
Willm's Temple de Whitney in Com' Oxon. = Isabella filia Hen. Euerton.
Tho. Temple de Whitney in Com' Oxon. = Alicia filia Joh'is Heritage de Burton Basset in Com' War.
Rogerus Temple filius et hæres.
Petrus Temple de Stow in Com' Buck. = Milicent fil. Joh'is Jykett in Com' Midd de Newington.
Cutbert Temple de Stanlake.
Anthonie Temple 2. fil.
Joh'es Temple de Stow in Com' Buck. = Susanna fil. of one of the heyrs of Tho. Spencer of Euerton in Com' Northamp.
Petrus Temple de Coton in Com' Warw.
Maria uxor Joh'is Farmer de Marlow in Com' Buck.
Susanna uxor Tho. Denton de Hillesdon in Com' Buck.
Katherina uxor Nich'i Parker de Ratton in Com' Sussex.
Millicent ux. Ed'ri Saunders de Brickswort in Com'Northa'.
Dorothea nupta Paulo Risley de Chetwood in Com' Buck.
George 2 fil. obijt s. p.
2 John. — 3. Alexand'.
4. Will'm. — 5. Peter.
Tho. Temple filius et hær. = Hester filia Michaelis Sandes de Eaton in Com' Buck.
Petrus Temple de Stow miles in Com' Buck æt. circa 30 annoru' 1622. = Anna filia et cohæres Arthuri Throckmorton de Pauesbury in Com' North'ton mil.
Anna filia unica ætatis 4 annor' 1622.

(Beaumont.)

ARMS. *Quarterly :—1. Azure, semée of fleurs-de-lis, a lion rampant or. 2. Azure, three garbs or, banded gules. 3. Gules, seven mascles conjoined or, three, three, and one. 4. Gules, a cinquefoil ermine pierced. 5. Azure, a lion rampant argent, crowned or. 6. Argent, an inescocheon within a double tressure flory counterflory gules. 7. Azure, three garbs or. 8. Gules, a lion rampant vair. 9. Azure, a fess argent between three cinquefoils or. 10. Argent, a maunch sable, in chief a crescent of the last for difference. 11. Argent, a fess sable between three birds (untinctured). On an escocheon of pretence or, three rere-mice displayed gules.*

CREST. *On a cap of maintenance azure, semée of fleurs-de-lis or, turned up ermine, a lion passant of the second.*

Ludouicus fil. Caroli R. Ceciliæ filij Ludouici 8. Regis═Alicia fil. et hær Vice-Francoru' et frater Caroli Regis Ceciliæ. | comitis Beaum'.

Henricus de Bellomonte Baro vocatus Comes Boghan ob. 14. E. 3.

Ludouicus de Bellomonte Ep'us Dunelm'.

Johannes de Bellomonte═Alianora filia Henrici Comitis═Ric'us Comes Arundell. obijt 16. E. 3. | Lancast' ob. 47. E. 3. | 2. maritus.

Isabella nupta Henrico Duci Lancastriæ.

Henricus D'ns de Bellomonte.═Margareta filia Joh'is Vere Comitis Oxon'.

Joh'es de Beaumont ob. 20. R. 2. fuit miles Garterij.═Katherina fil. et her. Tho. Eueringham de Laxton militis ob. 5. H. 6.

Ricardus Beaumont 2 filius.

Cicilia uxor D'ni Bo-treaux.

Elinora monialis apud Amsburie.

Henricus de Beau-mont miles ob. 1. H. 5.═Elizab. filia Willmi D'ni Willoughby ob. 6. H. 6.

A

Tho. Beaumont miles D'ns de Baqueville in francia 5. H. 6. fil. 3.═Phillippa fil. et hær. Tho. Marward de Quarter-mersh in Com' Leic.

B

z

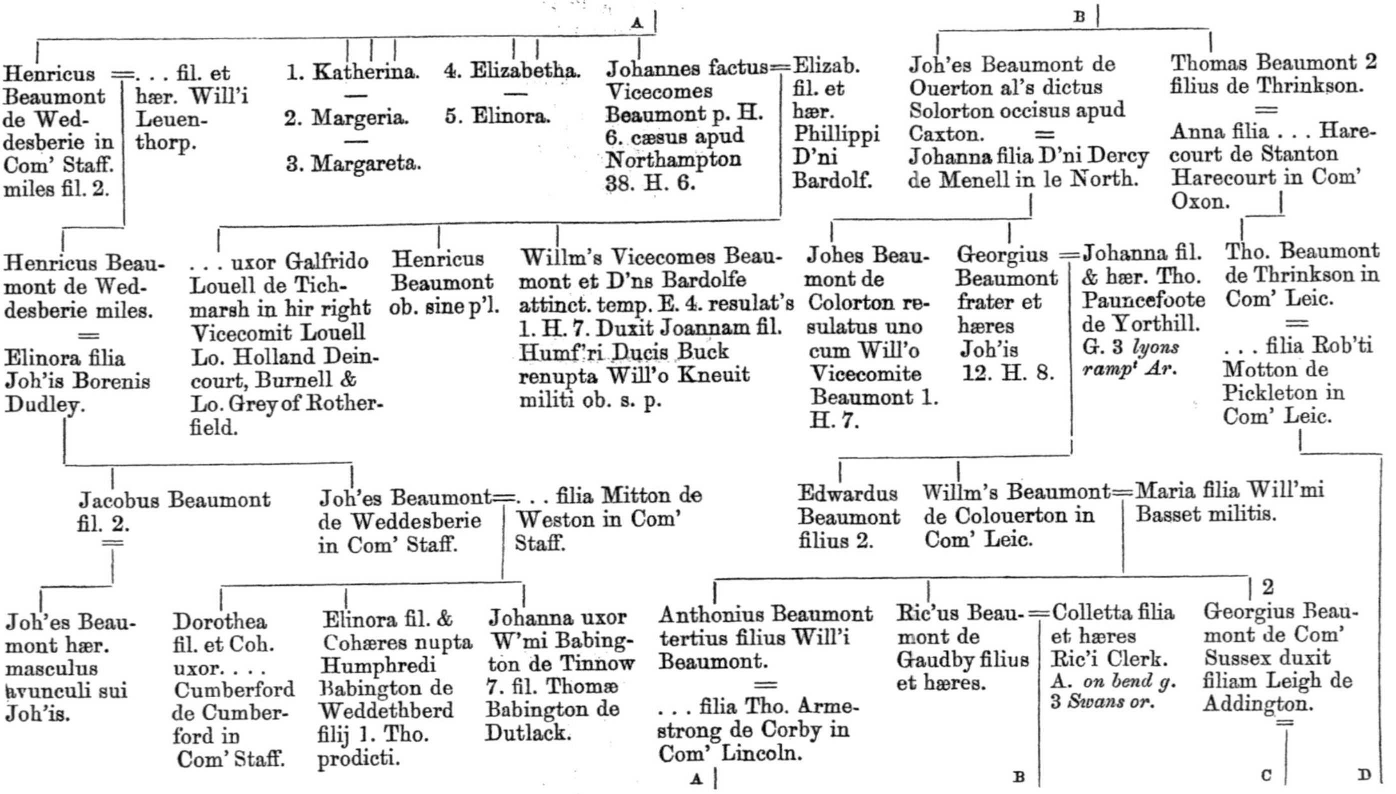

A |

Henricus Beaumont de Weddesberie in Com' Staff. miles fil. 2. =... fil. et hær. Will'i Leuenthorp.

1. Katherina.
2. Margeria.
3. Margareta.
4. Elizabetha.
5. Elinora.

Johannes factus Vicecomes Beaumont p. H. 6. cæsus apud Northampton 38. H. 6. = Elizab. fil. et hær. Phillippi D'ni Bardolf.

B |

Joh'es Beaumont de Ouerton al's dictus Solorton occisus apud Caxton. = Johanna filia D'ni Dercy de Menell in le North.

Thomas Beaumont 2 filius de Thrinkson. = Anna filia ... Harecourt de Stanton Harecourt in Com' Oxon.

Henricus Beaumont de Weddesberie miles. = Elinora filia Joh'is Borenis Dudley.

... uxor Galfrido Louell de Tichmarsh in hir right Vicecomit Louell Lo. Holland Deincourt, Burnell & Lo. Grey of Rotherfield.

Henricus Beaumont ob. sine p'l.

Willm's Vicecomes Beaumont et D'ns Bardolfe attinct. temp. E. 4. resulat's 1. H. 7. Duxit Joannam fil. Humf'ri Ducis Buck renupta Will'o Kneuit militi ob. s. p.

Johes Beaumont de Colorton resulatus uno cum Will'o Vicecomite Beaumont 1. H. 7.

Georgius Beaumont frater et hæres Joh'is 12. H. 8. = Johanna fil. & hær. Tho. Pauncefoote de Yorthill. G. 3 *lyons ramp'* Ar.

Tho. Beaumont de Thrinkson in Com' Leic. = ... filia Rob'ti Motton de Pickleton in Com' Leic.

Jacobus Beaumont fil. 2. =

Joh'es Beaumont de Weddesberie in Com' Staff. = ... filia Mitton de Weston in Com' Staff.

Edwardus Beaumont filius 2.

Willm's Beaumont de Colouerton in Com' Leic. = Maria filia Will'mi Basset militis.

Joh'es Beaumont hær. masculus avunculi sui Joh'is.

Dorothea fil. et Coh. uxor.... Cumberford de Cumberford in Com' Staff.

Elinora fil. & Cohæres nupta Humphredi Babington de Weddethberd filij 1. Tho. prodicti.

Johanna uxor W'mi Babington de Tinnow 7. fil. Thomæ Babington de Dutlack.

Anthonius Beaumont tertius filius Will'i Beaumont. = ... filia Tho. Armestrong de Corby in Com' Lincoln.

Ric'us Beaumont de Gaudby filius et hæres. = Colletta filia et hæres Ric'i Clerk. A. *on bend g.* 3 *Swans or.*

2

Georgius Beaumont de Com' Sussex duxit filiam Leigh de Addington. =

A | B   C   D

A B C D

Franciscus Beaumont filius et hæres miles =

Georgius Villers de Brokesby in Com' Leic. miles 1. maritus.

= Maria nupta Will'i Reyner 2. maritus. illa fuit Creata Comitissa Buck. p' Jacobu' Regem. 1618.

= Tho. Compton miles frater Will'i Comitis Northampton maritus 3. sup'stes 1619.

Anna ux. Will'i Brett de Rotherby in Com' Leic. — ... filia ux. Ashby — Dorothea ux. .... Hill de Com' Warr.

Aueria uxor Tho. Findern de Finderne s. p. — Henricus Beaumont Prebendarius de Winsor.

Nicholas Beaumont of Colouerton in Com' Leister. ob. 1585. = Anna filia Will'mi Saunders de Melford in Com' North.

Tho. Beaumont de Sussex habuit uxores. — Hen. Prebendarius de Windsor.

Filia ux. Comitis et Baronis Maxwell.

Huntington Beaumont.

Franciscus Beaumont 3. fil.

Sr. Henry Beaumont de Colorton in Com' Leic. miles ob. 1607. = Elizab. fil. & hær. ... Leois Ciuis London.

Sr. Tho. Beaum^t de Stoughton in Com' Leic. = Katherina fil. et hær. Thomæ Farnham de Stoughton.

Tho. Beaumont de Colouerton in Com' Leic. miles et Baronettus sup'stes 1619. = Elizab. fil. & hær. Hen. Sapcott de Elton in Com' Hunt.

---

2. Henricus æt. 4.
3. Thomas æt. 2.
4. Rob'tus.

Sapcott Beaumont fil. et hær. ætat. 6. 1619.

1. Elizab.
2. Katherin.
3. Francis.

4. Maria.
5. Elianor.

Thomas.
Anna.

Jana ob. s. p.

Jana uxor Will'i Temple de London Mercator.

Isabell uxor Hugonis Snousell de Belton in Com' Eboru'.

Anna uxor Joh's Dillon de Fordinghoe. — Elizab. ux. Joh'is Ashbornham militis.

Francisca ux. Wolstani Dixi de Bosworth in Com' Leic. — Maria uxor Ric'i Paramour de Loseby in Com' Leic. — Elinor.

Henricus Beaumont fil. et hær. Miles duxit Elizab. fil. Will'i Turpen de Knoptoft in Com' Leic. militis.

Farnam Beaumont 2 fil. — Thomas Beaumont 3 fil.

D

D

Isabella filia Law-=Joh'es Mr Rotulorum=Elizab. 2. fil. et
rentij Dutton de | perquisiuit manerium | Coh. Will'mi
Dutton in Com' | de Grace dieu in | Hastinges militis
Cest'. | Com' Leic. | 2. uxor.

Maria uxor Ric'i Storey de Bromston in Com' Leic.

Dorothea uxor . . . Rigmaden.

Edwardus Beaumont 2. filius.

Anna uxor Tho. Ashby de Loseby in Com' Leic.

Franciscus Beau-=Anna fil. Georgij
mont Justicia- | Peirpoint de
rius de Com'uni | Holme in Com'
Banco. ob. 12. | Nott.
Aprilis 1598.

Elizab. ux. W'mi D'ni Vaulx de Harroden.

Jana uxor Rob'ti Brokesby de Sholby.

Willm's Beau-=. . . filia
mont filius et | . . . Yore
hæres. | de Derby.

Christopherus Beaumont 2 filius.

Elizab. ux. . . . Suliard.

Johannes Beau-=Elizab.
mont de Grace | filia
dieu fil. et | Joh'is
hæres superstes | Fortes-
1619. | cue de
| London.

Henricus =Barbara fil.
Beaumont | . . . Anthoni
Miles ob. | Faunt de
1605. | Foston in
| Com' Leic.

Franciscus Beaumont
de Barrow in Com'
Derby aº 1607.
=
Elizab. fil. et her.
Simonis Brasbruge.

Edward Baumont
2 fil.

—

Willm's Beaumont 3. fil.

Elina fil. 1. ætat. 8.

2. Katherina æt. 4.

—

3. Maria æt. 3.

Johannes Beaumont fil. et hær. ætat. 12. 1619.

Franciscus Beaumont fil. 2. ætat. 11.

Henricus fil. 3. ætat. 9.

4. Geruais æt. 5.

—

5. George æt. 1.

Barbara.

(Bickerton.)

ARMS. *Argent, on a chevron sable three pheons of the field.*

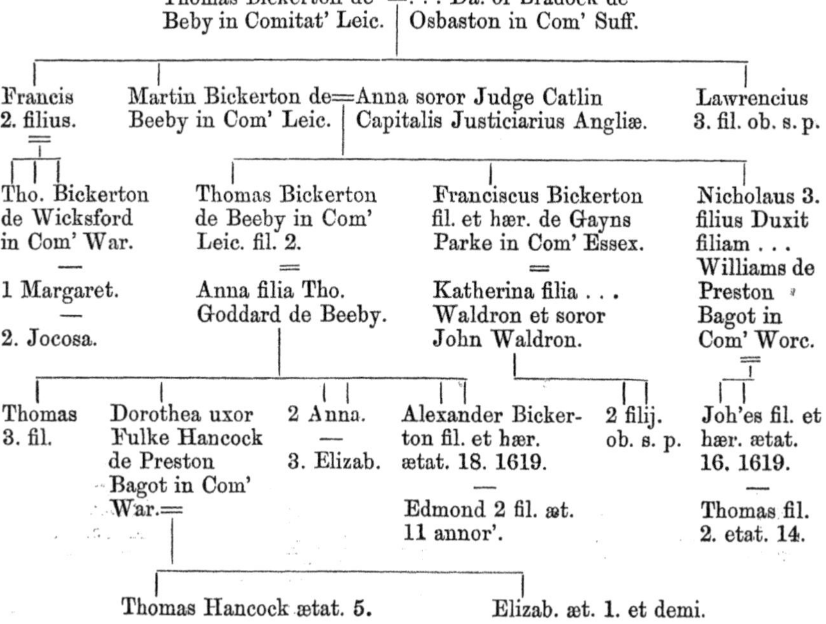

Thomas Bickerton de =... Da. of Bradock de
Beby in Comitat' Leic. | Osbaston in Com' Suff.

Francis
2. filius.

Martin Bickerton de=Anna soror Judge Catlin
Beeby in Com' Leic. | Capitalis Justiciarius Angliæ.

Lawrencius
3. fil. ob. s. p.

Tho. Bickerton
de Wicksford
in Com' War.

1 Margaret.

2. Jocosa.

Thomas Bickerton
de Beeby in Com'
Leic. fil. 2.

Anna filia Tho.
Goddard de Beeby.

Franciscus Bickerton
fil. et hær. de Gayns
Parke in Com' Essex.

Katherina filia ...
Waldron et soror
John Waldron.

Nicholaus 3.
filius Duxit
filiam ...
Williams de
Preston
Bagot in
Com' Worc.

Thomas
3. fil.

Dorothea uxor
Fulke Hancock
de Preston
Bagot in Com'
War.=

2 Anna.

3. Elizab.

Alexander Bicker-
ton fil. et hær.
ætat. 18. 1619.

Edmond 2 fil. æt.
11 annor'.

2 filij.
ob. s. p.

Joh'es fil. et
hær. ætat.
16. 1619.

Thomas fil.
2. etat. 14.

Thomas Hancock ætat. 5.

Elizab. æt. 1. et demi.

(Leigh.)

ARMS. *Quarterly:—1. Azure, two bars argent, over all on a bend gules in dexter
chief a mullet or for difference. 2. Or, three lozenges azure. 3. Ermine, on a
chief indented gules three ducal coronets or. 4. Argent, a fleur-de-lis sable. A
mullet for difference.*

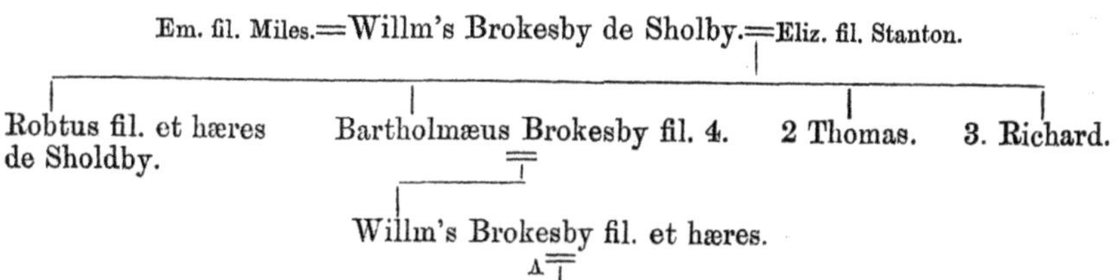

Em. fil. Miles.=Willm's Brokesby de Sholby.=Eliz. fil. Stanton.

Robtus fil. et hæres
de Sholdby.

Bartholmæus Brokesby fil. 4.

2 Thomas.

3. Richard.

Willm's Brokesby fil. et hæres.

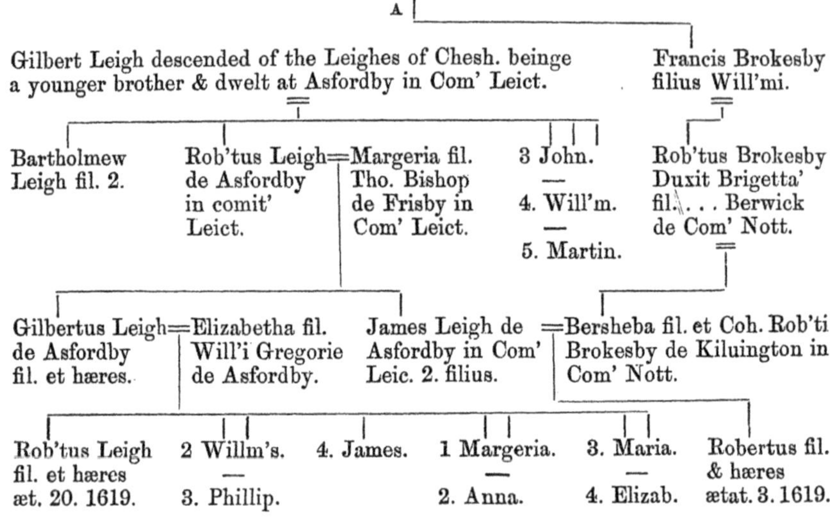

A |

Gilbert Leigh descended of the Leighes of Chesh. beinge a younger brother & dwelt at Asfordby in Com' Leict.

Francis Brokesby filius Will'mi.

Bartholmew Leigh fil. 2.

Rob'tus Leigh de Asfordby in comit' Leict.=Margeria fil. Tho. Bishop de Frisby in Com' Leict.

3 John.
—
4. Will'm.
—
5. Martin.

Rob'tus Brokesby Duxit Brigetta' fil. . . . Berwick de Com' Nott.

Gilbertus Leigh de Asfordby fil. et hæres.=Elizabetha fil. Will'i Gregorie de Asfordby.

James Leigh de Asfordby in Com' Leic. 2. filius.=Bersheba fil. et Coh. Rob'ti Brokesby de Kiluington in Com' Nott.

Rob'tus Leigh fil. et hæres æt. 20. 1619.

2 Willm's.
—
3. Phillip.

4. James.

1 Margeria.
—
2. Anna.

3. Maria.
—
4. Elizab.

Robertus fil. & hæres ætat. 3. 1619.

(Noone.)

ARMS. *Or, on a cross engrailed vert a crescent of the field for difference.*
CREST. *A double-headed eagle or, with wings displayed vert.*

This Coat & crest confirmed by W. Camden Clarenceux. 1611.

John Noone de Walton in Comitatu Lecestriæ.

Johannes Noone de Walton.

Georgius Noone de Walton in Com' Leic.=Jana, filia . . . Wymark de Com' Rutl.

Georgius 3. fil.

Thomas Noone filius 2.

Rob'tus Noone de Walton in Com' Leic.=Margareta fil. Francisci Cudden de Malbarton in Com' Norf. vel Suff.

Maria nupta Libio Derby de Walton in Com' Leict.

Franciscus Noone de Walton in Com' Leic. ætat. 32. 1619.=Katherina fil. Hen. Goodier de Powlesworth in Com' Warr.

2. Will'm æt. 20.

3. Robtus æt. 14.

(𝕰berard.)

```
            ... filia La-══Ricardus Euerard de Shenton══Anna filia et hær.
            tham ux. 2.  │ in Com' Leic.               │ ... Langham.
```

Stephanus Euerard de══**Jana fil. Tho. Babington de**   **Rob'tus Euerard de Shen-**
Hether in Com' Leic.   │ Rothly Temple in Com' Leic.   ton filius et hæres.

Thomas Euerard══**Francisca filia Tho.**   **Elizab. uxor**   **Maria uxor Tho. Samson**
de Hether in   │ Reeue de Holt Hall   Stafford Watts   de Leic. postea renupta
Com' Leic.   │ in Com' War.   de Barleston   Edw. Gifford.
                                      in Com' Leic.

Thomas Euerard   **Stephanus Euerard**   **Georgius**   **Henricus**   1 Elizab. æt. 13.
2. filius ætat. 4.   fil. et hær. æt. 14.   3. filius   4 filius   —
                     1619.   ætat. 2.   ætat. 1.   2. Jana æt. 6.

(𝕾tarkie.)

ARMS. *(Field untinctured,) a stork (untinctured).*
CREST. *A stork, holding in its beak a snake (untinctured).*

Robertus Starkie de Stretton in Com' Cestriæ Ar.

Thomas Starkie de Tonge══**Alicia filia Will'mi Dethick**
in Com' Leic. aᵒ 10. H. 7.   │ de Newhall in Com' Darb.

Rowland Starkie de   ══**Cicilia fil. Thomæ Winter de**
Tonge in Comit' Leic.   │ Com' Leic. temp. 26. H. 8.

Willm's   **Elizab. uxor ...**   **Georgius Starkie**══**Elizab. filia**   **Maria nupta**
1. filius   Jackson de   de Tonge in   │ Joh'is Pate de   Ric'o Marsh
ob. sans   Newbold in   Com' Leic.   │ Breeden in   de Segraue
issue.   Com' Leic.   │ Com' Leic.   in Com' Leic.

Ric'us fil. 2. æt. 45.   **4 Will'ms.**   **Joh'es Starkie**══**Katherina**   **Elizab. uxor**
—   —   de Tonge in   │ filia Joh'is   Edwardi Tilcott
Rowlandus 3. fil.   5. Edward.   Comit' Leic.   │ Dartnoll   de Packington
Chandeler in   —   ætat. 48.   │ in Com'   in Com' Leic.
London æt. 40.   6. George   │ Rutland.   —
                         ob. sine p'le.   Anna ob. s. p.

1. Elizab.   2. Anna   Georgius fil. et   Joh'es 2 fil.   Edwardus
æt. 15.   æt. 6.   hær. ætat. 13.   ætat. 11.   3. fil. æt. 9.

(Armeston.)

ARMS. *Sable, a chevron between three spear-heads argent, in chief a crescent for difference.*

CREST. *A dragon's head erased proper, charged with a crescent for difference.*

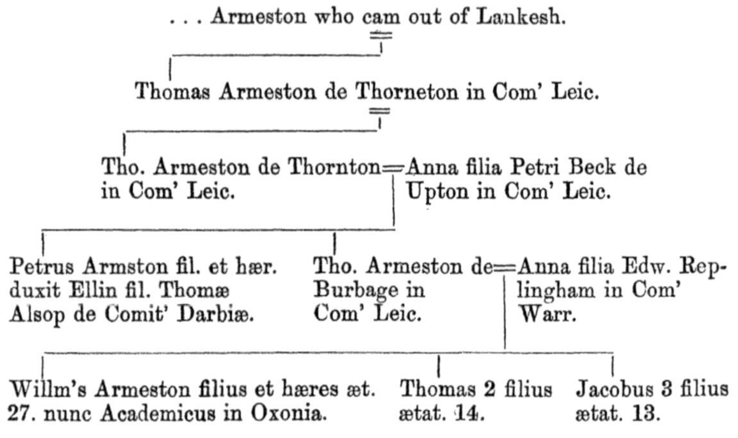

(Trimnell.)

ARMS. *Or, a cross engrailed gules, over all a bendlet azure.*

Rogerus Trimnell al's Trinnell de Com' Staff.

Tho. Trimnell 3. filius.   Johannes Trimnell de Com' Staff.=Anna fil. . . . Fawknor.   Rogerus Trimnell 2. filius.

Fardinando Trimnell 1 fil. ob. s. p.   Basill Trimnell de Stoke Golding in Com' Leic.=Lucia filia Abelis Makepeace de Chipping Warden in Com' Northamp.   Goditha nupta Waltero Britaine de Wincote in Com' Warr.

1 Dorothea æt. 16.

2. Maria æt. 15.

3. Jana æt. 13.

Willm's Trimnell filius et hæres ætat. 14.

Georgius 2 filius ætat. 10.

4. Lucia æt. 9.

5. Briget æt. 8.

(Corbet.)

ARMS. *Or, a raven sable, in chief a mullet gules for difference.*
CREST. *An elephant argent, trapped sable, surmounted with a tower, triple towered or (tinctured).*

Rob'tus Corbet de Morton in Com' Salopiæ.=Anna filia D'ni Windsor.

Andreas Corbet de Morton in Com' Salop fil. et hær. = | Walterus Corbet 2 filius ob. s. p. | Rob'tus Corbet de Stanardine in the wood in Com' Salop 3. filius.

Sr Rob'tus Corbet Duxit fil. D'ni St. John de Bletzo. 1 fil. = | Ric'us Corbet 2 fil. miles ob. s. p. | Vincentius Corbet miles 3. fil. Duxit filiam Humberston. =

Elizab. fil. et hær nupta Hen. Wallop militi. | Anna fil. et Coher. ux. Carey. | Andreas Corbet de=... filia Boothby Morton in Com' de Com' Derbie. Salop mil.

Hierome Corbet one of yᵉ Counsell in the marches of Wales 4 sonne. =Dorothea fil. Tho. Poyner de Bostow in Com' Salop. | Elizab. ux. Vincent Curson. | Margareta ux. Francisci Palmes militis.

Rogerus Corbet de Barton in in Com' Leic. =Jana filia ... Banester de Upton in Com' Leic.

Thomas Corbet fil. et hær. æt. 1 anni. 1619. | 1 Anna æt. 9. | 2. Jana æt. 5.

(Warde, *alias* Farmour.)

ARMS. *Vair, argent and sable.*

Thomas Warde who came out of Chesheire & had issue.

Laurence Warde al's Farmour de Hucklescot Grange in Com' Leic.=... filia ... Smith.

Jacobus 2. filius Duxit uxorem et habuit exitum. | Tho. Warde al's Far-mour de Hucklescot Grange in Com' Leic.=Katherina fil. Jacobi Abney de Willesley in Com' Derbiæ Armig. | Willm's 3. filius habuit exitum filiam unicam.

A

A |

Maria uxor Tho. Dilke de Godeby in Com' Leic.
=

Jacobus Warde al's=Gracia filia Anthonij Gray de Burbedg in Com' Leic.
Farmer de Hucklescot grange in Comit' Leic. ætat. 27. 1619.

Thomas 2. fil. Linnen Drap' in London ætat. 25. 1619.

Joseph 3. filius Scholler in Cambridg ætat. 21.

Thomas Dilke æt. 1. anni.

Katherin ætat. 1.

Thomas Farmer fil. et hæres ætat. 6. 1619.

Henricus 2 filius ætat. 4.

Jacobus 3. fil. ætat. 2.

(Beresford.)

ARMS. *Quarterly:—1. Argent, three fleurs-de-lis between seven cross crosslets fitchée sable, three, two, and two. 2. Argent, three garbs azure, banded or. 3. Argent, three eagles displayed gules within a bordure engrailed sable.*
CRESTS. *First, A badger passant sable. Second, A dragon's head erased or, gorged with a collar gules, charged with a fess indented azure.*

Conventio matrimonij inter Joh'em Barford de Barkeby in Com' Leic. et Margeriam filiam Joh'is Fowler Junioris cum dotalicio in terris in Barford, Thorpe Malford, Ardingworth et Sundelondes in Com' Northa' et Lubbenham in Com' Leic. Dat. 2° Nouemb' a° 21 E. 4.

John Beresford de Darby.
=

Joh'es Beresford de=Margareta filia Joh'is Barkeby in Com' Leic. 21. E. 4.
Fowler nupta 21. E. 4.

Rob'tus Beresford filius Johannis.=... filia et hær. Lole.

Willm's Beresford de Robottle et Shakerston.
=

Arthurus Berford de Shakerston=Dorothea fil. Joh'is Danuers de in Com' Leic.
Swithland in Com' Leic.

Dorothe uxor Michaelis Ashley de Wollaton in Com' Staff.

Adrian 2 fil. æt. 35.

Robertus Berford=Elizab. filia de Shakerston et Nelston in Comit' Leic. ætat. 40.
Thomæ Ashley de Patteshall in Com' Staff.

Arthur 3. filius æt. 35.

Georgius.
—
Thomas.
—
Edward ob. s. p.

1 Elizabetha.
—
2. Jocosa.

3 Isabella.
—
4 Margeria.

Joh'es Berford fil. et hær. ætat. 10. Annoru' 1619.

Franciscus filius 2 æt. 8.

Brianus fil. 3. æt. 6.

(Farmer.)

ARMS. *Sable, on a chevron between three lamps argent, flammant proper, a leopard's face between two mullets gules.*

CREST. *A dexter arm erect, couped at the elbow (untinctured), gauntleted, and holding a lamp argent, flammant proper.*

Barthomeus Farmer de Ratcliff in Com' Leic.=Margeria.

Humphr'us Farmer 3 fil. nupsit filia' ... Wikeman.	Joh'es Farmer de Rat-cliff in comit' Leic.=Elizab. fil. ... Borde de Comit' Buck.	Rad'us fil. 2.

1 Johannes. — 2. Will'mus.	Lawrentius 3. fil. nupsit filiam ... Steines de Huncot in Com' Leic.	Bartholmeus farmer de Ratcliff in Comit' Leic. ætat. 72. 1619.=Ursula filia Rob'ti Mottes de Whit-church iuxta Alisberie in Com' Buck.	Rad'us fil. 2 duxit Elizab. fil. ... Hill de Shinton in Comitat' Staff.

1 Barthol-meus. — 2. Johan-nes.	2. Edwardus æt. 22. — 3. Thomas æt. 21. — 4. Georgius æt. 19.	Will'mus 15. — Rad'us 13.	Johannes Farmer Filius et hæres ætat. 30. annor' 1619.=Maria filia Fran. Purifoy de Cacott in Com' War'.	1 Dorothea 16. — 2. Kathe-rin 9.	1 Mar-geria. — 2. Eli-zabeth.

Letticia æt. 4.	Franciscus Farmer filius et hæres ætat. 3. temp' visitac'onis.	Radulphus fil. 2. ætat. 1.

(Mountney.)

ARMS. *(Field untinctured.) A bend between six martlets (untinctured).*

CREST. *A wolf séjant, collared and lined (untinctured).*

Thomas Mountney de Mountneys Playne in Com' Norff.

Tho. Mountney de Mount-neys Plaine in Com' Norff. filius et hæres.	Will'mus Mountney Marcator de la Staple 2. filius.=Jocosa filia Tho. Whithill de Shepey in Com' Leic.	Stephanus Mountney 3. filus.

Willm's Mountney de Neobald Verdon in Com' Leic.=Margareta filia ... Taylor de Delahey in Com' Derby.

Dorothea uxor Will'i Hemsley de Burton sup' la Would in Com' Leic.	2 Katherina. — 3. Francisca. — 4. Margaret	Georgius Mount-ney filius et hæres ætat. 23.	Thomas 2 fil. Scholler in Cambridg æt. 22.	Willm's 3. filius.

(May.)

ARMS. *Gules, on a fess between eight billets or, a crescent for difference.*
CREST. *Out of a coronet or, a leopard's head gules, charged on the neck with a crescent*
for difference.

Thomas Maye de Faunt in Com' Sussex.

Thomas Maye de Faunt filius et hæres.

Ric'us Maye de Faunt,=Margareta filia . . . Dalley iuxta Mayfeild in Com' Sussex 2. fil. prope Tunbridg in Com' Cantij.

Thomas Maye de Com' Sussex miles.

Jeffrey Maye de Sutton=Joanna filia Will'i Cheney who cam out of Denston de Stonye Sussex ætat. 70. 1619. Stanton in Com' Leic.

Johannes fil. 2 ob. in Hibernia sine prole.

Dorothea uxor Edw. Twine.

Alicia nupta Tho. Wright de Sutton in parochia de Brough-ton Astley in Com' Leic.

3 Marya.
—
4. Katheria.

5. Margareta.

Ricardus Maye de Sutton=Presilla filia Tho. Cheyney in Com' Leic. Stiles de Walton ætat. 33. 1619. in Com' Northamp.

Willm's Maye fil. 2 nupsit Graciam filiam Luke Mortimer de Stonie Stanton in Com' Leic. ætat. 22.

(Gee.)

ARMS. *Gules, a sword in bend argent, hilted and pomelled or, in chief a crescent*
for difference.
CREST. *A dexter gauntlet erect proper, grasping a sword argent.*

Alexander Gee of Rothley in Com' Leic.

Edmundus Gee de Rothley=Grace fil. Tho. in Com' Leic. Baskeruile.

Ric'us Gee 2. filius Duxit filiam Joh'is Villiers.

Joh'es Gee filius et hæres.=Ursula filia Tho. Neuill de Holt in Com' Leic.

Rob'tus Gee fil. et hær. duxit filiam . . . Digbie et ob. sine p'le.

Johannes=Elizab. filia Joh'is Gee filius Hawbark de Joh'is. Stobleford ar.

. . . filia nupta Thomæ Wood-ford Ar.

Roger Gee.

Henricus Gee fil. et hær. of whom is descended Will'm Gee of Hull.

Thomas Gee duxit filiam . . . Poole de Withcocke.

A

A |

* Eustace Gee de Rothley in Com' Leic.=... filia et coh. ... Ellis de Com' Cestriæ.

| Briget ob. s. p. | Jone uxor ... Iues ciuis London. | Anna nupta ... Pudsey de Com' Eboru' | Willm's Gee de Rothley in Com' Leic.=Eliz. fil. ... Hart de Ashbourne greene in Com' Darby. |

Eustace Gee de Rothley in=Anna fil. Joh'is Sauage rector Ecclesiæ
Com' Leic. ætat. 30. 1619. | de Sutton Rodington in Com' Nott.

| Johannes Gee fil. et hæres ætat. 6. annor' temp. huius visitationis. | Willm's 2. fil. ætat. 3. menses 8. die' Septemb' 1619. | Francisca filia ætat. 3. annoru' |

** This descent in the original is on the side, opposite to Eustace Gee of Rothley and
fil. et coh. Ellis de com. Cestriæ.*

Fil. ux.=Willm's Gee 3. fil. Maior=Eliz. fil. Walteri Jobson de Kingston
prima. | of Kingston upon Hull. | upon Hull alderman.

| Anna nupta Rob'to Legard de Kingston sup' Hull. | Willm's Gee fil. et hær. duxit Thomazin filia' Doctoris Hutton. | 2. Walter. — 3. Samuell | Elizab. uxor Joh'is Stephens — Elianor filia 2. |

(𝕭𝖆𝖞𝖓𝖇𝖗𝖎𝖌𝖊.)

ARMS. *Argent, a chevron embattled between three battle-axes sable.*
CREST. *On a mount vert a goat statant (untinctured), attired and collared argent.*

To Will'm Bainbriges of Lockington in Com' Leic. by Will'm Flowre Norrey
14. feb. 1585. aº 26. Elizab.

Johannes Baynbrig del North.=Alicia fil.

| Rob'tus Baynbrigge de Lockington in Com' Leicest.=Isabella filia Will'mi Milgate de Manchester in Com' Lancast'. | Thomas 2. fil. |

| Will'mus Baynbrig de Lockington in Com' Leic.=Elizab. filia Edwardi Charde one of yᵉ Exchequer in Westm'. | Alicia uxor Tho. Hunt de Com' Derby. |

A|

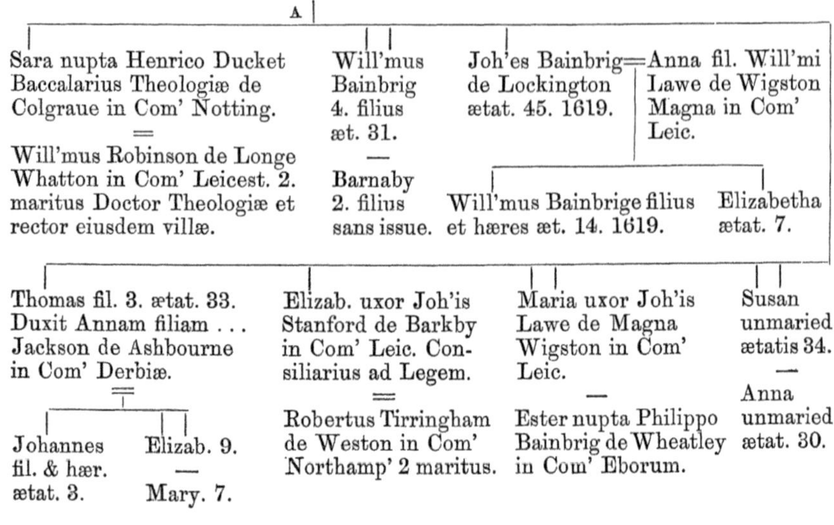

(𝕽𝖔𝖇𝖎𝖓𝖘𝖔𝖓,)

ARMS. *Vert, on a chevron between three stags statant or as many trefoils slipped gules, in chief a crescent for difference.*

Willmus Robinson descended out of yᵉ North.

(Eyton.)

ARMS. *Quarterly :—1. Or, a fret azure.* (EYTON.)   2. *Barry of six ermine and gules.* (HUSSEY.)   3. *Argent, a fess between three sinister wings sable.* (DERBY.)
CREST. *A lion's head argent, holding in his mouth a tun or.*

Ricardus Eyton de Perie in Com' Staff.═Maria filia Will'mi Brasbridge.

Edwardus Eyton de Gadsby in Com' Leic.═Elizab. filia Libiis Derby de Gatesby.

Symon Eyton duxit Mariam 1 filiam Tho. Ashbye de Loseby.

Anthonius Eyton═Maria filia . . . Gray de de Gatesby. Newton in Com' Leicest.

Henricus Pilkington de═Anna filia et hæres Simonis Eyton.
Borow in Com' Leic. filius Rob'ti Pilkington.

Isaack Eyton filius et hæres ætat. 14.

1 Damoris.   3 Presilla.
—   —
2. Apula.   4. Debora.

Henricus Pilkington filius et hæres ætat. 12.

2 Will'mus 8.   3. Rob'tus 6.   4. Thomas 4.

(Morton.)

ARMS. *Argent, on a chevron gules between three demi-buckles, tongues pendant, sable, a mullet or for difference.*

Willm's Morton de Bosworth in Com' Leic.
descended of Morton of Morton in Com' Staff.

Rob'tus Morton de═
Sutton in Com'
Leic. fil. et hær.
obijt apud Gils-
brough in Com'
Northamp.

Tho. Mor-═
ton 2 fil.
de Potters
Cotten in
Com' War.

Joh'es Morton
3. filius
Rector Ecc'liæ
de North Kil-
worth ob. sine
prole.

Willm's Morton de
Leicester 5. fil.
═
Alicia filia Will'mi
Borage de Leicest.

John Mor-═
ton fil. et
hæres.

Joh'es
Morton
2. filius.

Rob'tus Morton 1.
filius de Northkil-
worth in Com' Leic.
habuit exitu'.

Thomas
Morton
2 filius.

Will'ms Mor-
ton de New-
castell supra
Tine.

Thomas Morton filius Johannis.

A

A |

Nicholas Morton=Francisca filia Ric'i Yate de   Edw. Bowyer=Elizab. fil. et
de Bosworth in | Roughton in perochia de   de Bosworth. | Coh. Joh'is Ma-
Com' Leic. | Woruell in Com' Salop. | lorie militis.

Joh'es Morton de =Elizab. fil. W'mi   Edwardus Morton=Anna filia et heres
Quarenden in Com' | King de Seleby   filius et hæres de | Edwardi Bowyer
Leic. 2. filius. | in Com' Leic.   Bosworth. | de Bosworth.

Jana 2   Francis uxor Rob'ti   Johannes Morton 2. filius   Willm's Morton fil. et
filia   Slimun de Tickell   82. ætat. annorum 1619.   hær. ætat. 30 Anno-
bibit   in Com' Yorke   rum 1619. =
solu'-   =   Juditha filia . . . Ched-
modo   —   Maria filia Joh'is Allen   low de Ciuitate Co-
Aquam.   Nicholaus Morton   de Mountsorrell in Com'   uentriæ.
            3. filius æt. 23.   Leic.

Rob'tus Morton=Anna filia . . . Chettle   Anna uxor Geo.
filius et hæres   de Longe Whatton in   Gladwyn de Darl
                   Com' Leic.   in Com' Darby.

(𝕳𝖔𝖑𝖑𝖎𝖓𝖌𝖜𝖔𝖗𝖙𝖍.)

ARMS. *Azure, on a bend argent three holly leaves slipped vert.*

Hollingworth=filia Duncalf.

Hollingworth=filia Leuerseege.

Radulphus Hollinworth de Bushingthorp=Isabella filia . . .
in Com' L'ncolne whose father came fro' | Shaw de Com'
Mottra' in Chesheire. | Lincoln.

Francisca filia Tho. Saunder-=Radulphus Hollingworth de=Susanna filia Joh'is
son de Weston in Com' | Wheston in Com' Leic. duxit | Whitby de Comitat
Leic. relicta Will'mi Ashby | Emmot filia Will'mi Carre | Ebor' uxor prima.
3. uxor. | de Com' Lincolne 2. uxor.

Radulphus Hollingworth filius   Patience uxor Tris-   2. Ellina 20.   4. Elizab. 17.
et hæres ætat. 24. modo Aca-   tam Holland Ciuis
demicus Oxoniæ.   Londini.   3. Susan 18.
                                    =

George Holland filius et hæres ætat unius anni 1620.

(𝕾alisburp.)

ARMS. *Gules, a lion rampant argent, charged on the shoulder with a crescent for difference, between three crescents or.*

CREST. *On a mount (untinctured) a lion rampant argent, and charged on the shoulder with a crescent for difference, in dexter paw a crescent or.*

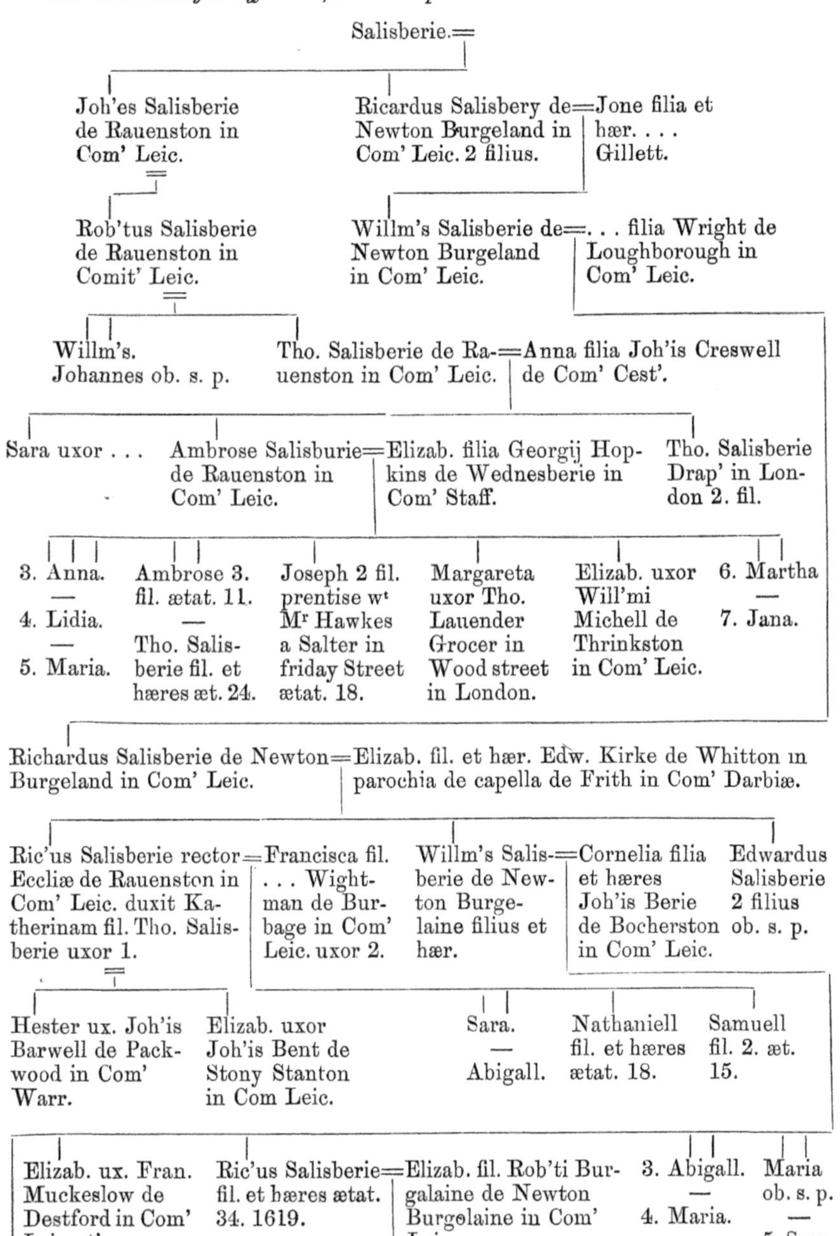

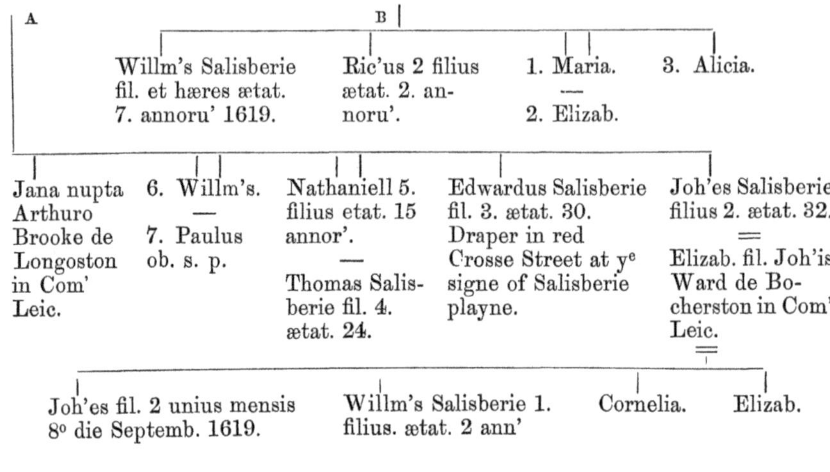

A   B

Willm's Salisberie   Ric'us 2 filius   1. Maria.   3. Alicia.
fil. et hæres ætat.   ætat. 2. an-   —
7. annoru' 1619.   noru'.   2. Elizab.

Jana nupta   6. Willm's.   Nathaniell 5.   Edwardus Salisberie   Joh'es Salisberie
Arthuro   —   filius etat. 15 fil. 3. ætat. 30.   filius 2. ætat. 32.
Brooke de   7. Paulus   annor'.   Draper in red   =
Longoston   ob. s. p.   —   Crosse Street at yᵉ   Elizab. fil. Joh'is
in Com'   Thomas Salis-   signe of Salisberie   Ward de Bo-
Leic.   berie fil. 4.   playne.   cherston in Com'
                             ætat. 24.   Leic.
                                                                       =

Joh'es fil. 2 unius mensis   Willm's Salisberie 1.   Cornelia.   Elizab.
8° die Septemb. 1619.   filius. ætat. 2 ann'

(𝕷𝖆𝖈𝖞.)

ARMS. *Quarterly :—1. Argent, six pellets, three, two, and one, a crescent surmounted
by a mullet gules for difference. 2. Gules, six billets or, three, two, and one,
on a chief indented three roundles (untinctured). 3. Per pale gules and sable,
a lion rampant argent, crowned or.*

Jasperus Roskin.=... filia et coh. Bellers.

Ric'us Lacy de Hallifax=Margaret Da. et coh. Jasperi Roskin
in Com' Eboru'.   de Melton Mowbray in Com' Leic.

John Lacy 3. filius   Seth Lacy fil.=Isabella filia   Leonard Lacy 2. filius Duxit
Duxit Elizabetham   et hæres.   Henrici Farrar   Joannam filiam Muston.
filiam ... Lissay.   de Hallifax.   =
=

1. Faith.   Mathew   Willm's Lacy de =Anna filia Joh'is   Elizab. nupta
—   Lacy.   Melton Mowbray   Digby de Welby   Tho. Frearch
2. Isabell.   in Com' Leic.   in Com' Leic.   postea Johanni
—   sup'stes 1563.   sup'stes 1563.   Elwood.
3. Modwen.

Johes Lacy filius et hæres.

1 Seth.   2. Thomas.   1 Elizab.   2. Mary.   3. Grace.

(Nicolls.)

ARMS. *Sable, three pheons argent.*

Nicolls del North tempore E. 4. et de Ecton in Comit' Northamp.

Thomas Nicolls de Pichley in Com' Northamp. et=Anna filia Joh'is Pell de Elting-
ib'm sepultus. ob. 29. Junij 1563 ætatis. 38. | ton in Com' Northamp.

Franciscus Nicolls=Anna filia   Edwardus=Maria filia=Augustinus Nicolls de
de Hardwick in   Dauidis   Bagshaw   Heminges   Faxston miles unus Justi-
Com' Northamp.   Seamour.   de London   de London.   ciarius de Comuni Banco
fil. et hæres.   1. maritus.   obijt 1617. sine prole.

Maria ob.   Franciscus Nicolls de Hardwick et=Maria filia Edw.   Johannes
virginem.   Faxston Ar. fil. et hæres Francisci   Bagshaw de   Bagshaw
         consanguinius et hæres Augustini   London.   filius et
         superstes aº 1619.   hær.

Maria ætatis 2. annorum.

Willm's Nicolls de Tilton   Susanna uxor Rob'ti   Margeria ux. Michaelis Purifoy
in Com' Leic. superstes   Manley de Com' Warr.   de Mussin in Com' Leic.
1619.

=   Anna uxor Ed'ri   Lodouicus Nicolls mercator
Jocosa filia Geo. Gifford de   Hasilrig de Theding-   London 3. fil, ob. s. p.
Botlebridg in Com' Hunt.   worth in Com' Leic.

Augustinus Nicolls   2 Will'mus æt. 2.   1 Maria 12.   3. Elizab. 6.
filius et hæres ætat.
11. 1619.   3. Francis æt. 1.   2 Anna 11.   4. Jane. 3.

(Gregory.)

ARMS. *Quarterly* :—1. *Or, two bars and in chief a lion passant azure.*   2. *Argent,
a saltire engrailed sable.*   3. *Azure, a lion rampant argent, crowned or, debruised
by a bend gules.*   4. *Ermine, a fess paly of six or and gules.*   5. *Sable, two lions
passant in pale argent, crowned or.*   6. *Vair, a fess gules, fretty or.*
CREST. *A demi-boar couped rampant sable, gorged with a collar or.*

Johannes D'ns de Grigorie=Matilda de Pekulton filia
de Freseley et de Asforby. | D'ni de Pekulton.

Ric'us iste dedit partem   Ric'us Gregorie   Nicholas   Walterus   Alicia nupta
terrarum de Fresley Ab-   Dn's de Freseley   2 filius   Gregorie   Hugoni, filio
batiæ de Lilleshull in   et Asfordby ob.   pater Adæ   3 fil. pater   Stephani de
perpetuam Elimozinam.   20. E. 1.   Gregory.   Ric'i Gregorie.   Erdwick.

A

A

Franciscus iste relaxauit Will'o de Percy ius
suum in aduocatione Prioratus de Selibred ac
terras in Soundon et Hasseta in Sussex p' finem
a° H. filij regis Johannis.

Dn's Franciscus
Gregorie despensator
Simonis de Montiforti
Comitis Leicest.

Johannes 2. filius.
—
Thomas 3. filius.

A° 46. H. 3. quidem Rad'us Gregorie leuauit finem
de terris in Iabsmith Gregorie in Com' Essex.

Radulphus Gregorie=... filia Petri
filius et hæres.   de Asfordebye.

Iste Thomas educatus
in Cantabrigia doctus
Clericus habuit mane-
rium de Asfordby.

Thomas Gregorie de
Asfordby sup'stes
21. Ed. fil. regis Edw.
=
Isabella de Segraue
hæres manerij de
Cateby. filia et hær.
Ric'i Segraue.

Willm's Gregorie 2. filius
duxit Aliciam filiam et
hæredem Roberti de
Cawley D'ni de Cawley
in Com' Warw.

Ricardus
4. filius.
—
Henricus 3.
filius cæsus
fuit in bello
in Scotia.

Johannes
Gregorie
2. filius de
Asfordby.
=
Margareta
uxor.

Franciscus
Canonicus
beatæ Mariæ
in pratis
Leicest'.
Doctor
Theoligiæ.

Willm's 3.
filius habuit
hæredita-
menta in
Thornton
et Desford.

Joh'es 4
filius fuit
escaetor
D'ni Regis.

Elizabetha
monialis
de Polles-
worth.

Fines de Anno p'mo
R. 2. Margareta
Gregorie de terris in
Rotherwick in Com'
Suth'.

Robertus Gregorie=... filia D'ni de Bosworth
de Asfordby.   relicta Hen. Harecourt.

Willm's Gregorie 1 fil. obijt
sine sobule masculo.

Joh'es Gregorie Armig' Escaetor=Johanna filia ... Billesby
D'ni Regis iu Com' Dorcest.   soror D'ni Will'mi Billesby.

Thomas Gregorie Armiger.=Alionora filia Ric'i Billesby de Com' Lincoln.

Willm's Gregorie de Asfordby.=Hellena soror et heres Joh'is Malin.

Thomas Gregorie fil. et hæres=Elizabetha filia Christ'.
Consanguineus et hæres   Wade mercatoris Couen-
Will'mi Dimmock de Eiton   triæ maioris eiusdem
in Com' Nott.   ciuitatis.

Willm's Gregorie
de Asfordby 2.
filius.=

3. Christopherus.
—
4. Edmondus.

Henricus
2. filius.

Arthurus Gregorie fil. et=Jana filia Joh'is Ferrers
hær. Thomæ Dn's de   filij Humphredi Ferrers
Stiuechall in Com' Warr.   de Tamworth.

Tho. Gregorie primogenitus ob. s. p.   Johannes Gregorie.   Rob'tus 3. filius.

A

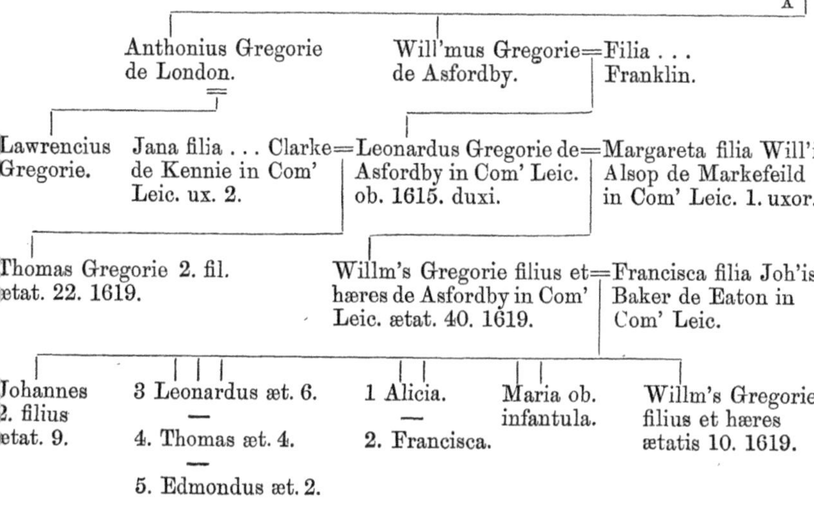

A |

Anthonius Gregorie de London.

Will'mus Gregorie=Filia . . . de Asfordby. | Franklin.

Lawrencius Gregorie.

Jana filia . . . Clarke=Leonardus Gregorie de=Margareta filia Will'i de Kennie in Com' | Asfordby in Com' Leic. | Alsop de Markefeild Leic. ux. 2. | ob. 1615. duxi. | in Com' Leic. 1. uxor.

Thomas Gregorie 2. fil. ætat. 22. 1619.

Willm's Gregorie filius et=Francisca filia Joh'is hæres de Asfordby in Com' | Baker de Eaton in Leic. ætat. 40. 1619. | Com' Leic.

Johannes 2. filius ætat. 9.

3 Leonardus æt. 6.
—
4. Thomas æt. 4.
—
5. Edmondus æt. 2.

1 Alicia.
—
2. Francisca.

Maria ob. infantula.

Willm's Gregorie filius et hæres ætatis 10. 1619.

(Gilbert.)

ARMS. *Field (untinctured) a leg couped at the thigh in armour proper, spur or, between two broken spears in fess argent, in chief a mullet for difference.*
CREST. *An arm couped at the shoulder, embowed in armour proper, grasping a broken spear argent, the point downwards, staff or.*

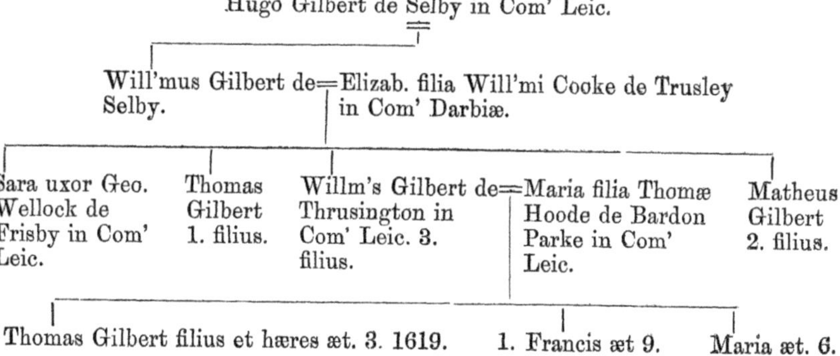

Hugo Gilbert de Selby in Com' Leic.

Will'mus Gilbert de=Elizab. filia Will'mi Cooke de Trusley Selby. | in Com' Darbiæ.

Sara uxor Geo. Wellock de Frisby in Com' Leic.

Thomas Gilbert 1. filius.

Willm's Gilbert de=Maria filia Thomæ Thrusington in | Hoode de Bardon Com' Leic. 3. | Parke in Com' filius. | Leic.

Matheus Gilbert 2. filius.

Thomas Gilbert filius et hæres æt. 3. 1619.	1. Francis æt 9.	Maria æt. 6.

(Goddard.)

ARMS. *Azure, on a fess between three hawks' heads erased or, five lozenges conjoined in fess vert.*

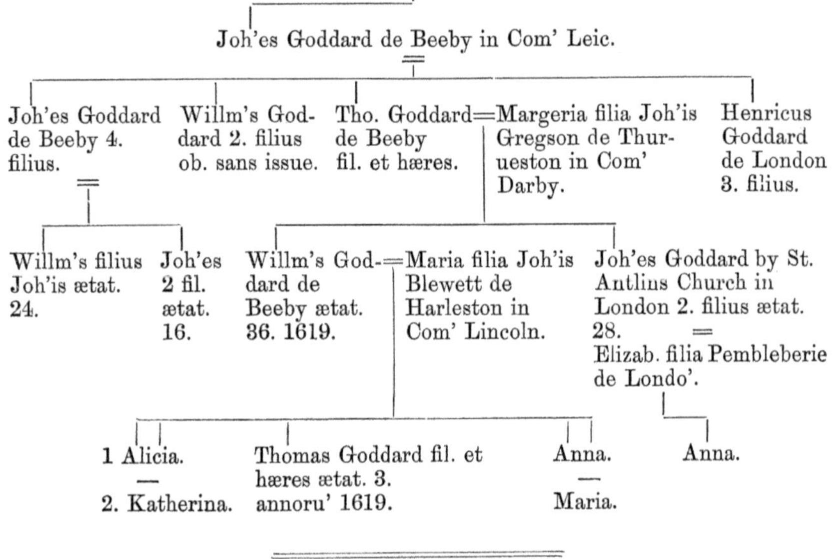

Willm's Goddard de Beeby in Com' Leic. descended out of Barksheir.

Joh'es Goddard de Beeby in Com' Leic.

Joh'es Goddard de Beeby 4. filius.   Willm's Goddard 2. filius ob. sans issue.   Tho. Goddard de Beeby fil. et hæres.═Margeria filia Joh'is Gregson de Thurueston in Com' Darby.   Henricus Goddard de London 3. filius.

Willm's filius Joh'is ætat. 24.   Joh'es 2 fil. ætat. 16.   Willm's Goddard de Beeby ætat. 36. 1619.═Maria filia Joh'is Blewett de Harleston in Com' Lincoln.   Joh'es Goddard by St. Antlins Church in London 2. filius ætat. 28. ═ Elizab. filia Pembleberie de Londo'.

1 Alicia. — 2. Katherina.   Thomas Goddard fil. et hæres ætat. 3. annoru' 1619.   Anna. — Maria.   Anna.

(Bainbrig.)

ARMS. *Argent, a chevron embattled between three battle-axes sable, in chief a crescent gules for difference.*

Joh'es Bainbrig de Wheatley in Com' Leic.═Alicia filia.

Rob'tus Bainbrig filius Primogenitus.   Thomas Bainbrig 2. filius.═Alicia fil. Rob'ti Palmer de West Broughton.   Joh'es Bainbrige 3. filius.

Willm's Bainbrig de Lockington.═Elizab. filia … Chare.   Anna fil. Ric'i Euerard de Shenton uxor 1.═Rob'tus Bainbrig de Asby de la Zouch.═Lucia fil. Willm' Stacy de Borrow in Com' Leic. 2. ux.

Joseph filius primus ob. sans issue.   Mathew 2. filius ætat. 14.   Rachell uxor Tho. Corbison de Polesworth in Com' Warr.   Martha. — Margareta. — Abigall.   Hester. — Berseba. — Susanna.   Sara. — Sara 2. fil. ob. s. p.

A

| A |

Anna uxor Humphredi Westwood de London Goldsmith. — Elizab. nupta Francisco Smith de London Grocer. — Joh'es Bain-brig filius 5. Doctor medicinæ Londo'. = Maria filia Rob'ti Willmet de Derby Pannari's. — Samuell Bain-brig 4. filius. = Maria filia Joh'is Watts de Instock in Com' Leic.

Johannes fil. et hæres æt 9. — Henricus fil. et hær. ætat. 10. — 2 Edward. — 3. Samuell ob. s. p.

Abraham 7. filius. — Nathaniell 6. filius. — Willm's tertius filius. — Edwardus Bainbrige fil. 2. — Thomas Bain-brige filius primogenitus. — 3 Maria. — 4. Ellina. — 5. Rebecca ob. sine p'le.

(Cotton.)

ARMS. *Quarterly :—1. Argent, a bend sable between three pellets. 2. Azure, an eagle displayed argent. 3. Gules, three birds or. 4. Barry nebulée of six argent and gules, a canton of the last.*
CREST. *An eagle displayed argent.*

Thomas Cotton who came out of Staffordsh. & lyued in Chesh. temp. H. 7.

Rob'tus Cotton de villa Leicest' et nuper Maior eadem villæ.

Tho. Cotton fil. et hæres ob. s. p. — Edwardus Cotton de Laughton 2. filius et hæres fratris ob. 1617. = Margareta filia . . . Villers de Hothorp in Com' Northamp. — Willm's Cotton de London 3 fil. ob. sine prole.

Tho. Cotton cleri-cus 2. filius duxit filiam . . . Young in Com' Warr. — Willm's Cotton de Loughton in Com' Leic. ætat. 66. 1619. = Anna filia Clemtis Smith de Ha'mel-ton in Com' Rutland. — Edm. Cotton de Lubinam in Com' Leic. 3 fil. duxit Annam fil. Will'mi Tarlton in Com' Leic.

| | | | 1 | 2 | 3 | 4 |

Nathaniell Cotton pri-mogenitus ætat. 25. == . . . filia Cliueroe. — Jonathan 2. filius ætat. 15. — Elizab. nupta Lawrentij Horton de Monsley in Com' Leic. — Martha uxor Ambrosio Saunders de Sibertoft in Com' North-amp. — Goditha uxor Will'i Parker de Lubnam in Com' Leic. — Anna nupta Joseph Leadoch de Bosworth in Com' Leic.

Filia.

A

5. Ruth.	Jana uxor Hen.	Samuell	Tho. Cotton de=Elizab. fil.	Joh'es
—	Sutton de	3. fil.	Loughton in	Edw. Shuke-	Cotton
6. Sara.	Galway in	ætat. 16.	Com' Leic'	brough de	2. filius
—	Conaugh in Ire-		fil. et hær.	Naseby in	ætatis
7. Dorothia.	land Clericus.		ætat. 24.	Com' North-	21.
				amp.	

Ann 1.	Mary	Thomas Cotton	Edwardus Cotton	William	Samuell	Robert	Henry
—	3.	son & hr	filius et hæres	Cotton	Cotton 3	4.	6.
Elizabeth		liuing 1649.	ætat. 2. annoru'	2.	sonn.	—	—
2.			1619. ob. s. p.			Eusiby	John
						5.	7.

(Caldwall.)

ARMS. *Quarterly:—Azure, a cross patée fitchée within an orle of étoiles or; and argent, on a fess indented sable three fishes' heads erased and erected or.*
CREST. *A cock's head or, beaked and combed gules, between two wings displayed sable, holding in his mouth a cross patée fitchee of the first.*

Thomas Caldwall.=Alicia filia . . . More de Douebridg in Com' Darbiæ.

Willm's Caldwall=Johanna filia	Rob'tus Caldwall	Ricardus	Thomas
de Burton super	Will'mi Fish-	4. filius.	Caldwall	Caldwall
Trent. 2. filius.	wick.		3. filius.	1. filius.

Rob'tus Cald-=Anna filia . . .	Edwardus Cald-=Maria filia	Johanne 4. filius.
wall de Whit-	Helmsted de	wall de Upton	. . . Skinner	—
ford in Com'	Ingerston in	Warren in Com'	de Com'	Joseph 5. filius.
Wigorne.	Com' Essex.	Wigorne 3.	Kent.	—
		filius.		Willm's Caldwall
				2. filius.

Talbott	Rob'tus =. . . filia Smith	Samuell Cald-=Dorothy filia W'mi
Caldwall	Caldwall	de Stoke in	wall 2. filius	Morton Alder-
filius et	fil. et	Com' Worc.	de Com' Leic.	manni Leicestriæ
hæres.	hæres.			relicta Baker.

| Edwardus Caldwall filius | Georgius Caldwall filius | Johannes 2 filius | Anna |
| et hæres ætat. 6. | et hæres ætat. 5. 1619. | ætat. 2. | æt. 1. |

1 Maria uxor	2 Anna nupta	Sara ux. Gerrard	Jane uxor	Presilla uxor	Rebecca
Joh'is Wes-	Edwardi	Dannet fil. et	Joh'is	. . . Nicolls	ob. sans
ton de	Purshull de	hær. Joh'is Dan-	Acton de	de Com'	issue.
Com' Cantij.	Purshull hall	net de Com' Worc.	Com'	Heref.	
	in Com'	militis.	Hereff.		
	Wigorn.				

(Eyre.)

ARMS. *Argent, on a bend sable three quatrefoils of the field.*

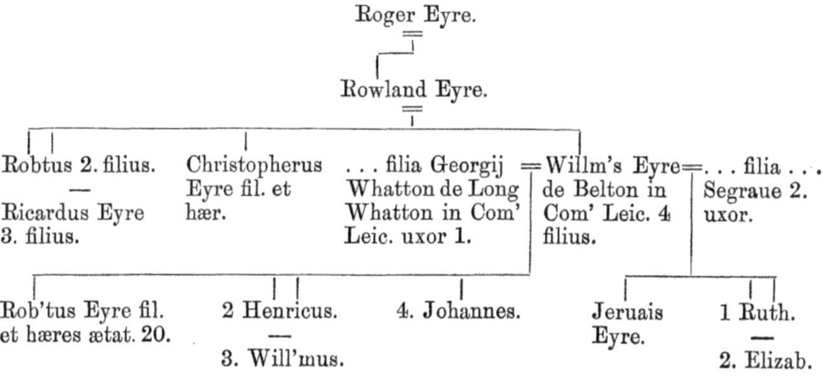

Roger Eyre.

Rowland Eyre.

Robtus 2. filius. — Ricardus Eyre 3. filius.	Christopherus Eyre fil. et hær.	. . . filia Georgij Whatton de Long Whatton in Com' Leic. uxor 1.	Willm's Eyre de Belton in Com' Leic. 4 filius. = . . . filia . . . Segraue 2. uxor.

Rob'tus Eyre fil. et hæres ætat. 20.	2 Henricus. — 3. Will'mus.	4. Johannes.	Jeruais Eyre.	1 Ruth. — 2. Elizab.

(Overton.)

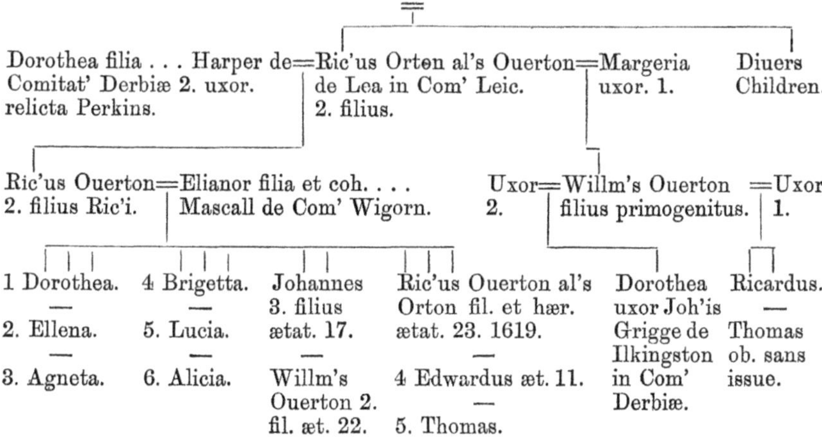

Ricardus Orton al's Ouerton de Lea in Com' Leicest.

Dorothea filia . . . Harper de Comitat' Derbiæ 2. uxor. relicta Perkins. = Ric'us Orten al's Ouerton de Lea in Com' Leic. 2. filius.	= Margeria uxor. 1.	Diuers Children.

Ric'us Ouerton 2. filius Ric'i. = Elianor filia et coh. . . . Mascall de Com' Wigorn.	Uxor 2. = Willm's Ouerton filius primogenitus. = Uxor 1.	

1 Dorothea. — 2. Ellena. — 3. Agneta.	4 Brigetta. — 5. Lucia. — 6. Alicia.	Johannes 3. filius ætat. 17. — Willm's Ouerton 2. fil. æt. 22.	Ric'us Ouerton al's Orton fil. et hær. ætat. 23. 1619. — 4 Edwardus æt. 11. — 5. Thomas.	Dorothea uxor Joh'is Grigge de Ilkingston in Com' Derbiæ.	Ricardus. — Thomas ob. sans issue.

(𝔖trelley.)

ARMS. *Paly of six argent and azure, in chief a mullet for difference.*

Nicholas Strelley a third sonne of the house of Strelley in Com' Derby.

Rob'tus Strelley de West=Joanna filia Nicholai
Langton in Com' Leicest. | Rowell de Com' Oxon.

Elizabetha uxor Edw. Chapman de Foxston in Com' Leic.

Nicholaus Strelley=Katherina filia Tho. Fransum de West Langton in Com' Leic. de Com' Glouc.

Margareta nupta Hen. Stone de Thornton in Com' Leicestriæ.

Sara nupta Joh'i Gottes de Estlangton in Com' Leicestriæ.

Elias Strelley=Gracia filia Joh'is Leife de Stamford in Com' Northamp. fil. et hæres ætatis 40. annoru' 1619.

Francisca nupta Edmundo Clarke de Church Langton in Com' Leic.

Katherina uxor Mawritij Brodgate de West Langton in Com' Leic.

Jane ætat. 14.

Henricus Stralley fil. et hæres ætat. 16. temp' huius visitationis 1619.

Nicholas 2. filius ætat. 9.

Margeria ætat. 18.

(𝔙owe.)

Willm's Vough=Margareta filia et hær. Joh'is Mitton whose de Halloughton auncester maried y⁰ Da. & hey. of Dester & in Com' Leic. Dester maried the Da; & hey; of Hackluit.

His office to be found in the Rolles for Halloughto'.

Leonardus Vough=Lycia filia . . . Antwisell de Stanton Wyuell in Com' Leic. 2. filius et hæres fratris.

Thomas filius et hæres ob. sine p'le.

Franciscus Vowe fil. et hær. obijt sans issue.

Thomas Vough =Agnitia filia . . . Dickingson de Peterborowe. de Halloughton in Com' Leic.

Agneta uxor 1. Blocksome et postea Mariott.

Jocosa 2. filia.

Thomas Vough de Halloughton=Thomazin filia Octauiani Fisher de in Com' Leic. Threkingham in Com' Lincolne.

1. Agneta æt. 17.

2. Elizab. æt. 12.

3. Francisca æt. 10.

4. Joanna. 6.

5. Margaret. 2.

Leonardus Vough filius et hæres æt. 17. 1619.

Thomas 2. filius ætat. 10.

Willmus 3. filius ætat. 4.

Johannes 4. filius æt. 1. anni.

(Dixon.)

Joanna filia Cannon=Ricardus Dixson de Rolston in=... Relicta ... Brough de
de Com' Essex.　Com' Leic. temp. H. 8.　Brough in Com' Leic.

Friswold ob. sans issue.
—
Audria uxor ... Astwell de Com' Northamp.

Margeria nupta ... Sharpe de Comit' Rutland.
—
Margareta uxor ... Dent de Hallaton in Com' Leic.

Willm's Dix-=Margareta filia son de Rols-|... Howe ton in Com' | relicta ... Leic.　| Bedell de Com' North- amp.

Ricardus Dixson 2. fil. ob. s. p.
—
Dorothea uxor Bedell de Com' Northamp.

Dorothea nupta Will'o Euerard de Barleston in Com' Leic.

Oliuerus Dixson de Kethrop in Com' Leic. 2. fil.
==
Anna filia Nic'i Armestrong de Desford in Comit' Leic.

Willm's Dixon de Rolston in Comit' Leic.
==
Anna filia Edw. Dudley de Clapton in Com' Northamp.

Johannes Dixson de Skrosbie in Com' Lincolne 3. filius.
==
Maria filia Joh'is Brian de Bullingbrooke in Comitat' Lincoln.

1 Maria.
—
2. Ruth.

3 Agneta.
—
4. Joanna.

Ric'us Dixson fil. et hæres ætat. 18.
—
Oliuerus Dixson 2. fil. ætat. 3.

Joh'es Dixson fil. et hæres ætat. 15. 1619.

Jone uxor Rob'ti Busby.
—
Margeria 2. fil. ætat. 9.

(Allen.)

Anthonius Allen de Marfeild in Com' Leic.

Anthonius Allen de Marfeild=Anna filia Edwardi Deepcup de in Com' Leic.　Rockingham in Com' Leic.

2. Georgius.
—
3. Edwardus.
—
4. Henricus.

Willm's Allen de=Katherina fil. Burrow in | Hen. Dilling- Comit' Leic. fil. | ham de Deane et hæres ætat. | in Com' Leic. 26. 1619.

5. Anthonius.
—
6. Ricardus.
—
7. Thomas.

1 Maria.
—
2. Anna.
—
3. Jocosa.

Thomas fil. et hæres æt. 3 annoru' 1622.

Briget ætat. 2. 1619.

Anna 2. filia æt. unius anni 1622.

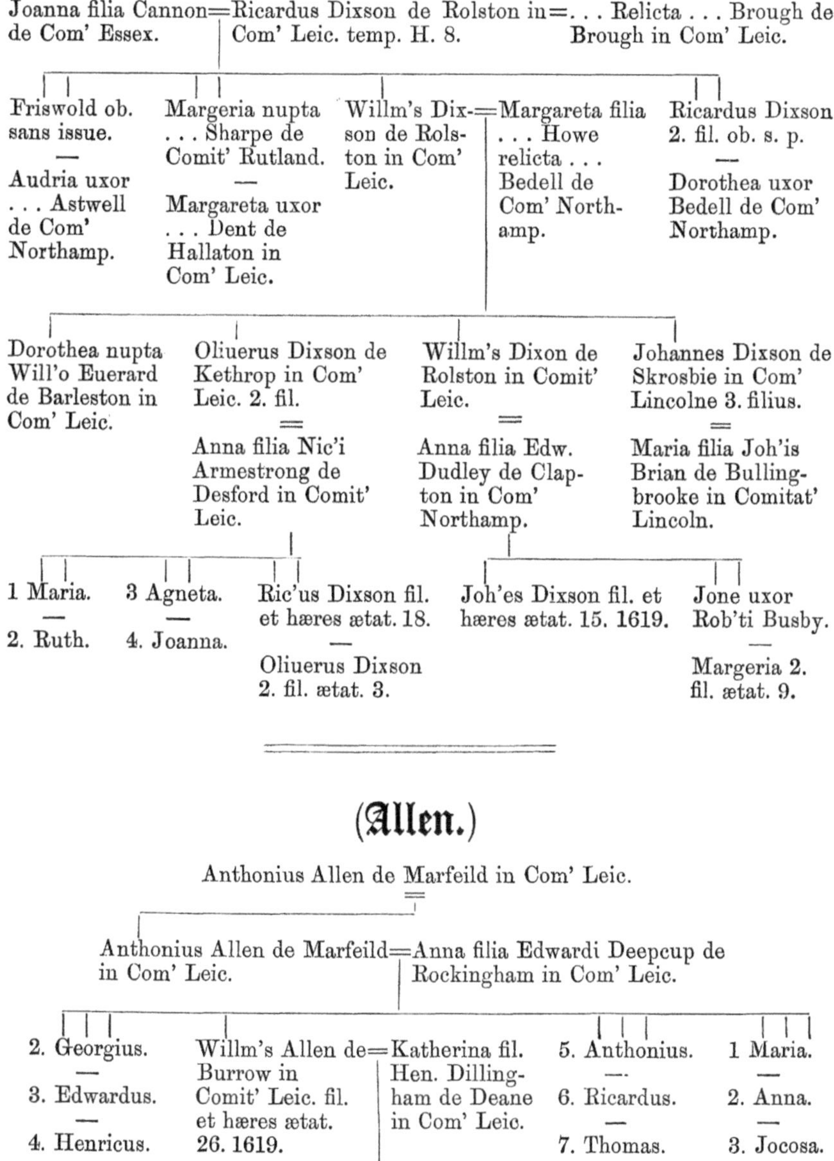

(𝕷𝖆𝖓𝖞.)

ARMS. *Quarterly :—1. Argent, on a bend between two fleurs-de-lis gules a lion passant or. 2. Argent, a chevron engrailed between three cinquefoils gules, on a chief of the last a lion passant or. 3. Gules, a crescent ermine within an orle of martlets or.*

CREST. *A mermaid (untinctured), wreathed argent and azure, holding in dexter hand a hawk's bell of the first attached to a string vert, at the end a tassel silver.*

. . . Filia Aslake de=Joh'es Lany de Cratfeild=Katherina filia . . . Yaxley de
Norfolk 2. uxor. | in Com' Suff. | Melleis in Com' Suff. ux. 1.

Aslack Lany mar & had issue.

Joh'es Lany=Maria filia . . . Pooley de Badley hall in Com' Suff.
Recorder of Ipswich in Com' Suff. fil. et hæres.

Tho. Lany of yᵉ Newark in Leist' 3. filius.
=
Gartrude fil. Joh'is Hunt de Lindon in Com' Rutland.

James Lany de Barwick maried & had issue.
=

Beniamin 4. filius ob. sine p'le.

Joh'es Lany fil. et hær. habuit 2. uxores.

Bassebon Lany et alij filij.

Thomas Lany fil. et hæres ætat. 33.

filius.

Anna nupta.

(𝕳𝖆𝖗𝖙𝖔𝖕.)

ARMS. *Sable, a chevron between three otters passant argent.*
CREST. *Out of a coronet or, a demi-pelican with wings endorsed argent, vulning herself gules.*

Rad'us Hartop temp. R. 2.=. . . filia Alexandri Moyne.

Prisilla uxor Oliueri Cooke.

Alexander=Ellina fil.
Hartop.

Phillippa uxor Geo. Holleis.

3 Marion.

4. Audria.

Johannes Hartop.=Margareta filia Tho. Bridemaine.

Maria uxor Hen. Leibourn.

Johannes=Cristiana filia Joh'is Williams.
Hartop 2. filius.

Henricus=Barbara filia Radulphi FitzRandolph.
Hartop.

Margareta uxor Thomæ Brokesby.

Ursula nupta Joh'i Ashley.

Rob'tus Hartop=Anna filia Joh'is Porter de Bretton.
2. filius.

Johannes=Jana filia Will'mi Inglebeard.
Hartop.

Isabella nupta Thomæ Blesby.

A

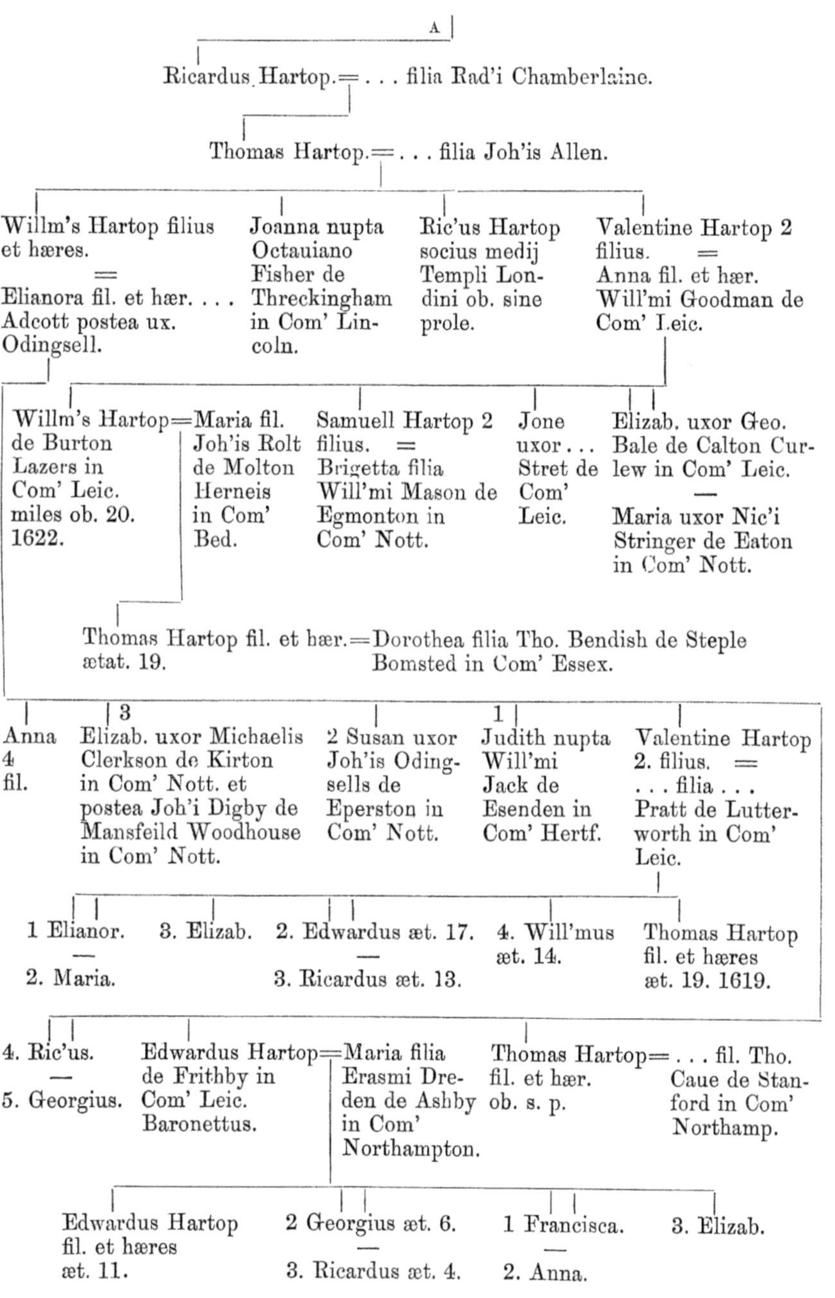
A
Ricardus Hartop.=... filia Rad'i Chamberlaine.
Thomas Hartop.=... filia Joh'is Allen.
Willm's Hartop filius et hæres. = Elianora fil. et hær. ... Adcott postea ux. Odingsell.
Joanna nupta Octauiano Fisher de Threckingham in Com' Lincoln.
Ric'us Hartop socius medij Templi Londini ob. sine prole.
Valentine Hartop 2 filius. = Anna fil. et hær. Will'mi Goodman de Com' Leic.
Willm's Hartop de Burton Lazers in Com' Leic. miles ob. 20. 1622. =Maria fil. Joh'is Rolt de Molton Herneis in Com' Bed.
Samuell Hartop 2 filius. = Brigetta filia Will'mi Mason de Egmonton in Com' Nott.
Jone uxor ... Stret de Com' Leic.
Elizab. uxor Geo. Bale de Calton Curlew in Com' Leic. — Maria uxor Nic'i Stringer de Eaton in Com' Nott.
Thomas Hartop fil. et hær.=Dorothea filia Tho. Bendish de Steple Bomsted in Com' Essex. ætat. 19.
Anna 4 fil.
3 Elizab. uxor Michaelis Clerkson de Kirton in Com' Nott. et postea Joh'i Digby de Mansfeild Woodhouse in Com' Nott.
2 Susan uxor Joh'is Odingsells de Eperston in Com' Nott.
1 Judith nupta Will'mi Jack de Esenden in Com' Hertf.
Valentine Hartop 2. filius. = ... filia ... Pratt de Lutterworth in Com' Leic.
1 Elianor. — 2. Maria.
3. Elizab.
2. Edwardus æt. 17. — 3. Ricardus æt. 13.
4. Will'mus æt. 14.
Thomas Hartop fil. et hæres æt. 19. 1619.
4. Ric'us. — 5. Georgius.
Edwardus Hartop de Frithby in Com' Leic. Baronettus.=Maria filia Erasmi Dreden de Ashby in Com' Northampton.
Thomas Hartop fil. et hær. ob. s. p.=... fil. Tho. Caue de Stanford in Com' Northamp.
Edwardus Hartop fil. et hæres æt. 11.
2 Georgius æt. 6. — 3. Ricardus æt. 4.
1 Francisca. — 2. Anna.
3. Elizab.

(Perin.)

ARMS. *Argent, on a chevron sable between three pine-apples slipped, reversed vert, as many leopards' faces of the field.*

Gilbertus Perin de Com' Salop.═Elizab. filia . . . Scrimshaw de Com' Salopiæ.

Thomas Perin de Ashby═Katherina filia Tho. Parret de Ashby
de la Zouch. │ de la Zouch.

Thomas Perin de Ashby de la═Anna filia Radulphi Potter de
Zouch ætat. 34. │ Lichfeild in Com' Staff.

Thomas Perin filius et   2 Elizabetha 6.   1 Katherina 8.
hæres ætat. 9.   —   —
annoru' 1619.   3. Sara ætat. 3.   4. Maria 3 menses.

(Ashton.)

ARMS *(Field untinctured) a mullet sable charged with an annulet or, in dexter chief a crescent gules for difference.*
CREST. *A boar's head argent, charged with a crescent for difference.*

Peter Ashton de olde Weston in Com' Hunt.

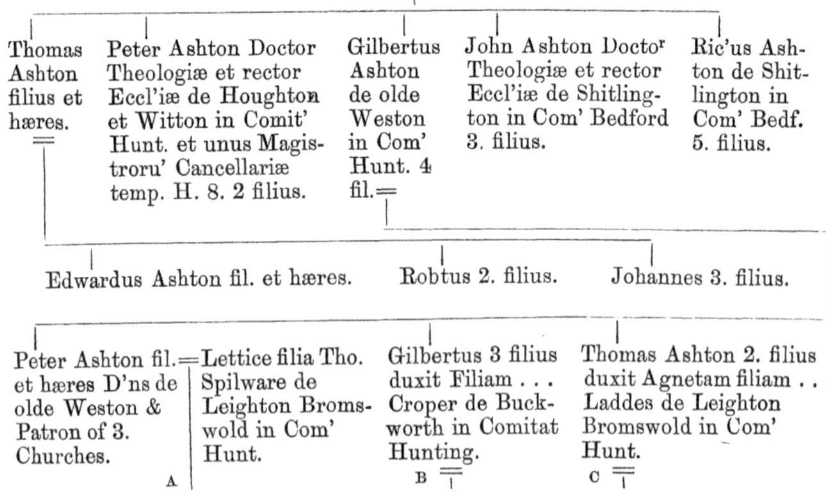

Thomas Ashton filius et hæres.

Peter Ashton Doctor Theologiæ et rector Eccl'iæ de Houghton et Witton in Comit' Hunt. et unus Magistroru' Cancellariæ temp. H. 8. 2 filius.

Gilbertus Ashton de olde Weston in Com' Hunt. 4 fil.═

John Ashton Docto^r Theologiæ et rector Eccl'iæ de Shitlington in Com' Bedford 3. filius.

Ric'us Ashton de Shitlington in Com' Bedf. 5. filius.

Edwardus Ashton fil. et hæres.   Robtus 2. filius.   Johannes 3. filius.

Peter Ashton fil.═Lettice filia Tho.
et hæres D'ns de │ Spilware de
olde Weston & │ Leighton Broms-
Patron of 3. │ wold in Com'
Churches. │ Hunt.
A │

Gilbertus 3 filius duxit Filiam . . . Croper de Buckworth in Comitat Hunting.
B

Thomas Ashton 2. filius duxit Agnetam filiam . . . Laddes de Leighton Bromswold in Com' Hunt.
C

A
Nicholas Ashton
de Magna Gleane
in Com' Leic.
=
Joanna filia et
Coh. Will'i Ward
de Burton Ouerie
in Comitat' Leic.

B
Arthurus Ashton
fil. et hæres habuit
exitu'.
—
Willm's 2. fil. de
Kembolton in
Com' Hunt.

Petrus
3. fil. de
Bramton
in Com'
Hunt.

C
Peter Ashton de
olde Weston
duxit fil. Tho.
Ekins de Cat-
worth in Com'
Hunt. =

Petrus Ashton filius et
hæres ætat. 30. Mr. of
Arte in Cambridg.

Leticia uxor Rob't
Hodges de magna
Glen in Com' Leic.

Thomas
2 filius
ætat. 21.

Tho. Ashton fil.
et hæres ætatis
dimiduu' anni.

Tho. Ashton de
olde Weston in
Com' Hunt. 3
fil.
=
Alicia filia et
altra coh.
Ric'i Tindall.

1. Katherina.
—
2. Francisca.
—
3. Margareta.
—
4. Elizabetha.
—
5. Agneta.

6. Rosa.
—
1. Johannes.
—
2. Humphrie.
—
3. Gilbertus.
—
4. Peter.

5. Johannes
ob. sine
prole.
—
Anna Maria
ob. s. p.

Rob'tus Ashton
de Olde Weston
fil. et hæres.
=
Katherina filia
et Coh. Ric'i Tin-
dall de Stinch-
comb.

Carolus Ash-
ton fil. et
hæres ætat 21.

1. Lettice.
—
2. Francisca.

Clifton Ashton
filius et hæres
ætat. 28.

Pawle Ashton 2.
filius duxit fil. et
hær.

(𝔇𝔦𝔤𝔟𝔶.)

. . . filia Carl-=Willm's Digbie de =. . . filia . . . Dixwell
ton 2. uxor.   Welby in Com' Leic. | de Com' Warwick.

Elizab. uxor
Humphredi
Vernam de
Quarenden
in Com'
Leic.

Thomas Digby fil.
et hæres qui ven-
didit Welby.
=
. . . filia Peto de
Com' Warr.

Edwardus Digby de Hol-
well in Com' Leic.
=
Ellina filia Rad'i Seche-
uerell de Hopwell in
Com' Derby.

Anna uxor
Sammuell
Creach de
Wartenby
in Com'
Leic.

1. Elizabeth.
—
2. Sara.
—
3. Penelope.

Johannes 2. fil.
ætat. 18.
—
Willm's Digby
filius et hæres
ætat. 21.

Edwardus Digby
primogenitus
ætat. 14.
—
Johannes 2 filius
ætat. 10.

1. Emma.
—
2. Jana.
—
3. Anna.

4. Tabitha.
—
5. Maria.
—
Nathaniell
ætat. 9.

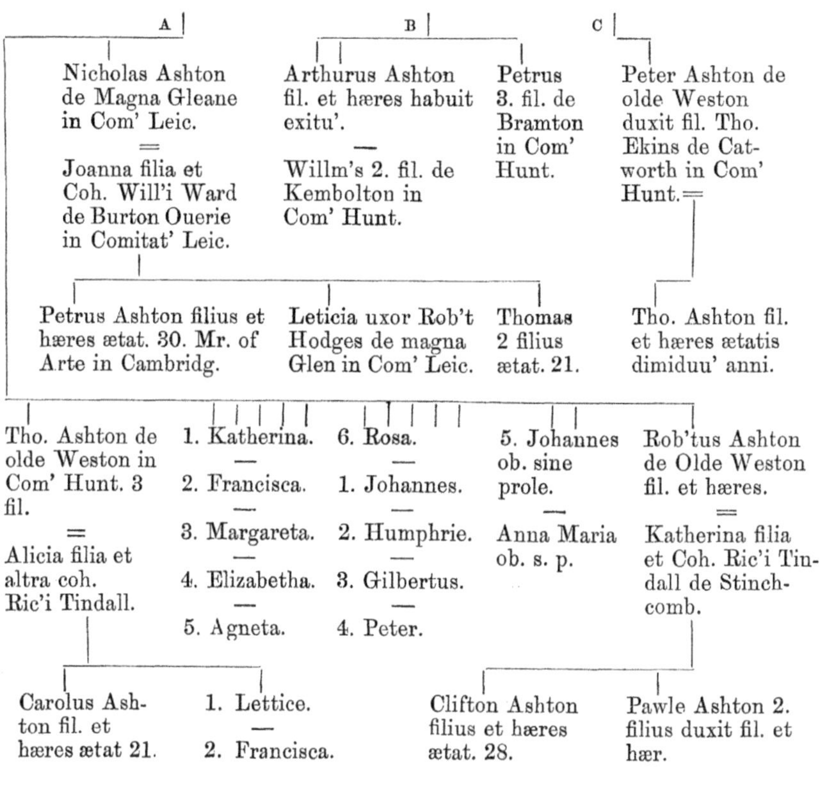

(𝔚ase.)

ARMS. *Argent, on a chevron sable between three garbs vert, banded or, as many étoiles of the field.*

CREST. *Out of clouds proper issuing rays or, thereon a dexter arm embowed in armour argent, garnished of the first, holding by the point a demi battle-axe erect of the second.*

John Wase de London Merchant temp. H. 6.

Johannes Wase de=Alicia filia et hær. Joh'is Bailey de Rotherby
Leicest' Merchant | in Com' Leic. relicta Will'mi Hill de
of the Staple. | Leicest' mercator Calitiæ.

Ric'us Wase de Leic.=Elizab. filia Georgij Meuerell de
temp. H. 8. | Throwley in Com' Staff. Armig'.

Thomas Wase de Rotherby=Anna filia Thomæ Cole-   Anna nupt. Will'o
in Com' Leic. temp. M. R. | clough de Com' Staff.   Widder de Com' Staff.

Margareta uxor Henrici   Elizabetha uxor Augustini   Ric'us Wase 2. filius
Fox de Magna Wigston   Olife. postea Tho. Armeson   Duxit Margeriam filia
in Com' Leic.   de Loughborow in Com'   Will'mi Brokesby de
    Leic'.=   Gadsby.=

Thomas Olife.   Elizabetha.   Anna Olife.   Katherina filia unica.

3. Alicia.   Anna nupta   Tho. Wase de   3. Edwardus.   Samson Wase fil. et
—   Georgio Allen   Hickling in   —   hær. nuptus 13. De-
4. Jana.   de South   Com' Nott.   4. Johannes   cemb'. 1586.
—   Croxston in   duxit Janam   ob. sine   =
5. Dorothea   Comitatu   filiam Henrici   prole.   Margareta filia
ob. s. p.   Leicestriæ.   Darker de   Erasmi Wildman
    =   Dalby in le   de Beby in Com'
        Wouldes.   Leicest'.

Willm's.   Margareta.   Susan nata 22.   Thomas.   Johannes   Thomas Wase
—   —   July A° 1602.   —   natus in   fil. et hæres
Valentine.   Anna.   —   Dorothea   Octob'.   natus 20. De-
—   —   Anna nata   ob. s. p.   1599.   cemb'. 1589.
Georgius.   Ellianor.   1595.

(Brookesby.)

ARMS. *Barry of six nebulée argent and sable, a canton gules.*
CREST. *A boar's head couped at the neck, bristled and tusked or.*

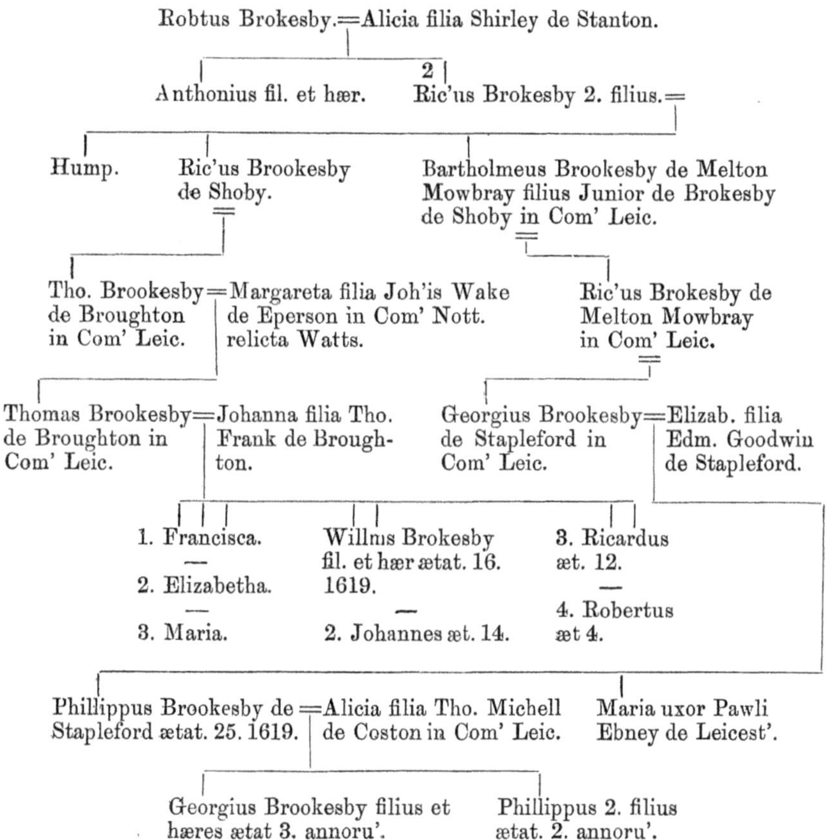

Robtus Brokesby.=Alicia filia Shirley de Stanton.

Anthonius fil. et hær.

2 | Ric'us Brokesby 2. filius.=

Hump.

Ric'us Brookesby de Shoby.

Bartholmeus Brookesby de Melton Mowbray filius Junior de Brokesby de Shoby in Com' Leic.

Tho. Brookesby de Broughton in Com' Leic.=Margareta filia Joh'is Wake de Eperson in Com' Nott. relicta Watts.

Ric'us Brokesby de Melton Mowbray in Com' Leic.

Thomas Brookesby de Broughton in Com' Leic.=Johanna filia Tho. Frank de Broughton.

Georgius Brookesby de Stapleford in Com' Leic.=Elizab. filia Edm. Goodwin de Stapleford.

1. Francisca.
—
2. Elizabetha.
—
3. Maria.

Willms Brokesby fil. et hær ætat. 16. 1619.
—
2. Johannes æt. 14.

3. Ricardus æt. 12.
—
4. Robertus æt 4.

Phillippus Brookesby de Stapleford ætat. 25. 1619.=Alicia filia Tho. Michell de Coston in Com' Leic.

Maria uxor Pawli Ebney de Leicest'.

Georgius Brookesby filius et hæres ætat 3. annoru'.

Phillippus 2. filius ætat. 2. annoru'.

(Farrent.)

Lawrentius Farrent de Moulton in Com' Hunt.═Elizab. filia Adæ D'ni Lumley.

Thomas Farrent fil. et hær.

Georgius Farrent de Filgraue═Alicia filia . . . Coonye de in Com' Buck. 2. filius. Comitat' Lincoln.

Maria fil. Ric'i Cooper═Tho. Farrent de Lut-═Johanna fil. de Warmington in terworth in Com' . . . Thorley Com' Warr. ux. 2. Leic. ob. 1613. uxor 1.

. . . filia nupta . . Winter de Comit' Glouc.

Maria unica fil. æt. 21.

3. Ricardus æt. 18.
—
4. Franciscus 10.
—
5 Jacobus æt. 6.

Thomas Farrent 2. filius ætat. 20.

Anthonius Farrent═Martha filia Anthonij de Lutterworth Mariott de Aston et in Com' Leic. fil. Ardingworth in et hær. æt. 27. Comitat' Northamp.

(Rudiard.)

ARMS. *Argent, treillé sable, on a canton gules a rose or.*

Rad'us Rudiard de Rudiard in Com' Staff.

Rad'us Rudiard fil. et hær. obijt sine prole.

Thomas Rudiard 2. filius.

4. Johannes.
—
5. Edmundus ob. s. p.

Carolus Rudiard 6. fil. ob. sine prole.

Jacobus Rudiard 3. filius.

Willm's Rudiard 3. filius.

Thomas Rudiard filius et hær. ob. s. p.

Johannes Rudiard 2 fil. Duxit Elizab. fil. . . . Bidell de Com' Cæst'

Beniamin Rudiard miles suruaior of the Court of Wardes.

Ric'us Rud- iard.

Lawrence Rudiard mar. & had issu.

Rob'tus ob. s. p.

Will'mus Rudiard═Margareta filia 3. filius Rector Joh'is Shilton de eccl'iæ Leices- Newbold in Com' triæ. Leic.

Johannes 2. filius.

Anna filia An-═Thomas Rudiard═Rebecca filia Nic'i thonij Luther filius et hæres Steward de Patishull 1. ux. æt. 40. 1619. in Com' Northamp.

Joseph 2 filius æt. 34.

Willm's et Willm's ob. sine p'le.

Anthonius fil. et hær. æt. 10.

Thomas 2 fil. æt. 9.

Nicholaus ætat. 2.

Richard ætat. 6. septimana 24. septemb' 1619.

(Roberts.)

ARMS. *Quarterly:*—1. *Argent, three pheons sable, on a chief of the last a grey-hound courant of the field, collared gules.* 2. *Per fess argent and gules, a pale counterchanged, on the first, three demi-lions rampant couped sable, crowned or.* 3. *Argent, on a fess sable three fleurs-de-lis or.*
ANOTHER. *The same, with a crescent for difference; impaling argent, two bars, and in chief a lion passant gules.*

Faith filia & h. . . . Pattinson═Edmondus Rob'tes═ . . . Soror Rob'ti
de Colman Street London │ de Wilesdon in │ Chester militis
ux. 2. │ Com' Midd. │ ux. prima.

Anna obijt   Edmondus 3.   Thom. Rob'tes 2. fil.═Anna filia Tho. Burnaby de
infantulam.   fil. unmaried.   de Com' Leic. │ Watford in Com' Northamp.

Elionora unica filia   Will'mus 2 filius   Thomas Rob'tes filius et
ætat. 18.   ætat. 13.   hæres ætat. 16.

Franciscus Robertes═Maria filia   Katherina ux.   Elizab. nupta . . .   Maria
de Wilesdon in │ . . . Barnes   . . . Ciampanti   Wyndouer pro-   ob.
Com' Midd. fil. & │ de Wilesdon in   Italiano de Com'   curator iuris   sans
hæres. │ Com' Midd.   South Italian.   Ciuilis.   issue.

Elizab. uxor   Barnes Ro-═Maria filia Alder-   Francisca ux. . . .   Jana nupta
Saunders.   berts │ manni Glouer de   Franklin de   Tho. Glouer
   filius et │ London et soror Tho.   Wilesdon in Com'   de London
   hæres. │ Glouer milit'.   Midd.   militi.

Barnes Rob'ts et Willm's Rob'ts   Johannes Franklin de Willesdon in
Gemelli fratres ætat. 14. 1619.   Com' Midd. miles ætat. 21.

(Sherman.)

ARMS. *Or, a lion rampant sable, charged on the shoulder with an annulet for differ-ence between three oak-leaves vert.*
CREST. *A sea-lion séjant argent, guttée de poix, finned or.*

Thomas Sherman de Yaxley═ . . . fil. Waller de Wortham
in Com' Suff. │ in Com' Suff.

Tho. Sherman fil.   Willm's Sherman Grocer   6. Francis.   3 Johan-   Ricardus
et hæres.   & Merchant of London   —   nes.   ob. s. p.
═   5. filius.   ═   7. Jeames.   —   —
. . . filia . . . Yax-   Faith fil. Joh'is Lany   —   4. Hen-   filia uxor
ley in Com' Suff.   de Cratfeild in Com'   8. Bartholmew.   ricus.   Lock-
   Suff.   —   wood.
A │   B │   9. Anthony.

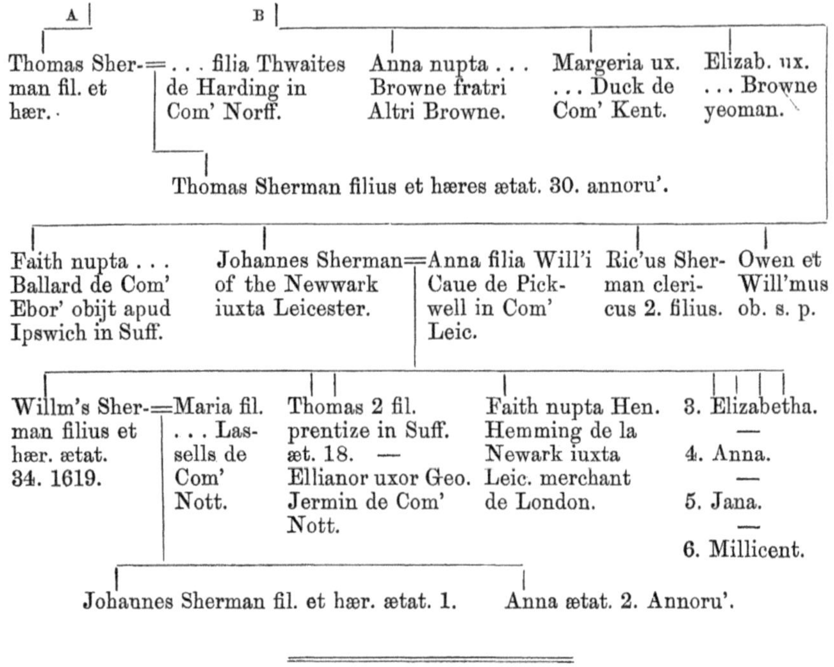

A |
B |

Thomas Sher-=... filia Thwaites   Anna nupta ...   Margeria ux.   Elizab. ux.
man fil. et   de Harding in   Browne fratri   ... Duck de   ... Browne
hær.·   Com' Norff.   Altri Browne.   Com' Kent.   yeoman.

Thomas Sherman filius et hæres ætat. 30. annoru'.

Faith nupta ...   Johannes Sherman=Anna filia Will'i   Ric'us Sher-   Owen et
Ballard de Com'   of the Newwark   Caue de Pick-   man cleri-   Will'mus
Ebor' obijt apud   iuxta Leicester.   well in Com'   cus 2. filius.   ob. s. p.
Ipswich in Suff.   Leic.

Willm's Sher-=Maria fil.   Thomas 2 fil.   Faith nupta Hen.   3. Elizabetha.
man filius et   ... Las-   prentize in Suff.   Hemming de la   —
hær. ætat.   sells de   æt. 18. —   Newark iuxta   4. Anna.
34. 1619.   Com'   Ellianor uxor Geo.   Leic. merchant   —
   Nott.   Jermin de Com'   de London.   5. Jana.
      Nott.   —
            6. Millicent.

Johannes Sherman fil. et hær. ætat. 1.   Anna ætat. 2. Annoru'.

(Hall.)

Anthonius Hall de Henwick in Comitat' Wigor.

Anthonius Hall de   Elizab. filia=Willm's Hall de Rederiff=Martha filia ...
Mathon in Com' Wi-   ... Dale   iuxta London et de   Lumley Draper of
gorniæ fil. et hæres.   de Rederiff.   Comitat' Leic. 2. filius.   London ux. 2.

Thomas Hall   2 Willm's.   Willm's Hall=Susanna filia Jacobi Freeman
fil. et hæres   —   fil. et hæres   de Neither Whitacre in
ætat. 40.   3. Henricus.   ætat. 22.   Comit' War.

Fil. et hær.   Martha filia unica ætat. 6. mensis 1619.

Jacobus Hall 2 fil. ætat. 20.   Elizab. uxor Tho.   2 Sara æt. 23.   3. Weblin
annoru' duxit Mariam filia'   Parker de London   —   Hall æt. 16.
Jacobi Collins de Hallaton   Milliner.   3. Maria æt. 18.   —
in p'ochia de Kinsberie in   4. Ricardus
Com' Leic.   ætat. 12.

(Griffith.)

ARMS. *Per chevron argent and gules, three stags' heads caboshed counterchanged.*

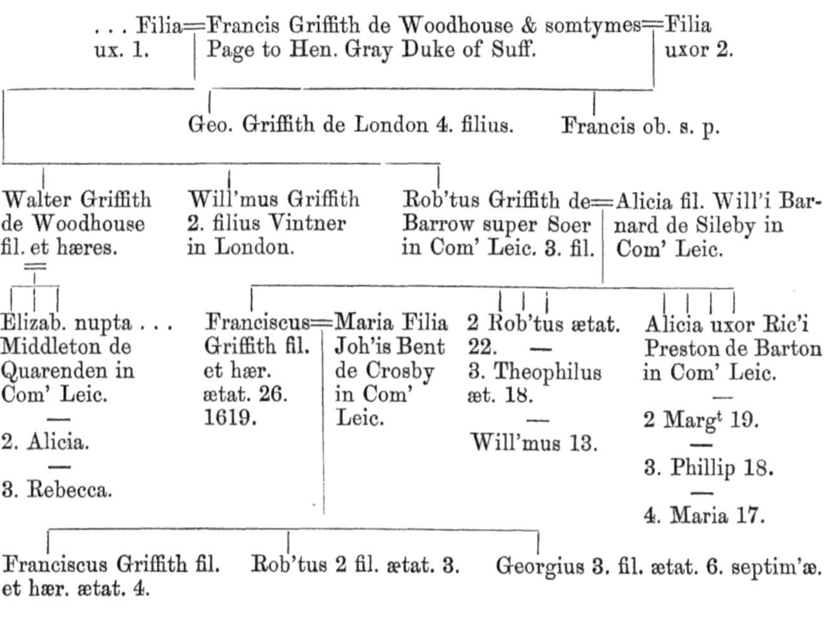

(Babington.)

ARMS. *Quarterly :—1. Argent, ten torteaux, four, three, two, and one, in chief a label of five points azure. 2. Azure, a cross flory or. 3. Argent, a fess vair azure and or, between three water bougets sable. 4. Or, a chevron gules, a canton ermine. 5. Azure semée of fleur-de-lis, a lion rampant or. 6. Gules, a lion rampant vair. 7. Argent, a bend componé gules and sable, cotised of the first. 8. Sable, two lions passant in pale regardant argent.*
CREST. *A demi-rere-mouse in pale affrontée, displayed gules. On the dexter side is written " The Creast is a demi Dragon gu." On the sinister against the wings, "false."*

Thomas Babington de =Editha filia Rad'i Fitz Harbert
Dethick ob. 13. Martij | de Norberie in Com' Darby.

Anthonius Babing-   Humphr'us Babington de=Elinora filia 3. et coh. Joh'is
ton de Dethick.   Temple Rodeley 5. filius. | Beaumont de Weddisberie.

A

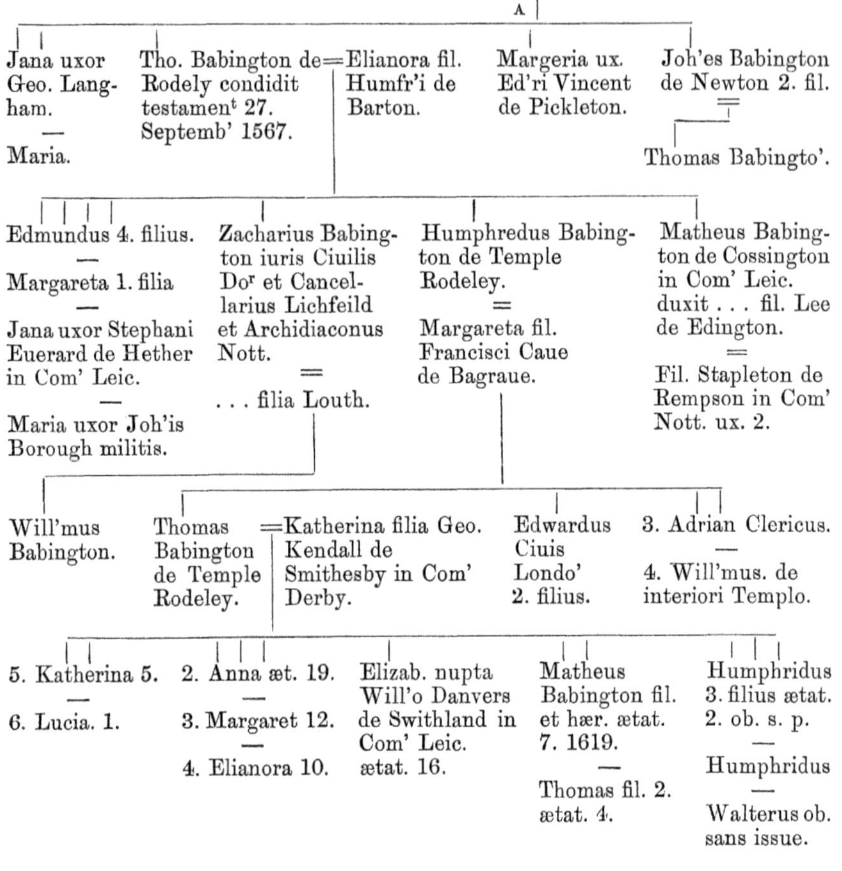

A

Jana uxor Geo. Langham.
—
Maria.

Tho. Babington de Rodely condidit testament 27. Septemb' 1567. = Elianora fil. Humfr'i de Barton.

Margeria ux. Ed'ri Vincent de Pickleton.

Joh'es Babington de Newton 2. fil. =
Thomas Babingto'.

Edmundus 4. filius.
—
Margareta 1. filia
—
Jana uxor Stephani Euerard de Hether in Com' Leic.
—
Maria uxor Joh'is Borough militis.

Zacharius Babington iuris Ciuilis Dor et Cancellarius Lichfeild et Archidiaconus Nott. = . . . filia Louth.

Humphredus Babington de Temple Rodeley. = Margareta fil. Francisci Caue de Bagraue.

Matheus Babington de Cossington in Com' Leic. duxit . . . fil. Lee de Edington. = Fil. Stapleton de Rempson in Com' Nott. ux. 2.

Will'mus Babington.

Thomas Babington de Temple Rodeley. = Katherina filia Geo. Kendall de Smithesby in Com' Derby.

Edwardus Ciuis Londo' 2. filius.

3. Adrian Clericus.
—
4. Will'mus. de interiori Templo.

5. Katherina 5.
—
6. Lucia. 1.

2. Anna æt. 19.
—
3. Margaret 12.
—
4. Elianora 10.

Elizab. nupta Will'o Danvers de Swithland in Com' Leic. ætat. 16.

Matheus Babington fil. et hær. ætat. 7. 1619.
—
Thomas fil. 2. ætat. 4.

Humphridus 3. filius ætat. 2. ob. s. p.
—
Humphridus
—
Walterus ob. sans issue.

(Brett.)

ARMS. *Gules, a fess indented between six billets or.*

Willm's Brett de Rotherby in Com' Leic. = Anna filia Anthonij Beaumont 3. filij Will'i Beaumont de Colhorton in Com' Leic.

Henricus Brett filius et hæres. = Margareta filia Tho. Seames de Ciuitate Gloucst.

Alexander æt. 32.
—
Arthurus æt. 27.

Anna nupta Lionello Cranfeild Comiti Midd. et Thesaurario Angl.

Georgius Brett filius et hæres ætat. unius anni 1622.

(𝔅𝔢𝔯𝔶.)

ARMS. *Ermine, on a bend engrailed azure three fleurs-de-lis or, in chief a crescent gules for difference.*

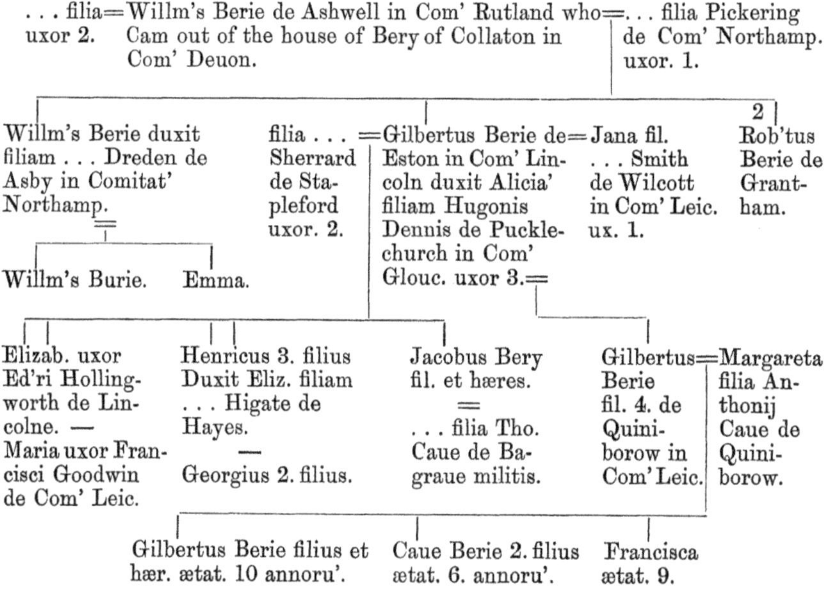

Facsimile Signatures of Leicestershire Gentry;
from the original loose papers of the Visitation of 1619_ Harl. Mss. 1195

Thomas Noble

William Clelin

Tho: Cave

Tho: Peryns

Tho: Staveley

W. Chamberlaine

... Ashton

Robt Breton

Thomas Brokesby

willm Neale

Phillip Brokesbey

Andrew ...

William Sutton

Jhon: Sherman

Nicholas Vessey

Tho: Vowe:

William Halle

Francis Griffith

William Dixon

Tho: Babington

INDEX OF NAMES.

Names in *Italics* have their arms blazoned.
  ,,   CAPITALS are the headings of pedigrees.
  ,,   Brackets ( ) are maiden names.
  ,,   ,,   [ ] are titles or surnames to titles.
= signifies "married to a."

Lounde—*continued*.
  Maria (Cave), 125.
  — = Sheffeld, 125.
Louth, John, 147.
  Juditha (Peck), 147.
  — = Babington, 206.
Lovell, Galfridus, 170.
  Margaret (—?—), 70.
  Nicholas, 70.
  Viscount, 170.
  — (Beaumont), 170.
Lovett, Anna = Earle, 4.
  Anna = Noell, 4.
  Elizab. = Cave, 126.
  Jane = Shirley, 26.
  Jocosa = Temple, 167.
  . Pinchpool, 152.
  Sir Robert, 4.
  Susanna = Cowper, 152.
  Thomas, 26, 126.
Lowe, Fifeild al's, 52.
  Goditha (Bent), 159.
  Hugo, 159.
Lowes, Isabell (Smith), 66.
Lowther, Sir Christopher, 24.
Lucy, Joane = Brasbridge, 43.
  Thomas, 43.
Ludford, Anne (Skeffington), 8, 112.
  Thomas, 8, 112.
Ludlow, Katherin = Abney, 154.
  William, 154.
Luffe, Agneta = Cowper, 154.
Lumley, Elizab. = Farrent, 202.
  Martha = Hall, 204.
Luson, Elizabeth = Yarde, 91.
  John, 91.
Luther, Anna = Rudiard, 202.
  Anthony, 202.

Mablethorpe, Ann = Nevill, 21.
Mackworth — (Hall), 46.
Madock, Jana = Everard, 142.
  Susanna = Wincoll, 156.
Madox — = Everard, 13.
Makepeace, Abell, 176.
  Lucia = Trimnell, 176.
Maldacum, Matilda = Cave, 125.
  Peter, 125.
Malin, Hellena (Gregorie), 188.
  John, 188.
Mallorye, 12, 58.
Mallorye, Mallory or Malory.
  Alice (Driby), 58.
  Beatrix = Baghot, 59.
  Dorothea = Cave, 126.
  Elizabeth, 59.
  Elizabeth = Bowier, 134.
  Elizabeth = Fenton, 58.
  John, 58, 134.
  Margery = Motton, 59.
  Margery (Turvill), 55.
  Mary (Humphrey), 62.
  Nicholas, 126.
  Roger, 58.
  Sir Antikell, 58.

Mallorye, Mallory or Malory—*continued*.
  Sir Thomas, 58, 59.
  Thomas, 58.
  William, 59.
  — = Staresmore, 5.
Mallowe — = Chambers, 51.
Malovell, 7.
Malson, Anna (Wilcockes), 136.
  Christopher, 136.
Maneringe, Marg*. (Brooke), 65.
  Roger, 65.
Manfeild, Edward, 131.
  Maria (Smith), 131.
Manley, Robert, 187.
  Susanna (Nicolls), 187.
Manning, John, 141.
  Margaret = Bale, 141.
Mannors, Francis [E. of Rutland], 30.
  Catherin = Ld Donlower, 30.
  — = Villers, 30.
Mansfeild, Katherin = Peper, 103.
  Richard, 103.
Manwaring, Charles, 65.
  Margery = Brooke, 65.
Marbery, Edward, 133.
  Elizabeth (Cave), 133.
  Margareta (Cave), 133.
  Thomas, 133.
Marbury, Elizab. = Lascelles, 155.
  William, 20.
  — = Cheselton, 20.
Markham, Anne (Langham), 12.
  Anne = Smith, 132.
  Thomas, 38, 132.
  — = Woodford, 38.
Marmaduke, Eliz. = Shirley, 26.
Marmion, Albreda = Camvile, 23.
  Galfridus, 23.
  — = Pilkington, 78 [*note*].
  — = Haselwood, 78 [*note*].
Marriott, Anthony, 202.
  Martha = Farrent, 202.
Marrow, William, 60.
  — = Ashby, 60.
Marsh, Agneta = Bent, 158.
  John, 158.
  Maria (Starkie), 175.
  Richard, 175.
MARSHALL, 103.
  Anna (Cave), 68, 126.
  Christian (Staresmore), 6.
  Francis, 103.
  Francisca = Gore, 85.
  George, 103.
  Gracia (Elkington), 85.
  Isabella (Milborne), 103.
  James, 103.
  John, 68, 103.
  Katherina (Champion), 103.
  Katherin (Nevill), 21.
  Margareta (Milborne), 103.
  Ralph, 21.
  Roland, 103.
  Sara, 103.

MARSHALL—*continued*.
  Sibilla, 103.
  Sibilla (Claxton), 103.
  Thomas, 85, 103.
  William, 103.
  — (Smith), 103.
Marson, Francisca = Gerveis, 71.
  Richard, 71.
Marstone, 101.
MARSTON or MARSTONE, 101, 102.
  Alicia (Payne), 101.
  Anna, 101.
  Anna (Hawes), 101.
  Anna (Marston), 101.
  Anna = Levins, 101.
  Benjamin, 101.
  Catherina, 101.
  Edward, 101.
  Elizabeth, 101.
  Elizabeth = Pratt, 101.
  Elizabeth (Savill), 101.
  Ellina = Collins, 101.
  Everard, 101.
  Gilbert, 100.
  Gracia = Moore, 101.
  Henry, 101.
  Jane, 101.
  Johanna, 102.
  Johanna (Bowman), 102.
  John, 101, 102.
  Katherina, 102.
  Katherina = Dillingham, 101.
  Lawrence, 101.
  Margareta (Hawes), 101.
  Margeria = Colman, 101.
  Maria = Jacomb, 101.
  Maria (Pickering), 101.
  Maria (Turvill), 101.
  Morell, 101.
  Thomas, 101.
  Tobias, 101, 102.
  William, 101, 102.
  — (Barret), 101.
  — (Goderich), 101.
  — (Payne), 101.
Martin, Alicia = Baghot, 150.
  Anne = Turvill, 55.
  John, 55, 150.
  Nicholas, 6.
  Ursula (Staresmore), 6.
Martival, 129.
MARTIVAL, 129.
  Agneta (—?—), 129.
  Anketinus de, 129.
  Fulco de, 129.
  Isabella (—?—), 129.
  Nicholaus de, 129.
  Ralphe de, 129.
  Robert de, 129.
  Thomas de, 129.
  William de, 129.
Martivaux, William de, 129.
Martiwall, William de, 129.
Martiwast, William de, 129.
Marvin, Eliz. = Cave, 126.
  Margaret = Everard, 142.
Marward, Thomas, 169.
  Phillipa = Beaumont, 169.

The Harleian Society,

INSTITUTED FOR THE

PUBLICATION OF INEDITED MANUSCRIPTS

RELATING TO

GENEALOGY, FAMILY HISTORY, AND HERALDRY.

President.

HIS GRACE THE DUKE OF MANCHESTER.

Vice-Presidents.

THE RIGHT HON. LORD MONSON.
THE HON. WILLIAM BRODRICK, M.P.
THE HON. HENRY ROPER-CURZON.
SIR GEORGE F. DUCKETT, BART., F.S.A.
SIR HENRY VAVASOUR, BART.
SIR JOSEPH RADCLIFFE, BART.
RALPH ASSHETON, Esq., M.P.
EVELYN PHILIP SHIRLEY, Esq., F.S.A.
R. E. EGERTON-WARBURTON, Esq.

Council.

W. AMHURST TYSSEN AMHURST, Esq.
GEORGE W. MARSHALL, Esq.
GRANVILLE LEVESON GOWER, Esq., F.S.A.
JOSEPH JACKSON HOWARD, Esq., LL.D., F.S.A., *Hon. Treasurer.*
THE REV. SAMUEL HAYMAN, M.A.
GEORGE J. ARMYTAGE, Esq., F.S.A., *Hon. Secretary.*
COLONEL JOSEPH LEMUEL CHESTER.
JOHN DAVIDSON, Esq.
JOHN MACLEAN, Esq., F.S.A.
WENTWORTH STURGEON, Esq.
JOHN FETHERSTON, Esq., F.S.A.
FAIRLESS BARBER, Esq., F.S.A.

Bankers.

LONDON AND COUNTY, 21, Lombard Street.

Auditors.

LIONEL G. ROBINSON, Esq., Junior Athenæum Club, and
Audit and Exchequer Office.
DUDLEY CARY ELWES, Esq., F.S.A., South Bersted, Bognor.

Rules.

1. This Society shall be called the HARLEIAN SOCIETY.

2. It shall have for its chief object the publication of the Heraldic Visitations of Counties, and any manuscripts relating to genealogy, family history, and heraldry, selected by the Council.

3. The Council shall consist of a President, nine Vice-Presidents, and twelve Members of Council, two of whom shall hold the posts of Secretary and Treasurer; and any four, including the Treasurer or Secretary, shall form a quorum. In case of equality of votes, the Chairman to have a casting vote. Any Candidate may be elected with the consent in writing of one Member of the Council, the Treasurer, and the Secretary.

4. Three Members of the Council shall retire in rotation annually, but shall be eligible for re-election.

5. The Annual Subscription shall be One Guinea, paid in advance, and due on the 1st day of January in each year; and Members elected after two hundred and fifty shall have joined, shall pay an Entrance Fee of 10*s.* 6*d.* in addition to their first Annual Subscription.

6. The funds raised by the Society shall be expended in publishing such works as are selected by the Council.

7. One volume at least shall be supplied to the Members every year.

8. An Annual Meeting shall be held in the month of June every year, at such time and place as the Council may direct; and due notice shall be sent to the Members of the Society at least a fortnight previously.

9. No work shall be supplied to any Member unless his Subscription for the year be paid; and any member not having paid his subscription for two years, having received notice thereof, shall cease to belong to the Society.

10. The Council may, at their discretion, pay the expense of transcribing from manuscripts whenever two hundred Members, at least, shall have joined the Society; but no payment in money shall be made to any person for editing any work for the Society.

11. No copies of the Publications of the Society shall be supplied to persons not actually Members, and each Member shall be restricted to a single Subscription.

12. An account of the receipts and expenses of the Society to be made up to the 1st of June in each year, and published with a list of the Members and the Rules of the Society in the following volume.

13. These Rules shall not be altered except at the Annual Meeting, and three clear weeks' notice must be given to the Secretary of any such intended alteration.

The Council have selected the Visitation of Rutland in 1618 *to follow that of Leicestershire.*

Report for the Year 1869-70.

On the 27th of March, 1869, two Members of the Society's Council invited several of their friends and correspondents to assist in the formation of a Society, having for its special object the publication of the Heralds' Visitations of Counties and other important Genealogical Manuscripts. By the 28th of May, fifty-eight persons signified their willingness to co-operate in the establishment of such a Society, and at a Special Meeting held on that day at 8, Danes Inn, the Honourable Henry Roper-Curzon in the Chair, the Officers of the Society were appointed and the Rules drawn out. The success that the Society met with was so great, that by the 28th of July no fewer than one hundred Members had joined, and from that time to the present this number has been gradually increasing, so that now it exceeds one hundred and seventy Members.

This great success may be attributed to the exertions of the several Members of the Council, and to the literary status of many of the original Members.

The Society has already published and distributed 'The Heraldic Visitation of London, taken by Robert Cooke, Clarenceux, in 1568,' edited by Joseph Jackson Howard, F.S.A., and George J. Armytage, F.S.A.

Camden's 'Visitation of Leicestershire in 1619,' edited by John Fetherston, F.S.A., will be ready for circulation in about a fortnight. This is a large work, and contains 207 pages of pedigree matter only. It will also include facsimiles of several of the signatures of the heads of families who entered their pedigrees at that Visitation, together with a very elaborate armorial and general index.

Sir George F. Duckett, Bart., F.S.A., has offered to edit a Visitation for the Society; and the 'Visitation of Nottingham,' to be edited by G. W. Marshall, Esq., LL.M., is ready for the press; and the three Oxfordshire Visitations are now being prepared by Mr. William Henry Turner, of Oxford.

The Society is now in a position to print Two Volumes a year, and it is hoped that the addition of another hundred Members will enable a third volume to be published; and it is believed that the issue of Three Volumes in return for the Guinea Subscription will place the Society in the foremost ranks of such Associations of this country.

The especial thanks of the Members are due to the Council of the Surrey Archæological Society for so courteously placing their Meeting-room at the disposal of the Harleian Council. Arrangements are now being made for the payment of a few pounds per annum to the Surrey Society, as it is considered desirable that this Society shall have a recognized place of meeting.

Harleian Society.

BALANCE SHEET FOR THE YEAR ENDING 31st MAY, 1870.

Dr.

			£.	s.	d.	£.	s.	d.
1869. 141 Subscriptions at 21s. . .			148	1	0			
2 ,, 21s. 6d. .			2	3	0			
3 ,, 20s. . .			3	0	0			
						153	4	0
1870. 37 ,, 21s. . .			38	17	0			
1 ,, 20s. . .			1	0	0			
						39	17	0
						£193	1	0

We have carefully examined the foregoing accounts, and find them correct in every particular and the payments supported by the necessary vouchers.

Dudley G. Cary-Elwes,
Lionel G. Robinson, } *Auditors.*

Cr.

	£.	s.	d.	£.	s.	d.
Receipt Stamps				0	8	4
Commission on Cheque				0	0	6
Advertisements—						
'Athenæum'	£1	8	0			
'Notes and Queries'	2	1	6			
				3	9	6
Incidental Expenses—						
Honorary Secretary				5	14	1
Honorary Treasurer				1	6	6
Circulars, etc.				6	12	0
Printing and Binding London Visitation				87	0	0
				104	10	11
Balance in hand on 31st May, 1870 . . .				88	10	1
				£193	1	0

List of Members,

CORRECTED TO JUNE 22ND, 1870.

G. Brindley Acworth, F.S.A., Star Hill, Rochester.
Edward Akroyd, M.P., F.S.A., Bank Field, Halifax.
Reginald Ames, Cote House, Westbury-on-Trym, Bristol.
W. Amhurst T. Amhurst (*Council*), Didlington Hall, Brandon.
Frank Andrew, Ashton-under-Lyne.
Ely Andrew, Mere Bank, Ashton-under-Lyne.
J. E. Andrewes, War Office.
Charles Frederick Angell, F.S.A., Grove Lane, Camberwell, S.E.
Francis R. Armytage, Balliol College, Oxford.
George J. Armytage, F.S.A. (*Hon. Secretary*), Kirklees Park, Brighouse.
The Earl of Arran, The Pavilion, Hans Place, S.W.
Ralph Assheton, M.P. (*Vice-President*), Downham Hall, Clitheroe.
Rev. Charles S. Atkinson, Harswell, York.
W. J. St. Aubyn, 68th Light Infantry, Fort Camden, Cork.
Charles Baker, F.S.A., 11, Sackville Street, Piccadilly, W.
Mrs. Baker, Ulster Terrace, Regent's Park, N.W.
Fairless Barber, F.S.A. (*Council*), Castle Hill, Rastrick, near Brighouse.
Joseph Gurney Barclay, 54, Lombard Street, E.C.
Thomas H. Bates, Mayfield, Wolsingham.
George Frederick Beaumont, Knowle, Fixby, Huddersfield.
Rev. Charles W. Boase, 33, Surrey Street, Strand, W.C.
W. Consitt Boulter, F.S.A., 6, Park Row, Park Street, Hull.
Edmund M. Boyle, Rockwood, Torquay.
Lieut.-Col. Bradbury, Huddersfield,
The Rev. William Bree, the Rectory, Allesley, Coventry.
The Hon. and Rev. R. O. Bridgeman, Weston-under-Lyziard, Shifnal.
The Hon. William Brodrick, M.P. (*Vice-President*), 20, Beaufort Gardens, S.W.
Thomas Brooke, Armitage Bridge, Huddersfield.
Francis Capper Brooke, Ufford Place, Woodbridge.
Percy C. S. Bruere, Middleham, Bedale, Yorkshire.
The Rev. Joseph Buckley, M.A., Sopworth Rectory, Chippenham.
W. E. G. Lytton Bulwer, Quebec House, East Dereham.
Charles John Burgess, Naval and Military Club, London, W.
Sir Bernard Burke, C.B., LL.D., Ulster King-of-Arms, Dublin.
The Dowager Countess of Carnarvon, Pixton Park, Dulverton.
George Alfred Carthew, F.S.A., East Dereham, Norfolk.
Colonel J. L. Chester (*Council*), 16, Linden Villas, Blue Anchor Road, Bermondsey, S.E.
Rev. Frederic T. Colby, B.D., F.S.A., Fellow of Exeter College, Oxford.
James Edwin Cole, Easthorpe Court, Wigtoft, Spalding.
F. S. Bermingham Pen Cole, Freemantle, Southampton.
Sydney Cole, Norwood Court, Southall, Middlesex.
James Coleman, 22, High Street, Blocmsbury, W.C.
W. H. Cottell, 1, Manor Rise, Brixton, S.W.
J. Gregory Cottingham, Edensor, Chesterfield.
W. Prideaux Courtney, Ecclesiastical Commission.
Mrs. John Woodhead Crossland, Thornton Lodge, Huddersfield.
Edwin Purves Roper-Curzon, Upper Sheen House, Mortlake, S.W.
The Hon. Henry Roper-Curzon (*Vice-President*), 47, Argyle Road, Kensington.
The Hon. Sidney C. Roper-Curzon, Upper Sheen House, Mortlake, S.W.
R. S. Longworth Dames, M.A., 32, Upper Mount Street, Dublin.
John Davidson (*Council*), 14, St. George's Place, Hyde Park Corner, S.W.
Robert Davies, F.S.A., The Mount, York.
Gordon Dayman, St. Giles's, Oxford.

Mrs. Fetherston Dilke, Maxstoke Castle, Coleshill, Warwickshire.
Robert Dowman, 'Manchester Guardian' Office, Manchester.
Henry Holman Drake, LL.D., St. Austell, Cornwall.
The Rev. The Count Dawson-Duffield, LL.D., Sephton Rectory, Liverpool.
Sir George F. Duckett, Bart., F.S.A. (*Vice-President*), Fangfoss Hall, York.
George F. Duncombe, 17, St. Stephen's Road, Bayswater, W.
Albert Edwards, Philadelphia.
The Rev. Henry T. Ellacomb, M.A., F.S.A., Clyst St. George Rectory, Topsham,
    Devon.
Wm. Smith Ellis, Hydecroft, Charlwood, Surrey.
Dudley Cary Elwes, F.S.A., South Bersted, Bognor.
V. Cary Elwes, Brigg, Lincolnshire.
Thomas Falconer, one of the Judges of the County Courts, Usk, Monmouthshire.
J. G. Fanshawe, Board of Trade, Whitehall, S.W.
William Fennell, Wakefield.
John Fetherston, jun., F.S.A. (*Council*), High Street, Warwick.
George Fitzwilliams, New York, U.S.A.
Edward Fitzwilliams, Philadelphia, U.S.A.
John Ribton Garstin, F.S.A., 21, Upper Merrion Street, Dublin.
Arthur Edward Gayer, Q.C., LL.D., Dublin.
Joseph Gillow, jun., Winckley Square, Preston.
Granville Leveson Gower, F.S.A. (*Council*), Titsey Park, Godstone.
Henry Sydney Grazebrook, Stourbridge, Worcestershire.
The Rev. Henry Thomas Griffith, B.A., North Walsham, Norfolk.
Gordon Gyll, Remenham House, Wraysbury, Staines.
Edward Hailstone, F.S.A., Horton Hall, Bradford, Yorkshire.
The Rev. H. F. Hall, M.A., High Legh, Knutsford, Cheshire.
Lady Frances Vernon-Harcourt, The Homme, Weobly.
William Henry Hart, F.S.A., The White House, St. Peter's Lane, Canterbury.
William Harvey, Harrold Hall, Bedford.
The Rev. Samuel Hayman, M.A. (*Council*), The Rectory, Doneraile, Ireland.
Lady Heathcote, Hursley Park, Winchester.
Thomas Helsby, 41, Princess Street, Manchester.
Robert Henderson, Bell House, Pitminster, Taunton.
Spencer Herepath, 15, Upper Phillimore Gardens, W.
Miss Francis Margery Hext, Lostwithiel, Cornwall.
John Hirst, jun., Dobcross, Saddleworth.
The Rev. C. W. Holbech, Farnborough, Banbury.
Daniel Dean Hopkyns, F.S.A., Weycliffe, St. Catherine's, near Guildford.
Joseph Jackson Howard, LL.D., F.S.A. (*Hon. Treas.*), 3, Dartmouth Row,
    Blackheath, S.E.
Rev. Edmund Jermyn, B.A., Nettlecombe Rectory, Taunton.
Joseph Jones, Abberley Hall, Stourport.
W. Stavenhagen Jones, 2, Verulam Buildings, Gray's Inn, W.C.
Edward B. Jupp, F.S.A., Carpenters' Hall, London Wall, E.C.
The Rev. F. W. Kittermaster, All Saints, Coventry.
Arthur John Knapp, Llanforsh House, Clifton, Bristol.
C. T. Lane, 3, Lombard Court, Lombard Street, London.
Arthur Larken, 53, Manchester Street, Manchester Square, W.
The Rev. F. G. Lee, D.C.L., F.S.A., 6, Lambeth Terrace, London, S.W.
Mrs. Littledale, 19, Queen's Gate Gardens, South Kensington.
Ben. Lockwood, Huddersfield.
William H. Dyer Longstaffe, F.S.A., Gateshead.
John Maclean, F.S.A. (*Council*), Pallingswick Lodge, Hammersmith, W.
Silvanus J. Macy, 21, West 47th Street, New York, U.S.A.
The Duke of Manchester (*President*), 1, Great Stanhope Street, W.
George W. Marshall, L.L.M. (*Council*), Weacombe House, Bicknoller, Taunton.
Bernulf de Clegg Mattinson, Oldham.
Walter C. Metcalfe, Epping, Essex.
Captain R. Molesworth, High Legh, Knutsford.
The Right Hon. Lord Monson (*Vice-President*), Gatton Park, Reigate.
Thomas H. Montgomery, 400, Walnut Street, Philadelphia, U.S.A.

Lieut.-Col. CHARLES THOMAS JOHN MOORE, F.S.A., Frampton Hall, near Boston.
FREDERICK J. MORRELL, St. Giles, Oxford.
EDWARD MORTON, The Villa, Malton, Yorkshire.
GEORGE MURRAY, Hartford House, Werneth, Oldham.
Miss NEWMAN, 6, Patshull Road, Kentish Town, N.W.
Miss CHARLOTTE NEWMAN, 6, Patshull Road, Kentish Town, N.W.
JAMES NEWMAN, 235, High Holborn, W.C.
CAPTAIN W. NEWSOME, R.E., Gravesend.
JOHN GOUGH NICHOLS, F.S.A., 25, Parliament Street, S.W.
WILLIAM JOHN O'DONNAVAN, LL.D., M.R.I.A., Foxcroft House, Portarlington.
EVAN ORTNER, 3, St. James's Street, S.W.
FREDERIC OUVRY, F.S.A., 12, Queen Anne Street, Cavendish Square.
The Rev. FIELDING PALMER, Eastcliff, Chepstow.
The Rev. J. T. PARKINSON, D.C.L., F.S.A., Ravendale, Grimsby.
DANIEL PARSONS, Stuarts Lodge, Malvern.
D. WILLIAMS PATERSON, Newark Valley, New York, U.S.A.
EDWARD PEACOCK, F.S.A., Bottesford Manor, Brigg, Lincolnshire.
Rev. A. J. PEARMAN, Rainham Vicarage, Sittingbourne.
CHARLES GEORGE PERCEVAL, Passenham Manor, Stony Stratford.
THOMAS A. PERRY, Bitham House, Leamington.
LEMUEL POPE, Cambridge, Massachusetts, U.S.A.
SIR JOSEPH RADCLIFFE, Bart. (*Vice-President*), Rudding Park, Wetherby.
The Rev. CANON RAINE, York.
ALEXANDER RIVINGTON, 27, Cleveland Gardens, Hyde Park, W.
The Rev. C. J. ROBINSON, M.A., Norton Canon Vicarage, Weobly.
The Rev. EDWARD ROGERS, M.A., Blachford, Ivy Bridge, Devon.
R. COXWELL-ROGERS, F.S.A., Dowdeswell Court, Andoversford, Gloucester.
The Rev. ROBERT ROE ROGERS, 104, Exmouth Street, Parkfield Terrace, Birken-
    head.
The ROYAL LIBRARY, Windsor Castle.
Rev. DAVID ROYCE, The Vicarage, Lower Swell, Stow-on-the-Wold.
JAMES RUSBY, 34, Manor Road, Wickham Park, Lewisham, S.E.
The DUKE OF RUTLAND, K.G., Belvoir Castle, Grantham.
EVELYN PHILIP SHIRLEY, F.S.A. (*Vice-President*), Lower Eatington Park, Strat-
    ford-on-Avon.
Rev. E. H. MAINWARING SLADEN, M.A., F.R.G.S., Alton Berners, Marlborough.
J. S. SMALLFIELD, 32, University Street, W.C.
CHARLES SOTHERAN, 81, Derby Street, Hulme, Manchester.
CHARLES STEWART, Royal Artillery, Government House, Jersey.
WENTWORTH STURGEON (*Council*), 25, Gloucester Place, Portman Square, W.
JOHN SYKES, M.D., F.S.A., Doncaster.
Miss CAROLINE C. THAYER, Boston, U.S.A.
T. G. TOMKINS, Great Ouseburn, York.
GEORGE D. TOMLINSON, Huddersfield.
HENRY TREHERNE, Latymer House, Brook Green, W.
GEORGE TUCK, New Road, Windsor.
WM. HENRY TURNER, 8, Turl Street, Oxford.
J. R. DANIEL TYSSEN, F.S.A., 9, Lower Rock Gardens, Brighton.
PHILIP TWELLS, M.A., Chase Side House, Enfield.
SIR HENRY VAVASOUR, Bart. (*Vice-President*), Holton Hall, Halesworth.
EDWARD WALTHAM, Stockwell, London, S.W.
R. E. EGERTON-WARBURTON (*Vice-President*), Arley Hall, Northwich.
EDMOND CHESTER WATERS, Upton Park, Poole.
FRANK G. WATNEY, 17, Pembridge Crescent, Bayswater, W.
Rev. JAMES WEBB, M.A., Clifton, Brighouse.
Lieut.-Colonel WESTON, Hunterstone House, West Kilbride, Ayrshire.
WILLIAM H. WHITMORE, Boston, U.S.A.
Miss WILLIAMS, Orchard Wyndham, Taunton.
Rev. EDWARD WILTON, West Lavington, Devizes.
R. H. WOOD, F.S.A., Crumpsall, Manchester.
CHARLES H. L. WOODD, F.G.S., Roslyn, Hampstead.
W. H. WRIGHT, Philadelphia.

PUBLICATIONS.